Knot of the Soul

Knot of the Soul

Madness, Psychoanalysis, Islam

STEFANIA PANDOLFO

The University of Chicago Press
Chicago and London

The University of Chicago Press, Chicago 60637
The University of Chicago Press, Ltd., London

Published 2018

27 26 25 24 23 22 21 20 19 18   1 2 3 4 5

ISBN-13: 978-0-226-46492-3 (cloth)
ISBN-13: 978-0-226-46508-1 (paper)
ISBN-13: 978-0-226-46511-1 (e-book)
DOI: 10.7208/chicago/9780226465111.001.0001

Library of Congress Cataloging-in-Publication Data

Names: Pandolfo, Stefania, author.
Title: Knot of the soul : madness, psychoanalysis, Islam / Stefania Pandolfo.
Description: Chicago ; London : The University of Chicago Press, 2018. | Includes index.
Identifiers: LCCN 2017006640 | ISBN 9780226464923 (cloth : alk. paper) | ISBN 9780226465081 (pbk. : alk. paper) | ISBN 9780226465111 (e-book)
Subjects: LCSH: Islam and psychoanalysis—Morocco. | Pastoral psychology | (Islam). | Mental health—Morocco—Religious aspects—Islam. | Mental illness—Alternative treatment—Morocco. | Islam—Morocco—Customs and practices.
Classification: LCC BP190.5.P78 P36 2017 | DDC 297.0964—dc23
LC record available at https://lccn.loc.gov/2017006640

for Yassine

CONTENTS

Introduction

Illness [is] the introduction of the living to the existence of the subject.

—Jacques Lacan[1]

Yet in the earliest times of the Islamic community the word *fiqh* was used to denote the science of the path of the hereafter, the recognition of the minute evils or subtle afflictions of the soul.

—al-Ghazali[2]

I said that *al-nafs* (the soul/self) is the yeast, the fertile land that Shaytan cultivates and tills; but he doesn't cultivate grapes, figs, and pomegranates! He cultivates desires, cravings, and longings, and with them blasting and bombs.

—the Imam

Do you know what madness is?

—the patient, to the ethnographer

A Map of the World

She wandered off to the other side of the roof, a side that bordered a house that had remained vacant and was now falling into ruin. I followed her. The roof had no parapet, and as we walked, me after her, the void gaped fifteen meters below. The roof terrace was crumbling, and in some places the surface under our feet nested dangerous holes. As I tried to guide her back to safer grounds she was unconcerned and kept walking, and told me that we were striding across a map of the world. Months later, after she had regained a shared sense of reality, she asked me if I recalled that day on the roof. She could still remember now, she said, her perception back then. In her perception of then we were walking on a topographic map of the world, a sort of world atlas that, as we walked, morphed into a boundless surface made of a succession of countries in which we disappeared as individual consciousnesses. "We were walking on a map of the world," she said, "we were becoming that map, and you had no idea."

There had been times of anxiety and fright, and times in which it seemed that we could live with the rhythms of the illness, its comings and goings, like the movement of waves on sand. It is perhaps because I had stepped on that map of the world with her, on the roof of a crumbling house that was literally and allegorically the world itself in its losing consistency and reality, that it became for me an exigency to learn to relate to that experience, one that had brought home for me glimpses of other histories, grids that had led me there without my knowing.

That image, morphing into the landscape and becoming a map that could not be read, has accompanied me for twenty years, and in the writing of this book. It registers the fading of the self in a cartography that can no longer be traveled, the dissolution of bodily boundaries into a flat surface that evokes eschatological scenes of world ending, or the mythical forms of shamanic cosmomorphism in a time of post-shamans.[3]

It is an image and a perception that would only too hastily be sanctioned as mad (but that was best described by psychoanalysts who attempted to think from within the experience of psychosis),[4] for it bespeaks an experience that is not unfamiliar to most of us in moments of lapse and estrangement, or in certain dreams, and provides glimpses into a dissolution of our "psychic skin" that is a tangible confrontation with the limit of life, a confrontation where subjectivity is both founded and at risk. Today, as I write this preface, that roof vision of a map of the world, witness to an inner catastrophe, seems prophetic of that other catastrophe, the collective vicissitudes of a region, where entire areas (in Iraq, Syria, Yemen) have been reduced to flat surfaces that have swallowed their inhabitants, memories, and modes of life.

Knot of the Soul started as an attempt to relate to an experience of madness through an ethnography. In the process, and through the vicissitudes of fieldwork, I encountered the question of the psyche and the soul, what the terms *psukhé* (psyche) in Greek and the European languages and *nafs* in Arabic literally mean and conjure. On that border of translation I sought to think the problematic of the cure in a contrastive proximity, between the thought of the unconscious in psychoanalysis, and the maladies of the soul in Islamic tradition, at a time of world changing and upheaval.

The method of this exploration became clear to me only in retrospect, for it is the result of a slow transformation of the gaze in the give and take of my ethnographic work, which made the psyche and the psychoanalytic cure appear through the lens of the *nafs*/soul, its carnal and spiritual life, its vulnerability, and its ontology of the Invisible (*al-ghayb*). What this disclosed was not just the possibility and actual presence of a contrastive dialogue between the psychoanalytic and the Qur'anic cure, but a spiritual-metaphysical dimension of the psyche itself.

There is of course a scholarly archive of this exchange, a history of the conversation between the psyche and the *nafs* at the modern inception of the discipline of *'ilm al-nafs*, the science of the soul (also modern psychology) in the Middle East, at the intersection of Sufism and psychoanalysis, as well as much older debates at the intersection of medicine and theology in Islam.[5] It is enough to mention that one of the translations of the Freudian concept of the unconscious in Arabic is *lā shu'ūr*, a term used by the twelfth-century Sufi Ibn 'Arabi to refer to the incommensurability and alterity of God.[6] Some voices in the history of psychoanalysis have highlighted a spiritual dimension of the unconscious and the reality of an ongoing psychoanalytic conversation with religious traditions, and likewise scholars of religion have acknowledged parallels with psychoanalysis.[7]

While this work is conversant with that archive, which has nourished its project from beginning to end, my insight is born of that less explicit and messier form of apprenticeship that is characteristic of ethnography. I encountered the problematic of the *nafs* in the therapeutic practice of a Qur'anic scholar and therapist who has been a key interlocutor in my work. In his commentary, and as an effort of listening, I worked through the medical-spiritual tradition of the *nafs* and its passions in Islam, on the trail of (among others) the twelfth-century jurist and scholar of the soul, Abu Hamid al-Ghazali. And inasmuch as I have come to this research with an interest in the psyche and in the topics of the unconscious, and through years of conversation with Moroccan psychoanalysts, it is in the site of the ethnography and in the biography of its author that the alchemy of concepts and their reciprocal work actually takes place. An example of this is when I realized, already well advanced into the writing of this book, and because a contingency of life made me revisit the conversations with the Imam, that the experience of trauma and loss, but also of desire, was now refracted for me through the lens of Qur'anic eschatological ethics as having the structure of the "ordeal" (in Arabic, *balā'* or *ibtilā'*): a divine trial to which the subject is called to respond.

That we might resemble a map inscribed and reinscribed upon, rather than already formed selves and consciousnesses, and that we might be vulnerable to disappearance into its grids, was also Freud's crucial insight. Freud had imagined the psyche as a topographic map punctuated by knots of significance and gaps of penumbra and forgetting, and in his 1930 *Das Unbehagen in der Kultur* he compared psychic space to the layout of a city.[8] The city in his example was a spatial agglomerate of different localities and neighborhoods, in their successive buildings, demolitions, and reconstructions around an original nucleus that could never be brought to light as such. In this sense, the layered grid of the city resembled the memory-work of the psyche, its imprints, pathways, displacements, condensations, and obliterations. Yet, Freud argued, the concrete space of a city existed in historical time and was subject to transformations that altered its morphology beyond return. The shapes of former buildings could at best be inferred from their ruins, ruins that themselves were not even the original remains, but "the ruins of later restorations made after fires or destruction." Psychic space, by contrast, was an archive characterized by the virtual copresence of multiple localities and times, where, as he put it, "nothing can ever perish—everything is somehow preserved, and, in suitable circumstances (when, for instance, regression goes back far enough) it can once more be brought to light."[9] The psyche as a topology was for Freud a metaphysical hypothesis, one that undid chronological time, and alluded to another, nonhuman time, beyond individual life and subjectivity. His reluctant exchange with Romain Rolland on the mystical notion of "oceanic feeling," a merging into the "unbounded," and the "sensation of eternity" it produced is a witness to this fact.[10]

Psychic time is scanned by repetition, the return to a site of traumatic inscription that, however, can be met only in its aftermath (Lacan compared it to ritual) in a spiral movement that Freud called *Nachträglichkeit*, the fact that events happen in a space of delay and retrospection, where future and past are intertwined, and contingency is the other side of repetition.[11] Yet the analogy of two spaces, the city and the psyche, and two rhythms or histories, the temporal and the non-temporal, suggested that they do have something in common, and the scene of the psyche can be glimpsed in watermark. What is common to both histories is the persistence of what Freud called *Trieb*, "the drive," a heteronomous force, which in the life of humans—at least inasmuch as human life is grasped in historical, worldly time—partakes of the eternal (and if we were to follow the archive of the *nafs* here we would say the divine), and yet can be seized only in the lacunas, the distortions, destructions, and transformations it produces, in the way it undoes and hides away the evidence.

It is in Freud's later works that the ambivalent quality of the drive (at once life and death) and its fatal trajectory were most closely explored, in relation to violence and self-annihilation, and the ambiguous remedy of identification, as an almost theological wrestling with the problem of evil, and in light of a question: What does it mean to be the subject, or more precisely the "host" of the drive? And to become capable of withstanding its life, wrestling with its violence, torment, and pleasures?

In the conclusion of his "Thoughts for the Times: On War and Death," written in 1915, "in the confusion of wartime in which we are caught" and still relevant in the wartime of today, after pondering the disillusionment of a war that had disclosed the unthinkable cruelty at the heart of what appeared as civility, Freud made an urgent call for that wrestling, and for coming to terms with the agency of the drive. It was not just a condemnation of the ravages of war, but a call to realize that we are directly concerned, whether at home or at the front, because of the implication of our desire. "*Si vis vitamin para mortem,*" he elliptically admonished at the end of his essay; "if you want to endure life, prepare yourself for death." "Could you bear the life that you have," echoed Lacan in one of his lectures, "if you didn't have faith in the limit of death?"[12]

What if the heteronymous agency of the drive were seen from the perspective of Islamic eschatological ethics as having the structure of the ordeal?

Knot of the Soul

Since Foucault wrote *The History of Madness* in the mode of an archaeology of silence,[13] much has happened in the field of mental health, as well as in the practices, technologies, and debates surrounding subjectivity, the body, the psyche, the brain, and the imagination, to reinforce his portrayal of the becoming unthinkable of an experience—an experience that, as such, had once summoned questions of truth, politics, ethics, life, and death. And yet in the contemporary world and in the context of global capitalism and its crises, the stage and voices of madness come to the fore again, and well beyond the protocols of public health and psychopharmacology; beyond, as well, Foucault's own historical framing.

The ethnography of madness that I pursue in this book asks what it is to think a lacuna, engage with an exteriority (Lacan called it "extimacy," *extimité,* at once intimate and irreducibly other) in the everyday, and in the space of writing itself. In dialogue with psychoanalysis and anthropology, as well as with Islamic theology and spiritual pedagogy, and from the particular context of Morocco today, the book asks, What are the ethical and political implications of such an engagement—which is also an engagement with human vulnerability and unreason, violence, and destruction—with the "non-temporal" and the scene of the soul? And what does it mean to pursue these questions in the vocabularies, imagination, and practices of a contemporary Islamic tradition, where they resonate within an ontology and a cosmology that grant a cardinal place to divine reality and discourse, and in dissonant encounter with psychoanalysis and psychiatry?

Conceived as an attempt at writing from the cusp of personal and collective experience, where in the folds of subjective articulation the sense of being is done and undone, the core philosophical project of the book addresses the problematic of subjugation and intergenerational transmission, and the possibility of writing from the midst of trauma, taken at once as a historical event and as a window into the vicissitudes of the soul.

Culture in Agony

In an address at the conference of Black Writers and Artists in 1956,[14] Frantz Fanon spoke of the disablement of culture and cultural creation—he called this disablement *déculturation*—as a strategic dimension of colonial domination, one that goes hand in hand with military occupation and the expropriation of territory: "The enterprise of deculturation is but the negative of a more gigantic work of economic, and even biological, enslavement (*asservissement*) . . . The enslavement, in the strictest sense, of the native population is the prime necessity. For this its systems of reference have to be broken."[15] Physical expropriation is "doubled by the looting of cultural schemata."

At the center of Fanon's address is the figure of the agony of culture: a cultural tradition reduced to the status of a living ghost, suspended between life and death. The goal of colonialism, says Fanon, at once psychic and military, is not to destroy the autochthonous culture, but to produce its unending agony (*agonie continuée*), a simulacrum of life in the suspended state of a culture undead. Culture in agony no longer supports being, thinking, and dreaming, generating new forms in a process of world making. Rather, "at once present and mummified, it testifies against its members" (*à la fois presente et momifiée, elle atteste contre ses membres*).[16] It is a "corps à corps" of the natives with their culture that attacks them from within, as a persecutory and yet desired object. Deculturation is intimately and reciprocally related to the modus operandi of racism, "in as much as the object of racism is no longer a person, but a form of existence," consumed by the incorporation of a murderous gaze.

The figure of agony is resonant of other of his texts from this period, where Fanon captured this experience in both Algeria and France,[17] as he described lives lived with the rhythm and tonality of an "unfinished death" (*mort incomplète*) and reflected on the implications of "perceiving life, not as the actualization of a fundamental vitality, but as the endemic struggle against an atmospheric death." (Atmospheric: that is, pervasive, environmental, infiltrating one's life and soul.) Or as he dissected the vocabulary of North African patients in France evoking their bodily ailments in a sacrificial mode, where pain, diffused and atmospheric, is the only available language, and the person becomes an unwitting witness of the destruction of a form of existence: "*Où as-tu mal? Partout, monsieur le docteur.*"[18]

Fanon returned to this point in 1959, calling for a close-up reflection on destruction, an attention to detail, in his discussion of the effects of colonial violence on the Algerian family and the Algerian physical landscape: "we must . . . walk step by step along the wound inflicted on the Algerian soil and the Algerian people." The colonial operation was aimed at dispersing, uprooting, and separating families: internment camps for the men, women left alone to support the children, violence against women and serial rape at military stations, men returning home with broken bodies and "the spirit inert." How could anyone think, Fanon asked, that in all this the Algerian family would remain intact, and that the hate of colonialism would not grow to immense proportions? "French colonialism since 1954 has wanted nothing other than to break the will of the people, to destroy its resistance, to liquidate its hopes."[19] Yet in that process, Fanon continued, the people dispersed and undead found a novel cohesion in that suffering, a spiritual community of pain, which became a rampart of the Algerian revolution.

An "undead" culture is one unmoored from its bearings and condemned to live among the ruins of its system of reference, its symbolic forms: "Such a culture, once alive and open towards the future (*l'avénir*), shuts itself up, fixed in the colonial status, caught in the yoke of oppression."[20] It is a culture that Fanon sees as incapable of performing its work, "the work of culture," *Kulturarbeit* (parallel to *Traumarbeit*, the "dreamwork"), which Freud had seen as the condition of possibility of human fellowship, in the sublimation of unconscious drives into symbolic and spiritual creations.[21] That failure and that loss are for Fanon the failure of the symbolic law itself. It must be acknowledged, he thought, rendered visible and felt before even envisaging the question of a renewed possibility of culture. In the given situation, "any pseudo-respect of the cultural institutions corresponds to the most elaborate sadism."[22]

What would it mean to reactivate the work of culture, or to imagine its impasse otherwise?[23] Fanon himself had gestured to a "leap" (*saut*)[24] as the creative offspring of a realization of loss, an interruption that is also a fugitive coming to life, one that resists hardening into an identity: "I find myself, a human being, in a world where words are fringed with silence; in a world where the other hardens interminably." "I am not a prisoner of History . . . I must remember at all times that the real leap (*véritable saut*) is bringing invention into existence."[25]

In a tone reminiscent of Fanon's depiction of agony, but in the spiritual-political figures of contemporary Islam, the Qur'anic therapist who has been a pivotal interlocutor in my ethnography over many years formulates the concept of "soul choking" (*taḍyīq al-nafs*)—a kind of medical-spiritual phenomenology of the soul, inspired by the Qur'anic depiction of the "constriction" and "expansion" of the *nafs* as an opening or sealing of the heart to the knowledge and the path of God. "Soul choking" describes in his words a crippling of the ethical faculty, a disablement of the soul fostered in existential and political trauma, in the confrontation with evil, and in the illness of melancholy as it leads to suicide. This is how he describes the experience of despair among the youth, crushed by the political violence of the state and the mass pull towards undocumented migration. Soul choking bespeaks the subjugation of the soul and the oppression of the collectivity; when life shrinks, death is generalized to a banality that makes it unthinkable, and the divine message is no longer heard in the heart. It is a state of unacknowledged and impossible mourning, when the soul weakens, surrendering to passions stirred by demonic insinuation, and loses divine guidance.

The ethical-political question becomes that of shedding light on and revealing such a state of things, in a disclosure that may be that of illness and even madness itself: a necessary shock, towards the reanimation of the soul. But, differently than for Fanon, in the practice of the Imam the choking agony is addressed through a pedagogy of imagination that is also a "jurisprudence of the soul," aimed at creating conditions in the heart for a renewed receptivity to the divine message. The stage is the Qur'anic liturgy of *al-ruqya*, a cure for madness and spiritual illness, where in the vulnerable space of an imaginal manifestation of the Invisible is marked the inception of a work of culture.

In my exploration of sites of presencing and repair on the ruins of and in the agony of culture, the work of Michel de Certeau has been a consistent source of inspiration. In his research on the sixteenth- and seventeenth-century European mystics—Diego de Jesús, Juan de la Cruz, Teresa de Avila, Jean-Joseph Surin—Certeau traced oral calligraphies of invention at a time of political and cultural crisis, and on the ruins of symbolic forms, exploring the possibility of transmission for a tradition uprooted from its system of reference. He described the mystics' style of dwelling and creating among the ruins of a tradition as an art of connecting to the generative "abundance of a source." "We must understand that the origin that was sought [by the mystics] is not a dead past. At issue is the advent of a 'voice' that speaks today in its avatars, and that infuses with its force the actual words that are uttered in the present."[26]

Certeau wrote of spiritual communities gathered around "manners of speaking" and "styles of doing" that nested their impermanent residence in the aftermath of culture, in the "night of bodies that can no longer find orientation in the signifiers of an established cultural tradition."[27] And yet in that void, and through the practices of oration and writing, they could carve a path towards an encounter with the divine, as a possibility open at the very site of agony.

At the border of the historical and the intemporal, the book unfolds in the space of most intimate, violent, and paradoxical attestations, of a culture "testifying against its members," and moves between two related and yet very different sites in a Moroccan history of madness: the psychiatric hospital and the reformist world of Islamic healing.

Knot of the Soul is based on several years of ethnographic research at a Moroccan psychiatric hospital (and school of psychiatry), and other sites and institutions for the healing and treatment of mental illness at the interface of modern psychiatric practice and the Islamic and vernacular "cures of the jinn" (*ʿilāj al-jinn*). From the periphery of these institutions it seeks to discern forms of the subject at the intersection of the clinic with other practices and discourses of alterity, madness, and healing: the long-standing afflictions and therapies of possession, and the practices and discourses of Islamic healing. This is a Qurʾanic medicine of the soul, based, in its reformed liturgy, on a prophetic medicine of the heart (*ṭibb nabāwī, ṭibb al-qalb*), a medical-spiritual tradition that is today witnessing a return throughout the Muslim world.

In the complex exchange of psychiatry, psychoanalysis, and Islamic healing new possibilities of the self are being debated and crafted, and questions of vulnerability, responsibility, ethics, justice, life, and death are brought to the fore. The dissonant encounter of psychiatry and Islam takes place in mental health institutions (psychiatric hospitals, rural clinics, associations of patients and families, psychoanalytic conferences), as well as through a field of Islamic psychology that directly engages Western psychological theories, challenging them and seeking to reinscribe them within an Islamic cosmological vision. This is paralleled by the renewal of the cure sanctioned by Islamic jurisprudence (*ʿilāj sharʿī, ruqya sharʿiyya*), in explicit contrast with vernacular cures. The impact that ensues is felt well beyond the space of the clinic, carrying implications in the domain of theology, ethics, and politics.

I conducted fieldwork at the Razi hospital in Sale between 1998 and 2003, and in 2002 for a continuous year: in the wards and the emergency room, with psychiatrists, residents, patients, and sometimes their families. I had come as an anthropologist (one who had published a book on subjectivity and memory in Morocco, and who was versed in the archive of psychological anthropology) to a psychiatric institution and milieu where, at that time, there were only psychiatrists, psychologists, nurses, and patients, and no position (if there ever is one) from which to only observe.

During that time, I also engaged in conversation with psychoanalysts and psychotherapists, participated in their seminars and conferences, covered some basic ground in psychiatry, and shared and debated my work with them and published in joint collections. This phase of the work is evoked in part 1 of the book, "Psychiatric Fragments in the Aftermath of Culture."

Between 2003 and 2012 the work took me outside the hospital, to the realm of the *ḥāla*, as the term is used to mean both an altered, mystical state and mental illness, and as this dwells in and adjoins everyday life, a neighboring other world around which relationships unfold. Part 2 of the book, "The Passage: Imagination, Alienation," is an ethnographic record of such neighboring other worlds, and their capacity for practicing repair as the search for forms: the imaginal reckoning of madness as "torment of life" and divine trial in the mural paintings of the man I call Ilyas, and an excursus to the world of undocumented migration, the passage of "the burning" (*l-ḥarg*, classical Arabic *al-ḥarīq*), conceived as a struggle of the soul (*jihād al-nafs*) and an eschatological crossing, an exit, from the agony of a slow death at home.

Since 2005, however, my conversation with the scholar and therapist I call the Imam has come to the foreground of my work, and the Qur'anic cure has grown as a second major research site. It became clear that no discussion of madness could spare the effort of engaging with modes of theological reasoning, as well as religious experiencing. Indeed, they summon us anew to the problematic of unreason in relation to truth, ethics, and politics—that had also been at the kernel of Freudian thought. Through the ethnographic argument of this book, I propose that in the contemporary redefinition of the Qur'anic cures of the soul some of the core preoccupations of the psychoanalytic approach, in the Freudian and Lacanian sense, are today being addressed. But opening up to this possibility requires admitting a subject whose freedom and finitude, responsibility and praxis are articulated in relation to God, and who is simultaneously ethically active in relation to others in a community. This is a priori excluded in much of contemporary psychoanalytic writing about Islam (with some exceptions), where the subject of psychoanalysis is posed as necessarily secular.[28]

And yet, when the "secularization of the *nafs*" is posed as a necessary requirement for the practice of psychoanalysis in Muslim cultures, the proximity of the psyche and the soul is paradoxically acknowledged, as in this statement by a prominent Lebanese psychoanalyst who points to the difficulty of telling them apart: "How to discern between divine knowledge and the knowledge of the unconscious, as long as the psyche (*nafs*) has not been subjectivized, secularized?"[29] My ethnography moves in the opposite direction, arguing for the productivity of taking seriously this overlap, and the participation of the knowledge of the unconscious in the ontology of the Invisible (*al-ghayb*) and divine knowledge.

The family relationship I pursue in the book between the psychoanalytic and the Islamic traditions is therefore not just analogical. It digs its roots into the intercultural exchanges around the thought of the trace and of the intermediate realm of imagination (*Mundus imaginalis/ʿālam al-mithāl*), and the problematic of divine manifestation and prophetic knowledge.[30] (I do not trace such exchanges in the book, necessarily limited in its scope, not least by my incompetence, but note that the intercultural exchanges that contributed to the psychoanalytic conceptual archive have been shown to be much wider than the Arabo-Greek connection, crucially including Persianate and Perso-Indian traditions.) This is registered in Freud's understanding of dreaming and the unconscious, where Freud borrows from Aristotle's theory of the memory trace, from ancient

Byzantine and Arab treatises of dream interpretation, and from the concept of *Imaginatio* as developed by Albertus Magnus, a thirteenth-century Scholastic writer, whom he sees as prefiguring his own theory of regression in dreams.[31] And it is shown in Lacan's persistent recourse to the European mystical tradition, as well as to Arabic and Islamic sources, Ibn ʿArabi in particular (by the intermediary of Henri Corbin). More fundamentally, it is registered in the centrality and insistence of the enigma of madness in their thought and lives.

Knot of the Soul traces the terms of a possible conversation between Islam and psychoanalysis in two related senses: on the one hand through an ethnographic exploration of the Imagination, and the problem of "figuration" and "exemplarity"; on the other, through an inquiry into what I call—following al-Ghazali (d. AH 505/1111 CE) as well as my ethnography of the jurisprudence of the soul with the Imam—the "agonistics of the soul," and the problematic of the internal otherness of desire in Islamic ethical-medical practices—a problematic that, I suggest, resonates in Freudian and post-Freudian thought. I am thinking in particular of Lacan's reflection on the ethics of psychoanalysis as a mode of engagement with the drive and its surplus enjoyment (*jouissance*), and as an "art of the limit," akin to the mystical play of courtly love, a concept he refines in explicit reference to Ibn ʿArabi.[32]

Histories of Madness

When I first started conducting fieldwork at the psychiatric hospital in Rabat I was told by a senior psychiatrist that the interns were required to read *Histoire de la folie* as an introduction to the contested history and rich imaginary of the field of knowledge and practice they were about to commit to. This is not because the hospital endorsed Foucault's philosophical idealization of madness, as the senior psychiatrist put it, but for the way the book explored multiple sites and configurations, including the early medical and spiritual or supernatural, while posing the problem of translation, which remained a daily conundrum in the emergency room and the wards. Foucault had shown that illnesses, whether they bore the same name or didn't, were not the same illnesses in different historical times (*"Il se peut que, d'un siècle à l'autre, on ne parle pas, sous le même nom, des mêmes maladies; mais c'est que, fondamentalement, il n'est pas question de la même maladie"*);[33] and yet he had also stressed that the experience of madness could not be reduced to a discursive construction, or to a kind of cultural relativism inflected with a fascination with the exotic, as the French had done during the colonial period, and as the ethnopsychiatric approach had proposed in the early postcolonial period.[34] The psychiatrist asked himself and me what it would mean to write a history of madness in Islamic tradition and in Morocco today.

This book is not a return of his question, because in my hands the question took on a whole different life and moved towards an exploration of lives and concepts that could never be returned to the sender. But as I taught Foucault's *History of Madness* over the years in implicit dialogue with my own research, I could see the thread of a conversation that remained active, and which can be felt in its displacements and new figurations.

Originally published in 1961, *History of Madness* can and has been read in many ways, including by Foucault himself, who kept amending the text in its later editions; yet the angle that is important for me here is Foucault's concern with the possibility of what he calls a "dialogue" of reason and unreason and with the "scandal" of folly itself, which in the Middle Ages and early modern Europe had been associated with the pathos of tragedy and the rehearsal in the human world of "irreconcilable cosmic tensions" expressed in visions of the apocalypse.[35] "Madness and non-madness," Foucault writes, "reason and unreason, are confusedly implicated in each other, inseparable as they do not yet exist, and existing for each other, in relation to each other, in the exchange that separates them."[36] *History of Madness* traced the silencing of that exchange.

I am less convinced by the "silencing" in Foucault's argument, standing rather with his critic Gladys Swain on the importance of recognizing the continuing presence of that exchange in the history of madness and in the life of patients. The dialogue of reason and unreason, she argued against Foucault, takes place in the space of an interval (*écart*) between the subject and her or his own madness, as a spark of reflexive insight. It has been well known to caretakers, nurses, and the famous concierge of Bicêtre that, in that interval, it is possible to communicate with the mad. There the mad person can relate to their madness, and the sane person to the insane.[37]

The travelers of the passage on Brandt's poetic and historical Ship of Fools, which Foucault chooses as an emblem of the status of madness at the dawn of European modernity, were figures of the Limit, between this world and the other, a limit that by their intercession gave itself to be felt. The intricate plot of Foucault's text traces the spatial logics and shifting configurations of the construction and exclusion of madness all the way to the nineteenth and early twentieth centuries' establishment of the hospital, between the diverse and disconnected realms of the government of territory, of medicine, philosophy, and the study of the soul (including a description of the *bimāristān*, the Persian and Arab hospital for the mad, where patients were treated with music and water therapies, and of the "cure of the soul," and a discussion of the soul and its passions at the interface of pneumatic medicine and metaphysics). But from beginning to end Foucault also pondered the experience of madness itself, *la folie*, and the way in which, in early modernity, the figure and experience of madness came to occupy the place of a penumbra of being that exceeded the transparency and mastery of knowledge, and was akin to the "thrownness" that had been at the center of his earlier writings on dreaming and the imagination. There he had described the dream as a coming to the fore of "existence" in the surrender of the personal subject: a surrender that was also an encounter with truth.[38]

Vision of Blindness

The voice of the therapist is reciting the Qur᾽an over the body of his patient, a woman, who is lying unconscious during the liturgy of the *ruqya*: at once a cure, a moral exhortation, and the opening of a stage of the soul. It is a scene from the end of this book. The Imam had begun with an evocation of the scene of Judgment, and the torments of fire, to force the invisible presence that refused to separate from that woman to repent and submit. Then suddenly his tone had changed, and the recitation had moved to a passage from Sūrat Yūsuf, the twelfth chapter of the Qur᾽an, which narrates the vicissitudes and trials of the prophet Joseph's life. It is then that the invisible presence had begun to speak, and, in the voice of a *jinn*, had recounted the life and hardship of the woman, as if recognizing the vicissitudes of her soul amidst the adversities and signs of Yusuf's trials.

"The best of narratives" (*aḥsan al-qaṣaṣ*) is how the Qur᾽an announces Yusuf's story: most beautiful, in the sense of a story aesthetically edifying and most exemplary; but also and more importantly in the sense of a narrative that contains "signs" and "lessons" (*āya*, *ʿibra*) for those willing to see them, signs that point to and contain a knowledge of the Invisible, beyond the reach of human perception, and hence of the cosmic reality of the revelation that is the Qur᾽an itself: "How many a sign (*āya*) is there in the heavens and on earth which they pass by (unthinkingly), and on which they turn their backs!" (12:103).[39] Yusuf's story has the nature of one such sign. It is "the account of something that is beyond the reach of perception" (12:102).[40]

It is a well-known story, punctuated by visionary dreams and scenes of instruction and exhortation about the truth of revelation, and closely related in its plot to the story of Joseph and his brothers in the Bible. Freud, an unwitting modern-day Joseph, granted with the gift of imaginative insight and a drive to grasp the "inner meanings of happenings," evokes the story (in the biblical version) in his *Interpretation of Dreams*, where he takes Joseph's divination of the king's dream of the seven cows as an example of the "symbolic method."[41] Like Joseph/Yusuf, Freud is an insistent reader of "signs," willing to risk his steps in the penumbra of life where the mastery of the plot must be surrendered, and exchanged for trust in the guidance of the Other.

The Qur'anic version of the story rehearses its worldly plot in vivid details as the unfolding of powerful, violent, and contradictory passions, betrayals, crimes, and hopes; but it keeps returning to a lacuna, a place or position of blindness, one that eludes human understanding and points to a gaze outside and yet also inside, beyond or beneath the surface of events, and even beyond the capacity to discern by subjects endowed with an extraordinary power of insight such as Yusuf and his father; an opacity and blindness that make manifest, as their obverse, the all-seeing and all-knowing reality of the divine. The narration alternates between the myopic perspective of this world and the all-seeing perspective of God, at moments intervening through direct speech as a voice over, as an exhortation to ponder the lacuna and the paradoxical vision of blindness.

Modern Qur'an commentaries such as that of Sayyid Qutb have attended to the urgency of the historical context of that revelation, at once as factual history and historical allegory, one that may instruct us in our own times of despondency and crisis[42]—the fact that the story of Yusuf, a prophet himself, was revealed to Muhammad in the days of hardship, when estranged from his people in Mecca and just prior to his exilic journey to Medina, when the world around him was hostile, his future clouded, but yet he was called to persevere in the effort. The ordeal of the prophet of Islam, exiled by his contemporaries and striving to found a new community, is mirrored in the trials of Jacob/Ya'qub, Yusuf's suffering father, who is subjected to the loss of two sons, and is treated as a fool for his visionary insight; and it is reflected in the ordeal of Yusuf himself, a child left to die in the desert by his envious brothers, rescued by a caravan but then sold as a slave, again rescued and adopted by a noble of the king of Egypt, but then thrown in jail because of the false accusation of the courtier's wife, who desires him, and whom he desired but renounced to honor the law of his God; all the way to the promise, contained in the final disclosure of the unfathomable logic of the events, when a forgiving and thankful Yusuf is reunited with his father and brothers: "But at last—when those apostles had lost all hope and saw themselves branded as liars, our succor attained to them. (. . .) Indeed, in the stories [of these men] there is a lesson ("sign," *ʿibra*) for those who are endowed with insight" (12:110–11).

And yet intertwined with the vicissitudes of the temporal world, and nested in the traumatic site of the ordeal, is the scene of the soul: the *nafs* (psyche and soul) and its transformations and transfigurations, at work in the imaginal space of the narrative, displacing the scene in the temporal world to a different order of reality, visible as if in watermark. And in fact in this section we find the much-cited verse (lit. "sign," *āya*) spoken by Yusuf himself, which defines the nature of the desiring *nafs*: "I am not trying to absolve myself, for verily the *nafs* does incite to evil" (12:53). It is a depiction of the *nafs* (soul, inner self, breath of life) as moved by desire and passion, but also of the *nafs* in the movement of becoming aware, and already prefiguring the other states of the *nafs* in its striving to purification. At this level, which is no longer that of historical reality, and yet is intertwined and immanent to it, the "best of stories" is the story of the soul in its journey, whose nature is to be moved by desire, at once the signature of its carnal, violent, and vulnerable character and the imprint of its origin and final destination in God. Such is the desire of the courtier's wife (who remains unnamed in the Qurʾan, but elsewhere is known as Zulikha),[43] who, as the poet Jami (d. 1492) suggested, should be read as an allegory of the *nafs* itself. It is a parable of the trials of the soul and its purification (*tazkiya*), as a result of the trials and battles of the embodied *nafs* and its passions. The erotic desire of Yusuf and Zulikha and the envy and greed of Yusuf's brothers are figures of the passions of the soul, the very ground on which the soul and the self can transform and learn to recognize the "signs" that can be a guidance in the world.

Between these two scenes, that of the temporal world and world of the soul, there is a questioning of the nature of the event—the accident, the hurt, the betrayal, the wickedness, the love—that is shown to have the character of the ordeal. This is the meaning of the terms *balāʾ* and *ibtilāʾ*, divine testing and the trial of faith, which in the Qurʾan and already in early exegetical (*tafsīr*) literature highlights the interpellation nested in the event, as a call to recognize the advent of a sign (*āya*) bearing witness to a divine disclosure.[44]

Seen from this angle, events in the temporal world are encompassed by a larger frame within which human history appears as opaque, spotted by zones of penumbra, and interrupted by lacunae that must be acknowledged. The incommensurability of human and divine knowledge—and the reliance on an external, heteronymous law, one that guides through "signs"—is a key lesson of this story. For openness to the inner meaning of happenings requires the capacity to suspend judgment and welcome the penumbra of knowledge, which in the world of the visible attests to the Invisible—the "realm beyond human perception" which manifests itself as blindness. We may call it the "unconscious," *al-lā shuʿūr* (that which is without or beyond the reach of consciousness), an unknown-known, as did early translators of Freud borrowing the term from Ibn ʿArabi, but we must bear in mind that from the perspective of God the unconscious is divine consciousness.

"People are asleep, and when they die they awaken," writes Ibn ʿArabi, citing a hadith in his "ringstone of wisdom of light in the word of Joseph," reflecting on the paradoxical relationship of consciousness and unconsciousness, imagination and revelation, God and the world, in terms of the example of the shadow. God's essence self-discloses through its shadow, and the world, including our lives, belongs to the realm of the shadow, a manifestation of God, unrescindably and intimately connected to its source, and yet infinitly distant from it: "Know that what one calls 'other than the Real' and which is referred to as 'the world' is, in relation to the Real, as a shadow is to an object. It is the shadow of God. (. . .) This divine shadow's locus of manifestation, which we call the world, consists only of the identities of contingent things . . . This shadow extends over the essences of contingent things in the form of the unknown invisible."[45] At once necessary and inadequate, interpretation is a bridge between forms as perceived in the historical world, or in the world of the soul, and the divine essence of which they are shadows. Yusuf's story is a pedagogy of the shadow.

And this leads us to the scene of judgment. The reader who is too quick to identify the culprit in the story (Yusuf's brothers, the woman) will be confused by the unfolding of the events in the realm of worldly happening as in the world of the soul. For as stated multiple times in this Qurʾanic chapter, understanding the "inner meaning of happenings" (*taʾwīl al-aḥādīth*) is not an easy task, and in all cases only partly accessible to human beings, even those, such as Yusuf and his father, endowed with the capacity to perceive the realm beyond human perception and to attain knowledge of the future through visionary dreams. What from the perspective of the temporal world is experienced as a calamity may prove a gift in the world of the soul, or vice versa.

The question posed by the story, in the end, is that of the capacity to receive the lesson ("indeed in the stories of these men, there is a lesson for those endowed with insight"), and learn to read the "signs" presented and concealed in the event. What does it mean to be the subject of trauma, of calamity, of the passions of the soul? And to welcome the event as an "ordeal" (*ibtilāʾ*) that at once seizes and addresses one? This is a question that when asked and engaged may shift the coordinates of the real.

The Work of Death

Searching for a way to visualize the *punctum* of this work, I have repeatedly returned to the image and the concept of the Serpent in the mural painting by the man I call Ilyas, whose life and art I discuss in the second part of the book. The painting portrays a giant creature that Ilyas describes as a serpent, and registers—or as he says "stores"—an experience of madness. The image had emerged ready-made, thrown, as it were, on the wall. Ilyas received it as the advent of an autonomous imaginal form—an image whose reality is independent from the eye or the mind of the beholder, an imaginal coming to presence. All this happened before I knew Ilyas. When we met he was beginning to whitewash the walls of his apartment, to cover over the serpent and send it back to its latent state. In that interim, which I argue granted him a particular kind of gaze, Ilyas offered an interpretation (*tafsīr*) of the painting.

> If we want to understand the painting, there is the serpent, it is the torment of life (*humūm l-ḥayāt*): life when it is hard, when it is painful, is like a serpent. . . . As for the sword (*sayf*), the Sword is the force that conquers (*ghalaba*) all things: next to the sword, he [referring to himself in the third person] wrote in Arabic *Lā ghāliba illā llāh*, "No one is victorious except God," because God, praise and glory on him, only God is the cause of all things. [Meaning that] all that happens in the life of creatures, of human beings (*insān*), all human beings suffer and endure, their successes and their failures, it happens with the permission of God.

Ilyas's mode of witnessing was what he called *taʿbīr* (expression, figuration, symbolization), which I thematize in the book as the interval of figuration. I follow the most expansive sense of *taʿbīr* as a crossing from one world into another. It is at once the interval and its crossing, between incommensurable experiences, spaces, and times. The serpent, for Ilyas, was the "torment of life." It was the agony of the soul itself.

Our conversation spilled over into the writing of this book, and led to considering the forms of relation to what Ilyas figured as the serpent. It is from that angle that we attempted to rethink the conundrum of madness.

What would it mean to receive the disturbing address of the serpent? And for me to register that address in an ethnography?

This is an elusive and yet crucial possibility of ethnography, which I understand with my own life as an ethnographer to mean the writing of the Other, not one that fixes the other person or culture in place as an object of knowledge but one that allows itself to be pierced and guided by the Other, at once an elucidation and a working through.

Was this a problem that concerned solely the ontological consistency of Ilyas's world, with its serpents and visions, or was it instead also something else, and more fundamental beside: not the ontology of the anthropological other, but instead the enigmatic address of a different kind of Other, which summons each of us in a singular way?

Taʿbīr is a mode of engaging with the "torment of life," and with that neighbor that is also one's soul. The task of *taʿbīr* for Ilyas was not just aesthetic, nor was it simply psychological: it was ethical. His use of the concept designated a particular kind of efficacious image, one that can become the operator of a transformation. It was an image that stored the affect of a state, the encoded memory of self-annihilation, and, at the same time, made possible a certain confrontation.

Ilyas's paintings were sites of encounter with an Other that could never be completely mastered or even diagnosed, rendered discursive, or narrated into stories—an Other that nonetheless was woven into his life (and ours) as at once a potentiality and a risk. At moments the serpent, oppressive and consuming, claimed full dominion over the space of the home, as in the acute spells of Ilyas's illness; at other times it could be circumvented, eschewed, agonistically engaged, or encircled in a dance. Over the years of our conversations I came to realize that the interest of his paintings was not just their therapeutic potential (in itself undeniable). Beyond the dialectic of the cure the paintings were themselves an ethical engagement with the incurable—with the serpent, that uncanny and ever-present neighbor.

Freud was not unfamiliar with the problematic of the serpent. He gave it different names—among them "the uncanny" (*das Unheimliche*) and "the death drive" (*der Todestrieb*). One could say that the project of psychoanalysis as he intended it is an effect of that disquieting familiarity with an intimate neighbor, as well as a mode of engaging and eschewing it. This reflection spanned Freud's major works, from the early speculations on the "neighbor" (*Nebenmensch*) and the affective trace in the charting of neural pathways (his first topographic map),[46] to the reminiscences and ecstasies of hysteria, the enigma of self-dissolution in melancholia and in the "unease" (*Unbehagen*) of culture, and his speculations on life, repetition, and trauma.

I am thinking here, however, of a peculiar letter Freud wrote in 1922 to the Austrian writer Arthur Schnitzler, himself a topographer of the uncanny. Freud had never met the famous writer, and wrote to send him well wishes on his birthday, making the "too intimate" confession:

> I think I have avoided you from a kind of reluctance to meet my double. Your determinism as well as your skepticism—what people call pessimism—your being seized by the truths of the unconscious and the instinctual drives in man, your undoing of our conventional cultural securities, the insistent preoccupation of your thoughts with the polarity of love and death; all this moves me with an uncanny feeling of familiarity. (In a small book entitled *Beyond the Pleasure Principle*, published in 1920, I tried to reveal Eros and the death drive as the original powers whose interplay dominates all the riddles of life.)[47]

Indeed, in a short text titled "The Work of Death" (*le travail de la mort*) the psychoanalyst Jean-Bertrand Pontalis writes of the central and enigmatic place that death occupies in Freud's theoretical project as well as in his own life, which, he notices, was marked for Freud not only by a tormenting angst but also by a number of somatic symptoms, including cardiac arrhythmia, a fact that points to the uncanny intertwining of signs and resistant somatic materialities.[48] Pontalis argues that the work of death in Freud is a silent carving—an "antagonistic work of unbinding"—that arguably traverses and drives both the project of psychoanalysis and the lives of Freud and his patients. It shows in the very lacunae of Freud's argument, in the specific style that Freud describes as his "limping," and from his repeated admissions of inadequacy. The work of death is insistent and elusive and by its nature is resistant to analysis; it manifests itself in the enigma of repetition, and in the "fainting" of the subject that for Freud is associated with trauma. But if trauma can be said to be one of the figures of the work of death, this is only because, as Freud posits it in *Beyond the Pleasure Principle*, trauma exposes the impossible experience of a time before time, before human and even organic existence.

Freud does not explicitly address the ethics of engaging with this "work of death" other than by opening his own life and work to the enigma of alterity. Pontalis, on the other hand, writing in the shadows of Freud, does explicitly articulate the ethical dimension of that engagement in terms of a "tending towards" (*se porter à la rencontre*) of both trauma and the work of death. Tending towards the antagonistic work of death is a never-resolved engagement with the incurable, with the violence and the heteronomy of desire, with madness, and with the materiality of the soma: with the scandal and enigma of alterity. It is an engagement that, Pontalis tells us, inaugurates the movement of life in its erotic and ethical dimensions. *Taʿbīr*/figuration was for Ilyas such a mode of "tending towards." My ethnography is as well.

The Original Syntax

The ethical-eschatological legacy of psychoanalysis I am attempting to reclaim is a legacy that traverses and interrupts, in the form of a countermove, what in 1933 a young Lacan had dubbed as "the bourgeois theory of psychology," its "Cartesian machine" and its organo-dynamism, and their related "naïve realism of the object"—as well as "the bourgeois philosophical conception of the human being as originally endowed with absolute moral freedom, and individual responsibility."[49]

Against a "bourgeois psychology," whose instrumental task, Lacan saw, even in its humane expressions, was to optimize the adaptation of labor to a Fordist economy as a kind of human engineering, Lacan opposed a psychoanalytic ethics of being summoned by the interpellation of madness as the scanning of a "time of the End," in the psychiatric hospital, listening to the delusions of patients, as well as in the quotidian dimensions of life. What did this mean? This meant, conceptually, but also ethically, to situate the risk of madness at the very heart of life and subjectivity, not as a contingent malfunction, or organic pathology (as Lacan argued in 1946 against French psychiatrist Henry Ey)[50] but as the "metaphysical" question of an ever-present virtuality: the virtuality of "a fault (*faille*) opened up in its essence." If for the modern science of psychology and later psychiatry madness was a problem of a primarily juridical nature (for it disturbed the assumption of individual moral freedom and responsibility, and thus needed to be codified), for Lacan it brought to the fore the radical vulnerability of the human subject, determining at once its potentiality and its being-in-danger.

> Thus rather than resulting from a contingent fact—the frailty of its organism—madness is the permanent virtuality of a fault (*faille*) opened up in its essence. And far from being "an insult" to freedom, madness is freedom's most faithful companion, following its every move like a shadow. Not only can

> man's being not be understood without madness, but it would not be man's being if it did not bear madness within itself as the limit of his freedom (*s'il ne portait pas en lui la folie comme limite de sa liberté*).[51]

"The limit of freedom," for Lacan, is the ontological insufficiency of the human, its fundamental dependency on the externality of an "Imago" in which the subject is at once alienated and constituted. It is also the intimate alterity of desire itself, later conceptualized as the intimate exteriority of the drive (*Trieb*). The Imago, Lacan explains, should be understood in the full magical resonance of the term, its deathly fascination, its internecine rivalry, its relationship with a death. It is a foreign and most intimate neighbor. The human subject is born as ontologically insufficient, subjected to the calling of an externality, which constitutes the geological "fault" (*faille*) of its essence.

In the writings of the young Lacan (resonant in this sense with Foucault's early reflection on the experience of unreason as a manifestation of Judgment Day in modernity), an ethics of being summoned by the experience of madness is one that ponders the limits of freedom, the ambivalent bonding to an intimate neighbor, and the impersonal agency of the imagination, as in other times and other traditions one pondered death as an ethical work. This meant (in the direction of the Freudian concept of the unconscious, and beyond) to appreciate yet without romanticizing it the production of significance in "another scene," independent of intentionality and consciousness, and which in Lacan's early work was the Other Scene of psychosis. Indeed in his 1933 essay on the "Problem of Style" Lacan pondered the impersonal productivity of delusion, and invited the reader to appreciate the "knots of significance" that emerged from their midst, which, much like myth and stylized poetics, engendered, he said, complex symbolic forms and at times provided the "original syntax" of an epoch.[52] Other times and civilizations, he noted, had been much better equipped than we are to appreciate and channel the force of what was capable of being communicated in such "delusional" forms.

Unending Cases

Knot of the Soul reflects a commitment to ethnography as both empirical research and a philosophical project. Its method is to trace and stage in its writing a casuistry of examples, "passages" and "figurations" in the sense discussed above, as well as "cases," if one is to rethink the Freudian strategy of allowing a multiplicity of voices and their struggles and counterpoints to emerge, beading singularities in a paradigmatic form, in order to outline a form of life and produce, by the same turn, a particular angle of vision.

The stories, or "cases," are themselves theoretical sites of elucidation. Concepts emerge within the ethnography, and are brought into conversation with other concepts. Diegesis, mimesis, and exegesis are intertwined, and it is in that way that I hope the book will be read. The ethnography is more than just a description of the there-and-then of its anthropological object, be that contemporary Morocco, psychiatry, the life of patients, psychoanalysis, Qur'anic cures, or the Islamic ethical tradition. It has the nature of a coming to the fore, an encounter, with a world and a tradition, but more fundamentally with what Ilyas called the "torment of life."

I take writing not simply as a matter of genre (in the sense, for instance, of a literary genre of ethnographic writing that pays attention to the poetics of description and evocation) but, acknowledging Maurice Blanchot's intimation in *The Space of Literature,* as the site of a "passage," a passage to another side of the real, where the subject recedes and the world comes to the fore in the impersonality of the image.[53]

Such a *passage,* I argue, following my interlocutors' Arabic conceptual vocabulary—and the terms of an Islamic tradition of the Imaginal where the image is a modality of presence, and cosmic existence is identical to imagination (*khayāl*)[54]—is the cipher of the relation between loss and expression, between this world and the other. The insistent terms, which we have encountered in the previous pages, are *ʿibra* and *taʿbīr*: *ʿibra,* "a passage or bridge across incommensurable places, spaces, languages, or times, as well as the incommensurability of the spaces themselves; a moral example, a lesson to be drawn from things past, events, portentous signs or histories; the passages of migration, translation, or conversion, and the crossing of death"; *taʿbīr,* "expression and figuration, giving form, imaginalization."[55] The sense of passage is also implied in the Arabic term *ḥāla,* "state" or "condition," "altered state," and therefore also pathological state and "case," which is a recurrent and important term in the book. For me, such a "passage" directly concerns the practice of ethnographic writing, as a double responsibility to the real in the sense of both the document and its transfiguration.

Two texts and styles have been on my mind as I thought of cases in relation to this ethnography: the first is the journal of a cure, by the psychoanalyst Marion Milner, who wrote the daily record of her sessions with a schizophrenic woman named Susan, in a style akin to a "mutual dreamwork rather than a cumulative process of understanding."[56] The sessions became part of their lives over many years, often including Susan's drawings, remade by Milner to better understand them, attempting to allow the space and time from which something could emerge on its own, and where both therapist and patient were, as Milner put it, "in the hands of the living God," delivered to the heteronomy and guidance of an Other, where "outcomes are no longer the point."

The second, very different text is Fanon's collection of ten case histories from the Blida-Jontville psychiatric hospital in Algeria.[57] Fanon listens, and invites us into the fact of madness that bears witness to the real of an unending war, and the temporal indeterminacy of trauma, pondering that vulnerability exposed, and renouncing the mastery of an exit, or the resolution of the cure.

His discussion of cases opens on a cautionary note: "*mais la guerre continue*" (but the war goes on). The war is unending, and even when it seems to have ended, it returns, or reopens its wounds in the temporality of the aftermath; and when we think we can locate an event, the time of trauma sends us backwards and forwards, in a labyrinth of shadows and replicas (*reéditions*) from which there seems to be no exit. How are we to receive this warning? On the one hand the all-pervasive character of the war, colonial and anticolonial, sets the condition for an "*atmosphere de guerre totale,*" a climate of total war, which is the fertile ground of mental illnesses, and of an impairment that will persist well after the war is over, and sometimes forever. The violence of war, Fanon tells us, is itself the continuation or extension of the violence of the colonial system, in its labor of undoing, and the two become indistinguishable. And indeed, if one is to follow that analogy, which takes us back to the question of trauma and time in *Black Skin, White Masks,* the unending war is also the unending temporality of trauma, in the overlapping of the racist structure of the colony and the sociogeny of the psyche. "When does a historical catastrophe become traumatic?"[58] On the other hand Fanon is inviting us into the zone of that unending, summoning us to the midst of illness and unreality. The cases he presents in series A, "*troubles reactionnels,*" related to a traumatic event, and series B, bearing witness to the climate of total war in Algeria, are offered as fragments without resolution, or as situations where what is disclosed in the exchange with the therapist is the uncertainty of the event, the fact of belatedness, and the co-presence of earlier traumas. Fanon listens, and appreciates the symptom that bears witness to the war, more vividly and eloquently than any historical work.

From one fragment of life, or encounter, to another, part 1 of this book, "Psychiatric Fragments in the Aftermath of Culture," attempts to apprehend and describe a scene doubly marked by an urgent request (for listening, for recognition, for care, by the patients) and, at the same time, by the impossibility of inhabiting the available cultural or modern medical institutional references. This, for two reasons. One is the lack of concrete access to modern psychiatric and biomedical care, and of juridical and political rights—a situation that makes any claim to health rights essentially empty. The second reason is a form of subjective homelessness. So much is expressed in the hiatuses, the silences, of encounters in the psychiatric ER. And then, in the context of the hospital, and in several of the cases I consider in the book, there is the impossibility of the cultural reference itself, the inability to find healing in the sanctioned locations and vocabularies, in the cures of the jinn and the sanctuaries of saints, and even the cruel and persecutory reversal of the signifiers of cultural belonging. This is a central theme in the narratives of the men and women I met in the hospital, and it is a site of reflection in the book. It exposes the conundrum of an attachment impossible to dissolve, the death grip of a "culture in agony" that is unlivable but that won't let one go.

And yet, in the midst of the Islamic Revival of recent years, other understandings of illness and other kinds of therapy have appeared, granting a new authorization to practices that had been both foreclosed and rendered incommensurable on the grounds of the hospital and in the larger discourse of national public health. Unlike "traditional" cures, associated with spirit possession and the cult of saints and debased by colonial and postcolonial health institutions, reformed Islamic cures, known as *ʿilāj sharʿī* ("cures according to the Shariʿa," or "lawful cures"), draw legitimacy from a renewed investment of the medical-spiritual tradition of prophetic medicine (*al-ṭibb al-nabawī*) and an integral understanding of human life and subjectivity in relation to God.

This is the subject of part 3 of this book, "The Jurisprudence of the Soul," the longest and the last one I completed, and to my eyes, the most important and the most incomplete. It is based on nine years of intermittent conversations with the scholar and therapist I call the Imam, concerning the Qurʾanic cure of madness, the nature of the soul and its faculties, the agonistics of the *nafs*, the disablement of soul choking, the question of illness and divine trial (*ibtilāʾ*), the law and the "path to the hereafter," as well as on witnessing *ruqya* sessions and writing the stories of some of his patients. The concluding section, "The Passion of Zulikha, a Dramaturgy of the Soul," is written as the journal of a cure and in the imaginal space opened by the liturgy of the *ruqya*. It is an ethnographic illustration of what I called above "the art of the limit" as a form of working through, and as a modality of testimony at the intersection of the personal and the collective, the self and the other, the living and the dead, the human and the divine.

In the cures practiced by the Imam, psychic/spiritual illness is understood in terms of a problematic of societal self-transformation in a time of social and moral crisis. The conceptual roots of this etiology extend into a classical Islamic understanding of the soul, its organs and faculties, its forms of embodiment, and its capacities for witnessing through the work of the imagination—an understanding of the soul that is grounded in the Qur᾽an and in the commentary of the medieval Muslim scholars Ibn Sina, al-Ghazali, Ibn Qayyim al-Jawziyya, and Ibn Kathir, among others, in their encounter with Aristotle, Galen, and Plotinus. The contemporary spiritual cures recover this understanding of life in order to address the conundrums of contemporary existence; and in doing so they reach to a generative kernel in the tradition, directly challenging the ideological construct of postcolonial modernity.

However, the shariʿa cures exceed the context of political-ethical critique that has framed many of the practices and debates of the contemporary Islamic Revival, for they are anchored in an approach to illness that conceives of the subject as a vulnerable being of passions. From this angle, the question of ethics is posed differently, and more ambiguously, than in the vocabulary of perfectibility that holds a prominent and authoritative place in this Islamic ethical tradition. The task of perfectibility, or, as al-Ghazali called it, the training or dressing of the soul and of character (*riyāḍat al-nafs*), remains an important dimension, as it is in the more general ethical project of the Islamic Revival. Shariʿa cures, however, are staked on a confrontation with forms of destruction that are at once internal and external to the soul and the self; they exemplify and perform the ontological and ethical risk of a being of desire, who struggles with its passions in a *jihād al-nafs*.

In the account of the soul I strung together from my conversations with the Imam over the years, imagination carries a pivotal role, both as a faculty of the personal soul and as an autonomous realm of cosmic existence. The Imam stresses the formative power of the imagination—the formative faculty (*taṣawwur*), the imaginative faculty (*takhayyul*)—in its capacity to configure, form, and de-form, and he shows the way images have an effect on the heart (*al-qalb*), the spiritual center of being. For images, he says, contain the affective form of a life design.

His therapeutic and pedagogical interventions are aimed at a repossession of imagination, which is also a decolonization of desire, for he considers that, in our time, it is through a coopting of the imagination that human beings, Muslim and not, are reduced to captivity and oppression. To understand his plea we will need to cast aside the notion of imagination as fancy, phantasy, or even mental representation, and instead appreciate the way imagination is here the faculty of the soul that makes possible discernment, knowledge, and a wrestling with truth that is the tending towards of the subject.

It is in this sense, I argue in the book, that a conversation is possible between the ethics of psychoanalysis and ethics in the Islamic tradition. A reflection on evil, violence, and despair is central to the practice of these cures, for the realm of madness is fraught with theological and existential risks. They provide nuanced and differing ways of asking questions, on the terrain of a spiritual struggle (*jihād al-nafs*) that is never resolved, and that in that impossibility of resolution attests to the presence, vulnerability, and activity of an ethical subject. In that interval it becomes possible to both listen to and engage with the "torment of life" in its singularity.

Postscript January 2016

> In the middle of the eighth [fourteenth] century, civilization both in the East and the West was visited by a destructive plague which devastated nations and caused populations to vanish. It swallowed up many of the good things of civilization and wiped them out. It overtook the dynasties at the time of their senility, when they had reached the limit of their duration. It lessened their power and curtailed their influence. It weakened their authority. Their situation approached the point of annihilation and dissolution. Civilization decreased with the decrease of mankind. Cities and buildings were laid waste, roads and way signs were obliterated, settlements and mansions became empty, dynasties and tribes grew weak. The entire inhabited world changed. The East, it seems, was similarly visited, though in accordance with and in proportion to (the East's more affluent) civilization. It was as if the voice of existence in the world had called out for oblivion and restriction, and the world had responded to its call. God inherits the earth and whomever is upon it. When there is a general change of conditions, it is as if the

> entire creation had changed and the whole world had been altered, as if it were a new and repeated creation, a world brought into existence anew.
>
> —Ibn Khaldun, *The Muqaddima: An Introduction to History*[59]

When this manuscript was in its final stages, the Maghreb and the Middle East—as is well known—entered a phase of upheavals, transformations, and destruction that remain ongoing. Demonstrations and revolts furrowed Morocco as well. It became clear from the first days that the uprisings were the expression of an existential condition: the condition of what I refer to in this book as "soul choking" (*taḍyīq al-nafs*) in the vocabularies of the Imam, and describe elsewhere, particularly in section 6 of this book ("The Burning"), in the lexicon of despair of Moroccan youth themselves in relation to what they called "the slow death," as formulated in the horizon of undocumented migration. (That section was originally written when the risked crossing of the Mediterranean could not have predicted, if perhaps did prefigure, what would become the fast and massive death of migrants and refugees from wars in the region in years to come, which turned the Mediterranean into an underwater graveyard.)

The uprisings articulated new forms of collective agency, forms of the political and the spiritual beyond juridical rationality and self-preservation (what people then called the overcoming of fear). While often couched in a language that demanded institutional accountability, freedom, and democracy, their voice and actions have also marked an interruption, perhaps most poignantly exemplified in the acts of self-immolation that in 2011 and 2012 took place in Tunisia, Egypt, and Morocco, situated at the ambiguous and morally troubled border of suicide and testimony. Irrespective of the outcome of the uprisings, this confrontation with the limits of relation and life has engendered an angle of vision—a kind of anamorphic mirror that revealed the machinery of subjugation and a desire for the reclaiming of life.

The five years that have lapsed since January 2011 have witnessed the rapid succession of hope and despair, of the imagination of possible new worlds and the catastrophic registering of forms of life being annihilated. Popular revolts and revolutions were followed, in some cases (Egypt and Tunisia), by attempts at dismantling the infrastructure and machineries of postcolonial authoritarian states, and by the tensions and violent suppressions and restorations that ensued, both internally and in the confrontation with larger geopolitical interests. In Morocco an initial uprising was muffled by the promise of reforms, the fear of internecine violence, and the vivid memory of a history of state violence and suppression. While

Egypt underwent multiple upheavals, repression and its restoration, Syria, Yemen, and Iraq have been ravaged by unending war and the rise of civil and sectarian strife that laid cities and countryside to waste, causing overwhelming devastation and death, and as I am writing the end is not in view. This prompted a massive movement of refugees to neighboring Jordan, Lebanon, and Turkey (with refugees reaching all the way to Tunisia and Morocco), and since 2015 to the European Union in what has been labeled the "European refugee crisis." Images of bodies floating on the Mediterranean, of Syrian corpses on the beaches of Turkey and Greece, of Syrian and other refugees waiting on the train tracks and pushed back in Budapest, tear-gassed in Macedonia, and welcomed in Vienna flooded the world media in fall 2015, producing paradigmatic portraits of victims and totems of humanitarian care, and registering a European anxiety of invasion, alternately constructing the refugees as phobic objects (bringing the reality of war and death into the intimacy of bourgeois homes), instrumental objects of neoliberal governmentality and humanitarian care, and objects of narcissistic enjoyment.[60]

How might this recent history be accounted for *otherwise*? How might we ponder and mourn the dead beyond the drive to instrumentality and appropriation? How could an accounting of this recent history at once register the hope and desire that animated the revolts, and reflect on the destruction that ensued, through the traumatic legacy of a former history of revolts and suppressions that has punctuated the region? From the "disastrous" ending of World War I[61] to the establishment of modern colonial states, the wars of liberation, and the unfinished work of "independence," from the Maghreb to the Mashreq, and the newness of the catastrophic present, what would it mean to approach this moment as at once a repetition and what Ibn Khaldun called "a general change of conditions"?

In the third part of the book, "The Jurisprudence of the Soul," I trace a conceptual configuration in the Islamic ethical-eschatological tradition that associates the experience of calamity with the event of divine trial, moral and existential questioning through the notion of *ibtilāʾ*: "to put to test," through accident, through adversity, through contingency, through illness, through migration, through poverty, but also through health and plenty, success and fulfillment. I draw the centrality of this concept and its crucial relevance for understanding the present moment from conversations with the Imam, who appeals to this notion with reference to the ethical conundrum of the subject's responsibility in the encounter with illness as in the context of personal or collective calamitous events; specifically, the fact of undocumented migration and the risk to life this entails, and in our most recent conversations, the ethical implications of the current catastrophic events, from war and destruction in Syria, to sectarian strife, to the rise of the "Islamic State" and its appeal for some European and Middle Eastern youths.

The concept of *ibtilāʾ* is instantiated in a well-known passage of the Qurʾan: "Every soul (*kullu nafsi*) shall have a taste of death: And We test you (*nablūkum*) by evil and by good by way of *fitna*, and to Us you must return" (Qurʾan 21:35).

The stress on responsibility is central. *Ibtilāʾ* is a paradigm of decision, testing, in the passage through the world understood as ordeal. In the words of the Imam, "testing and contingency are a rule of the cosmos (*ibtilāʾ sunnatu kawniyya*), but the question is what one does in the confrontation with it." The configuration of *ibtilāʾ* as "accident" and "testing" crosses the boundary of the personal and the collective, the medical and the political, the realms of politics and of the soul. "Endurance" of calamity is thus not just a normative compliance. It is a sign of awareness of God's lesson, a lesson for those who have insight. An endorsement of one's destiny in the fullest vital sense.

PART I

Psychiatric Fragments in the Aftermath of Culture

ONE

Testimony in Counterpoint

> The lines of force, having crumbled, no longer give direction. In their stead a new system of values is imposed, not proposed, but affirmed, by the heavy weight of cannons and sabers. The setting up of the colonial system does not of itself bring about the death of the native, autochthonous culture. Historic observation reveals, on the contrary, that the aim sought is rather a continued agony than a total disappearance of the pre-existing culture. This culture, once living and open to the future, becomes closed, fixed in the colonial status, trapped in the joke of oppression. At once present and mummified, it testifies against its members.[1]
>
> —Frantz Fanon

> Begin by not assuming that you understand . . . It is precisely for having always radically misrecognized, in the phenomenology of pathological experience, the dimension of dialectics, that psychiatric clinic has been led astray. If you understand, so much the better, keep it to yourself, the important thing is not to understand, it's to attain the truth.[2]
>
> —Jacques Lacan

A late morning in May 1999—the grassy area around the emergency ward where visitors had been waiting in little groups is now empty and burned by the sun, while the narrow hallway of the prefabricated ER building is packed with patients and their families waiting their turn to be received by the psychiatrist on call. Amina arrives late, escorted by her father. Cutting across the thick line of patients, she approaches the head nurse at the reception counter and demands to see "her doctor," Dr. N. The head nurse tells her that she'll have to come back another day, she doesn't have an appointment in "post-cure," and doesn't seem to be in need of urgent care.

Her father comes up to the counter to plead; he looks old and exhausted, says that they have come from far away, have traveled since dawn in a long-distance bus. A nurse recognizes the young woman: she's been hospitalized here before. She comes from the backcountry, a village next to Sidi Slimane, in the Gharb region; "a familiar face," he says. By complete chance Dr. N. happens to be walking through the hallway; I am with him and we are in the midst of conversation. He sees her. "A former patient," he tells me. "She's come a long distance, we can't send her back." He turns to her with a smile of recognition, welcomes her. She smiles back. He explains to me that she had been his patient two years before, in the locked ward, where she had remained for over three months. He directs her to a room, and invites me to come in with them.

These were the last few months the old ER building was in use. In 2000 the emergency unit moved to a new building outside the compound of the hospital proper, and adjacent to the new substance abuse center (*Centre de prévention et de recherche en toxicomanie*) that opened the same year. The old ER had been a temporary addition on the grounds of the hospital founded in 1963, which included four pavilions built in the exposed concrete architecture of the modernist 1960s in Morocco: two locked wards, one for men and the other for women, and two open wards (*cliniques*), one for men and the other for women, where patients in less acute condition and who could pay were cared for. There was an administration building, which had been the original nucleus of the hospital, built by the French prior to Independence in the neoclassical colonial style, a cafeteria open to the patients, and, far at the end of the hospital grounds, in the middle of the garden, the prefabricated building of the ER (*al-mustaʿjilāt* in Arabic, *les urgences* in French). It only had a few rooms, which fulfilled the double and heavy purpose of urgent care and post-cure. There were no beds, and the patients admitted in emergency were sent directly to the wards. The new ER was instead a semiautonomous unit of the hospital, with its own team of psychiatrists and nurses, and dormitory-style rooms where patients were kept in observation until they could be moved to the hospital ward or discharged. My fieldwork, which had started in 1999 in the old ER building and the wards, was resumed in 2001 and lasted until 2003, in the new emergency unit, the wards, and the staff meetings. But the impact of the first encounters in the old ER building remains indelible, as is the voice of Amina.

Much later, I am writing in the margin of that voice, on that day and many other days, over the span of the several months during which I met with her, her psychiatrist, and her family on the grounds of the hospital. My words are woven in interstices of her own recitations, recollections, and silences, in the hiatuses of the biographical, medical, and juridical narratives that were and could be told of her, attempting to register in the writing, as well as in the analytic reflection, as a form of listening and of response, the impact of Amina's presence and her absence and the enigma of what she called her madness. I attempt to register the performance of her voice and the multiplicity of other voices that can be heard through hers, those to which she bears witness, unawares, and the voices of those for whom she wills to testify, the emblems of a generation choked off and violated, casualties of modern life that can no longer speak in their names. They are shadow presences summoned to the scene of our conversations, other voices and echoes that exceed the terms of the psychiatric contract and the economy of the institutional encounter, where illness and pain can only be authenticated as standardized and atomized suffering. At a time when the narrative and cinematic representations of traumatic events are central pieces in the construction of evidence and cultural reality, occupying the core of medical and juridical institutions and rationalities, human rights practices, and media markets, I attempt here to carve a space for reflection, translation, and research that might drift aside, in an "untimely" fashion. Drifting aside, as well, from the still crucial debates on how trauma, witnessing, and biography exemplify and deploy strategies of global power, or how, in a related sense, they become enabling or disabling idioms within larger logics of the state, as grounds of appeal, compensation, recognition, or inclusion.[3] It becomes important then, for an anthropological ethics of listening, and what I call registering, to ponder Benjamin's reflections on how translation is a practice of alterity, and to keep in mind Lacan's warning that the other can be "*reconnu*" (recognized) but never "*connu*" (known); that difference between recognizing and knowing scans the possibility of encounter.[4]

It will then be a question of a singular life, apprehended within the particular and constraining frame of an encounter within the physical space and discursive terrain of the psychiatric institution; apprehended as well in the back and forth of an exchange that I attempt to capture here in the mode of performance—the only one that might grasp the taking place of an utterance, the said and unsaid of a dialogue, the moments of opacity, and prove capable of describing the stakes of subjectivity and culture at a moment of questioning. I choose a strategy that might be called miniaturist, for I think that in following the meanderings of particular lives one might better apprehend the articulation between heterogeneous and even clashing vocabularies and registers of experience, whose continuity is lived with violence and is illegible in a representation of culture, for belonging itself poses a problem.

Amina is perhaps twenty-five. Dressed in a dark blue jelaba with a white headscarf tied under her chin, urban style in the countryside, she has green eyes and an intense expression. At our first meeting in the emergency unit, the psychiatrist asks her father to leave us and wait outside. He addresses her: Does she recognize him? She smiles. Of course! He is Dr. N., her doctor (*ṭabīb dyālī*, my doctor). She says that she's glad to see him. Speaking Arabic with the intonation and turns of phrases of her local vernacular, she tells a story I follow with some difficulty, in which the frightening image of a man chasing her with a knife is intertwined with an account of the solitary pleasure she takes in listening to songs on a cassette player. "You want the truth? I'm afraid of a guy, a killer of souls" (*n'awdlik l-wāqi'? kankhaf min waḥd ddri qātil r-rūḥ*).[5] She tells us that she's still a virgin (*'azba*), begins to cry, and then addresses me directly—me, a woman with an uncertain role, seated a few steps from the psychiatrist. She is still a virgin, she repeats; it's visible just from looking at her, right? The other day a man approached her by the side of the river in her village and insulted her, accusing her of being *fāsda* (defiled, a prostitute). She answered that this wasn't true, that she was an honorable woman, that she didn't work in the orange tree plantations anymore, and that she took her medications every day. At this point she begins to cry and implores Dr. N. to give her a prescription.

Dr. N. remembers her story and the context of her previous illness; he asks some standard questions in order to assess her orientation to time and place. He explains to me that Amina was hospitalized two years earlier for three months (a long time in this hospital and according to the law that regulates psychiatric hospitalization),[6] in response to a state of severe confusion linked to a traumatic event: her repudiation on the night of her wedding. In her fragmented account today, Amina summons three scenes that keep coming back like a refrain during our conversations over the coming weeks: her "expulsion" the night of her wedding ceremony, her confinement within the enclosure of a saint (*sayyid*, a saint and a sanctuary), and her arrival at the hospital in an ambulance of the *protection civile*, the paramedics of the emergency rescue. "Her story is incoherent but is not unreal," Dr. N. tells me. He attempts to weave the pieces together, and insists that although her experience is painful and fragmented and might even be delirious at moments, it remains anchored in reality. That violent reality must be acknowledged. At the time of her first hospitalization, Amina received a diagnosis of "*bouffée delirante*" (acute psychotic episode), under the rubric of what was then described as a hysteric personality. Dr. N. was her psychiatrist then, and that had been his own assessment at the time. But now he defers his diagnosis, cautiously limiting himself to pointing out the role of trauma in her symptoms and experience, as well as in his own interpretation of the patient's state. He opens the door and beckons her father to return.

The father reports that Amina has lost her mind again—"that thing came back to her, the madness came back again" (*arjaʿ lah dak shī, arjaʿ lha l-ḥumq*). In Moroccan Arabic, *l-ḥumq*[7] is a figure of raging madness, beyond all symbolic mediation by the jinn or the other beings with whom it might be possible to relate or engage in combat. In its radical generality, *l-ḥumq* evokes the *junūn* of Qurʾanic resonance,[8] a concept in Arab medicine,[9] and a figure in poetry: madness beyond treatment or return. In the vernacular understanding, *l-ḥumq* is recognized by its intractability in interpersonal relations, as in the saying *l-ḥmāq kaydrib b-l-ḥajar* ("the mad person throws stones"). It indicates a loss of agency and a state beyond thinking; as such, it is different from delusion or obsessive seclusion in an inner world, states conveyed by other metaphors and vocabularies of madness.

The father contradicts his daughter's story, explaining that the hospital was the only option after she threatened her mother and sisters with a knife. Amina begins to cry once again. Dr. N. proposes a stay at the hospital: *Naʿsi?* Would you like to sleep here, rest a bit? The expression is commonly used to indicate hospitalization, but here, in Dr. N.'s voice, it carries a comforting, caring connotation. After a moment of hesitation, she declines, and he scribbles a prescription—Nozinan, a neuroleptic ("to sedate her," he explains later, suggesting that he doesn't think she is actually delusional), and Tegretol, a mood regulator. He schedules her for an appointment the following week. Amina asks me if I'll also be there. She has, she tells me, a photo to show me. I promise to come. With this exchange she establishes the rules of a game so to speak, suggesting that, however imperceptibly, she will be the one directing during the following months, pulling invisible threads and diverting the institutional configuration of the therapeutic relationship. A game in which we will all become entangled and where no one, psychiatrist, patient, or anthropologist, will remain in their assigned place, but is involved as an interested party, in the events and their making.

Amina showed herself to be caught in a web of losses that had the repetitive, tragic scansion of a fate. In the institutional space of the hospital, and in the clinical encounter as she experienced it (at least as she conveyed that experience to me once I became a factor in the story), at issue for her was the possibility of bearing witness—at once to the injustice that had become her fate and to her pain. Of bearing witness, as well, as Dr. N. and I came to realize, to the fate of an absent collectivity, a vanished people or a people to come, the dead and the unborn, for which she offered her antiphonical call. (Antiphony, Nadia Serematakis tells us, is the back and forth of a lament, which "hears" and "speaks" on behalf and in the voice of the dead, creating reciprocity and connectedness for both the dead and the living.)[10] The scattered form of her narration mirrors the dismembering of a life, echo of other losses, Amina's own, as well as those of a generation for which she elects to become the voice. It is "the new generation," she says, the youths "who went to school but failed," and to whom she keeps returning in our conversations; the youth who give themselves to death, "take their lives" (*intaharū*), in the river by the side of her village. Amina casts herself as their "representative," in an act of mourning that is also a testimony in a court of law: "To 'witness,' 'suffer for,' and 'to come out as representative for' are narrative devices in laments that fuse jural notions of reciprocity and truth claiming with the emotional nuances of pain. (. . .) The concept of trial here evokes the 'judgement of the dead,' the notion of ordeal, and the last opportunity to be witnessed and represented by the living."[11]

Her story and her life elude anthropological and even psychiatric exemplarity: they unfold in the mode of reverie, the mark of an experience of fear, where the criteria of truth become uncertain. And yet in her telling, as if by the gesture of a reverse hagiography—one that writes catastrophe in the place of miracles[12]—Amina speaks a truth of a different order, beyond the circumstantial sequencing of events, and offers her life as the exemplar of a historical condition—that of a collectivity from which she knows herself to be banished—and yet on behalf of which she is perpetually mourning. The "injustice" that determined her fate overflows her individual life, becoming transfigured as the cipher of a collective dispossession. Her lament is at once an attestation of loss, and a poetic gesture of repair.

Amina poses the question of the present—one out of joint and dismembered—through her search for "evidence" and an appeal for testimony, a word and concept to which she turns in its multiple semantic and juridical configuration. *Al-shahāda*, from the verbal root *shahida*, to testify—in the sense of being present, of seeing with one's own eyes, of having a personal experience of something, of attesting to that experience with one's life—is the same word from which the legal term for witness (*shāhid*) and the modern administrative term for certificate are drawn.[13] *Shahīd* is also the classical (and modern) term for martyr, ultimate testimony of faith in the sacrifice of self. Most importantly here, the *shahāda* is also the utterance of the formula *ashhadu an lā ilāha illā llāh,* "I bear witness that there is no god but God," by which one becomes a Muslim.

In this story, the testimony in question is the hybrid progeny of this constellation. It emerges in the quasi-juridical establishment of a truth of the self through the intermediary of the modern state's techniques of veridiction (official papers, certificates, identification cards, photos, evidentiary exhibits of a circumstantial justice) and by means of procuring recognition from the institutional others to whom she appeals (the public health physician, the judge, the psychiatrist, the anthropologist). But the truth sought after in this way is also that of speech—in the Lacanian sense of *parole*—which makes itself heard through the transference with the psychiatrist and in a nonclinical sense with me; and through the performance of a symptom (what she calls her madness) that articulates Amina's own registering of a collective history's traumatic real. In Lacan's words, key in her recitation is "what plays the part of resonance in speech. For the function of language there is not to inform but to evoke" (*ce qui, dans la parole, fait office de resonance. Car la function du langage n'y est pas d'informer, mais d'évoquer*).[14]

The criteria for truth are thus not simply circumstantial or epistemological but also ethical. Ultimately, this is what Amina calls her challenge: "I am defiant" (*anā ʿāṣiya*), she will say, "I stand up to my challenge." It is the challenge of constituting herself as a witness to a social and existential condition, one of dispossession and banishment from the here and the now, and of recounting the advent of her madness as an ordeal that is the theological sign of an injustice (*ẓulm*, a theological concept). She is a witness (*shāhida*), in this sense by way of her exemplarity, yet she bears witness to a collectivity. In a more radical sense, it is her pronouncement of dereliction, her declaring herself without witnesses, without connection or guarantee, which evokes her position as *shahīd,* here approaching the sense of witness-martyr. She will say: "God is the only witness, and as for me, I don't have any [human] witness, no one, who will testify for me." But unlike the case of the martyr, for Amina the enunciation of pain does not find completion in death; it is transmuted into voice.

Amina's story unfolds against a plurality of spaces that reject and invalidate one another, where she seeks to find an anchor, and from which she is violently repulsed at every turn. They are the loci of family and genealogy (stories of names, of the father, of the mother, of the mother's cousin and the paternal aunt, of bewitchment, of unpaid debts, of betrayal and rejection); of marriage (*khaymatnā,* our home, our "tent") which reveals itself to be a site of deceit, abuse, and repudiation; of work, the orange plantation where she works as a day laborer, paragon of colonial and postcolonial capitalist exploitation, of uprooting from the protection and constraints of village life, opening to the pleasure, the violence, and the risk of sexuality exposed and violated; and finally, even the loci of healing: the sanctuary, symbol of protection in the ritual life of her community, which becomes for her a theater of violence and forced seclusion; and the hospital, where she arrives bound in ropes, brought by a male cousin, in the ambulance of the *protection civile*, "mad among the mad" (*ḥamqa maʿ l-ḥummāq*), she will say. From this succession of uninhabitable spaces, an abduction of place, issues the forced choice of a departure. At first, she takes leave of herself into the nonplace of madness—"flying up to the sky," as she puts it, and being swept away by the wind. She then finds rest in a "borrowed dwelling" (I steal here an expression from Teresa de Avila in the account of Certeau), at once imagined and born in speech, the production of a home or a "station" that is not her own and that she pieces together with her psychiatrist from the midst of her illness, moving towards the possibility of finding a voice, a transfigured voice, and a reconfiguration of belonging in exile.[15] In my reading I attempt to grasp the articulation of voice, its appearance and its loss, and propose a reflection on the voice-in-pain (*al-ṣawt*, "the voice," with its corporal and poetic connotations), understood here as "song"—the song of the patient in the emergency room—with regard to its power to recapitulate a life.

Before entering the labyrinth of her story, as well as that of our relationship, I want to ponder Amina's determination to bear witness to a history larger than her own and which attests, she says, to both her madness and her pain. This points for me to a theoretical knot in the way the shattering force of traumatic symptoms, experiences that resist inclusion in an everyday temporality, exceed the boundaries of individual lives and point to the spectral presentation of a collective history, as summoning of and from the dead. I understand Freud to be making this point in *Beyond the Pleasure Principle*,[16] where reference to destructive "mechanical" events of war injuries and railroad accidents, and to the traumatic nightmares that awaken the survivor in "another fright," develops into a larger discussion of the enigma of death at the root of life. A kind of legacy is passed on in the mysterious tendency of the living to return to a state outside of life where all individuality and subjectivity subside. All this suggests that it is not "trauma" per se that is important to Freud's reflection, but rather the "beyond" it exemplifies. Yet Amina's antiphonal call conjures a "beyond" that, in the Islamic tradition from which she is speaking, carries a spiritual ethos and a theological status, one Freud could only gesture to indirectly in his speculative reflection.

With some important exceptions,[17] psychoanalysis and psychiatry have been scarce to address the spectral presenting of a collective history in the experiences of madness and trauma. At the hospital some psychiatrists registered the uncanniness of listening, for us "normal people," to fragments of non-sense, the intrusion of a raw real that is not addressed to us, but addresses us nonetheless. One could reject that address, retreating beyond psychiatric classifications and diagnosis, or instead feel concerned, Dr. S., a female psychiatrist, told me.

It was 2002. The emergency room was filled with voices that echoed fragments of the historical present—the bombing in Afghanistan, the uprising in Palestine, the international War on Terror. My notes mention a man who claimed to being sodomized every day by a horde of fifty men bearing the names of states, "Nigeria, Nicaragua, Nik [sexual intercourse], Nike [the sport clothing brand]," who destroyed his "American [sport] clothes"; another talking about the liberation of Jerusalem, yet another seeking "sanctuary against the army of criminals sent by Bush," and who begged to be admitted as an inpatient. After an intense staff meeting in January 2002, Dr. S. made a comment that ran contrary to her entire psychiatric training:

"It is as if we are called to witness, as involuntary addressees, petrified fragments of social commentary, of a collective speech, delivering themselves as impersonal statements in the saying of psychotic patients. They can't possess their own history and yet that history tells itself to us, a history that eludes them and concerns us, that makes us reflect on the status of our own history. How are we to receive that saying?"

The Abduction of Place and the Palimpsest of the Voice

Writing from a still-colonial Algeria, and in the aftermath of the massacre of Setif in 1945, where thousands were killed in the repression of an anticolonial uprising, Kateb Yacine tells the story of the twentieth century as the visionary account of the advent of a present in ruins (*présent en décombres*).[18] Staging itself through the shadows, reminiscences, and voices of the characters of his novel *Nedjma*, Kateb's traumatic present is born from the channeling of multiple other worlds; worlds centuries apart that exist side by side as tangible scars in the life of persons and territories, and that secrete overlapping narrations in the tragic and always mythological deployment of history. At once inactual and uninhabitable, the here and now projects itself in the temporality of ruins. It withdraws from the gaze, resists factual accounts, and manifests itself fleetingly in the shudder of bodies, in gestures and dreams beyond memory, in the voices and echoes of a story—the story of Nedjma, a woman, the elusive "Star," as well as our own. In the dismembered space-time of the novel, Kateb's characters lend a ventriloquized voice to "the ruins steeped in the blood of our veins, the ruins we carry in secret, without ever finding the place or the time suitable for seeing them: the inestimable ruins of the present."[19]

Forever lagging and impossible to grasp other than in the elusive forms of a "dream beyond memory,"[20] the vertiginous temporality of the novel proclaims the violent expropriation of the present by the brute force of colonial domination. It is a theft seized by Kateb at once in its raw historical singularity (as in the scene of murder and rape at the wedding-turned-orgy of an aging and drunken French colon) and as the spectral return of other conquests and other crimes—the ghostly recurrence of ancient Roman military campaigns, the Turks, the Arabs, and the French invasions—and of a "prior" imprint in the physical body of both the person and the land.

The time-space of ruins becomes for Kateb the site of an epistemic uncertainty that manifests itself in a conspicuous impossibility of establishing the facts,[21] in the sense of a police investigation and of conventional history: *Nedjma* is also the story of two murders and their circumstantial reconstructions. Yet, epistemic uncertainty points also to a radical doubting of identity, a threshold of madness, that is formulated in the text as a questioning of the origin—the psychotic question—in the genealogical sense of kinship and filiations, and in the historical sense of a possible account of the past. At the origin of social life here are incest, murder, and rape. The result is a certain mad quality of the narrative, which performs the impossibility of reconstituting the history of the subject and of a collectivity otherwise than in the repetitive metamorphoses of a trauma.

Kateb stages the unspeakable secret of the social law: its criminal core, sealed by murder, rape, and incest, by colonial occupation, by the confusion of genealogies, the falsification of fatherhood—by the failure of transmission, save the transmission of crime. Exhausted by successive expropriations, disoriented and violated, the self is but the splinter of a broken jar: "Nomad of a prematurely exhausted blood, I had to be born in Cirta, the capital of the vanished Numidians, in the shadow of a father murdered before I even saw the light of day; I who was not protected by a father and who seemed to live at his expense the time he might have yielded to me gradually—I felt like a piece of broken jar, an insignificant fragment from an age-old architecture."[22]

It is a rootless account of the destruction of a culture, and of culture as such. Culture in the sense of a symbolic archive and the living potentiality of a tradition; the sense implied by the epigraph from Fanon above. Culture, as well, in the Freudian sense of *Kultur*: the capacity for ethical existence via the sublimation of destructive drives.[23] Kateb echoes Fanon's remarks about how the plundering of autochthonous cultural schemas and the breaking of symbolic references go hand in hand in colonial domination with murder, expropriation, and military occupation. Yet, and here is the important difference, in the poetic form of the story, Kateb's text performs a visionary return to the obliterated sites of the looted tradition, which through the novel is granted a second chance. Caught between the violence of colonial relations and the "rage of the ancestors"—the climax of the story takes place in the mythical tribal land—he declares the abduction of place and the impossibility of inhabiting the symbolic sites of belonging. But he also gives birth—a second birth—to both place and culture, to the possibility of a collective memory, through his gesture of writing, in a modality of consciousness that resembles a trance.

It is in dialogue with Kateb's intuition, and by the intermediary of the story of Amina, that I raise in this section the question of the abduction of place, of community, and of the modalities of their repossession. "Place" in the literal sense of a residence, a space, a body, and a community where "being" might reside; in the juridical sense of being authorized to do something; as well as in the sense of something that happens, that takes place.

In the gaps and impasses of Amina's story, I address complex questions concerning the obliteration of indigenous therapeutic practices and ways of relating to illness; the foreclosure[24] of schemata of body and illness that are both conjugated in the multiple voices, practices, and texts of a tradition, and rooted in the unconsciousness of language, and of somatic, psychic, and spiritual attitudes. The obliteration began to take shape during the French Protectorate (1912–56), when vaccination campaigns and the struggle for the eradication of infectious diseases went hand in hand with penal indictments of the exercise of "indigenous medicine," the confinement of natives to their villages for reasons of public health, the militarization of modern medicine, the struggle against the "indigenous mentality," and what the director of Health and Public Hygiene in Morocco named "the dictatorship of health."[25] An active eradication was later pursued by postcolonial medical institutions that inherited French hospitals and policies and situated themselves antagonistically vis-à-vis other practices and conceptions of illness while remaining unable to provide a viable alternative for the health needs of large underprivileged segments of the population.

The result today is a sense of dispossession and a feeling of anger for many, but also, for a growing number who come to recognize themselves in the position of the patient, an imagined inclusion, one that fosters the anticipation of listening, and the possibility of appealing to the modern institution. On this complex and ambiguous scene there is, on the one hand, the predicament of Moroccan psychiatry, with its colonial legacies as well as a history of early postcolonial experiments in deinstitutionalization and alternative care; a history that accounts for a certain indeterminacy in diagnostic criteria, and which allows for flexibility and improvisation in the margins of institutional practice; a history that is specifically modernist, in that it registers the experience of a rift, the desire for an elsewhere—in the form of a hospital bed. On the other hand, there is the continued presence of other therapies and understandings of illness within a vernacular and a reformist theological framework, and of other practices, both foreclosed and rendered incommensurate on the grounds of the hospital and in the larger discourse of national public heath.

During the first days in the emergency unit, Dr. N. is my guide, as well as an interlocutor according to an unspoken but mutual choice, in recognition of an affinity between our nonetheless very different ways of framing questions. He is a psychiatrist sensitive to the ambiguous experience of patients caught between the superimposed and incommensurable worlds of this modernity; he is sensitive to their pain, their silences, and their speaking Arabic or Berber in an institution where patients' records are written in French (a colonial legacy in the administration of health in Morocco). For the psychiatric encounter is based on a mechanism of unequal translation, in which medical discourse controls the criteria of validity and intelligibility: translation between languages (Arabic or Berber and French), between interpretations of illness, between experience and its representation, and between vocabularies of demonic inspiration and the languages of modern medicine as these are embodied by the psychiatrist and imagined by the patient. An asymmetric translation that echoes and amplifies the chasms and the obliterations that furrow the world outside the institution.

Dr. N. is aware of all this. He is trained in phenomenological psychiatry (French training in the colonies and early postcolonies), at the school of Henry Ey, Minkowshy, and Binswanger, which emphasizes the register of meaning in the lived experience of the patient and in the context of a life-project, instead of reducing the patient to the symptoms of an illness according to psychiatric semiology. He is motivated by an ethos of social critique, has a perceptive ear, and is cautious when exercising diagnostic judgment, which he nonetheless sees as a necessary dimension of his clinical work, and a key responsibility of the physician. We look for a transactional language, a shared vocabulary somewhere between his medical posture and my anthropological questions. As we casually gaze out the window of his office at a group of women sitting on the lawn around a young female patient and immersed in an animated exchange whose words we can't hear, I ask Dr. N. how he fares with this cohabitation of contiguous and rival worlds in the physical and cognitive space of the hospital. Dr. N. does not say. His reply is in the concrete unfolding of his clinical work, in his choice to devote himself to the patients who each day crowd the narrow hallway by the door of his office (rather than to the institutional politics of the hospital), and whom he receives with hope, sadness, and often with a sense of impotence. We speak of "culture," culture in the speech of his patients, in the psychiatrists' act of listening, in the hospital records. "Culture" is a key word here,[26] designating in the discourse of the hospital the "traditional" spaces of belonging, representations of illness, possession by the jinns, healing by the saints, magic, and sorcery.[27] As in the compendiums of Moroccan folklore written down by colonial ethnologues and administrators, these representations are fixed, the counterparts of a reified modernity: the prerogative of an Other who also often happens to be the patient. Psychiatrists speak of "cultural factors" in the elaboration of delusional themes, and even sometimes of resorting to culture as a defense mechanism. But when one listens more closely, culture reveals itself as the actual site of fracture, of loss, of a severance. It disturbs and questions. As another psychiatrist once told me, "I situate myself in the experience of the break, in the rift," in, that is, the position of an assumed exile from language, culture, and memory, but also, in a more subtle sense, in the very site of this cleavage.

As an external observer at the daily staff meetings in the psychiatric unit, where each morning are debated the incoming patients' files and respective case assignments, I measure the inadequacy and possibility of an anthropological approach that would propose something other than simply documenting and reflecting upon the patient's ambivalence vis-à-vis the symbolic sites of belonging. For these are reduced on one side to a catalogue of empty forms, and are experienced on the other as an uninhabitable home—unlivable, but also unforgettable.

First, medical discourse: The official mode is that of a struggle that is twofold, a militant distancing: from the sites of cultural identification in the life of patients, on the one hand, and from the colonial representation of the indigenous psyche on the other. Psychiatric discourse situates itself against the racist, colonial representation of the Arab mind, which postulated its essential irrationality in the name of cultural-racial difference; and it opposes to it as a necessary antidote modern psychiatry's insight into the universal nature of psychopathology ("schizophrenia is the same everywhere"), its humanistic bias and stress on social reform, access to care, and the destigmatization of mental illness. On the home front, on the other hand, medical discourse battles the affective attachment of patients to the sites of cultural and religious belonging, and most importantly, it struggles against what it labels "traditional therapies" (the "indigenous medicines" of colonial times), which constitute, from the standpoint of institutional psychiatry, the main obstacle to the rationalization of treatment. On the side of patients, in turn, disidentification takes a different form: The hospital is the option of last resort, turned to only after the failure of a therapeutic quest that has taken them to healers and to the shrines of saints; or else it is forced upon them by the police. In the experience of many patients, this estrangement is the site of an exile to which they have been violently subjected, or that they have somehow actively sought instead.

Dr. N. is familiar with my research. Our daily conversations are a hesitant search for shared ground. Mine is an open-ended project, somewhat at odds with a professional milieu that emphasizes nosography and diagnostic specification, and for which it is problematic to conceive of a study outside of the parameters of a given disease entity (acute psychosis, mood disorder, suicide). Such a lack of specification disturbs, yet it also allows for a certain cautiously probing mode of questioning. What is it to offer diagnosis, to listen to a patient's speech, to be called in (and for) by that address, and by the loss of sense it makes audible?

What is it, for a psychiatrist like Dr. N., to be able to hear, between the lines, the other sites of both an utterance and an illness that together extend out well beyond the hospital walls, their roots reaching into other interpretations of illness and practices of healing, while also investing himself right here, in the space of the hospital, and in the terms of its institutional codes? I am told by almost everyone I meet, in a matter-of-fact manner that at once acknowledges and bypasses the question, that until recently, the area just outside the perimetral walls of the hospital was a place of consultation for many traditional and Qur'anic healers. What is it for a patient to speak in the emergency room, to answer the evaluation protocol, with the concealed or barely disclosed background of an altogether other perception of her illness, even as she addresses her symptom to the institution of modern medicine? And what is it to be the recipient of such a therapeutic request for a psychiatrist, the ambiguous addressee of an ambiguous request, mediator of an exchange doubly foreign and twice marked by translation? (As for me, at least for a time, this conundrum remained a central question. I began to train myself and read in psychoanalytic and psychiatric terms, met with patients on a daily basis, and was myself troubled by their experience of illness. I quickly came to realize that the possibility of listening, and of speaking, is not incompatible with a reflection within the terms of psychopathology.)

Near the end of the consultation that took place the following week, Dr. N. asked me whether I wouldn't like to speak with Amina alone. "She'll speak to you differently," he said. The ambiguity of my position at the hospital came into play. In the eyes of the psychiatrists, I am, as an anthropologist, a specialist in "culture," but in a place where the notion has little currency, identified as it is both with colonial practices and forms of knowledge and with what is perceived to be the archaic irrationality of the patient's mentality. And yet, inasmuch as psychiatrists profoundly perceive and inhabit that ambiguity, by virtue of their own clinical practice and biographies, they are also reaching, in a certain way, for an anthropological attitude and kind of listening. It is thus that I found myself occupying a paradoxical place: that of the interlocutor to whom an incipient questioning is addressed, but a question that is hardly possible to formulate.

I explain to Amina that I'm not a psychiatrist, but that I work at the hospital with the patients and doctors as a researcher. I tell her that I talk to them about their experiences, and that I'd like to speak with her, if she is interested and if she agrees to it, about both her life and her illness. I have met with her over a period of three months, both in the informal space of our conversations one-to-one, and in the structured space of consultations with Dr. N.

My listening has not been a clinical one; neither "clinical" in the psychiatric sense of diagnostic attention to a symptom of psychopathology, nor in the psychoanalytic sense of listening to the unconscious and whatever symptomatic signifier might be borne by the patient's utterance. Attempting to open a different kind of space in parallel, I listen closely to Amina's stories, ask her questions, and respond to the questions that she asks me; I am affected by her story and by her request. For on the one hand, without a therapeutic goal, my ethnographic ear is less targeted or controlled: I record the account in its entirety, I reflect on the nuances of vocabulary, on the impasses of the narration, and I try my best to situate them in a larger context, a social context, but also that of a religious tradition in which concepts such as "injustice" or "error" have a theological resonance. On the other hand, this process of listening has its own effect within the space of the clinic. It is far from impermeable to desire and the interlacings and transfers of the ethnographer's story, and her own projections, which remain inscribed in the deepest motivations of her research (as is the case with research in general). For his part, in encouraging me to meet Amina in his absence, Dr. N. hoped to listen to her otherwise, so to speak, through my ear. Besides which there is Amina's story itself, the way it stirs a psychiatrist quite versed in the living conditions in rural areas, which his own background happens to share. (Amina and Dr. N. are both from the Gharb region in Central-Northern Morocco, a formerly swampy area traversed by the Sebou river that was drained in the early years of the Protectorate and became the site of large scale capitalist agriculture, with a layout of irrigation canals, colonial farms and small peasant villages where the workers lived with their families; an infrastructure that lived on in postcolonial times.)

Since adolescence, Amina had worked in orange plantations, singing with women in the fields and in the trucks that brought them back home at night. Eventually she had been given in marriage to one of her mother's cousins. The night of her wedding would become one of violence and shame: kicked out, thrown into the street, she was accused of not being a virgin (*fāsda*, corrupt and impure) and of *zinā* (illegitimate sexual intercourse). This is the traumatic core of her story, to which Amina returns insistently both in her clinical meetings with Dr. N. and during our private conversations. But the story is told as a complete account only by her father, to whom she delegates the task of reporting the facts. Countless times, when the psychiatrist questions her and she can't bring herself to speak, Amina gestures toward the closed door: "*Bba ygullek*" (my father will tell you). By speaking in her place, by simultaneously lending her a voice and confiscating it, the father bears witness to her story. But this is an "official" testimony that only reproduces, in its own way, the violence it narrates. From her lips, this story will be told only in fragments, through the rubble of scenes, in their spectral repetition, often involving multiple characters—

other faces, other violences, other masculine figures of betrayal, other accusations of immoral conduct.

I discussed the clinical dimension of Amina's story with several psychoanalytically oriented psychiatrists, at the hospital and elsewhere. An analytic reading would emphasize the complex role of actors within the extended family, and evince the play of identifications and the failures of symbolic transmission across generations that, for the subject, translate into a barred path.[28] In her own way, this is what Amina emphasizes in her account by revealing the entanglement of the most intimate aspects of her story with the machinery, exclusions, and phantasms of collective life in the postcolonial nation.

In a work on psychosis and "the space where the 'I' can 'take place,'" psychoanalyst Piera Aulagnier reflects on the entanglement of psychic processes and historical traumas in situations of violence and social crisis, racism or the colonial occupation in its intergenerational configuration, where historical reality "intensifies" (and sanctions) a phantasmatic construction, such that the symbolic pact that would authorize the subject to exist is "falsified." For Aulagnier the pact—which she calls a "narcissistic pact" to emphasize its nature as an early affective tie—is what inscribes the child into the group before the fact, conscripting parental figures, particularly the mother, into playing the role of spokespersons (*porte-voix*) of its collective discourse. The "narcissistic pact" permits the subject to project herself or himself into an ideal community, to have a place and a title through which she or he can articulate a singular voice within a chorus of other voices. But there are situations in which the pact is "falsified at the outset" by the dynamics within the family or by the group, which refuses to grant the person what Aulagnier calls a *"droit de cité"* (a right to belong)—or proposes an exploitative, slavish, and unacceptable contract. The subject is thus arbitrarily dispossessed of the place that would have been her own, through a history of exclusions within the family, a history that often enough is mirrored in the social world. Such entanglements can drive a person crazy. The lived historical reality of childhood is superimposed with a phantasmatic construction, such that making sense is possible only through delusion—the sole remaining path by which the subject can continue to exist.

> In a number of psychotic anamneses one is struck by the doubling effect social reality has come to enact. Rejection, mutilation, hatred, dispossession, all these situations characteristic of the predicament of psychosis, are found enacted in real and concrete life—and not just fantasized—in the way society, the group, the state, relate to the person. From the moment that the "I"

> discovers the world beyond the family, at the moment the subject looks to the world for a sign that would grant her citizenship (*droit de cité*) amongst her peers, she can only find there a verdict that denies her this right, and that offers no more than an unacceptable contract. Accepting the terms of such a contract would imply that the subject submits to becoming nothing more than a worthless cog in service to a machine which doesn't hide its intention to exploit or exclude him.[29]

At our second meeting, and after the psychiatrist left the room, Amina shows me an old photo ID. "I was still a virgin then . . . it shows on my face, doesn't it?" I ask her to tell me her story: How did she get to the hospital?

"It's a long story (*qiṣṣa ṭwīla*) . . . I came because I was sick (*jīt hit kunt mrīḍa*) [she reconsiders], I was married and was divorced (*kunt mjwwja u ṭallaqt*), he divorced me and I was a virgin. He divorced me, and I came out in the dark of night (*kharjt f-llīl ya khtī*), they threw me out, my sister, they spit on me. And now, if I pursue him in court, I'll have him, won't I? Women are traitors, they say . . . It is I, not he, who would have had illicit sex! They took me to the doctor, had me examined, they found me a virgin. I have the photo, and the certificates, four certificates. A presentiment of something, my heart knew (*qalbī aʿlam*)."

She starts to cry, her father interrupts. He retells the story, explains what happened on their night of shame, when their entire family had been thrown out ("They threw us out!" [*jraw ʿalīna*], she yells). Amina listens, intervenes, clarifies, contradicts. The father recounts the struggle against humiliation, a battle that takes place on the stage of the law—the law of the state: attestations of virginity, medical and police reports. The day after the incident, they got these certificates, and pressed charges against the husband at the police station. The husband demanded official verification, a virginity test from a public health physician, and official doctor (*ṭabīb lmakhzen*, a physician of the state.) The physician attested to Amina's virginity. At that point she interrupts her father's account: "He said, You're still a virgin (*gel, nti baqa bint*) . . . He said, Go, show them the certificate, and if they don't acknowledge your rights, I'll go with you all the way to the public prosecutor of the King!" Amina reports the doctor's testimony with gratitude: "May God elevate his soul!"

The husband's family apologized, and once again requested Amina's hand in marriage. It is a murky and ambiguous story, which remains so despite all efforts to decipher it (my own, as well as those of Dr. N.); a story that disappears as a narrative to become flesh in Amina's misfortune and illness, voicing itself in her complaints and accusations. The story is one of jealousy and money, the dowry money that the husband's family accuses Amina's father of having "eaten," money that the father would have insisted on returning had he not been able to demonstrate his daughter's virginity, the "corruption money" each party accuses the other of having paid to the representatives of the law, so that they might prevail in the matter. Add to this the rivalries and entangled relations between the families of the mother and father, the husband being a cousin of Amina's mother, who had herself arranged and wanted the marriage.

It all appears to be a matter of families of different social and economic status, that of the mother (and the husband) being richer and more powerful than that of the father, an agricultural worker without resources. Amina will invoke her poverty countless times—that of her father, and her own, as well as the poverty of her abused femininity, the poverty of women in a world ruled by men: "Women don't have a chance, if he wants to divorce, he divorces" (*nsa' maʿndhā khubza, ila bgha iṭallaq iṭallaq*). With regard to her father, poverty is weakness: "He's poor, and the poor have no place in this world" (*drawiysh, mskīn, mabqash yaʿish fin had l-maqām drawiysh*). By contrast, the husband's father is the president of the city council and has an emigré son in Italy and a taxi business in town. Yet by virtue of his weakness, Amina's father is also implicated in her misfortune. It is his paternal uncle's wife that she accuses of witchcraft, of putting a curse on her marriage out of jealousy.

And there is the fear of the social gaze, the "eye" of the neighbor. The mother insists that Amina be returned to her husband. The father resists, wishing to spare his daughter further hardship and not wanting to return the dowry.[30] One day when her father was traveling, and with her mother's collusion, Amina was taken back to her husband's family at night and by taxi, a scene that she describes as an abduction. This time the marriage is consummated. Ten days later, the husband's family had her undergo a medical examination, to make sure that she was not pregnant. They then brought her to court, where she was lawfully divorced, this time "before the judge." The father reports, "In court the judge said to Amina, 'You're going to divorce.' She replied, 'Never without my parents.'" In the father's account, the judge had him sign a paper by which he renounced his rights (*tanāzul*).[31] "Later when I myself was in the courtroom, the judge said to me, 'Your daughter is going to be divorced.' I asked why. 'This is what she did, and today she's divorced. As for you, no one owes you anything.'" And Amina returned to her parents' home.

One year later, the descent into madness. When they told her he remarried she couldn't stop thinking about him; she became fixated (*tkhmmam*), the father says. She says, "I flew up," *thazit*—levitation, being swept away by the wind, like a leaf or a plastic bag. She says, "I burst open," *tfajart*—rupturing of a wound, explosion, but also a connotation of fury, eruption of rage. She concludes, "I took leave of my mind, I fell on my bones," *kunt kanghīb ʿalā ʿaqlī u kanthaḥ b-l-adam*—an expression that means to fall and to enter an altered state. She interprets her state using a coded expression, a fainting that is a loss of self, a being swept into madness. *Kanghīb*, from the verb *ghāba*, is a signifier of absence and estrangement, and well beyond a vocabulary of madness. It belongs to the language of trance, of dream (a taking leave of self that is at once a voyage and an opening to an Outside, from which a voice can be heard), and of poetic creation, but also to the language of madness, and of possession by the jinn.[32]

(When Amina says *kanghīb* here, the meaning is at once coded and unstable, being rooted in a phenomenology of madness linked to the loss of self through possession by the jinn and other modalities of the failure of reason, while also being simultaneously addressed to the space of the psychiatric institution and to the presumed universe of the psychiatrist (*kanghīb ʿalā ʿaqlī*, "I was absent from my mind," is a translation offered to the psychiatrist). *Kanghīb ʿalā ʿaqlī* is in this sense an image of madness that resists a simple assimilation to any one lexicon, or any one universe of interpretation.)

I ask whether they visited a *faqīh*, a Qurʾanic healer in "the cures of the jinn" (*ʿilāj al-jinn*), or whether they paid a visit (*ziyāra*) to a sanctuary. First a *faqīh*, the father says, and adds after a pause, "He wrote [magic squares] for her, *katiblhā*"; he burned incense, and said that Amina wasn't "touched," which is to say, possessed by spirits: "she doesn't have the sickness of the touch" (*gel, ma ʿandhash marḍ l-qis*), she isn't possessed by a jinn. Amina stubbornly refuses to have her misfortune ascribed to "possession": "I wasn't 'touched,' I wasn't! *ma ʿandish l-qis, ma ʿandish*, I become absent from my mind and I fall on my bones, *kanghīb ʿalā ʿaqlī u kantah b-l-ʿadam . . .*"[33]

After the healer, the ritual visitation to the sanctuary of a saint (*sayyid, maqām*). This is a paradigmatic site of healing in Maghrebi culture. These rounded vaults punctuate the Moroccan countryside, centers of saintly lineages, complex institutions where gift and countergift are exchanged in the search for healing and a pious life, and that sometimes specialize in the reception and care of the mad, and at the very least offer a sacred refuge, a shelter, a door and a caretaker, where the ill may seek rest and dreams of deliverance.[34] But the site of the saint becomes here a theater of rejection, of repudiation. The scene, described in the voice of the father, evokes the space of a rending, a radical loss of symbolic protection. Amina returns to the event in each conversation: door closes, clothes fall to the ground, screaming; it is the void of symbolic protection. "They shut me in" (*sheddū ʿalayya*), she says, an imprisonment that is a repetition of the first scene, which Amina calls "the expulsion" or "the exit" (*kharjt*, "I went out"). The site of the saint is drawn into the strangeness of her delirium. Once again, it is her father who recounts the story.

"She screamed," he says, "she didn't stop screaming (*katghawwat*), and after a moment we brought her to the saint, the sanctuary built around a saint's tomb, we had her circle (*dwarnāhā*) [the sanctuary from the outside—a circumambulation ritual], and it was raining. A man said to me, 'Bring her in!' (*dkhalhā*). As I got her inside, the door shut—I don't know if she's the one who closed it, or if the door closed all by itself . . ." Amina intervenes, crying, "No! It was closed by the will of God!" "When we returned the next morning," the father continues, "I'd just gotten to the door with the keeper when she came out, she'd opened it herself." "I opened it myself, God knows that I opened it myself," Amina insists, crying. "She was screaming," her father continued, "she'd taken off her clothes, her clothes were on the ground, fallen down with everything else. That's what happened . . . After that, I brought her to the hospital (*ʿand ṭbīb l-makhzen*, literally the physician of the state). I brought her first to the authorities (*ʿand l-makhzen*) [here the police], and they gave me a paper for the hospital [a police order for psychiatric evaluation]."

In this place of refuge par excellence, the sanctuary—the very image of symbolic protection within the culture—Amina lost all refuge. Undressed, that is to say, to the letter, in this scene of destitution, unprotected by any *kswa* (covering, clothing), in the space of the *kāsi*, or the saint, the "protector," who abandoned her, just as she had been separated off and abandoned by others in her surroundings: her mother, who released her to the man who would reject and shame her, and who is her cousin; her father, who didn't have the courage or the capacity to protect her, and who, unable to make a place for her in the world, speaks and lives as her proxy; her father's sister, who put a curse on her to prevent her marriage; her sisters and brothers, who insult her and call her "the madwoman"; the people of her village, men and women for whom she will always be marked by an indelible stain, that of the illegitimate sexuality of which she's accused; and then men in general, her ex-husband, but also the others, imagined and not—spectral faces, voices that call her, insult and judge her . . . Only her grandmother took her in. "I've been raised by my grandmother" (*anā mrbiya ʿalā ḥanna*): read to the letter, it means "grandmother," but in Arabic it also resonates with "affection" (*ḥanān*). "I'd borrowed from her character, shared her nature, and she died."

Later on, during a discussion with Dr. N., Amina returned to the scene of the saint. She declares herself exhausted, tortured by a pain on the right side of her head. "It's *la tansio*," she says. From the French *tension* (referring to high blood pressure), *tansio* is a corporeal figure for "nerves," connoting the propensity for fits and crises of madness.[35] I ask her about the origin of this pain. "My head . . . they took me prisoner, in chains, they chained me, and they had me circle around a *sayyid*, his name is [she tries to remember] . . . What's his name? They brought me to the *sayyid*, and they shut me inside, and father came, and he freed me, and me, it's my grandmother who raised me, it's my grandmother who educated me, my grandmother whom I love (*anā mrbiya ʿalā ḥanna*), and she died. Don't make me cry, my sister. No, do make me cry."

There is both the actual event to consider, that of her "expulsion," as a specific rupture in Amina's life: the accusation of not being a virgin, its inscription in her body, and the way that this break plays out in the family's history, between the families, and in relation to the institutions of modern life (the stakes of virginity, but also the story of money, and migration to Europe), as well as the symbolic significance of that event: "expulsion" from a world, from a universe of references, interruption of a transmission, breakage. In this sense, the event in the sanctuary marks the failure of tradition, not of that tradition that would be the counterpart or residue of a reified modernity (the fossilized tradition that Abdallah Laroui rightly denounces in his critique of the Arab ideology of modernity),[36] but of tradition as continuity, *traditio*, transmission, as the possibility of a belonging to come in which the place of the subject will not be confiscated by violent arbitrariness. The circling (*dwarnāhā*, said her father, "we made her circumambulate") of the sanctuary represents the violence attendant upon a return to the scene of origins, where the healing word of the saint could not be heard, much less received. The name of the saint is thrown into oblivion, and the site of tradition—the origin—becomes the origin of a concatenation of violence—the confinement, and then the loss of consciousness, the undressing, the screaming.

This theme of violence at the place of origins—which manifests itself as the violent place of identity—was present in the accounts and delusions of other patients whom I met at the hospital: Reda, who refused to speak

Arabic, and felt devoured by his mother tongue and by what he called the "agents of tradition"; and Haddiya.

Dr. R. had come to see me after I presented my project and previous research at a plenary staff meeting at the hospital during the first months of fieldwork—the beginning of a hesitant conversation. She was completing her residency, a woman in her early thirties, originally from a small town in northern Morocco. She said that several of the residents wanted to talk more about their own call to psychiatry in relation to a sense of severed cultural belonging, a *"crise d'identité."* And she told me the story of Haddiya, one of her patients, a young woman from a rural area she was discharging that day from her third hospitalization. She saw that story as an allegory of the question I was trying to understand (and perhaps as well something she saw in the perplexity of her own clinical work). Haddiya had been brought to the hospital by her husband and brother tied in ropes, in the midst of a psychotic episode. I later read in her hospital file how she had refused food for days and lay naked on the floor hiding under a blanket and refusing all contact, how when approached she replied in injurious and sexualized language, physically kicking people away, eventually complaining that she was being tortured, that she had been thrown into a well. The file, written in French, like all hospital files, by several different hands, contained no mention of the elements in Dr. R.'s account. Haddiya had been diagnosed with a *bouffée delirante*, an acute psychotic episode.

It all started at a saint's tomb, Dr. R. reported, a sanctuary not far from her village, where Haddiya said that a spell had been cast on her by her brother-in-law, a healer who practiced harmful magic: he himself, she claimed, was a madman (*ḥmaq*). A few months after this event she lost her mind. Her husband took her to a healer, who believed that Haddiya had been struck by a jinn, and performed on her the "falling cure" (*ṣarʿ*). But the cure failed. The *ṣarʿ* is a ritual where, by the recitation of Qurʾanic passages over the body of the patient, the healer induces the jinn that struck the person to present itself and speak. The person falls into a deathlike state, a "disappearance" or "loss of consciousness" (this is what the term *ṣraʿ* means in Arabic), and from that unconsciousness rises the voice of the jinn, with whom the healer engages in a struggle, aimed at forcing the jinn to disclose its name, the first step towards its defeat.

I had published an article on this ritual, and had given Dr. R. a photocopy a few days before. She knew that I understood the importance of naming, both of the person and of the jinn, and how that ritual enacts a wrestling of identity and alterity. But when Haddiya fell unconscious and the healer asked to reveal "her" name (the name of the "other" in herself, as is customary in depossession liturgy), she replied with her own name: *"Anā Haddiya."* Dr. R. interpreted this reply as her challenge to the healer; she had refused to submit to the rules of the discourse of possession, and to the masculine and patriarchal rule that the healer embodied. But her victory had been short-lived. She got worse, and was brought to the hospital tied in ropes. At the ER registration a nurse asked her name, in what is a routine administrative gesture. In a "changed" voice she replied, *"Anā jinn,"* I am a jinn.

Why was Dr. R. telling me this story? Was she pointing to a transgression, the fact that her patient had dared not host the voice of the jinn, had challenged the healer with her own name, refusing to be healed in the name of a desire for self-determination, a desire to extract herself from the entrapment of oppressive kin relations, a transgression she had later paid for with repeated hospitalizations, the jinn taking revenge on her in her mad utterance? Or perhaps the psychiatrist was pointing to an impossibility, a failure of the cultural idiom, an inability of that idiom to provide Haddiya with an access to the passage through the Other in which the subject could reemerge, in which, in the mimetic instability of a possessed utterance, the patient/jinn could find a position from which to speak?

"She was able to complete the *ṣarʿ* at the hospital," commented Dr. M., a senior psychiatrist, who in his own clinical practice was inspired by a dialogue with psychoanalysis. The hospital, in his view, had functioned like what D. W. Winnicott called a "transitional space," where something could be articulated that found no room for expression within the parameters of her world, a world that she experienced in the mode of persecution. He told me about *The Piggle*, Winnicott's account of his psychotherapy with a little girl, which he conducted as a kind of pathos-theater: "The dramatization of the child's inner world enables her to experience and play with those fantasies which most disturb her. This occurs in small doses and in a setting which has become safe enough through the skill of the therapist."[37] Haddiya's statement "I am a jinn" was in Dr. M.'s view such a dramatization. It was an attestation of the life of the unconscious in the paradoxical sanctuary that for some was the hospital.

Dr. R. was not sure. For her, Haddiya had formulated the terms of a question, in the exchange of institutional places, and in the unstable interval between the two utterances: I am myself, I am the jinn, I am myself, I am another, I am here, I am there, I don't have a place, I strive to create a place. And she had failed to find a resolution. Or, perhaps, she had gestured to a beyond of resolutions, as she painfully staged and inhabited the space of the rift.

In a different way, that question could be said also to be Dr. R.'s own, shaping her decision to become a psychiatrist. A predicament that in Dr. R.'s view, as in the view of several of her senior colleagues, was uttered every day in the speech and through the symptoms of patients, in the way that speech and those symptoms addressed the medical institution with an urgent request while eluding it at the same time, reaching elsewhere, to other vocabularies and interpretations, and more fundamentally, to the reality of a loss, a loss hallucinated in the visions and delusions of patients; a loss that was both acknowledged and denied by the institutional gaze and its protocols—by the ambivalent gesture of what, paraphrasing Certeau on the nature of the historiographical operation, might be called the "psychiatric operation" (at once archiving away—the dead, the mad—and reencountering them in the penumbra of the archive).[38] Hiding naked under a blanket on the unfurnished hospital floor, an embodiment and literalization of "exposure" as the ultimate portrait of destitution in the Moroccan and Arab cultural imagination, appealing to a literal figure of protection (the blanket, that is, also linguistically, to dress, to cover, to protect), Haddiya manifested her torture, facing a chasm on both sides. Dr. R.'s story, not solely the story of a patient, contained the outline of an urgent questioning: to find an access to language and voice within the testimonial act of their loss.

This predatory violence of the origin is often expressed via the image of poisoning or witchcraft (*siḥr*), in the idea, for instance, of a poisoned collective meal that "activates" the incorporation of a deadly reference, or in a ritual that turns into a misfortune, and whose stage is sometimes the tomb of a saint. (Once again, an interpretive clue is in Kateb Yacine's novel, where the characters make a last journey to the mythic and originary scenes of the tribal ancestor Keblout, which becomes a destination of death and a figure of lethal affiliation. The last survivors of the tribe reject and kill those children of the same lineage who went away, learned French, and embraced a life in exile. Kateb specifies that the literal meaning of this ancestral name is "broken cord.")[39]

In the everyday practice of the hospital, these themes of a collective reference turned lethal are routinely understood as the anecdotal imagery of a psychotic symptomatology. For in a strictly psychiatric reading, the content of a delusion is accidental. Yet during daily staff meetings, where psychiatric and psychodynamic interpretations of the patient's cases are pitted against each other in debates around the table, it becomes clear that psychiatric semiology is not the sole frame evoked at the hospital. The theme of a predatory identity, or of a cultural origin turned lethal, could be read, from an anthropological standpoint, as the expression of an ambivalence toward the sacred within the culture (for example, that surrounding the notion of *baraka* in a long tradition of Maghrebi anthropology). But this reading effaces the historical dimension of the phantasm—its being blurred with reality—as well as the experience of the subject's despair. On the contrary, it is necessary to consider these themes of predatory violence on the self, of imprisonment and bewitchment in the traditional sites of belonging, in a literal sense. They are imaginary experiences of the impossibility of symbolic reference, phantasmatic elaborations of a fundamental anguish specific to a historical condition.

Amina was brought to the hospital by police order. Her memory of arriving *mselsla*, "tied up in ropes," accompanied by a cousin (*wld khaltī*, once again a maternal cousin), is at once an image of imprisonment and deliverance.[40] This third scene in her account, the abjection of her arrival, reenacts her night of shame and her confinement in the sanctuary of the saint.

> The ambulance—the ambulance brought me, and dropped me off without chains (*labilans, labilans jabatnī hatatnī matluga*). . . . The day they brought me here they told me go in, and I told them, do I have to go in with the mad (*maʿ l-hummāq*)? I recovered my reason (*anā wllit bi ʿaqlī*), the pills, I buy them myself, *Roche* in French, I buy them myself, that's what happened. I won't throw the pills away, I need them, my sisters insult me, you, you're an idiot, *nti hbila*, and I say to them, let me be crazy, at least I'm crazy but in peace, but you? You are the ones who are crazy!

She found a place to rest at the hospital, she says, and yet it's there that she was swept away the farthest, that she truly took leave of herself. Mad among the mad, she says. When one day I asked her what madness is, she told me of times when she went out naked in the ward, onetime bleeding during her period, unaware of her body, or of her state, or of the nurse who was charged with her care. "I was absent from my mind, I lost my reason" (*kunt ghayba ʿalā ʿaqlī*).

—Why did you take your clothes off?

—Because of the night I was sent away.

She repeats her family name, the name of her father. Not the genealogical patronymic, but the family name (*kunya*), as it appears on her national identity card.[41] This is the name the nurse called out three times a day, when medications were given out: Amina voices it that way, in the anonymous call of the nurse, the summons to the place assigned to her by the psychiatric institution. It's a proper name whose literal meaning evokes images of battle, of virility and explosion. She chants her name, playing with its different meanings, at the same time a curse and a protection. Family names bring us back to the theme of kinship, and of witchcraft (*siḥr*), and the spell that she claims was cast on her. Among her kin, there are those who wish her misfortune, try to destroy her, so that she'll never know the happiness of having a husband and child. Her assertion, "I wasn't touched [by the jinn], I wasn't" (*ma ʿandish l-qis, ma ʿandish!*), is counterbalanced by an accusation of witchcraft, "my uncle's [paternal] wife cast a spell on me" (*saḥaratnī mrt ʿammī*). I understand this as a cry of anguish in the midst of an intimacy turned lethal. Witchcraft itself is a logic of imprisonment, which maps subjection to an arbitrary, inscrutable, absolute power, often associated with the family and a lethal disruption of social ties.

It is not by accident that witchcraft occupies a central place in the imaginary of illness and modernity in Morocco, in the speech of patients, as well as in the exegeses of numerous Qur'anic healers. Peter Geschiere's work is relevant in this context, for it shows, outside of any therapeutic frame, how the proliferation of witchcraft logics in Africa is a specifically modern phenomenon that stages and attempts to explain the "speculative" development of social inequalities, of poverty, wealth, and the abuse of power, and relates as well to a growing deterioration within the sphere of family intimacy and social relations.[42]

The witchcraft accusation is Amina's appeal to the psychiatrist, a call for a different kind of listening within the "foreign" space of the psychiatric hospital. (Redoubling of the scene of expulsion in an "exit" that might mark the beginning of another life.) This is how Dr. N. himself receives it. He asks her about her lack of trust in others. "I can't trust" (*mantiqsh*), she cries: "I come home and I make my own food, I eat alone, I don't allow anyone to prepare my food because"—she pauses deliberately, to emphasize her words—"because I have been thrown out on my wedding night, 'my night' (*liltī*). But if they dared accuse me of not being a virgin, if he dared throw me out in the middle of the night, I also made him suffer."

Dr. N. intervenes, he seems moved. "Why can't you trust?" She can't trust human beings, Amina replies, and turns the question back to him.

"What is it, who is it, that makes a person crazy? What is the source of madness?"

It is a troubling question, and Dr. N. receives it as such, refusing to reduce Amina's pronouncement to the objectified impersonality of "culture." And yet in the general currency of the hospital, every reference to witchcraft is understood as the deployment of an ancestral cultural trait. *Siḥr* (witchcraft) is treated as a traditional figure of persecution from which paranoid schizophrenia, an acute psychotic episode, or an obsessional neurosis can all draw their psychopathological themes (becoming "witchcraft delusion," *délire de sorcellerie*). Psychiatrists are careful to specify that the cultural representation is not in itself pathological, but merely a mythological theme that becomes pathological once appropriated as a thematic motif by the architecture of a delusion. Yet listening to Amina's speech means something other than making her the object of a cultural representation, even in its psychopathological deployments. It is to receive her speech as a gesture, the possibility of a question, which opens the space of her singularity.

I think of the critique of the taken for granted practice of "understanding" patients, and understanding in general, in a cutting remark Lacan made to the participants of his seminar on psychosis: "Begin by not assuming that you understand. . . . If you understand, so much the better, keep it to yourself, the important thing is not to understand, it's to attain the truth." Further on, in a discussion of the concept of truth in psychoanalysis, Lacan defines the terms of a fundamental distinction between "comprehension" (*compréhension*) and "listening" (*écoute*). The first fixes the other in place, the second is dialectical, grasps the possibility of a questioning, of a movement, a transformation.

Back to Amina:

"It's the wife of my [paternal] uncle who did witchcraft on me" (*saḥaratnī mrat ʿammī*).

"Why?"

"Because of the marriage (*li juwaj*). Because she has two daughters who are unmarried . . . they spent a lot of money just to harm me, she set her children against me, she was jealous, and she didn't want me to marry . . ."

"How do you know? Did the healer find the witchcraft (*siḥr*)?"[43]

"The healer? I didn't need a healer to tell me. I had a spell put on me, I know it all by myself (*anā tsḥart, ʿraft rasī kifesh*), I stepped over a flask of 'haunted water' (*nqqezzt ʿalā wāḥid al-māʾ dyel muluk*), a flask of water from the seven wells, simple water, like that." She takes a bottle of water from the desk, pours it on the floor and steps over it. "And later, when my hands were decorated with henna [on the first day of the bridal celebration in the marriage ritual], my hand started to tremble."

She returns to the expulsion on the night of her wedding, to the court decision, and to her madness. If there were justice on earth, her husband would have been condemned to five years in prison (the penalty for rape in the Moroccan penal code), and she herself wouldn't have ended up at the hospital. But instead he's the one who sent her to prison, which is to say to the hospital, and he's the one who stayed home, in "our home, our tent" (*huwa saiftnī lhabs, u huwa ga'ad fī khaymatnā*). Amina calls upon a logic of restitution: her madness is the result of an injustice and an unpunished crime. She wouldn't be ill if her husband had been taken to court and judged guilty. "It's witchcraft" (*hada tuwkal,* bewitching by bodily incorporation), "the type that makes people run . . ."

Amina draws an analogy between her fate and that of other casualties of modern life, the young people who had been schooled, who studied, and who ended up taking their lives in the river next to her home. These young people who had been "enlightened through education" (*qarīn*), who had been initiated into the world of modernity, of writing and learning, still couldn't fly far in a world that was closed to them. So they fell out of life: "So many youngsters commit suicide here in the wadi, the river, not our people (*min 'andnā*), not people from our village, I'm telling you frankly, the people from Sidi Qacem [the neighboring town]: their young people commit suicide, all in the river, the ones who studied and didn't succeed (*llī kayqraw llī qarīn, llī qarīn u manjhush u la dak shī, kayntahru*)."

In spite of the fact that she hasn't been to school, Amina recognizes herself in the experience of these youth, who aren't "from our home," strangers to "our home," like she is. She shares with them a painful consciousness (*wa'ī*) of modernity, and of an impossible self-realization, which may turn to suicide as an affirmation in death. She refers to her banishment in a language that is at once theological and juridical, shaped by her repeated visits to courtrooms and police precincts. It is in the vocabulary of testimony that Amina affirms her abandonment: "God is the only witness," *shāhid huwa llāh,* it is the Muslim testimony of faith, "but as for me, I haven't got any witness, not one person, who would testify for me [except for God]," *u anā mabqash shī waḥed ishāhid lī.*

To witness is an obligation in the Qur'an: "And witnesses must not refuse when they are summoned [to testify]" (Qur'an 2:282). Testimony, the fact that others will attest for me, and that I exist as a proof in their witnessing, is a pivotal concept in Islamic law.[44] (Until the thirteenth century the rule of testimony was considered, within the frame of juridical debates, a supreme hermeneutical criterion for establishing proof.)[45] It was in constituting us, Dr. N. and myself, as witnesses in the juridical sense of *shuhūd*, that Amina created a space for herself in the clinical sessions. The production of evidence in a style inspired by the courtroom (the ID photo, the certificate of virginity, her medical prescriptions), by the rule of *shuhūd* (I exist in the testimony of others), and the "tie" fostered in the relation of transference, made possible the pronouncement of her ordeal, of her being in pain.

Amina's words point to a gap in the texture of experience, a place where language meets silence. At that limit, there can be a coming of voice. A transformation of living substance in its afterlife. (Walter Benjamin: "For in its afterlife—which could not be called that if it were not a transformation and a renewal of something living—the original undergoes a change. In the pure language, which no longer means or expresses anything but is, as expressionless and creative Word, all information, all sense, and all intention finally encounter a stratum in which they are destined to be extinguished.")[46]

Anthropologists have written about modes of bearing witness to the dead and the paradoxical connectedness fostered in an encounter with alterity—what Seremetakis calls an ethics of antiphony. In the Greek ritual space of laments that she describes, the "chorifea" and her living listeners and vocal interlocutors become the literal and physical "representatives" of the dead person. They become the "face of the dead" (*prosopos*) in the world of the living, translators and intermediaries between worlds, opening a space where the dead can become present in their absence. The voice of laments circulates and touches the community of mourners as the "shared substance" of an exchange between the living and the dead, screaming the claims and the pain of the departed, and enabling a socialization of loss that constitutes, she says, the "substance" and the ground for the inscription of a collective memory.

In a context severed from the ritual stability of the Greek laments, and in a text that is itself an offering to and a conversation with the dead, Veena Das traces the gestures, utterances, and silences of feminine grief in the aftermath of the faceless violence of the India-Pakistan Partition in 1947, a violence, she posits, that is impossible to account for other than through a gesture of mourning that renounces narration, sheltering the exposure of being under a mantle of silence. For she shows that, at its core, intercommunal violence falsified the integrity of the symbolic law, the law of generation, of kinship and language, as well as the law of the nation, revealing their intimate criminality and delivering being to a radical loss of shelter and protection. In that ravaged landscape, Das suggests, only a feminine work of repair capable of carving a space of life at the very sites of violation and loss, as a commitment to relationship and life, can open the possibility of reinhabiting the world. The characters of Asha and Munjit in Das's text have resonated for me with the voice and life of Amina, and her paradoxical gesture of connecting to a community to come in the very movement of her own dispossession.[47]

Despite their resonance with the story I am telling here, these modalities of mourning presuppose the persistence of a collectivity in place, one spiritually capable of hosting the "stranger" and having access to the symbolic language of burial. The witness, as Seremetakis writes, in Greek *marturion*, is also a coded message composed of two incomplete halves, one each in possession of the sender and the recipient. "Completion and decipherment of the message required joining the two parts."[48] Not unlike the *sumbolon* and the "*tessera*" evoked by Lévi-Strauss and Lacan, made of two halves of broken pottery that become a token of recognition and the "password" in the symbolic exchange that testifies to the existence of a community, the *marturion* inaugurates and presupposes a symbolic universe, a culture, where the two halves may be capable of recognizing each other. It is the collective practice of laments, its prosody and linguistic structure, the presence of a community of mourners that will receive the message incarnated in the voice, taste "the shared substance" and pick up the refrain, which provides the symbolic frame within which the mourner can become a representative of the dead.

But the *tessera* is missing in Amina's life. The symbols fail in their capacity to ground the truth of the subject and summon the community to the possibility of mutual recognition. They are, in the image of Kateb Yacine, fragments of a broken jar, forever severed from their context, temporally and spatially adrift.[49] Taking seriously Amina's claim that her "folly" attests the perpetration of an injustice, and speaks in the name of the dead and the disappeared, means to ponder the reality of the loss of the symbolic itself; to explore the aftermath of culture, the realm of the "broken jar," and the possible worlds that might be born in that vision of ruin. And it means to allow for the possibility that the experience of madness—an experience Amina claims as such, in the hospital ward, and in the failure of all established paths to healing—might itself be a modality of witnessing.

It's in the midst of her scattered reminiscences that Amina begins to sing. She sings "right here" (*hnaya*), in the consulting room of the hospital, here where we are talking. Her father has just left the room. Her tone changes, becomes more personal, intimate. Then, abruptly, she cries, and says: "I went out in the night, in the dark of night, my sister (*kharjt f-llīl ya khtī*), they bewitched me, or I don't know what, they say a woman who is pure is better than all those wizards . . . and myself, I am made of silk, my heart is white, when I walk out I smile, when I come back I hail, can I give you a song (*ngullik waḥed l-ghonia*)? Forgive me, if you can listen, I want to sing right here (*bghit nghahnni hnaya*) . . ."

She begins to sing softly. Her voice, in the style of *l'ayṭa* (a musical genre whose name means to call out, scream and weep), fills the space of the "right here" (*hnaya*) as her call, her appeal, and her cry. "Right here," in the time of the now, a precipitate of her life. Her voice (*al-ṣawt*), rising and descending, is a counterweight to her being swept into madness. "I was swept" (*thezit*), she had said.

Ila bghiti tmshi ghir sir
Wash wellah ash ndir?
Jarḥati qalbī wash ndir
myat marra mashī ghir hadi

If you want to go, Leave.
Oh God, what to do?
You broke my heart, What to do
A hundred times, not just this time

And I also want to sing this poem for you [Stefania]:
ya hadak l-ghādi u sallem 'ala duk nās
awlad bladī wash huma labās
gulilhum anā ghadi-a-f-dunya ḥawās

O Traveler: greet them for me
Ask my countrymen, how they fare
Tell them: I am wandering the world without aim
[I am losing my grip on this world].

She composes the words of her songs in the style of the songs she chanted with the girls in the fields, improvised sung poems in the mode of antiphonal call-and-reply inspired by scenes of everyday life, the hardship of work, the pains of love, loss, and betrayal. Her songs are reminiscent of *l'ayṭa* ("the calling"), a musical-poetic genre from the planes of central Morocco, and are inspired by the art of *shaykhāt* (feminine plural of *shaykh*), the women singers and dancers who from well before the colonial period performed at men's gatherings and in ritual festivities. In the Moroccan masculine imagination *shaykhāt* are associated with sexual licence and carry an ambiguous aura, colored with desire, stigmatization, and insult; but also a paradoxical freedom, independence from men, and courage of openly speaking the truth.[50]

Singing erupts from Amina's speech without warning; narrative gives way to fragment, to the visualization of rhyme. Syntax is ruptured at times, melody almost gone, and the words chase and crisscross one another on the path of secret associations. Rhyme alone: standing vestige of the extinction of sense: synergy of sense left on hold. And her speech of pain opens onto a ciphered energetic, a breathing of rhythm. Her song is a precipitate of her life, marking itself in the dangerous temporality that Benjamin had called the *Jetztzeit*.[51] This is the time of "now," a space of unstable enunciation, here-there (*hnaya*), suspended between the loss of meaning and its possibility. The song opens a path, weaves a link, a contact in the space of transference. Her voice that rises and falls (*al-ṣawt*) is a counterweight to Amina's experience of being swept away into madness.[52] She says, "I was lifted up" (*thezit*).

External to the order of narrative, the voice of the song appears and settles in the body, at once present corporeality and inscription of alterity, emergence of an elsewhere, of another voice—not unlike the way the voice of a jinn suddenly makes itself heard through a change of timbre, and in the absented and deathlike body of the patient.[53] But Amina refuses all correlation between her misfortune and the vocabularies and liturgies of spirit possession because, among other reasons, appealing to the jinn would be a way of avoiding the designation of those responsible for that which, in her opinion, is an injustice in the human world, an injustice that should be denounced and punished.

As I listen to her song on my tape recorder, I wonder about the origin of this voice, born in "counterpoint" to the scene of the psychiatric institution, with regard to the assignment of her presumed role as patient, and with regard to a code: that of hospitalized madness.[54] (Her own name again, called out in the third person at the moment of dispensing medications by the anonymous voice of the hospital nurse.) I use "voice" here in two senses. On one hand, the song exists as concrete reality, in its poetic and its medical interpretation: *al-ṣawt* with its corporeal connotation of breath, of melody, of physical sound prior to its enunciation, at once anticipation and recapitulation of meaning. In the exegesis of poetic enunciation by the oral poets with whom I worked in southern Morocco, for instance, the "voice" (*ṣawt*) of a poem in singing is a whispered melody in the form of a "la-la" at the beginning of a composition, by which the singers, as well as the listeners, recognize the "word" (*kalima*, poem) that will follow.[55] The voice (*ṣawt*) of a poem is a condensation and an anticipation of the poem in abridged form, a crystallization and sonic image of the poem. And in this sense the "voice" is an announcement, a premonition that contains, in its condensed materiality, poetic expression itself.

In his monumental opus *Kitāb al-ḥayawān*, the ninth-century Arab scholar al-Jahiz elaborates a theory of the voice that subsumes both the poetic and the medical sense, as an energetic agent with an ambiguous power of destruction and healing (as discussed by Mohammed Hamdouni Alami, who draws the implications of al-Jahiz's poetics of voice and emotions for a theory of Islamic art). Al-Jahiz cites an Andalusian physician who describes how the melodious voice penetrates the body, circulates and purifies the blood, calms the heart, and delights the soul. And he explains that melody (*al-nagham*) springs from an overflow of discourse (*al-manṭiq*, logic) and expresses that which language cannot formulate in its ordinary logic.[56]

In his *Introduction to Arabic Poetics*, the Syrian poet Adonis has a compelling discussion of the corporeal materiality of the voice as "song" in early Arabic poetry (specifically its *qaṣīda* form). Yet he concludes that such corporeality and immediacy do not and should not have a place in modern aesthetics, being incompatible with a preoccupation with modern form and critical thought.[57] His modernist position is different from that of Kateb, who in *Nedjma* and in his other works points to the loss of experience as an inaugural event in modernity, but one that opens a space of mourning haunted by a lost and yet insistent voice that makes itself heard through a carving of form.

On the other hand, I use "voice" here to mean voice in an ensemble, a structural configuration, musical ensemble (or institution of collective life) where each instrument takes on a different voice according to the harmony of the composition. This double meaning—corporeal and structural—of voice is in play when Theodor Adorno speaks of "counterpoint" (as well as "counter-song") in his writings on modern music. There he attributes to voice so understood a primary role as a condensed image of modern subjectivity, and speaks of the "enigmatic" and "irreconcilable" nature of this way of being a subject, for which, he says, music and art constitute critical and privileged observatories. For modern counterpoint disfigures the harmony of the ensemble, and confronts us with "the paradox of a multivoiced music without a community."[58] Counterpoint is the violent trace of an existential condition marked by an "indescribable tension." It is the product of an "opposition," a struggle, which puts into play "the nuances and contrasts of the soul divided against itself, and against the world."[59] For contrary to medieval polyphony, where, Adorno writes, there is no dominant theme and the subject exists only in relation to a collectivity, modern counterpoint remains true to the bourgeois idea of the sovereign subject and its emancipatory aspirations, all the while demonstrating its impossibility. Voice in modern counterpoint is the result of a violent combat in a field of power, between a dominant subject or theme and another subject, at once subordinated and independent. Instead of reinforcing the dominant subject as an accompanying voice, the other voice "involuntarily condenses into counterpoint and then continues to play a major role in the rest of the work as an independent counter-subject."[60] Here resides for Adorno the difficulty of modern listening: in an ensemble of voices that appear simultaneously, one must learn to listen to them as a plurality in which each one is independent and singular, while at the same time discerning their entanglement in a dispositif of power.

It is somewhere between these two senses of voice that I situate the experience of Amina in the psychiatric hospital—corporeal expression, material and "insubordinate" (*ʿāṣiya*, defiant, her word), yet which is rooted in a field of power of which her voice is the trace and "condensation," in Adorno's sense of the word. Her voice unfolds as "independent counter-subject" vis-à-vis the discourse of the psychiatric institution (on madness and illness, as well as on identity and culture), from which she borrows the central problematic of her saying while she also displaces it. It also speaks in counterpoint vis-à-vis the bureaucratic apparatus of the Moroccan state, its mechanisms of exclusion and its forms of legitimation, to which Amina takes recourse in her quest for protection against being crushed and destroyed. A destruction that is an annihilation of self, and that she calls her "bewitchment," the fact of being caught in a logic of intimacy turned lethal: her madness, but also her abuse and arbitrary treatment in the sphere of social and parental relations, side by side with the "impotence" and "invalidation" of cultural references. In a less obvious way, and in the gray zone of forgetting, Amina posits herself as countersubject with regard to these very references. Thus, to a certain extent, and from the inside, she manages to tear herself from their grip, while attaining a certain horizon, a preliminary condition of any act of reoccupation. For counterpoint, "simultaneously violent and impotent," acts as the "condensed image" of emancipation.[61] This position in "counterpoint" is characterized by an impossible desire for emancipation at once affirmed and denied. It crystallizes into a countersubject that is forever scarred by power games it can't escape, and is threatened by the risk of losing its way with the loss of self: by the event of madness. To this, Amina concedes no virtue of emancipation. It is this position in "counterpoint," contradictory and "irreconcilable," that paradoxically permits her to grant a place for the voice, in the sense of the corporeal voice (*al-ṣawt*), which can sing at once the being swept up in madness: the eclipse of the subject, and its struggle (*ʿāṣiya*). But there is more that remains unimaginable from the standpoint of Adorno's argument. We can hear it in Amina's song of errance and error, "I am wandering in the world without an aim," and in the enunciation of her dereliction, "God is the witness, and I haven't got any witness, not one person, who would testify for me," both of which cast her interpretation of her own life in an ethical-religious perspective. Adorno presents modern counterpoint as a structure of sovereignty that at once enables and fails the subject, against the foil of medieval polyphony and its anchor in the community, and against, as well, philosophical notions of the free and autonomous subject. But for Amina, God is a third term, in relation to which the "independent counter-subject" constitutes herself on the mode of striving and in the midst of impossibility. In parallel to the voice (*sawṭ*) of her song, hailing an absent community through the call of her pain, we may think of the sung poems in the genre of *madḥ* (praise to God and the Prophet), where the contrapuntal participation of the audience and the divine inspiration of the panegyrist undermine the sovereign subject and its emancipatory aspirations and open on another scene of the voice. There an other imagination of counterpoint might be possible, where Amina's speech heralds not the aspiration of a bourgeois modernity, but a life in the memory of God.

Amina never sings with Dr. N. She only does so with me. But the psychiatrist knows, and Amina knows that he knows; he had listened to her voice on a cassette tape, a recording of one of our conversations, where she'd sung the poem that summons him personally to the place of witness (he, a psychiatrist receptive to the experience of suffering and social exclusion, and himself from a rural background, a "countryman" in the song): *Awlad bladī wash huma la bas* ("People of my country, are they safe and sound") / *Gulihum anā ghadia f-dunya hawas* ("Tell them I'm losing my grip on this world. I am wandering without aim").

The next time around, during her consultation with Dr. N., Amina is in a good mood. She reports having visited a saint's tomb (another sanctuary) with her girlfriends. What did she ask of the saint? asks Dr. N., smiling. Nothing at all, she says. She just lit some candles. She bursts out laughing, with that contagious laugh of hers. The psychiatrist laughs with her, and I too am drawn into their laughter. I didn't ask anything, she repeats, laughing. Then after a moment, she replies with a saying: "You say: marriage? O God make me a cripple [if I desire it]" (*gāllik: juwaj? ya'ṭenī 'awaj*).

She turns to Dr. N., with a serious tone: "I sang for her" (*ghannit lhā*), she says, pointing at me with a movement of her head. Dr. N. nods that he knows.

Her song, my presence, the implications of my anthropological fieldwork at the hospital, and the unconscious transference of stories and affects: all this pushed Dr. N. to suspend his clinical judgment for a time, and to listen instead to her voice. The voice of Amina in the clinical sessions had changed into the voice of her song. What is said, what is articulated in her voice, is also his, hers, theirs, mine: not because Amina speaks a common truth, even less a universal one, but because each story, each trajectory of life, is tied to the other in its singular knot, an untranslatable spot that can be spoken only by the other. We should ponder here the effects of this triangulation, the consequences of my presence, an informal presence, in the back and forth of clinical exchanges. But, more importantly, we should ponder the fact that both the enunciation of dereliction—*anā mabqash shī wāḥid ishhad li*, I don't have any witness left—and her song can be uttered, and what's more, experienced, in the relationship of transference where, according to D. W. Winnicott, "the thing past can be experienced."[62]

In his paper "Fear of Breakdown," Winnicott writes of the foundational function of transference in enabling a person to traverse an experience of the limit. To the space of transference he relates what he calls a "queer sort of truth"—the fact that "what is not yet experienced did nevertheless happen in the past." The insight is particularly relevant, he says, in the case of patients who have a compulsion to look for death and must sometimes traverse a "breakdown," or live through an experience of destruction in order to fully enter life for the first time. Winnicott argues that in such cases a psychotic illness is not in fact an illness, but a defense organization relative to a "primitive agony," a death unknown and unexperienced, which the self encountered at the dawn of life. The point of therapy is "to reach the bottom of the trough" under the guidance and shelter of "the auxiliary Ego of the analyst," so that "agony" may be experienced in the transference. Each of us, Winnicott implies, has in one way or another been exposed to trauma understood in this sense, and each of us may one day traverse a "breakdown":

> The breakdown has already happened, near the beginning of the individual's life. The patient needs to "remember" this, but it is not possible to remember something that has not yet happened, and this thing of the past has not happened yet because the patient was not "there" for it to happen to. The only way to "remember" is for the patient to experience this past thing for the first time in the present, that is to say, in the transference. This past thing then becomes a matter of here and now, and becomes experienced by the patient for the first time.[63]

Something on this order might have "happened" for Amina with "her doctor," on the foreign and unwelcoming grounds of the hospital. Could we explore the conceptual possibility of a family resemblance between the work of "testimony" as understood in Amina's account—bearing witness and being at a loss of witnessing—and Winnicott's understanding of the work of transference?

A conversation with Dr. N., during a break we take together at the hospital's cafeteria. We talk about what we're doing with Amina, of the possibilities in her life, of the interlacings of history, and the traps here, for each of us. She's doing better; he confirms this in his clinical evaluation. He's reduced the dosages of her medications. Yet he's pessimistic as to whether she will recover permanently, get married and go back to social life, even though, in his opinion, in another context she might very well. For even if, on the basis of a comparative study, the World Health Organization has determined that the forecast for psychoses and other severe psychiatric illnesses is better in countries of the global south because there is throughout a more communal involvement with the ill (what the lived experience of belonging to a "community" might be not having been defined), nonetheless, Dr. N. considers the exclusion to which Amina is subjected, which amplifies the phantasm of abandonment with a concrete reality, one of rejection and irremediable social marginality.

A senior psychiatrist at the hospital, Dr. N. fosters a humanist ethic with regard to the clinical encounter; he suffers from having to work in a permanent state of emergency, with respect to the difficulty of trying to establish in it continuity in the therapeutic relationship. He suffers over the loss of patients—who often are without the material means to pay for their medications or even their trips to the hospital—as well as the overwork that prevents real listening, and that socializes the residents into the habitus of a mechanical routine. (A political question, before even becoming a therapeutic one, it evokes in perhaps not so different a context Fanon's decision to resign from his post at the psychiatric hospital of Blida, Algeria, in 1956.)[64] Dr. N.'s secular pessimism encounters, via a different path, the theological diagnosis of the Imam (see part 3 of this book), who relates mental illness, and the proliferation of *siḥr*-related delirium with its predatory logic of bewitchment, to the growing social inequality and injustice at the planetary level. Yet it is under these very conditions, which are routine in the exercise of psychiatry in postcolonial situations,[65] in emergency (in Benjamin's sense), and at the margins of institutions, that a practice of experimentation can be initiated capable of opening a way into the daily cohabitation with impossibility, and that can take up the question of the subject—of self-transformation—and pose it in a new way. Amina has the last word in this hesitant quest for such a horizon.

Our last conversation (I was leaving the next day). Amina distressed, but lucid, off medications for several days: We meet alone, in a little office inside the locked women's unit. She recounts having left for the sea, twenty kilometers on foot, to look at the water and swim. The girls from her village don't go to the beach, which every Sunday fills with city folk under their parasols. For her, the sea opens the horizon. She is anxious, speaks of a woman in her village who has insulted her, beaten her, and treated her like a prostitute. It came to blows, and when Amina yelled for help, "I would tell her, my sister, Naima come to my rescue!," her sister replied, "Go on, get away from me, you're crazy."

She calls herself *'āṣiya*: defiant, protesting, refusing to abdicate. She is crying, stops crying, states with determination: "Don't worry about me, I won't cry, no longer cry, now I will speak" (*deba ghadi nhdar*). And: she wants to get married and have a child, to stop this life of wandering without aim. She tells me of her mother, in a back and forth of resentment and affection. Her mother enrages her, wasn't a good mother to her, pushed her to roam about, "she said to me, go hit the streets (*siri tejji*), wander the villages (*sir ll duwar*)." But then immediately afterwards, "She's sweet, poor mama, in her life she too knew violence and abuse (*ḥarb qaḥra*)."

She begins to sing:

Ayurtuni, shkan sbabī,
anā ra mriḍ u 'ayan yak a l-ummi,
anā mriḍ u 'iyan bik 'ayruni,
anā mriḍ u 'iyan kif jralī,
anā mriḍa

You [people] insulted me, what have I done,
I am sick [masculine form], I hurt, O my mother,
I am not well, I hurt, they curse me by your love,
I am sick, I hurt, what happened to me,
I'm sick [feminine form].

As the grammatical subject approaches the feminine, as it comes to designate her own speech, Amina abruptly stops singing:

> You take medication to calm yourself, and if you don't take them . . . My sister, I've visited all the doctors, I've been to the police, they said to me, "Make a declaration"; he's the one who should have been sentenced to five years in prison, if he'd been sentenced to prison, I wouldn't have had to see this hospital. I don't know if it's a spell (*ma ʿraft wash sḥur*), [again she begins to sing] *dayr bik u biya, ula men ʿand allah, anā qabla lih* [the song ends], I don't know if it's a spell, which was cast around you and me, or if it is the will of God, in that case I accept it.

Suddenly Amina addresses me in an official tone as though making an official declaration. It's an ambiguous speech, suspended between police testimony and court proceedings. "I am stating in your presence" (*ghadi ndeclarer bik*), she says, "through your intermediary"—me, the anthropologist with my tape recorder—where she "declares" a different truth. She says, "I want to get married and I . . . Say it [to herself], be brave, 'I want to get married or I want to roam the streets. Go ahead, record that on your tape recorder!'"

"It's recorded."

"That's enough (*iwa safi*), I'm done."

By way of a provisional conclusion, let me recapitulate Amina's winding path between different modalities of witnessing, through the risk of losing herself in madness, and the counterpoint (and counterweight) of the voice. For in their aftermath, in the very idea of counterpoint and of the enunciation of an independent countersubject within a field of power, there is the indication of a possibility of place and relationship. Counterpoint in such a sense is at once an acknowledgment of the subject's "struggle" for affirmation, to escape being crushed—she calls this her "insubordination" or "challenge" (*anā ʿāṣiya*)—and her subjugation to a power mechanism that eludes her, and that represents for her a crutch or a template in the reformulation of a possible real. Between these two, in the nocturnal shapes of a dream beyond memory, we find the glimpse of a return to a forgotten landscape.

It is not a matter of situating Amina in the finality of a recovery, or of accounting for the clinical evolution of her illness. To do either would be to miss hearing the specificity of her claims, which point us instead in the ambiguous direction of a third space with regard to the classifications of health, be it based on demonological or psychiatric logics. I should mention that some years after our conversations, and her visits to the hospital, Amina was leading a rather normal life in her village (as related to me by Dr. N.), and intermittently visited Dr. N. at the mental health clinic in a nearby town, where he is now the director. Yet it is not a matter of recovery, at least in my reading of her story, but rather of moving away from a problematic of the "exception," if exception is understood in the juridical sense of a sovereignty that subjugates. From the estrangement of her "madness" in the name of which she is expelled, but that also grants her an askew angle from which to gaze at her contemporaries, Amina ponders the predicament of the youth "who studied but didn't succeed," those who give themselves to death in the river by the side of her village. She herself has embarked on an intermediate path, in a deep recognition of the pervasive nature of violence and deceit. ("I don't know if it's a spell, that was cast around you and me, or whether it's God's will. If it is, I accept it.")

In what is neither a sovereign defiance through death—the realization of a logic of exclusion—nor a request for inclusion in the institutions of a community already in place, Amina embraces her position as a stranger, all the while calling on the bureaucratic apparatuses of the state, and on her status as patient, toward imagining a succession of provisional positions, each attained from within her imprisonment, by which she "condenses" a voice.

What then is the status of that voice that springs up and fills the space of the "right here" (*hnaya*), the "here, now" of the psychiatric emergency room, of the doctor's office, but also the space of the present, where "a tradition grows remote," and where one has "the experience of a fundamental defection, that of [. . .] the institutions of sense?"[66] What is the relationship between the voice-song at the hospital, and the cry, the fainting, the undressing, in the saint's sanctuary? Amina's voice surges from a tearing and a displacement; and a second rupture, a displacement onto the incomprehensible scene of the psychiatric institution, where she is both "mad among the mad" and sheltered from the system by which she has been banished. By the song at the limit of silence, and in the enunciation of her abandonment, she fashions herself into a being who speaks from and in the name of an absence (*ghayba*), a position gained here at the margins of the psychiatric institution. Her song and her utterance are born from the lack of witnesses, of those who would vouch for her, from the extinction of ties, the end of relationship, from her inability to speak. But to testify to that abandonment, as well as to her madness, she must have a witness. "I testify" (*ashhadu*), one reads in the classical dictionary *Lisān al-ʿarab*, means that "I know and I show something, I attest it" (*anā aʿlamu wa ubayyinu*), with my presence as a witness (*shāhid al-hāḍir*). Amina renders the *shuhūd* cowitnesses of an event, of a life, of a loss, by the fact of receiving her fragmented account, of acknowledging her disclosure of "evidence" (photos, certificates) to which they can attest. But also, and more fundamentally, they are witnesses of an absence and an agony, which in her story "take place" through her song. In this way the song itself testifies, as the "representative" (but not representation) and crystallization of a life. It is *shāhid* in the same sense as the stones that mark the place of the corpse in Muslim cemeteries, and which are called *shuhūd* (witnesses). External to the order of the story, as a voice over, the singing voice attests to the possibility of meaning while bearing the impression of its loss. This voice (*al-ṣawt*) comes from "another place" and settles in the body. It is at the same time a present corporality, "here, now," and an impersonal agent of strangeness, an inscription of alterity.

But if we consider Arabic poetics, and the specific poetic practice of oral poets from the Moroccan south, this phenomenology of song closely recalls that of the springing forth of poetic language. For the poem springs forth from an absence (*ghayba*), the poet taking leave of his very self, and returns to the forgotten site of an event. The last word is the poet's:

> How many times have I encountered my story in these poems. I sing them, the "words," and the wound that burns in my heart (*l-ḥarr lli f-gelbī*) finds a voice and can be released. You see, when I begin to sing a poem, when I throw it, I find the voice (*l-ṣawt*) and my being completely melts into this voice (*keyttekhsha bih d-dmagh dyālī*). For when you sing a poem, you're in it with your soul and your senses, you find yourself immersed in a real (*wāqiʿ*) of something that happened to you long ago, and all your longings (*shawq dyālik*) and your essence (*jwareh dyālik*) vibrate in your voice, and in its modulations.[67]

In this way Amina realizes a transfiguration of her "real" (*wāqiʿ*)—of the intolerably unthinkable that has reduced her to silence, and of the experience of annihilation out of which her voice is nevertheless reborn. This, for a time, brings her back to this side of madness. Within this phenomenology, the transfiguration of the *ghayba*-madness (*kanghīb ʿalā ʿaqlī*) into *ghayba*-poetry realizes, within the space of the hospital, an operation of resymbolization ordinarily associated with the saints (*siyyid, walī, sādāt*). In this way, in the other space of the institution, there is an indication of a possible transmission, and the formulation of a being-with to come.

TWO

The Hospital

It is as if, in the effort to make sense of itself, the Orient turned into an archaeologist and rediscovered superseded forms of Western consciousness. Inasmuch as each time it is the West that provides the elements of the discussion, one might be tempted to say that it confuses us on purpose, by artificially keeping alive a few of its older sloughs. This would be wrong, however, for it is clear that these two societies, slowly interpenetrating, can only dialogue in terms of religious consciousness at first, then political and finally technological consciousness. . . . Yet, [there is a] time-lag effect (*décalage dans le temps*). . . . Our consciousness, in Morocco, drifts between the determinations of the past and the call of the future. It dwells in the peculiar temporal category of an anterior future . . .

—Abdallah Laroui[1]

Art. 11—L'hospitalisation dans un service public ou un établissement privé de psychiatrie ne peut avoir lieu qu'au vu d'un certificat délivré par un médecin psychiatre qualifié mentionnant de façon détaillée et précise les anomalies du comportement du malade et concluant à la nécessité de l'hospitalisation. (. . .) Le certificat ne peut être délivré par un médecin parent ou allié au deuxième degré inclusivement du malade ou de la personne qui demande l'hospitalisation de celui-ci.

—Dahir n° 1-58-295 du 21 chaoual 1378 (30 avril 1959) relatif à la prévention et au traitement des maladies mentales et à la protection des malades mentaux

The Dahir of 1959

Shortly prior to the hospital's founding—and three years after the Independence of Morocco—a royal decree (*dahir*) instituted the charter of

Moroccan psychiatry. The law designated the agencies in charge of the "prevention and treatment of mental illness and the protection of mental patients," as specified in the title of the decree; regulated psychiatric hospitalization and treatment; specified the responsibility of each agency; and outlined the protocols for the protection of patients. Described as ahead of its times, and not just for Morocco, and for this reason only partly implemented in the following twenty years, this is the law that—with the 1974 amendments—is still in use today. Modernist in its inspiration, the *dahir* situates psychiatry in terms of safeguarding a patient's rights against the social institution of the family and the risk of abuse, whether personal or political; a risk perceived to be immanent to the bonds of reciprocity and obligation characteristic of extended families in Middle Eastern cultures. In this way, the law constitutes psychiatry under the ambivalent sign of both surveillance and freedom. Yet in a context in which psychiatric care touches a relatively small fragment of the population (and this not just because of a much debated cultural reluctance, but also due to the scarcity of institutional and financial means), the political project of the *dahir* takes on a specifically local dimension, one that is both utopian and exemplary. In its rupture with cultural institutions and the tutelage of the family, it institutes the imagined possibility of another listening, to which recourse is possible in an appeal for justice, as we saw in the case of Amina; but it also unleashes a force that can seize one by the legitimate and arbitrary violence of the state, as in the case of the youths from poor urban neighborhoods who are often brought to the ER by police at night.

I was introduced to the text of the *Dahir* by Dr. P., then director of the hospital, who stressed its centrality for my research and gave me a copy from the hospital library.[2] For those who saw the institution of psychiatry as quintessentially violent, he said, the 1959 charter law made clear that Moroccan psychiatry stood on the side of patients, and was animated by an emancipatory and anticolonial vocation, participating in the project of a new society, against the "French politics of asylums" and the racialization of care that had characterized medicine during the Protectorate. In the asylum-style hospital of Berrachid, created by the colonial administration in 1920, and whose population had grown to 2,000 inmates in 1955, patients were segregated by religion and race: European and "Muslim" (Moroccan) patients were kept in separate wings, and received differential treatment.

By the 1959 law, all decisions concerning issues of mental health, as well as the hospitalization of patients, are put under the responsibility of psychiatrists. The law mandates the establishment of psychiatric hospitals and mental health centers in all provinces (a goal that remains unrealized); limits hospitalization to three weeks, renewable up to a maximum of six months; enforces and regulates detailed clinical records in the hospital files; and states that hospitalization takes place "at the request of the patient, or of a public or private person acting in the patient's interest, or in the interest of the public safety (*ordre public*)." Inasmuch as a significant number of patients arrive at the psychiatric emergency room accompanied by the police, this point is of importance. A family member or a public official may request hospitalization by filing a police complaint: but the final decision rests in the hands of the psychiatrist who is mandated by law to act in the patient's best interest, ascertaining whether he or she is actually in need of psychiatric care, and no ulterior motives are guiding the actions of the family or for that matter of the state authorities.

Specialized medical knowledge then, the ability to discern "anomalies of behavior" and attribute a meaning to them, is at once a judicial tool and a guarantor of the patient's freedom, acting in the interest of civil society. The modernist vocation of postcolonial psychiatry is attached to each individual physician as a responsibility. Yet, uncomfortably nested in the phrasing of the law is a century-old colonial narrative relative to the characterization of the indigenous culture (Muslim or tribal) as one that subjugates the person and makes autonomous subjectivity impossible. Protecting the rights of patients in 1950s Morocco implied that patients were conceived in their individuality as subjects of care solely qualified by their (psychiatric) illness, understood as exclusively their own—not as the expiation of a past or collective history, not as the expression of an interpersonal or societal malaise, not as the effect of an external agency—a premise health practitioners themselves understood to be a fiction. Regardless, and however complex the colonial history, the result today is that the responsibility of/for "freedom" is an ambivalent dimension of the psychiatrist's call.

An amendment to the law published in 1974 (*Circulaire* of April 23, 1974) instituted the decentralization of mental health via the creation of "psychiatric regions," geographical areas gravitating around specific hospitals (so that Amina, from her rural town some hundred kilometers away, would be sent to the Sale hospital). The amendment also accelerated the dismantling of the asylum by mandating short-term care and promoting the creation of mental health centers in low-income neighborhoods and rural areas. This however remains far from fulfilled. In 2005 there were in Morocco 300 psychiatrists (203 in public psychiatric units, 83 in private practice, and 14 in military hospitals), 650 psychiatric nurses, 4 psychiatric centers and medical schools of psychiatry (in Sale, Casablanca, Fes, and

Marrakesh), 7 specialized psychiatric hospitals, and 17 psychiatric wards integrated in general hospitals, for a total of about 3,000 psychiatric bed capacity (for a population of 34 million). Despite all this, psychiatric care continues to function under conditions of relative emergency, understaffed and underequipped, especially outside large urban centers. A reform project unveiled in 2015, in line with international psychiatric trends and spearheaded by the organization of patients' families, revisits the role of families and communities in a perspective of "*reinsertion*," recovery and social rehabilitation, and specifies the protocol of patient consent, albeit remaining within the overall framework of the 1959 *dahir*.

The Hôpital ar-Razi in Sale, today one of the four schools of psychiatry in Morocco, was established in 1963 as a model psychiatric institution aimed at replacing the French style asylum of Berrachid. J. L. Rolland, the first director of the hospital (and of *Santé Mentale* in Morocco), was a French psychiatrist and psychoanalyst who in his practice (in Morocco for a time) and writings focused on the new question of anomie and the phenomena of urbanization and modernization, bilingualism and the effects of colonization, the formation of an urban lumpenproletariat, the spread of drug addiction and crime, and their destructuring effects on the ego. In the spirit of its inception, the hospital has grown as a site of treatment, teaching, and research, reaching out to the community and taking an active role in the public debate on pressing social issues.

Located at the site of a shrine, Sidi Ghazi, the hospital is named after Muhammad Ibn Zakariyya al-Rāzī, the famous tenth-century physician and polymath. Patients call the hospital Sidi Razi in a willing confusion of the two names, the mystic's and the physician's. The main hospital compound is composed of four pavilions, ranch-style buildings arranged at some distance from each other in the midst of a garden, two women's and two men's wards, each including one "open" clinic which is also a paying ward, and one closed ward, where patients in acute or dangerous chronic conditions, psychiatric prisoners (*medico-legaux*), and those unable to pay the hospital fees are assigned. In all, there are 276 beds. A library, seminar room, and office space for the *chefs de service* adjoin the two clinics. The emergency room was, until 1999, located in an isolated building at the edge of the hospital grounds, which also served as the site of post-cure consultations. In 2000 it was relocated outside of the hospital perimeter, in a newly renovated building that also hosts the new Center for the Prevention and Research of Substance Abuse (Centre Nationale de Prevention et Recherche en Toxicomanie, CNPRT).

The original structure from the early years of Independence is the Service

Fermé Homme, the men's closed ward. It remains the most emblematic and challenging destination for incoming psychiatrists today. The recent history of the hospital revolves around this ward, which was headed in the 1970–80s by a psychiatrist and psychoanalyst, Dr. B., who had started with a group of young psychiatrists the project of an "open institution" inspired by experiments in what Jean Oury had called "institutional psychotherapy," and Franco Basaglia's "therapeutic community," but also by the medieval therapeutic form of the Arab and Muslim *bimāristān*, a space of communal life where lunatics were treated with music and song. Families could come to have meals and spend the day with patients, nurses were involved in decision making, and artists (especially painters: it was a decade of blossoming for Moroccan abstract art) were invited to share their work at the hospital. In the experience of several psychiatrists, the end of this period of openness came about as a disappointment, still difficult to discuss today. The experiment was associated with the ethics of psychoanalysis and its practice of transference and countertransference, with the contestation of medical hierarchies and with a larger dream of social reform that could spill out from the grounds of the hospital into society, carrying a message of democratization and social justice. The staff mentioned the daily familiarity with patients in the wards (because the offices were located inside the ward), the sharing of meals and early morning conversations in Arabic: the utopia of a therapeutic experiment that made space (also architecturally) for a dialogue of reason and unreason, leaving room for the expression of patients. Then came the time of exclusion, and the reorganization of the hospital under a new leadership, with new priorities. Dr. B. left for a private practice, and has since created a parallel pole of reflection and critique on psychopathology and subjectivity, with a group of psychiatrists from the hospital who come to his seminar bringing the experience and doubts of their clinical work. At the hospital, the men's ward was remodeled, and the staff's offices were relocated to the external perimeter of the building, minimizing the contact between doctors and patients outside of the formal space of clinical consultations.

Under the new leadership, as well as in response to a changing epistemological scene (the turn from psychological to biological models in American psychiatry, and the development of the neo-Kraepelinian disease paradigm), the orientation shifted to an attempt to meet the standards of international psychiatry. This triggered an internal debate on the redefinition and standardization of diagnostic criteria, which at the time were fluid and left to the judgment of the therapist. DSM IV was introduced but not operationalized, and was in fact met with widespread resistance, because the orientation of clinical work (systemic and etiological in character) was inspired by French psychiatric semiology and psychopathology, with a reference to the phenomenologically inspired work of Henry Ey. The diagnoses of melancholia, acute and chronic psychosis (*bouffée delirante*, schizophrenia, paranoia, dementia, paraphrenia), manic-depressive psychosis, and sometimes hysteric psychosis, neuroses (obsessional neurosis, hysteria), alcoholism, hypochondria, were dominant, with the recent addition of *état limite* (borderline) depression and drug addiction, and not yet a specific definition of posttraumatic states. Reading the hospital files, it was clear that if the lack of standardization had been responsible for the inaccuracy of some reports, it also made possible a deep exploration of the patient's experience of illness and of life, leaving the mark of a creative interpretation. Over time, diagnoses fluctuated and changed, as the result of reassessment and multiple hospitalizations. While some took that indeterminacy to be the sign of an underdeveloped practice, others (influenced in this by their engagement in the wards, as well as by theoretical developments in psychoanalysis and the philosophy of science—reading Gaston Bachelard, D. W. Winnicott, and Gisela Pankow to make sense of their experience in the hospital) saw it as a unique chance for a creative listening to patients, and for the development of new therapeutic approaches. Such was the opinion of Dr. M. in particular, who pushed me to read Winnicott and Pankow, and who chose to make medical and political sense of the hospital as a space of "play," in the sense Winnicott elaborated in his work *The Piggle* (the diary of his psychotherapy with a little girl).

It was a time of reflection and instability, when the "international" question—what makes a reliable diagnosis—stirred up complex and very local issues, ranging from the way patients' symptoms and clinical interviews were written down in hospital files to the adequacy of the French language to represent illness narratives in translation, from the way Moroccan cultural themes played a role in the structuring and vocabulary of psychotic delusions to a renewed research interest in vernacular Moroccan and Islamic understanding of madness.

La psychopathologie marocaine

"Nothing durable can be done in the field of public health if the dominant mentality does not evolve," wrote Dr. Jules Colombani, then director of the Ministry of Public Health and Hygiene in Morocco in 1921. "We must take the pulse of its evolution every day. I will only cite, as an example, the many difficulties we have encountered in our attempts to transform the regime of insanity (*régime des aliénés*), difficulties we have hitherto been unable to overcome."[3]

Since the beginning of the century, colonial health officers in Algeria had been confronted with the imperative of seizing the indigenous mentality, cognitive processes, and sense of self. The outspoken task of the Algiers school of psychiatry, founded by Antoine Porot in 1918 and inaugurated by his paper "Notes de psychiatrie musulmane,"[4] was to study "the indigenous mentality," to better understand its pathology and make it progress effectively. The views of the school were inspired by Lévy-Bruhl's theory of "primitive mentality."[5] Porot borrowed from Lévy-Bruhl the hypothesis of a pre-logical cognitive function characterized by a predominance of visual over conceptual representation, of allegorical memory over logical reasoning, and of temporal simultaneity over diachronic periodization. But Lévy-Bruhl's phenomenological explorations were aimed at understanding other forms of cognition in their own terms, and eventually led him to pursue that hypothesis in the philosophy of modern science and in a dialogue with Einstein. Porot's racist appropriation, instead, bent Lévy-Bruhl's ideas towards a theory of the pathological mind. A *mentalité indigène prémobide* was described in terms of lack of the concept of time, deficiency of the critical faculty and inability to think conceptually, both related to a fundamental inability to symbolize, and to an excessive development of the mimetic faculty. Arabs were prisoners of the image, Porot said, and this explained the diffusion of what he called *les troubles de la mimique* ("mimeological disorders"): contagious hysterical states, which often grew into collective hysteria.

Toward the end of the colonial period, in the late 1940s and 1950s, a new approach was developed in Morocco against the racist orientation of the Algiers school. In an attempt to rethink the complex interpenetration of cultures issued from the colonial encounter, and to understand the destabilizing psychosocial impact of modernization, the *Groupe d'étude de psychologie de l'inconscient et de médecine psychosomatique* (Research Group on the Psychology of the Unconscious and Psychosomatic Medicine) gathered in Casablanca several French psychiatrists and *médecins militaires* around the person of René Laforgue, an expatriate French psychoanalyst, former friend of Sigmund Freud, and former president of the Societé Psychanalytique de Paris.[6]

The position of the group was elaborated in a series of articles published in the journal *Maroc Médical*. The approach was empirical, research oriented, open to understanding cultural difference and change. The contributors reflected on the attitude French mental health officers should assume towards indigenous medicine and age-old beliefs, and on the responsibilities of psychiatry vis-à-vis the social traumas of modernization, urbanization, and increasing proletarization, "a true drama in the psychosocial evolution of a country whose traditional structures are shattered, and that does not seem prepared to quickly come up with novel institutions."[7]

A crucial feature was the focus on culture—the attempt to situate psychopathological affections within the sociocultural context in which they were produced. The task, in the wake of "the American school of cultural anthropology," was to formulate a theory of the Moroccan personality structure (*personalité marocaine de base*—Igert cited Kroeber and Kluckhohn). Partly conceived in the appreciation of human difference, but also in strident denial of the violence of the colonial encounter, this also served to identify the areas where sociocultural personality traits would be dysfunctional in the process of modernization.

Maurice Igert's 1955 "Introduction à la psychopathologie marocaine" is an articulate exposition of this approach. Opening with the notion that "an initiation to Moroccan psychopathology should be an invitation to journey," Igert—a military physician turned psychoanalyst—reflects on what it entails, for European health officers, "to establish a contact with beings governed by internal laws other than our own": fundamentally different, and yet so closely related in daily commerce. ("The contact between French and Moroccan people is no longer that of two cultures that exist as two independent realities, but that of two human societies that have a certain common history, common interests in partnership and, obviously, some areas of friction.")

The idea is to identify "the cultural tensions generative of neuroses" specific to the Moroccan cultural milieu. Igert's text oscillates between the desire to "journey," listening to the stories of possession and suffering he analyzes, often with psychological insight, and the drive to produce a chart of sociocultural features with pathological potential. The detailed observation of Bouzoukri, a soldier admitted as a patient to the *Centre Neuro-Psychiatrique des Troupes du Maroc*, includes long sections of the man's direct narration. It is an effort at listening to a psyche other than one's own, and to the "mythical themes" of a delirium, which, Igert writes, are "not so foreign to us after all."

But the task of mapping the configuration of Moroccan psychopathology prevails, leading Igert to diagnose the neurotic orientation of the culture as a whole. Moroccan personality is characterized by "mental plasticity," "suggestibility," and the collective alienation of a society that cannot sanction the insanity of the mentally ill, but instead shares and validates their delusional tales of possession by the jinns. The real obstacle towards the possibility of emancipation and cure is therefore, for Igert, the "unlimited tolerance of the Moroccan social milieu vis-à-vis mental disorders that draw their themes from the very sources of collective belief"; for "as long as the individual remains faithful to this common source, he cannot be considered as insane (*aliené*)."[8] And, in the Freudian spirit, for a cure to be possible, alienation must be recognized.

The cultural tensions "generative of neuroses" are described as structurally conflictual features of the Moroccan patriarchal family, related to "the profound impregnation of Islam" in the culture. "Psychological plasticity" and the inability to take responsibility for one's acts are a consequence of what Igert see as "the Islamic cultural system." A tyrannical cultural superego associated with the paternal configuration of father-sultan-God led to an excessive identification of the children with an all-powerful father. The impossibility of finding resort in a mother who was hierarchically inferior and culturally devalued determined the "imbalance of the trio father-mother-son, "which in Europe makes possible the acquisition of individual autonomy." This caused the "absolute subordination" to paternal authority, which destined "the son's aggressiveness to total repression," and in turn led to its neurotic conversion into a flurry of symptoms. This submission made impossible the development of self-confidence and "individual sovereignty."

Igert's conclusion was that, "other than evading into spirituality, an avenue that is indeed wide open in the cultural milieu, he [the son] will have the sole option of bending. . . . Thus [he] develops a remarkable mental plasticity. . . . In the eyes of the psychiatrist, this plasticity represents a simple defense mechanism encompassing a vast field of reactions, ranging, according to its modalities, from utilitarian and banal lying, to hysteria, passing through simulation and suggestibility. This cultural trait marks Moroccan mental pathology with certain typical features, particularly the manifestations of individual and collective hysteria."[9] Magical and religious practices, the belief in spirits (and particularly the role of "castrating female spirits" such as ʿAisha Qandisha, that expressed the "occult revolt of Moroccan women"), indigenous healing, the place of saints in the society and the many varieties of Sufi mysticism, were all, for Igert, coherent manifestations of the neurotic personality structure.

Cultural Uncanny

At the conference on the Psychothérapie du Patient Magrébin, forty years later in Casablanca, the characterizations *medicine indigène* and *mentalité in-*

digène were updated by the qualifier "traditional." For they now designated a domain of practice and belief specific to a society that was the psychiatrist's own—which it was and yet wasn't, for its tense was an archaeological past. The domain had a name, *le magico-religieux,* a term recycled from colonial ethnological accounts to designate the realm of what was beyond the line of modernity. Descriptions of trance lent body and image to this space, evoking the slashing of Hamadsha devotees at the Festival of Shaykh al-Kamel, or the chaining of the insane to the columns of Buya ʿOmar's sanctuary. All the papers emphasized the need to study "traditional therapies," and sometimes proposed a classification of the range of practitioners (soothsayers or Qurʾanic scholars, talisman writers or exorcists), and proposed a translation of traditional symptomatology in the Freudian vocabulary of psychoneuroses—hysteria, above all.

Looked at from this angle, the situation bore a certain resemblance to the colonial project of seizing the *mentalité indigène,* all the while enforcing a policy of the Ministry of Health and Public Hygiene. For the Protectorate's attitude towards "indigenous medicine" had itself had many faces. The French fascination with the realm of the *magico-religieux* (Durkheim's *sacrée*) had inspired monumental works such as Edmond Doutté's 1909 *Magie et religion dans l'afrique du nord,* a survey of magico-medical beliefs and techniques based on a detailed study of classical and vernacular Arab treatises of magical and prophetic medicine. By systematizing and classifying indigenous medical knowledge, works such as *Magie et religion* gathered a dispersion of practices and techniques into an encompassing field, creating the possibility of "indigenous and Arab medicine" as a modern object of study. This attitude went hand in hand with a ban on the exercise of indigenous medicine, and with the militarized enforcement of what Dr. Colombani, the director of the Ministry of Health and Public Hygiene in Morocco in the 1920s and 1930s, called *"la dictature sanitaire"*—the Dictatorship of Health.[10]

Yet, beyond superficial parallels with the colonial policy of health, what emerged from the Casablanca conference, from the silences, the imprecisions and omissions in the characterization of the "traditional" realm, was a sense of malaise, an embarrassment with the object of knowledge that is absent in the colonial discourse. *Les thérapies traditionnelles* seemed inaccessible. This determined the fact that no serious comparative discussion of technique seemed possible.

It was a troubling question, involving the subjectivity of the therapists themselves. Strategic in a different sense, the psychiatric subjective positioning vis-à-vis *les thérapies traditionnelles* was structured by a claim of incommensurability,[11] pertaining, rather, to a register Freud designates as "the uncanny."[12] Disquieting unfamiliar familiarity, unhomely homeness, of what has fallen beyond the line, and returns as an urgent questioning from an archaeological beforehand.

Variously argued in the Freudian and Lacanian vocabulary by psychoanalysts, or in the nosological idiom by clinical psychiatrists, the main objections to the possibility of engaging in a dialogue with "traditional therapies" were two. The first was a caveat on cultural relativism. To treat indigenous psychotherapies as a culturally specific form of healing, and an effective one, meant to replicate the colonial operation of circumscribing an indigenous mentality—and pathology—as something essentially specific to a dominated race, in this case "one's own." The colonial psychiatry of Antoine Porot and the Algiers school of psychiatry was the example at hand.

The second and most crucial objection had to do with the assessment of traditional therapies from the point of view of modernist norms of subjectivity. Predicated on projection, suggestion, mimicry, and the displacement of agency onto imaginary entities (the jinns, or other persecutors), traditional therapies reproduced and reinforced an alienated structure of the self.

To state that one is bewitched (*mshūr*), as patients often declare in the psychiatric consulting room, amounts to saying "it is not me"; my suffering comes from elsewhere, others are the cause of the harm. To say one is possessed (*majnūn, mskūn, mshiyyer*)—a statement seldom uttered in the first person, because it is an enunciative prerogative of the healer and because, in a fundamental sense, it pertains to the unutterable of the psychiatric encounter—is to be unable to assume one's own suffering and desire, to push agency outside of the ego. It means to be neurotic, possibly schizophrenic—and, in all cases, fundamentally alienated. Rather than challenging that alienation, traditional therapists are seen as operating from within it and putting it to work.

In its systematic form, the discourse of contemporary Moroccan psychoanalysis about its Other revolves around the themes of "suggestion," "mimetism," and hysteria, and the alienating status of the subject's "other voice." I was induced to debate with psychoanalysts both by my own interest in the theory of the unconscious, and because of the realization that in contemporary Morocco an anthropological study of the therapies of the jinn that did not take into account—theoretically as well—their dialogical implications with the technique and discourse of psychoanalysis and psychiatry on the one hand, and with Islamic thought on the other, is fated to follow the steps of the colonial studies of indigenous mentality.

What does it mean to assume a subject position in the context of the "therapies of the jinn"?

This is the question I posed to a number of psychoanalysts in the 1990s. The answer was peremptory: from within the therapies of the jinn there could be no access to subjectivity—to a subject position in the Lacanian sense. For the "cures of the jinns" are predicated on imitation and identification, and allow no responsible engagement of the subject of speech. They are comparable to the hypnotic treatment of hysteria in the prehistory of psychoanalysis; and it is on hysterical symptoms that they are most (and solely) effective.[13]

As in the dedoublements of Anna O. (Josef Breuer's famous patient),[14] who split into a *"condition seconde,"* as Breuer and Freud called it, an other consciousness, speaking a language other than her own, the jinns speak through the person. Or they make the person speak, as in the case of the Rat Man studied by Freud, who is afflicted by voices that tell him things he cannot recognize as his own. But unlike psychoanalysis, which is interpretative, the cures of the jinns operate through "suggestion" and the displacement of agency onto imaginary entities. And it is known that Freud abandoned therapy through hypnosis and developed psychoanalysis instead, because suggestion can temporarily eliminate the symptom, but it cannot cure. "There is the greatest possible antithesis between suggestive and analytic technique," Freud wrote,[15] for one works by veiling, the other by unveiling. One works by producing illusions, and adds alienation to the alienation of the illness; the other uncovers the truth of the subject.

This is essentially why contemporary Moroccan psychoanalysts, who reformulate the problem within a Lacanian vocabulary, say that traditional therapies remove the symptom by adding alienation to the alienation of the illness. They mimic the ailment they are presumed to heal; the self becomes the passive recipient of demonic action, and the "I" is lost in the lure of its identifications. Like a trompe-d'oeil, traditional cures operate exclusively in the register of the Imaginary, without ever reaching the dimension of the Symbolic—the order of responsibility and assumed subjectivity. And since the Imaginary is the register of alienation and *méconnaissance,* these therapies are said to be unable to free the "true speech" of the subject. (Lacan's own interpretation of the story of Anna O. contradicts this reading, inasmuch as he presents Anna's poetic recollections under hypnosis—her trances—and the symptoms of her psychic body as the advent of true speech, made possible by the transference with her doctor.)[16]

My fieldwork at the psychiatric hospital started as an attempt to answer these questions. In a certain way the problem that I was confronted with on a daily basis during my fieldwork, and that I sought to register in the stories of patients, is whether patients themselves were able, in their transactions with psychiatrists, to appropriate a space not entirely bound by the terms of either modernist psychiatry or of a culture no longer in place—a culture suspended in a zone of "agony," as Fanon writes, experienced at once as inactual, and active in the form of a haunting. Amina in the previous section, and Reda, whom I discuss further below, bore witness to the impossibility of inhabiting the sites of symbolic protection and belonging. Amina's condition worsened when her father brought her to a *siyyid*, a sanctuary where the mad are traditionally brought to find refuge and seek healing. Reda perceived himself as "devoured" by the Arabic language as his mother/tongue.

THREE

The Jinn and the Pictogram: "The Story of My Life"

al-jinn khilāfu al-ins (the jinn is the other and the like of the human)

—*Ibn Manẓūr, Lisān al-ʾarab*

I ask Hind to repeat into my tape recorder the story about the origin of her illness that she had told me a few days before in the locked ward. That day she had spoken very fast, in an impersonal style, as if about someone else. She had been admitted to the hospital two days earlier for a relapse of the manic-depressive illness for which she had been an intermittent patient there since she was fourteen. Once again, on a police order (in the report, OP, "[*raison d'*]*ordre public*"). She came accompanied by two of her sisters and a police officer. The updated note in her file following her admission reads: "*Patiente logotique, idée délirante de grandeur. Rechute SMD dans état maniaque. Psychose maniaco dépressive à prédominance maniaque. Pas de syndrome dissociatif*" (Patient with logorrhea, delusional ideas of grandeur. Relapse of manic-depressive syndrome (MDS) in a manic state. Manic-depressive psychosis with predominance of mania. Absence of dissociation).

It was hard to follow. She had complained of the theft of her jewelry and her cell phone by a dark-skinned jinn, a spirit creature, and had mentioned the men who called her on that phone, rich and powerful men, Saudi businessmen and police chiefs, the men who wanted her. She evoked the pleasures and the filth of those encounters, and kept making leaps into the larger historical and political context of the country, of which her body, desired and violated, was the imaginal battlefield. Like Amina, and other women patients I met at the hospital, Hind is fond of singing. She sang the songs of legendary Egyptian singer, Abdel Halim Hafez, who, she said, told the story of her life. Our conversations are punctuated by her singing, and by the voice of Abdel Halim in a cassette player to which she turned to find words and tune in the gaps of her saying. I wanted to understand her experience of voice, as something different from speech and narrative—posterior or anterior—and yet engaged in a relationship with it. In the process, I realized that for Hind the voice was inextricable from what she called her tie to *al-ghāyb*, her connection to the world of the Invisible. That tie was instantiated by a jinn, who had accompanied her since her adolescence.

JINN (invisible being, spirit creature, demon; *al-junūn*, madness, possession): The verbal root encountered in this book carries the multidirectional sense of concealing, covering, and hiding, and spans in its various forms such diverse meanings as garden, Paradise, fetus, tomb, jinn/demon or invisible being, possessed person, the mad one, and madness. The root *j-n-n* appears 201 times in the Qur'an, 22 times as the noun *al-jinn*, the invisible beings God created from fire. References to possession or madness in the Qur'an are used most often to assert that the Prophet is not mad or possessed, that his state of connection with the divine is not equivalent to madness and is the opposite of possession (Qur'an 34:46). *Al-junūn* as such does not appear in the Qur'an, but is found in Quranic commentary, as noted in the classical Arabic dictionary *Lisān al-ʿarab*: *"futina bi-l-junūn"* (the one seized by madness/possession), where it is also said that, *al-jinn khilāf al-ins*, "the jinn is the other and the like of the human," and "there are those who say that the jinn is different than the human being because it is invisible."[1] In E. W. Lane's dictionary, *al-junūn* is glossed as "originally signifying a state of possession by a jinnī or a jinn, diabolical or demoniacal possession, and hence meaning loss of reason; or madness, insanity, or unsoundness in mind or intellect, or deficiency of intellect. It may generally be rendered as possession or insanity."[2]

In 1921, Freud introduced the concept of affective tie in *Group Psychology and the Analysis of the Ego* (*Massenpsychologie und Ich-Analyse*),[3] an important and enigmatic text developing a line of thought that furrows his "second topography." In that work so disparately understood by generations of readers, Freud explores the nature of the bond of identification, the affective tie, in the constitution of the individual self, while at the same time questioning the nature of the political tie: the machinery of sovereignty, collective bonding and depersonalization in the unconditional surrender to an all-powerful leader. Alternating between the registers of the self and of the "mass" (the "mass," not the "group" of the English translation) Freud shows that the affective tie constitutes the self mimetically in a piecemeal fashion as a compound of ties, that is, of identifications; but also that, by the same turn, it is a primary cause of self-undoing—for the "*Massen*" is a depersonalized collective entity without will and without reason, which surrenders to the coercive authority of the leader (*Führer*).

Freud distinguishes between two desires, both underpinning the mechanism of identification: the desire for "having" the other as a libidinal object, and a more fundamental, more "ancient" and "mysterious" passion (his words) the passion of "being," becoming the other—because the subject is not. It is this second desire (Freud called it narcissistic) that is key to a new and paradoxical way of conceiving relation and being as a violent movement of becoming a self by becoming another, becoming the other by incorporation and destruction, by mimetic borrowings from heterogeneous materials, by metamorphosis and surrender, in a passion of life and death that is both creative and destructive. It is significant that Freud's reflection on the ambivalent dynamics of identification within the unstable field of the self (which is constituted in the process) is also a reflection on power and sovereignty—on the coercive power of the narcissistic chief, who is also in his text the hypnotizer, the ego ideal, and, in the end, death itself—the alterity in which all power dissolves.

In *Group Psychology*, as in other works from this period, Freud turned back to the enigmas of his early explorations of hypnosis, hysteria, and paranoia. Rather than tracing the symbolic stuttering of the subject in a field of unconscious revelations, he ponders the mysterious "tie," its predatory propensities, and its creative potentialities. In the ambivalence and the risks of the affective tie there is a confrontation with madness, and with what Freud called the "daemonic" forces at play in the mapping of destiny. We might begin to understand Hind's attachment to the jinn who shared her life since she was fourteen in the mode of the Freudian affective tie, its ambivalent passions, violent propensities, and creative possibilities. But this type of approach, if it is to be elucidating, requires a displacement of psychoanalytic concepts through an understanding of the Islamic ontology of *al-ghayb*, the Invisible world, realm of divine manifestation and subtle essences, populated with spirits, and the dimension of the soul.[4]

A first reading of her thick hospital file, covering seventeen years since Hind's first hospitalization in 1984 (in 2001 she was thirty-two), in the changing handwriting of medical school residents and psychiatrists who had succeeded each other at the hospital over the years, conveys the portrait of a turbulent teenager, and then youth, and then woman and mother, halfway between the home and the streets, her life of "unbridled" sexuality an open challenge to the cultural norms, in and out of a family of the poor urban petite bourgeoisie: her mother worked as a janitor at a hospital, and was later referred to in the medical file as *"sans profession"*; her father, a shopkeeper who left them and remarried; a schizophrenic brother, described as "stabilized"; and a sister described as a prostitute (*prostitué*).

Since her first hospitalization when she was fifteen, there is mention in her file of *"idées de possession,"* "ideas of possession by a jinn Gnawi who requests her release from the hospital to attend the trance dance."[5] The qualifier "Gnawi" (an adept of the Gnawa) is not explained in the chart because readers are presumed familiar with the Gnawa brotherhood, a spiritual and musical *ṭarīqa* (path) whose adepts claim genealogical or adoptive descent from West African slaves, and cultivate an intimate relationship with jinn. The Gnawa are musicians and healers, who can divine illness and heal by activating and transforming a somatic memory of slavery. They perform a liturgy called *al-ḥadra,* "the presencing" ("the trance dance" in the medical chart), where music and song create a bridge between the visible and the invisible, inducing spirits to manifest themselves in the body of those who respond to their "tune."[6] The "jinn Gnawi," then, halfway between afflicting demon and Gnawi healer, is a dark-skinned spirit who belongs to the tribe of jinn who are summoned on the stage of the *ḥadra* ceremony.

Hind went to school until the end of middle school, and there she learned French and classical Arabic, read the "Thousand and One Nights" (she claims to be Qamar Zaman from the tale of Qamar Zaman and Princess Badur, unconcerned that Qamar in the tale is a prince and a male), and gained access to the popular cosmopolitan Arab culture of Egyptian songs and TV soap operas. But her recurrent fugues, related to her manic states (at fifteen she is recorded in the hospital file as living in illegitimate union with an older man, at thirty-two as coming home each night with a different man), increasingly determined the trajectory of her life, and she slowly found herself in the descriptive role of a prostitute—a role that, in her conversations with me, she both decried and reclaimed: for the eroticization and the degradation of her own body and discourse actively participated in the phantasmagoria of her life.

Because of her state of *sakan* (from the verbal root *sakana,* to dwell, inhabit, share residence), a permanent state of possession, one that is not resolved through exorcism or the diverse set of cures known as *ʿilāj al-jinn* ("the cures of the jinn"), in a different context she might have become a healer (*shawafa*, "seer") based on her life-long relationship to a jinn. She might also have joined the Gnawa brotherhood, for the illness and the identity of the jinn Gnawi might have initiated her into their way. But she didn't. She did try to pursue that path of healing, repeatedly visiting shrines and spending months attached by chains in a sanctuary for the mad.[7] But each time she returned to the hospital. Once, according to her patient file, she even checked herself in at the police station, to avoid being tied up in ropes by her sisters.

Hind sees herself has having an illness, an illness that has dismantled her life: "My education is lost to me (*ḍaʿit f qraytī*), my daughter is lost to me (*ḍaʿit f bintī*), my husband is lost to me (*ḍaʿit f rajlī*). This illness (*l-marḍ*) is all that." As is well known in the psychiatric clinic for manic-depressive patients (also known as bipolar), she would take medications for a while, feel normal again, and then stop her medication, and eventually her "state" (*ḥāltī*), as she calls it, would come back, during its season. The return of her "state" (*ḥāla*), a word that she repeats and even screams, coincides with the return of the jinn: "When I am not sick I have the sense that I have never been sick, and then this time comes, summer comes, and the sickness hits me (*kayjini l-marḍ*), and my man takes off. The Gnawi comes, and separates me from my love."

The Gnawi, the jinn, is therefore also a personification of her illness, of her intimate relationship with her "state." In this sense, it could be seen as an imaginal double, in a space of eroticized suffering in which her "psychiatric illness" participates. He "tortures her" (*itkarfes ʿalaya*), the jinn, she says, pushes her to wander the streets, incites her to have sex with other men, fills her house with black bugs; but he also makes love to her, gives her pleasure, and she desires him, speaks of him as beautiful and as a great lover. *"Kaydaiʿni u kayṭalaʿ fiya lmanubel, la noblesse"* ("He wastes me, ruins me, and brings out my nobility"), and the men love her, and then he separates her from them. *"C'est la vie, on n'a pas choisi"* ("Such is life, we haven't chosen it"), she repeats as a refrain, concluding that there is nothing to do, she is bound to *l-ghāyb*.[8] (The Invisible here is the ontological dimension of the nonmanifest in Islamic cosmology. The jinn is real, and can't be read as an objectification of the illness. It is the other way around: the invisible presence manifest itself with, or as, the illness.)

Now she is in the open ward, the *clinique femme*, medicated (on a neuroleptic and a mood regulator), showered and dressed in a pink gown, the long black hair gathered in a ponytail. She's listening to songs on her cassette player and singing along. The music is on for the entire time of our conversation, as it will be during conversations to come. It is a cassette of songs by Abdel Halim Hafez, an Egyptian singer, composer, and actor who performed and produced music from the late 1950s to the 1970s, an artist who transformed the field of Arab music and was gifted with a unique voice compared in stature to that of Umm Kulthum. A sad hero, he was loved by countless Moroccan women, and by women and men all over the Middle East; he was born in poverty and quickly became an orphan, and once he became famous gave back to the poor, but died young, killed by a chronic illness that consumed him to the end.

Woven on the sonic backdrop of Abdel Halim's songs, and borrowing words or entire expressions from the lyrics that provide her with narrative crutches at crucial moments, Hind's recitation revisits an original scene, a scene she presents as traumatic, and in which she locates her *sakan*, her possession or, in her words, "the snatching" of her self, and her state of being inhabited, as the onset of her illness, instinctively timing her story on the tempo of the songs—songs she knows by heart and has sung a million times.

The event has a mythical character and displays themes recurrent in her story: an ambivalence from and towards her mother; a polarity of purity and filth in both literal (the bathroom, the garbage) and metaphorical (nobility, mystical purity, prostitution and abjection of both herself and her mother) terms—a polarity also played out in the reckoning of her relationship with the jinn; her abandonment; and the loss, the "waste" of everything that counted in her life. This first scene also locates the onset of her illness in a specific demonic environment and etiology: water, the *ḥammām* (public bath, site of purification but also a paradigmatically haunted place), the school toilet, and the malevolent utterance of a girl, "the poison of her words."

Her recitation is a theatrical dramatization, in which she shifts between vernacular Moroccan Arabic, French, and classical Arabic, as she takes on different "voices," or aspects, of her story (in the musical, compositional sense I discussed in the previous section), and in such a way that the languages themselves are affectively charged and participate in the pathos of the telling. Statements about "nobility" and "purity" are made in classical Arabic, the bulk of the story is told in vernacular Arabic, while French is used to mark emphasis, or to explain to me things about the jinn—using the colonial language of hospital files as a protection, a shelter.

It happened at school, I was ten. A girl came, and said that Hind's mother is a *ṭayyaba* in a public bath. And when the girls teased me that my mother gave massages and filled up water buckets in the *ḥammām*, I fainted in the bathroom, and lay there for two whole days, in the school's bathroom, until the janitor came to clean and found me, and ran to tell the schoolmaster, and the schoolmaster called my mother, but my mother was away at my sister's wedding. When my mother came back she found that I had been snatched by the jinn, Hind had become another (*wllat Hind waḥda khra*). I was inhabited in my being (*tsekent fī dhātī*), and I couldn't stop screaming. I wandered in the streets without an aim, I wandered around with the homeless, I ate from the garbage cans, I ended up in a state (*ḥāla*) [long pause] *cas interdit* [in French, dramatic change of voice], an untouchable. Thank God, today I am again in good health. That girl [speaking about herself in the third person]: her mother was off the right path (*kharja ṭrīq*). And yet my mother was the noblest, the purest of all women (*ashraf al-nisā'*, in classical Arabic), Rabi'a 'Adawiyya, my mother, people called her Rabi'a 'Adawiyya in our neighborhood [a classical figure of purity and resistance in Muslim hagiographic literature. A woman mystic from early Islam, a slave, she sang poems of love and praise to God]. Rabi'a 'Adawiyya, men attempted to push her into sin, to force her into prostitution, but she resisted, locking herself into a room and singing for God.

And that mother of mine was *mbdd'a*, she was a libertine and a sinner, and she pushed her daughter to wander the streets, to stray off the right path with the Saudis.[9] But myself [switching to classical Arabic], I am a root that is pure (*nuqla ṭayyiba*), I am a tree that is pure, my branches are pure, my origin is pure. My father is a man, his name is Muhammad, they told me he died [moment of disorientation, then continues, in solemn tone]. The poison thrown by that girl [in the school] shows its effects (*kaydhar*). My education is lost to me (*ḍa'it f qrayti*), my daughter is lost to me (*ḍa'it f bintī*), my husband is lost to me (*ḍa'it f rajlī*). This illness (*l-marḍ*) is all that. What shall I do?

At this point in our conversation, the jinn manifests himself on the scene. Hind whispers to me that "that man" (*hadak sayyid*) is present with us *now*, and then explains (in French) that he's black, and he makes a whistling sound, and she's frightened of him. She says that he is a "jinn from the believers" (*mū'min*), and that to meet with him she pulls him up with a bucket from the bottom of the well, sees his reflection in the water, and then pours the water over her body. "I love water, water and perfume" (jinns also love water and perfume).

Under the gaze of the jinn, present with us but invisible to me, Hind begins to sing a song by Abdel Halim, the song Abdel Halim dedicated to Hassan II, the then king of Morocco, "Water and Vegetation." She stops singing and says: "Abdel Halim, branch of a dark tree[10] (*Abdel Halim, al-ʿandalīb al-asmar*). He [the jinn] is Abdel Halim, he [Abdel Halim] is that man [the jinn] (*ha huwa had sayyid*). He talks about me (*il parle de moi Abdelhalim*), I think he tells about me, he tells my story: "Fatat ganbina" ('She passes by me'). In all those songs, he tells about me, he sings about me, the story of my life (*qiṣṣat ḥayātī*), [she begins to sing] *qiṣṣat ḥayātī ya nās* [from one of his songs, 'Nibtidi mnayn il-ḥikāya' ('Where are we to start the tale?')]." She loses the tempo. Fumbles through the lyrics and suddenly says: "*Huwa* (he)."

—Do you know him? [to me, assertively]

She tells me about the man she married, her daughter's father, and about how he—the jinn—cause her husband to leave her. He left her, and migrated to France.

—I am sick; it is not my own wish (*anā mrīḍa, mashī khaṭrī*).

—Why did he push him to leave you?

—I am married to the Invisible (*al-ghāʾib*), the black man.

C'est la vie, on n'a pas choisi ("such is life, we haven't chosen it")—she repeats this as a refrain. She begins to sing again, a song by Umm Khulthum, "I dread something in the future." "I am Qamar Zaman [from "One Thousand and One Nights"].[11] You see Zaman [*zamān*, as noun: time, the world, fortunes and their reversals], *zamān* is God's will. Don't trust anyone, don't commit to anything, the earth turns and returns, one day you are the head, the next you are the feet."

The reversal of her fortune turns into that of her country, which is "tortured," corrupted and pure, shaken by destructive and erotic passions and vices. "There is no balance, no justice, only theft and corruption in this land." Suddenly realizing the potentially dangerous implications of her assertions, she concludes that she's a madwoman (*ḥamqa*), and she can say what she wishes; she is not accountable for her words. She begins to sing again.

Hind's relationship with the black jinn, who tortures her and gives her pleasure, causes losses in her life, and sometimes, she says, gives her life, is a peculiar form of cohabitation. It is a paradoxical form of relation (of a nonself to a nonother) that could be described, borrowing a concept from Sylvie Le Poulichet (a psychoanalyst who has written insightfully on attachment, addiction, and the subjectivities formed in a relationship with death), as the emergence within the self of an *objet inconnu*, an unknown and unknowable object, that the self encounters, introjects, passionately invests, and in the end becomes. That foreign object, which is not properly speaking an object, has the capacity to lend an image, and a body, in situations in which body and life cannot be reinvested or just invested: "the object-of-creation takes then the function of an *intimate foreign body* that can be affectively invested."[12]

It is Piera Aulagnier who pursued Freud's ponderings on the "affective tie" in their complex implications for an understanding of creative processes as well as of psychotic phenomena. Elaborating on an energetics of the trace Freud had sketched in his early work,[13] Aulagnier adds to the Freudian distinction of primary and secondary processes a third and "prior" register, which she calls *le processus originaire*, "the originary process," whose mode of representation, prior to the possibility of representation itself, is not the image but the "pictogram." Her theoretical reflection is directly related to her clinical experience with schizophrenic and severely psychotic patients, and is a response to an interrogation on the vulnerable and unstable nature of subjectivity, as structurally open to the possibility of madness.

The pictogram is at once the trace, the psychic carving, of the original encounter between the infans and the world, and the self-generated inscription that makes that encounter possible. It is an affective metabolization of the infans's own body, self and other at once, in the mode of incorporation and of annihilation. In psychosis, she writes, this "pictographic reservoir" or "background of representation" (*fond représentatif*) comes to the foreground producing the defensive work of delusion, understood as the desperate attempt "to make speakable and meaningful affective experiences born from a representation in which the world is reduced to the specular reflection of a self-generating, self-mutilating, self-rejecting body."[14] Yet Aulagnier sees psychotic phenomena on a continuum with what she calls "moments of *fading* of the I," moments most of us will experience at some point during our life.[15]

The pictogram is active, productive, and effective, but also inaccessible to knowledge otherwise than through its phantasmic metamorphoses and energetic deployments. This is why the obliterated trace is at work in intergenerational transmission. In a patient case study reminiscent of Frantz Fanon, Aulagnier shows the workings of such immemorial transmission, whereby the trace of forgotten inscriptions is played out in the shaping of reality over four generations and across vast geographical distance, and a racialized phantasm is realized back and forth in marriages, filiations, and violent intimacies between white France and colored Madagascar. And if one is willing to follow Freud in his study of the work of latency in the shaping of a cultural tradition in his last work, *Moses and Monotheism*,[16] the pictogram is also the register of the transmission of culture. The question is whether and when the play of obliterated traces may give way to transformation, to the possibility of being with others, and to the encounter of newness in repetition.

But for Hind there is another scene of the pictogram. The jinn is real, and her experiences, as she emphasizes, pertain to the realm of the Invisible, *al-ghāyb*. We may think of the meaning of the singer's name, the singer who, she tells me, is also the jinn: Abdel Halim, Slave of the Patient, namely of al-Ḥalīm, one of the names of God, but from a verbal root that means to dream, to have visions and insight.

To reflect on how Aulagnier's pictogram, that affective obliterated trace, may translate in the realm of the Invisible, requires addressing the question of the soul and its resonance in the space of the hospital.

The opposite also applies. Solely comprehending the passionate connection between Hind and the jinn from within the logic of the Invisible, spirit possession and healing would not do justice to the oxymoron of Hind's position, for in her own understanding the jinn *is also* a visible manifestation of her manic depressive illness. As documented in the hospital files, and described in the words of the psychiatrists who have attempted to treat her illness since she was fifteen, her bond to the jinn (what the hospital files call her "delusion") is "encysted," as an otherness that has become an unrescindable part of her self. Hind is incurable: deliverance is not an option for her. In different circumstances the cohabitation might have made of her a healer. But instead she is tied by a solitary bond to the dark-skinned spirit, who shelters and tortures her. Certain features of her condition, her cohabitation, are common to the experience of demonic and divine cures, in both the vernacular and the ethical Muslim tradition: an emphasis on the "effect," the "trace," of what cannot be recollected otherwise than through the rawness of affect; and a questioning of submission in her relationship to the jinn, of surrendering to the dominion of an unjust other, who holds her in his control. The nature of that submission is debated between different ethical and theological approaches to the cure in Islam, the key point being that submitting to God is surrender of a fundamentally different sort, one that cannot be described in terms of coercion.

In Hind's story, but also in her actual existence, the encroachment is originary. The self is born with the jinn. The jinn sings the story of her life, with the lyrics of Abdel Halim's songs; Hind plays his songs in her cassette recorder, and sings along in her own voice, which is also his voice.

What is the nature of such displacements? For Hind, the displacements are consummated in a phantasmagoric space of eroticism and abjection, prominently staged on her physical body (her liquid encounter with the jinn when she pours water on herself to meet him). What the jinn and the singer voice, and the effects of that voice, has to do with the energetic of the obliterated trace—in the body, in the voice, in the life, in a scene that is simultaneously of this world and the Other.

And thus the question lingers of the stakes of this kind of inquiry, and of the possibility of addressing these questions from the standpoint of another conceptual and experiential world—a different border zone of theory: the repertoire of Islamic thought, medicine, and practice, and the possibilities open within the Muslim tradition and the Arabic language. It is the subject of part three of this book, and particularly the section on the "jouissance of the jinn."

FOUR

The Knot of the Soul (and the Cervantes Stage)

A young man and a woman sitting on a bench in the waiting area of the emergency room, a crowded hallway in the old modular compound at the edge of the hospital grounds. The man is wearing jeans, has slightly long hair and the look of a university student. He is pale and tense, moves restlessly and gazes through the room with a sense of imprisoned rage. The woman is older, wears a *jellaba* and a headscarf. The man was brought that morning by an ambulance of the *protection civile*, on a police order, RP, *"requisition de police." The police car is still outside the building.*

The head nurse keeps an eye on the patient, for until the psychiatrist on call decides on his hospitalization or his release, the patient is held in police custody. They came from Tiflet, the head nurse tells me, a town that was once just a weekly market where tribal populations met, which became an army station during the Protectorate, and is today a large town and growing sprawl in the rural hinterland of Rabat. The woman is the patient's mother—it is she who filed the police complaint. I try to imagine what exasperation, what lack of exit led the mother to that resolution. I am waiting for Dr. R., a young woman psychiatrist, with whom I have agreed to share the day on call.

I write in a margin of the encounter that took place that day, in light of encounters that followed with other patients and in different circumstances, but in the wording, and concrete features of a particular life, as that life presented itself to me that morning in the emergency room. My reflections, in the form of a circumstantial commentary, address questions raised by the young man himself in his speech, and related to his perception and imagination of "modern times" in its confrontation with a "cultural home" he experiences as unlivable. It is a confrontation that takes place on the battlefield of his own body and life, but that by its nature concerns a whole society—as in a way a society and the possibility of a common life are called in his speech. Spoken from his uncanny experience (which is partly inaccessible to his interlocutors), his questions point to the tear of a failing transmission—the impossibility to inhabit a tradition. They voice the violence of cultural identity in the postcolonial nation, and an essential homelessness, which is that of his madness, but is also, in a different sense, the experience of his generation. Yet, at the same time, his questions bear witness to a struggle for existence and creative elaboration, for a possibility of resymbolization, fought on the very ground of the ER interview. Punctuated by a reiterated request for a lawyer, "a lawyer who may speak in my behalf and defend my rights," his discourse is a paradoxical appeal to the law, the law of the state and the institution of psychiatry, in a plea to be recognized as a subject.

Reflecting on questions of public health in the *banlieues* of French cities and in the context of irregular migration, Didier Fassin argues that the biopolitical reduction of being to "bare life," to the silence of a suffering body, grants to the excluded an ultimate and paradoxical recourse to the law.[1] He calls this agency "biolegitimization," a right issued from the loss of all rights and communal affiliations, and shows how the biopolitical operation is literally incarnated by migrant subjects of irregular status, for whom illness becomes the only possible ground of appeal in their request for inclusion.[2] But unlike the case of Europe, in the situation I attempt to apprehend becoming a biopolitical suffering body does not grant a paradoxical juridical inclusion.

The appeal to the institution of care must be understood differently, in a space of impossibility that is also the ground for the imagination of life. I trace in this section a paradoxical gesture of appeal, an appeal to the law of the state, the "constitution of the King," but an appeal that doesn't provide for access to citizenship, for it rejects existing ties and affiliations, and is instead spoken in an ambiguous utopian zone, where creation and loss are intertwined in the singularity of a marginal life.[3] (Yet in 2016, when, agitated by mounting nationalism and xenophobia, Europe is shutting its door to waves of refugees and migrants, when France treats providing meals to refugees as a crime, when the city of Paris puts boulders under its freeways to prevent refugees from sleeping under the bridges, when Hungary and Poland set up barbed wire and mobilize the army to halt the entrance of refugees from the Balkans, and when refugees nonetheless make their space in the city without its recognition, humanitarian reason may have reached its limit and turning point, and inclusion, access to citizenship, even of the biopolitical sort, may have become a thing of the past.)

How to think the aftermath of the subject of psychoanalysis without necessarily resorting to the categories of psychopathology? How to address the present sociocultural, political, and spiritual upheaval without surrendering to comforting psychosocial diagnoses? Some directions are found in the Freudian approach itself. Identification, as we discussed earlier, which underpins the processes of contemporary mass society as well as the formation of the ego, is "more ancient" than the contractual, symbolic mode of relation; it is a "passage through the Other" in which the "I" is both founded and revoked.[4] Developing this line of thought would lead, among other things, to questioning the irreducibility of the boundary between subjectivity and psychosis, exploring the troubling and unstable interfaces of subjectivity and depersonalization.[5]

In relation to these questions the story of Reda, the young man I was to meet in the emergency room, provides a number of unexpected answers. As with many youths at the onset of psychosis, or simply someone whose psychic skin is less impermeable, Reda takes it upon himself to articulate a malaise larger than his own, that of a collectivity of which he becomes an echo. From the rage of the torture he feels, inflicted on him by a cultural home he experiences as unlivable, Reda moves to a creative interpretation of his madness, opposing to that intrusion, to that shrinkage of vital space, something other than a search for identity: a kind of "comedy" (his term) he also designates as "the Cervantes Stage," a play that transforms alienation from within madness itself. His answer displaces the terms of the question, and suggests that if we pay attention to the concrete specificity of particular lives, and the philosophical resources found in living traditions envisaging possible other worlds, we may glimpse the inception of a renewed *Kulturarbeit*, a novel articulation of unspeakable cultural truths. Here, in the margins of a psychiatric encounter.

Shadow Theater of Modernity

As is often the case, there is tension in the emergency room. Dr. R. is opening the official seals, reading the letter from the police. Then she looks at the man and asks his name in Arabic. The mother replies that his name is

Reda, and that he's thirty. But Reda is not listening. He complains loudly about her, his mother, speaks French and addresses Dr. R. directly. Says that his mother doesn't understand him, couldn't possibly understand him, she is illiterate and ignorant, unable to even count six by seven.

Dr. R. interrupts him, in Arabic (visibly not to exclude the mother, who doesn't understand French, from the conversation): "*U nta ʿarfti?* (And you, can you do it?)," she asks. Reda is reluctant, annoyed by the obvious, finally says, "forty-two," and insists that he shouldn't be in this hospital, that he requests a lawyer, he demands his rights: "*Je demande un avocat, je demande mes droits!*"

"*Elle veut me rendre fou* (she wants to make me crazy), she forced me to consult with a *faqīh* (Qurʾanic healer) against my will." Reda insists on speaking French, ignoring the injunction of Arabic, the psychiatrist's refusal to reply in the language of his choice: the colonial language, the language of the hospital files, but also, for him, the language of his scientific studies[6] and of his literary journeys, a language his mother doesn't understand. It is the only language in which he is able to articulate his request, his appeal to the Other, embodied in the room by this frail young woman sitting behind a desk.

"Why should I take medications? *Khod dwa* (take your medications), she orders; I should instead take a lawyer because of the suffering she is inflicting to me. As for this language I am speaking [French], she [his mother] is illiterate and we are entering the twenty-first century."[7] He repeats this in Arabic, perhaps to make his mother feel the humiliation: "*Makatfehemsh lfranse, maqariash* (she is illiterate, doesn't understand French), while I have a Troisieme Cycle, a doctorate in mathematics" (the mother signals to the psychiatrist that this corresponds to reality).

I ask Reda about his education:

> I have a university degree, a *maîtrise* with equivalence in the French system, pure math, logic. I am a logician, only I disguise myself, and instead play my literary games (*je fais des jeux de littérature*). I studied pure mathematics, pure logic, I have a degree in linear algebra (*ʿarfti ashna hiya la géometrie algébrique*), do you know what that is? [violently to his mother]

"I don't know anything (*ma 'arfa walu*)," admits the mother.

Reda turns to his mother aggressively and says in Arabic, "Why did you take me to the healer (*ʿalesh dditini ʿand l-faqīh*), against my will, and with the fire department? Why? To feed me herbs (*ʿashūb*) and potions, nutmeg (*lgusa*) and fennel (*ḥabt lḥalawa*) to subjugate my will. I can still understand a girl who does that, she desires you and puts *twkkel* in your food, feeds you a magical couscous to make you marry her . . . But this woman?"

And then to the psychiatrist, and to me, in a mixture of Arabic and French: "They made me swallow meals of God only knows what, dog and cow brains . . . excrement (*les dechets*), cow dung they mix in with couscous, and much much more. In our region laboratory experiments are made with couscous!"

Insisting on using Arabic as the language of the interview, Dr. R. asks Reda whether he really thinks that his mother put magic in his food. Reda replies in French that he is suspicious, he doesn't trust her, her cooking, her food. Exasperated, the mother denies having put anything in the food, and Reda replies that in any case her cooking is poisoning him, and appeals once again to the mediation of the law, a law that might speak in his behalf—literally, to a lawyer: "I request a lawyer, a lawyer who may defend my case, for all the suffering that I endured with this woman . . . [repeats in Arabic], because I have suffered so much. . . ."

The scene in the emergency room becomes a trial, in which Reda is at once plaintiff and defendant. It is a trial and a self-defense made possible by the summoning of the institutional code, calling subjects in the position of patients, protected by the recognition of their illness, as stated in the law of 1959. Reda's passionate self-defense, like his request for mediation, is a testimony of his struggle for creating a "place," a space in which it may be possible to exist. The absence of place is a poignant feature of Reda's claustrophobic speech, aimed at pushing back an aggression, distancing an invader, striving to protect the possibility of a vital movement threatened at his core.

Reda is upset, the atmosphere is tense. I recall the anxiety, and the way his voice affected me, thinking that the psychiatrist must be affected as well. Because the drama that was unfolding before our eyes, resonated as something larger than a personal or a family affair. It overflowed the specificity of his personal history, and resonated for me (and how could it not for Dr. R.?) as a historical and political affair. In that overflowing, the possibility of a personal history was reduced (or imprisoned, in the vocabulary of *Daseinanalyse*) in what Ludwig Binswanger calls "the splitting off of experiential consistency into alternatives, into a rigid either-or." Reda, his voice, his body, became a rift where the cleavages of Moroccan modernity, the ideology of modernity, intersected and clashed, the same cleavages by which his life was furrowed, and that underpin the possibility of this hospital scene. The psychiatrist, the mother, and I were at once spectators and characters on the scene of this recital.

Twkel: Topography of the Unlivable

As I listen and listen back to Reda's words in the transcript of that conversation, I attempt to follow his figures of speech, as one follows the images of a dream.

He outlined the main themes at the outset, in a sort of poetic condensation. Poisoning and incorporation by ingestion, cannibalization, illiteracy, the theme of the mother. She wants to make me crazy, she wants to kill me. And, "we are entering the twenty-first century": exit and forward movement—science, mathematics, logic, and geometry, education by the intercession of the foreign tongue. Murderous persecution by "her cooking," her food and her magic, and by the intimate relationship his mother entertains with the *faqīhs*, traditional healers and agents of traditional culture. The magic Reda refers to and specifically names is itself called *twkel*, from the Arabic root *akala*, to eat (in this passive form of the verb, to be devoured, eaten away, destroyed). *Twkel* is a technical term, the name of a magical operation and of a form of illness attack described in manuals of healing and magic, and it is a key notion in the vocabulary of affliction, in the discourse of healers as well as patients and their families. Unlike other conditions, more directly related to the jinn, complaints of *twkel* are rarely censored in the illness narratives of patients in the hospital, because of its perceived equivalence with psychotic symptoms of persecution (by poisoning, or more "culturally specific," in terms of a "delusion of sorcery"), or of its more bodily, physical connotation. Intentionally harmful *twkel* can be obtained by natural means (attempting to kill a person with poisonous plants or other toxic substances mixed in food or drink), but in its most dreaded form it is *siḥr* (sorcery), a quest for power involving the intervention of the jinns, in the realm of death and the manipulation of the forces of harm.

In the explication of a Qur'anic healer and scholar of *fiqh* jurisprudence (who is the protagonist of part 3 of this book) with whom I discussed this point, if *twkel*'s destructive force, as *siḥr*, is channeled through magical operations that summon the malevolent intervention of a jinn, its origin, its source, is always in an envious passion, a devouring desire of the person to incorporate and/or annihilate the other. A desire and a rivalry, he added, that have become endemic in the current conditions of social injustice, in Morocco and in the world, generalizing the model of *siḥr* to a global struggle for power and destruction.

Unlike the healer I am quoting, who is a real interlocutor and acute clinician and exegete, *faqīhs*/healers kept returning as phantasmatic figures in the emergency room discussion with Reda and his mother. In Reda's account they are persecutory agents, pointing to a secret complicity between his mother, his cultural milieu, and the forces of tradition, in the insatiable passion to subjugate others, him, and "enslave his free will."[8] In his mother's account, by contrast, the mention of a *faqīh* traces the secret map of a quest for healing, in the hometown, the neighboring region, and all the way to the capital, Rabat; a quest the mother cannot fully acknowledge in the psychiatric context, where that idiom of illness is invalid (and couldn't fully acknowledge in general, for the realm of the jinn is ontologically elusive), and that she imputes to Reda himself. It is he, she says, who speaks of the jinn, who complains of being possessed, who seeks the cures of a *faqīh*, although she admitted later to having herself sought their intervention repeatedly, even without her son's approval or physical presence, as when she stood in line with her son's photograph in her hands at 5 a.m. at a healer's door—for the popularity of the young *faqīh* was such that petitioners had to take a number to be received, as one did in the hospital. That healer told her that Reda was *mqiws*, "touched" by the jinns (*tqas*, had been touched, registering the event of an initial entanglement), and gave her an amulet that she stitched in his pillow; yet another *faqīh* diagnosed that he was struck by a *jinniya*, a she-demon, and prescribed the sacrifice of a ram. With great difficulty, she said, she gathered the money to buy the ram, and called the ʿIssawa brotherhood to perform the trance dance, and brought in Reda with a stratagem, so that he might be smeared with sacrificial blood, fall into a trance, and be healed. Reda danced all night to the rhythm of the music, but did not "fall" (*ma taḥ-sh*, that is, into a trance). In the end he got up and left, and didn't come home for several days.

In Reda's account, the image of couscous is the condensation of his haunting, pregnant with what Freud called *Unheimlichkeit*—the uncanny unfamiliarity of what is at once intimate and foreign. Drawn from the Maghrebi repertoire of magic, feminine magic in particular, couscous becomes for Reda a figure of the murderous forces of the home that threaten his psychic and physical integrity. Echoes in his words of well-known magical recipes aimed at destroying an enemy or subjugating another person's will, recipes mentioned in magical books, but even more in the anonymity and terrors of rumor: such as the secret practice of digging out a corpse in the cemetery and mixing the couscous with the hand of the dead, or seasoning it with excrement and other bodily scraps, before feeding it to the victim. Couscous is an emblem of the most familiar and intimate, the definition of the communal meal itself, prepared by the maternal hand on Friday and other holidays, offered as *ṣadaqa*, charity to the poor, eaten in common at holy festivals in the space surrounding a sanctuary. In some legends, human settlements are said to have been founded around a *gsa'*, a large wooden couscous plate, as in a mythical narrative from a region in the south about a *gsa'* full of couscous brought by angels that descended from the sky, in the midst of an open space in the palm groves; people gathered to eat the miraculous meal, and from that gathering a community was born and a new settlement was built at that site.

But for Reda the communal meal becomes a lethal threat. This possibility was already inscribed within the affective ambivalence of the image of couscous, metonym of the identification with the group, which disclosed its destructive pole in the magical use. Yet the historical contingency of colonial and postcolonial expropriations in Reda's experience, and the way that contingency took a specific form in his life, and rehearsed itself through him, painfully and madly, suggests that we should approach that image as something more than cultural psychology, or as the inherent reversibility of symbols.[9] To belong to the "we" of the cultural identification means to swallow that meal, and to be killed.

"It is you! you took me [us] to the healers in Tiflet (*nti lly dditina 'and lfuqahā, f tiflet*)! I never agreed to go. I am vulnerable and sickly (*je suis maladif*), and you made me do unbelievable things . . . the *faqīh* would order me to smoke his magical writing on the blue paper of the sugar loafs, to vomit and smoke my vomit, I don't know, this woman is going to kill me with her healers!"

"It was to seek a cure for you," says the mother.

> [Now in Arabic] Cure me, she says! What cure, and what doctors? Why did you take me to the healer, to push me to my ruin, [in French] because I have eaten something, she fed me something, she'd grab me, she'd say eat eat eat! She said, go to the psychiatrists of our town, go to the healers!

If eating and being fed/devoured imply the omnipotence of the mother tradition, the illiteracy of the mother suggests impotence and amputation. It is an impotence that bears a sign of forbidden entrance, interrupted trajectory, lack of exit. *"Elle est analphabète et on rentre dans le 21ème siècle"* (she's illiterate and we are entering the twenty-first century).

The mother's illiteracy is the son's loss of voice, if he doesn't manage to get away, to distance himself, escaping their capture ("it was to elude the grip of these two *analphabètes*," he will say later on in the interview, referring to his parents). The *we* of "we are entering the twenty-first century" indexes a desire of community, to rejoin those who "enter" the future, those who *have access*: to the world, to language, to the Self. Exit and forward movement: science, mathematics, logic and geometry, education by the intercession of the foreign tongue. In this configuration "reading" understood as a form of resistance and an inalienable right holds a central place in what should be understood as Reda's *requisitoire*, at once a self-defense and an indictment.

In "the twenty-first century" Reda finds sanctuary against the persecution of the "home" that returns to attack him from the outside, menacing and deadly. His insistent request for a lawyer is an appeal to mediation—or better, insulation. The insulation of a "skin" that may contain and draw a boundary, the mediation of the law of the state, by which he may declare his right to exit, and of the law of discourse, the possibility of an authorized speech. It is Reda's struggle against the annihilation of himself.[10]

Dr. R. asks Reda, "Don't you hear voices (*makatsmaʿsh aṣwāṭ*)?" suggesting in her question that he might. A standard question to establish the presence of psychosis, and, possibly move towards a diagnosis of acute psychosis, paranoia, or schizophrenia. In psychiatric semiology, "voices," auditory hallucinations, are intrusive injunctions coming from the outside, which can be aggressive or injurious, give orders, or provide an external commentary. In psychoanalytic terms, they witness a tear in the subject, a hole, filled by the work of delusion, that ultimate retreat.

The psychiatrist's question marks a metamorphosis in the scene of Reda's speech.

Reda does not deny it. He does indeed hear voices, attacks coming from the outside, just like this voice that is addressing him now. He assumes the place assigned to him by the institution, and from there operates a displacement, wards off the threatening voice:

"At night," he replies to the psychiatrist, "and when that happens I rehearse Cervantes' voices, as if I was staging a play. I fight back with literature, he concludes in Arabic (*et alors je fais jouer les voix de Cervantes, comme si je faisais la comédie. kanharrab b la littérature*) . . . I escape, and save myself with it (*kanharrab b la littérature*)."

Then to his mother, in Arabic: "You don't know Cervantes, you don't know anything, this is suffering, you only know how to make couscous . . ."

It is at that point that the anguish of persecution gives way to an imaginary experience of creation, a "flight" of the imagination, where Reda stages his characters in the open spaces of a literature in the foreign language.

We—his interlocutors—will not witness the immediacy of his flight.

Reda presents his experience in the form of a reflection, offered in the distancing mode of commentary. Because for him what is at stake is a "retreat," an exit into another scene where the self may be rescued. Granting to it the status of a concept, Reda calls that other scene *Le Stade Cervantes* (the Cervantes Stage). "It is a stage that exists in literature," he explains, but that sometimes he experiences in life. This "Stage" has the configuration of an Intermediate World, an intermediate world that in Scholastic and Neoplatonic philosophy corresponded to the Imagination. In reading Don Quixote, Reda could absorb Cervantes's Neoplatonism and the idea that the active imagination is capable of "remaking reality" creatively.[11] I say this with a term of comparison in mind, one to which Reda does not refer explicitly but with which he is clearly familiar (from his comments, later on, on the nature of spiritual entities): *al-ʿālam al-khayāl*, the "intermediate world of the imagination" in Arab and Muslim tradition, and particularly in the Neoplatonist theophany of the thirteenth-century Sufi Ibn ʿArabi.

The literary identification by which Reda says to "escape" and "fight back" (I will return to the double play of his expression) oscillates between the roles of Cervantes-the-author and Don Quixote-the-character—between a controlled staging of madness in a baroque self-reflexive literature, and the madness without return of the wandering knight, prisoner of his imaginary combats, suspended between the books and the life. Yet, for Reda, all this happens in solitude, because rare are those who, in his surroundings, in his small town as in the emergency room, are familiar with Cervantes, Don Quixote, and the story of the windmills. And this independent of the fact that Cervantes, the historical author, was in his time influenced by the reading of Arab texts, and in particular by the narrative strategies of the *One Thousand and One Nights*, as well as, perhaps, by the reflection on madness and healing the *Nights* represents.[12]

> I wake up very early in the morning just to read, because with the crisis of the economy, there are no jobs, there is so much unemployment, and we live in Yacob El Mansur [a low-income neighborhood in Rabat], there is so much noise during the day, it is impossible to read!

Reda had registered my reaction at his mention of Cervantes, and a connection was created between us, a connection through reading. Physically foreign, with a foreign accent in both Arabic and French, a "researcher," from his perspective analogous to him, I am perceived to have complicity and am included as a character in his tribunal.

In this as in other public hospitals, where the majority of the patients speak vernacular Arabic and are unfamiliar with medical and psychiatric concepts, the staff makes use of what they dub *la langue du patient,* a language of trade supposed rhetorically to be "that of the patient," loosely codified and deployed in the effort to make possible clinical interviews across experientially incommensurable conceptual worlds. It is a vocabulary based on the implicit and reductive assumption of a one-to-one translatability of symptoms, or, more precisely, of the referential transparency of psychiatric symptomatology, which, whatever its symbolic expression, will necessarily translate into its true referent, that of a recognizable disease. *Al-waswās,* for instance, that demonic haunting, maddening whispering in one's ear, temptation of unreason, which is a central figure of madness in the Qur'an as well as in everyday speech, becomes the equivalent of obsessive neurosis, or, in DSM IV terminology, obsessive compulsive disorder. Hence to make a differential diagnosis the psychiatrist will attempt to isolate *"lwusuwās"* from the "voices" of schizophrenia.

Or when the presence of a jinn is at issue (in the complaints of the patient, never in the questions of the psychiatrists, unwittingly registering, by that reticence to enter the "patient's discourse," the vulnerability and risk of the "psychiatric operation"),[13] the task is to detect the symptom behind: the question becomes whether the jinn, or voice, is internal or external to the subject, and what the patient replies to that voice. As a senior psychiatrist put it at a staff meeting, discussing the case of a young man haunted by a jinn who, rather than *speaking through him* (as happens in trance), never stopped *talking to him*: "From a purely psychiatric point of view what we want to isolate is the type of symptom, beyond the anecdotal figure of the jinn, which is drawn from our available cultural repertoire and is not interesting in itself. We know that there is something embodied (*incorporé*), which causes the patient to do certain things, which gives orders to the person. It could just as well be a device implanted by the CIA in his body. From the semiological point of view in all these cases, we have one and the same symptom, which we recognize as *automatisme mentale.*" It is the risk, and the violence, of concepts in translation, when translation no longer discloses the foreign nature of language, but becomes instead the apparatus of appropriation and reduction to the same.

Wash katsma' aswat f-udnik? (Do you hear voices in your ear?) Formulating the question in Arabic is not obvious, even though it is done all the time. Because in the larger sense indexed by the Arabic language and rooted in the specific way of experiencing subjectivity exemplified in the discourse of the jinn, as well as, at a more philosophical level, in the ecstatic dimension of religious experience, hearing voices is not equal to madness. Or at least a certain madness, a certain "exit" from the self, is foundational for the possibility of subjectivity and truth. The Qur'an was revealed in a visionary dream, by the voice of an angel speaking in Muhammad's ear. Revelation, as argued by Fethi Benslama in his book on the Qur'an, is the result of a moment of an ultimate existential risk, a passage through madness in which the Prophet might be lost, but that instead gives way to the interpretation of the Voice as divine utterance—an interpretation made possible, and literally engendered, by the feminine intercession of Muhammad's wife, Khadija, on whose "lap" the divine's message becomes audible and can be received.[14]

Later in the interview, his mother tells us:

> Once, when he was first sick, during the time when he was praying a lot, he vanished for three weeks, went out into nature, into the wilderness (*kharj ll ṭabīʿa, f-l-khalaʾ*). He spent his days and his nights there, he took his books with him, said he was going to read his book to the land! He walked from Tiflet to El-Hajeb through the countryside, he slept outdoors and begged for food.

Reda counters that all this is none of her business. He turns to Dr. R., and to me, in French:

> I searched and searched in the books, I was forced to hide the Italian language, because you realize, *chez nous*, in Tiflet, it's impossible to show it in public . . . because I love languages, I love reading, I love nature, it is my right, I request a lawyer immediately. It is my right to do what I wish, here in Morocco, it is my right! I respect the Constitution of the King, and I demand a lawyer, a lawyer here and now!

"*Kanharrab b la literature* (I save myself with literature)." *Kanharrab*, a fleeing from an aggression, a dangerous situation, an attack or an invasion. A fleeing that is also a distancing, a departure that can save oneself. *Kanharrab*, "I escape," resembles and, in Reda's use, rhymes, with *kanḥarrab*, "I fight back, engage in a struggle," as in an armed counterattack: "I fight back with literature." (They are two different words, one with *h*, to flee, the other with *ḥ*, to wage war). For Reda literature is a "counterdelirium": as in the *Quixote* imaginary creation is an antidote to the maddening confusion of perceived reality. It is comparable to the counterdelirium of witchcraft, according to Favret-Saada, as well as to the counterdelirium of literature for Deleuze. But unlike the aggressive metaphor of witchcraft, the saving doesn't reestablish the "self" as full presence, for what departs, what is no longer there, is precisely the self that is saved, that is both lost and saved. "I flee/fight back with literature," that is by way of literature, but also literally "with it," with the books on my back, for a life of wandering with "my" characters, the other voices, on the stage of "my" comedy, the Cervantes Stage, the *mise-en-scène* of the voices. Myself, Don Quixote, Cervantes' mad reader and wandering knight. The Cervantes Stage is "another scene" where all persecuting others have vanished, including himself as a narcissistic injury. It is an "open empty space," *l-khala'*, where he can be alone and find sanctuary, with his stories and his books. In this place Reda reads to nature (*al-ṭabīʿa*): an empty listening, the only interlocutor that, he feels, doesn't reduce him to silence.

Later, after his hospitalization, in a room in the men's locked ward, I ask Reda about his encounter with literature. He tells me about the public library in his hometown, where people don't read, are illiterate, and don't speak foreign languages (but they do speak Berber and Arabic!); about reading Voltaire, and his passion for Dostoevsky and Cervantes. He read *Crime and Punishment*, but it is *Don Quixote* that really had an impact on him. When I ask him why "literature," he explains that since he started having difficulties in concentrating (this is how he speaks of the "strangeness" of his condition), he had to abandon his scientific studies and began to read—to dig into literature (*fouiller dans la littérature*). And why Cervantes? I asked. He returned the question to me, do I know the story of Don Quixote? "Don Quixote has read all the books," he explains, "the books of world history, and he wanted to fight with the windmills, and for his love Dulcinea wanted to show himself a great knight, and this is why he took on traveling with his friend Sancho, but most often, in fact, with no one [he laughs]. He doesn't do any harm, to anyone, but the important thing, the important thing is that each time he creates a story for himself (*chaque fois il se crée une histoire*)."

Translations

According to the structure of the clinical interview, Dr. R. moves on to the mother. She must collect information about family history and the early signs of the illness. There emerges, at this point, an important issue of translation, predicated on a play of reciprocal projections and on a certain complicity in *méconnaissance*. To proceed, there must be a sense of common ground, a common ground that both parties assume is lacking. The psychiatrist must translate her diagnostic concepts in terms the mother can understand, in vernacular Arabic and in images borrowed from everyday language, without however surrendering to the presumed interpretative schemata of the mother, that of possession by the jinn; the mother must describe her son's condition in terms the psychiatrist can accept and validate, that is, she must objectify and translate her own experience of his state as if in a foreign language. This double translation produces important alterations that cannot be recognized by either party. Misrecognized too is the disquieting sentiment that, even when they seem to have reached an agreement on the representation used, saying for instance that "something is ringing in his head," each interlocutor situates this image in her own symbolic frame of reference, which is at odds with that of the other. They know this, Dr. R. and Reda's mother, but can't acknowledge it, and perhaps even formulate it. They can't, because the institution itself, its symbolic efficacy, requires that silence.

And things are even more complex if one considers that the psychiatrist, Dr. R., even though she is external (by choice, by chance, and by historical reason), is not at all foreign to the symbolic universe of Reda's mother, who could easily be her own mother. This fact raises the unresolved and in a way unspeakable question of cultural belonging as open injury and interrupted transmission. And, at the same time, if one considers that the mother came to the hospital to contain, control, and help her son, but also for a desire impossible to avow, to be able to speak her own rage.

Dr. R. turns then to the mother, and asks in Arabic when her son's illness began. The mother relates how Reda started to "change" (*tghayyer*) two years earlier, when he suddenly embraced religion and took on assiduous praying. Even the dawn prayer, at the mosque, in the middle of winter. "What's wrong with praying?" Dr. R. counters. Attempting to construct her case, the mother speaks of the old men's surprise at Reda's sudden religious turn, for he used to drink and to smoke. His prayer was not "natural" (*kayṣalli ṣalāt mashī ṭabiʿiya*). What else was "strange"? asks Dr. R.

"Yes, strange (*ghrīb*)!" The mother struggles to represent that strangeness: speaks of her son's sleepless nights, his aggressive tone, the transformation of his bodily expression. He was no longer himself (*mabqash kimā kān*), she concludes.

The psychiatrist provides a vocabulary, "Did he look at himself in the mirror, did he notice a transformation in his image?" "Yes, and he would talk to himself, at first he'd stop if we walked into the room, then didn't care anymore, would just go on speaking to himself in our presence." And he hit another boy with a knife, she adds. "When?" the psychiatrist asks. "Just a few months ago, and he spent two months in jail, that's what finished him up." The psychiatrist interrupts the mother; she wants a chronological account, "from beginning to end," and asks whether Reda complained about his strangeness, whether he felt the world around him was becoming uncanny (*gharīb*).

"He complained that something was ringing in his head (*katsonne lih shy hajja f-rrās*), that he was possessed, 'there is a jinn in me' (*kaygullik mskūn, rah fiya jinn*)."

Dr. R. makes a gesture of recognition, moving towards a possible diagnosis. The mother acknowledges her gesture in silence, with what I read as a sense of relief. Only later, after the psychiatrist left us alone in the room, did she state that those signs, "that juggling of the limbs and the speaking to himself, the ringing of something in his head," were signs of demonic possession, and they were not the reason she had come to the hospital. She had come because of Reda's drug habit, his hashish smoking, because she thought the hashish might have got to his head, and, in that case, he would be treated with hospital drugs. In a way, she hoped so. Because in that case doctors could do something; Reda would take medications, and perhaps he'd be cured. But for a demonic possession, the hospital can provide no cure.

Afterwards, I ask myself whether the truth of the mother was in that discreet revelation of her interpretive universe, which she had omitted in her conversation with Dr. R., or instead in the story she was able to tell, after her son's departure, and because of the intent listening of the psychiatrist, in the foreign country of the psychiatric institution.

L-ʿuqda nafsiyya: The Knot of the Soul

Later, after her son was escorted to the men's locked ward, Reda's mother spoke differently. Her tone changed, and the anguish that froze her as a character, forced to speak the phantasm in the scene of her son's persecution, loosened into voice and made possible a different account. The story of her own pain, and the way it crystallized into the "knot" of her son's existence. Yet, as stories of suffering in situations of oppression are rarely innocent in their address and rhetorical scope, her story is an ambiguous one, where her pain is both revealed and deployed in an ultimate appropriation.

It is Dr. R. who can receive her speech within the constraining space of the emergency room. And the mother speaks of a wound, a "knot of the soul" (*l-ʿuqda nafsiyya*), with an evocative expression by which she reckons the intertwining of her suffering with that of her son, and laments his fate as an offspring of her own. He's "knotted" (*muʿaqqad*), she says, with an evocative "intermediate" concept, a bridge between two worlds of interpretation—at once an image of bewitchment from the vocabulary of magic, and the term for "complex" in that of modern psychology.

The knot of the soul is the hidden wound, physically expressed by the urinary incontinence that accompanied Reda from childhood and through his adolescence; a wound hidden inside, and suddenly exploded to the outside, into the other world of his illness. But the *ʿuqda nafsiyya* is also the knot of her own soul: her unhappy marriage, her alcoholic husband, the violence of her evenings, the sleeplessness of her nights, her tears. The husband, a policeman who beat her, and Reda, the little boy who watched the violence, who cried and later interceded for her with his father. The eldest of her children, he saw everything, and was traumatized. She uses the technical term *ṣadama* ("shock," "trauma"), a term she learned from her children who accused them, the parents, of having traumatized them. Yet despite all this Reda was managing, despite the "knot," the knot remained hidden, and he could succeed in school, the only one of the children to have had an education. But when he got his university degree and didn't find a job, when he found himself on the street, unemployed, a *chômeur*, all that came out in the open, like a blister, impossible to contain.

Now that the children have grown up, she decided to file for divorce. She was lucky because her husband did not oppose her request. She sought a divorce to try to give Reda a chance. She knows, she says, that it is her own injury that implanted itself into the life of her son, and is slowly destroying him. She suggests that I go to visit him in the ward. He will be glad to talk with me.

Don Quixote and the Cervantes Stage

Sitting on his chair without moving, Reda has been listening in silence to his mother's description of his state. But when she mentions his experience of possession by a jinn he protests, in Arabic, that the jinn are also God's creatures, that they are found everywhere in the world, and that they are mentioned in the Qurʾan.

The mother talks about his drug habit, his use of hashish, and the recent degeneration of his state. Not sleeping, wandering on the beach in Rabat, talking about the jinn. Her son protests, "*C'est le Stade Cervantes dans la littérature* (it is the Cervantes Stage in literature)."

Irritated, Reda starts speaking a sort of Italian or Spanish (he had asked me where I was from), his own linguistic creation, in which can be recognized the name of Don Quixote. The mother explains that when he's feeling bad Reda starts speaking other languages, "French, English, Italian, and Berber . . . he's good with languages . . ."

Dr. R. is moving to a conclusion. The mother hesitates, "I feel I forgot something." And the psychiatrist asks her whether Reda ever claimed to be a prophet. The mother nods, *"Imām l-Mahdi,"* she says, "you're right, I forget some things, once he told me that a woman appeared to him in his sleep, and told him, 'You are the son of Maryam, you are *l-Imām l-Mahdi,* he said this to his father and myself . . .'"

Reda protested in French, "This is Cervantes, am telling you . . ."

The psychiatrist asks him directly, "Are you a prophet?"

"No! That's absurd," he protests, "it is a manner of speaking, like Cervantes' (*c'est une façon de dire, comme Cervantes*). It is manner of living, I do this, every once in a while, it is my way of going on living, I make literature in life. . . . I invent and re-create . . . (*c'est ma façon de vivre, de temps en temps, je fais également de la littérature dans la vie . . . j'invente et je reinvente*)."

"What is it that you invent?" asks Dr. R., interested, for the first time, in exploring Reda's site of flight, his recurrent recourse, from the beginning of the interview.

> Stories such as those she's relating, stories with jinn. They say, for instance, back at home, that certain men have love affairs with she-demons. God created the jinns, and those jinns exist in our religion as terms for creatures. But no one was ever married to a jinn. The same thing that happens in literature, when it is applied to the practice of living, every once in a while I use terms such as jinn or jinniya, to live *Le Stade Cervantes* in life. Just to get away from those illiterate ones.

"What is this that you call *'Cervantes Stage'*?" asks Dr. R., in Arabic this time, stressing the quotation marks, as if not to validate Reda's concept as her own.

"In any case, this is what I call it. It means to make use of imaginary characters at certain times, to speak with the windmills (*tahuna*)," Reda repeats in Arabic, aware that the audience might not be familiar with Don Quixote.

Dr. R. stops listening, asks the mother whether they ever took her son to the hospital or to a *faqīh*. At his mother's reply Reda becomes angry. Siding with him for the first time, Dr. R. addresses the mother in a scolding tone. She is moved in her modernist sensibility, closer to Reda, in fact, in her own experience: "Who are the healers your son is complaining about?"

"They are well known in town," says the mother defensively. I ask her what the healer's diagnosis was; "touched" (*mqiws*, by the jinns), she says, and starts talking about his excessive washing as evidence of possession (demons are said to like water). Reda counters that it is his right to wash, to be clean, "it is called hygiene."

A nurse comes in, and escorts Reda to the locked ward. On Dr. R.'s quick notes, which will never become a formal patient file, there is mention of psychotic symptoms, pointing to a psychotic personality and possibly an early onset of schizophrenia.

Later, at the ward. Reda is brought down by a nurse, who waits outside the door because the patient is "not cooperating" and opposes his hospitalization. Alone for the first time, we talk in a room by the main patio. About literature, Don Quixote, and what makes it difficult for him to concentrate. He asks me about my nationality (he already knew in fact) and again starts speaking a sort of invented Italian that turns into Spanish and finally breaks into incomprehensible speech. Language hardens as a wall between us, and against this wall our conversation dissolves. When I come back to visit him the next morning, I learn that he has fled the hospital, climbing a high wall.

The Intermediate World

Yet aware of the risks of speculation (reducing Reda's suffering to my desire to understand), of that particular sort of appropriation that is anthropological interpretation, I attempt to reflect on the status of that other place, *the Stage*, where Reda retreats (*kanharrab*), and from which he fights back (*kanḥarrab*), in the rough moments of his illness as during the ER interview. The Stage to which he bestows the status of a theory, in which he is both a character and the director, and which is the site—rhetorical, existential, physical—of his surrender to the Other and his desire for self.

I am encouraged in this reflection by the ambiguity of my position, a position I so often experienced as frustrating and even paralyzing, always external to the action, if also enmeshed in it (the anthropologist listening, asking questions, feeling directly concerned, affected, yet unable and unauthorized to "cure"), but which can be enabling of an oblique interpretative space, a space of proximity, marginal to action and decision, a peripheral zone of speculation and critique. In attempting to inhabit this space, I am inspired by the strategy inaugurated by Reda himself, his "appropriation" of Don Quixote, which is also a dispossession of himself, and his multilayered use of characters and rhetorical figures by which, like the Spanish *hidalgo,* he labors at creating a multidimensional space where his uncanny experience of the world may find expression and elaboration. In this sense, his strategy can be called, as he does, literary.

Literature, writes Deleuze in one of his last essays, is the opposite of phantasm. Phantasms fix identities in place, personalize characters, and seal possession, while literature is a process of dispossession, a becoming-other that dwells in a zone of proximity (*voisinage*), and is never saturated by an identity: "literature begins only when a third person is born in us that strips us of the power to say I."[15] In this sense, Deleuze says, literature is health—a vulnerable health (*une petite santé*) that almost lost itself, in its experiences. It is born from within delirium, as a movement of straying, becoming foreign, from the mother tongue (from the Mother), from the madness of ideological identifications, and it transforms them from within; a becoming other that opens onto "visions," "ideas" that are not the projection of an ego and can become the singular-collective utterance of a people to come.

Reda has discovered his literary "procedure" in the work of Cervantes, where he encountered his own story in an exemplary form, translated into a foreign language. Thanks to this discovery, which coincided with his first realization of a feeling of strangeness in his experience of the world, he has taken on the practice of literature, which he intends from the point of view of the character as well as from that of the author. It is not by chance that in his literary search through Voltaire and Dostoevsky in the town library of Tiflet, Reda settled on *Don Quixote,* the text that raises the ambiguity of character and author, ironical distancing and imaginary capture, life and fiction, to the principle of its narrative structure.

(Reaching back stenographically to the political questions raised earlier, it could be said that "literature," in Reda's use and as read through Deleuze, discloses an unforeseen possibility of *twkkel,* the food poisoning, the murderous "us" of the collective identification. Literature opens for Reda the possibility of negotiating his debt to a traumatic cultural transmission, in the form of a not-yet or no-longer us. While the objectifications of his modernity ideal are rigid, as the saturation of knowledge in a self-sufficient totality, the moving and multiple identifications of the Cervantes Stage are fluid.)[16]

To phrase the question in terms closer to the clinical concerns of psychiatrists, it would be wrong to reduce Reda's procedure to the deployment of a delusion, or to the commonly observed quest of patients at the onset of psychosis, trying to make sense of and "rationalize" their experiences of growing strangeness in terms of a fantasy, which is then systematized into a delusi[illegible]uction would miss the dimension of struggle in Reda's expe[illegible]erating the sense in which his search is meaningful, and his ex[illegible] of otherness less unfamiliar than one may be willing to acknowledge. This was also the reaction of the psychiatrists at the hospital when we discussed a draft of this section: expressing the question in a diagnostic idiom, they said that if Reda had most likely a psychotic personality, he was however not fully psychotic, thanks to an element of creativity and to his ability to self-reflect.

First, Reda's symbolic geography. The Cervantes Stage, as a topological elsewhere, is an effect of withdrawal, of breaking the ties with "home" in all its forms: the family, the hometown, vernacular Arabic (the mother tongue), the space of the everyday, social relations and traditions. It is the result of a radical disaffiliation of which Reda is at once the victim, the character, and the author. This "retreat" is a vital distancing from the mother, figure of the uninhabitable home, and from the magical logic of *twkkel*, the envious incorporation of the other. But the distancing is more than just a withdrawal. It is a departure, a journey, the metamorphosis of the self in a theater of imaginary forms, where the possibility of self-realization gambles with the risk of nonreturn.

Reda becomes Don Quixote who, like himself, has read "all the books of history" and has given up all ties for a life of travel in the meadows of the imagination; Don Quixote who, like himself, lives at a time-lag with his contemporaries, a temporal disjunction, speaks a "dead language" full of references they don't understand, because he himself has renounced their recognition. But Don Quixote is tricked by the confusion of imagination and reality. Reda says this in full knowledge, as he looks at himself from the critical perspective of the author. He smiles and says that it happens to him too, sometimes, to fight against the windmills: he calls it living the Cervantes Stage in real life.

Yet in his conception of the Stage there is the trace of a possible mediation. To the psychiatrist's question, "What do you invent?" Reda replies that he invents stories of jinn, jinn that he enacts in the *mise-en-scène* of voices to live the Cervantes Stage in real life, because, he says, *"il faut garder la distance de la présence"* (one must keep the presence at distance); jinns that he glosses as "terms for creatures" in the Qur'an (*termes de creature dans le Qur'an*), and compares to figures of speech, when one practices literature in life. At once a space of language, where words materialize as images, and a cosmic realm populated with jinns, the Cervantes Stage is an intermediate world, a world of metaphors. But if jinns are metaphors it is because they are "terms for creatures," Reda says, as he describes the ontological status of invisible beings in the Qur'an. "Literature" is a modality of the Invisible (*al-ghayb*). It is a metaphysics of imagination.

The Cervantes Stage becomes then the site of a possible mediation, a passageway between delusion and creation, where the rejected terms of cultural identification, the remains of an inaccessible tradition, are reencountered, and can be symbolically transformed. For a moment the threatening otherness of the persecutory interpretation (the poisonous communal meal), becomes for Reda a literary experience. As he puts it, "one must keep the presence at distance." "*Inquietante familiarité*" (in Certeau's words), *fréquentation de l'Autre*.

Interlude: Islam and the Ethics of Psychoanalysis

> Le fou fait peur car il nous renvoit à nous mêmes. Il nous renvoie de manière exacerbée ce que nous même vivons comme souffrance . . . Moi le fou me fait avancer, le fou me fait refléchir, le fou est mon maître.
>
> The mad are frightening because they reveal ourselves to us. They mirror in an extreme form a mental pain that we also experience. . . . The mad person helps me understand, pushes me to think, is my teacher.
>
> I listened in the sanctuaries; what I heard is approximately what I hear in my office. As an analyst, I play dead; in the sanctuaries people talk to the dead.
>
> —the psychoanalyst[1]

> Il n'y a aucune raison que nous nous fassions garants de la rêverie bourgeoise.
>
> —Jacques Lacan, *L'éthique de la psychanalyse*

July 2008. An evening meeting in Rabat, at the office of a psychoanalyst, interlocutor and friend of many years. The waiting room filled during the day, people in waiting, in pain, in delusion, old and new patients, with their families, talking, in Arabic, in French, comparing experiences, offering and asking advice, youths, alone, reading a magazine as they wait. A separate small waiting room for patients in analysis, and a playroom for the psychotherapy of children, set up in the kitchen of this apartment transformed into an office, at this address for twenty-five years. Now, after the last patient has left, the waiting area has become a seminar room. Windows closed, still too much noise from the street, the air conditioner on. Sitting in a circle, the members of an informal seminar on psychosis and psychoanalysis that has been meeting in this office for ten years, and in which I have been an intermittent participant, a seminar that has now reached a critical impasse.

The quandary is whether the group should dissolve (the host is calling for a pause of reflection, an interruption, a symptomatic registering of crisis) or instead file the paperwork to charter an association, taking on an active institutional role, both at the level of a psychopolitical intervention in the ever-growing zones of social abandonment in the Moroccan cities, particularly with the youth, and at the level of curricular initiatives in the medical schools. Discussion of what a psychoanalytically inspired intervention in dispossessed neighborhoods would look like, of the risk of unwittingly participating in the apparatus of the security state, and the importance of siding with the youth; a mention of the experiments with social psychoanalysis in Brazil and Argentina, a model to rethink, taking psychoanalysis beyond the couch, but in a context, the Moroccan one, where psychoanalysis would have to change form. (A psychoanalytic association would be adding to the existing Societé Psychanalytique Marocaine, SPM, founded in 2001,[2] transforming what had previously been the Association Marocaine de Psychothérapie, AMP, to the Association Marocaine de Psychiatrie, the Moroccan branch of the International Psychiatric Association, and a proliferation of new associations and societies, dedicated to the psychiatry of children, autism, substance abuse, migration, to the victims of political trauma, and others—institutions to which members of this informal seminar have individually contributed and joined.)

Three main questions circulated in the room, born of a troubled pondering on the responsibility of psychoanalysts at this time in history, and in the specific context of Morocco, the Middle East, and the Islamic world. The first question can be glossed as follows:

What is the responsibility of psychoanalysts and psychiatrists in a society deeply fractured and internally hollowed by ever growing inequalities and material and symbolic dispossessions, and by state violence and abuses carried on from colonial times well into the postcolonial present, which are implicitly encouraged by the political and economic requirements of an unequal global order? The first National Survey of Mental Health,[3] which was realized in 2005 over the national territory under the auspices of the Ministry of Health (with the MINI diagnostic interview in vernacular Arabic translation), and with direct input from several Moroccan psychiatrists and psychoanalysts, sharply indicated that forms of despair had taken hold of large sectors of the population, and manifested themselves in psychopathological symptoms, hieroglyphics of pain that were also political inscriptions. Most of all, this showed in the unusually high rate of major depression across age and gender groups (26 percent of the total population). Independent of methodological questions concerning the reliability of the statistics produced by the survey, the publication of the report had the effect of a traumatic awakening. The initiator of this group had been on the board of the survey and had advocated the publication of the report at the Ministry of Health (for a commitment to truth of a different nature, which, he said later, might in this case be produced by a disclosure of numbers), but, in a different sort of symptomatic disclosure, the survey was withdrawn from the public eye following heated reactions in the national media. The image of the nation portrayed in the looking glass of the survey was too hard to bear.

The second question had to do with the collective realization of psychoanalysis's growing marginality, and this precisely at a time when attempts were being made to institutionalize its public voice in Morocco and the Middle East.[4] This is how the discomfort in the room can be rendered, spoken in the specificity of particular voices:

How to bring psychoanalytic knowledge, ethics, and practice to the fore in a situation in which there were just a handful of trained analysts, little public interest, really, outside of the francophone elite, and no resources that might enable young psychiatrists to undertake a personal analysis or a clinical supervision. Was "the transmission of psychoanalysis"[5] in this context (as the intergenerational and intercultural passing on of a debt, or a gift) possible, or meaningful, at all? What were the historical forms, and the available sites, in today's Morocco for what Lacan had called an active listening (*écoute*)?

The third question had to do with a positioning vis-à-vis what was felt as an interpellation from the field of Islam, the Islamic movements, and the sea change that induced. For the seminar members, all of whom were confronted on a daily basis with patients who spoke their pain within frames inspired by religious vocabularies, the problem was how to relate to the call of Islam in a way that rejected the general turn towards a diagnostic use of psychoanalytic concepts as a political mode of intervention, and that refused to participate in the construction of "Islam" as an Other, opening instead a space of critique and self-questioning. What, they were asking, was the responsibility of a psychoanalytic ethic and practice in a context where questions were raised, all the way to the level of the symptom, in the terms of another tradition, a tradition that, in a complex sense, was also the psychoanalyst's own, in vocabularies that could find no equivalent in translation, and in terms that should be called theological?

The seminar had started as a space where a small group of therapists presented difficulties and impasses in their clinical work and read together on the theory of psychosis. It was also a space where some reflected on the persistent and overwhelming presence of healing practices that addressed illness as a manifestation of the harmful agency of demonic entities. The presence of those practices, dubbed *"thérapies traditionnelles"* in psychological circles,[6] often a co-presence, since the afflicted pursued several therapeutic approaches at once, had been for psychoanalysts a challenge that called for a reply—one that often, particularly in the context of Moroccan psychiatry, came in the form of an ambivalent rejection.

But there were exceptions. One of the seminar members, a Lacanian psychoanalyst, used to tell of how, upon his return to Morocco from training in France, feeling the inadequacy of an analytic practice of the unconscious in the face of the organization of the symbolic at home, he embarked on a journey to visit sanctuaries known for healing the mad. These places are marked as burial sites of saintly figures, where the sick and their families seek healing through the release that would come in dreams. In his reckoning, sanctuaries were *lieux de parole* in the Lacanian sense, sites where being could come to the fore in the "revelation of speech," in the vision, and in the ear of death: *"J'ai écouté dans les sanctuaires; j'ai écouté à peu près ce que j'écoute dans mon cabinet. Moi, je fais le mort. Eux, ils parlent au mort* (I listened in the sanctuaries; what I heard is approximately what I hear in my office. As an analyst, I play dead; while instead they talk to the dead)."

Since the early 2000s the question of religion had supplanted for psychoanalysts and secular intellectuals the preoccupation with the problem of "traditional therapies" as a source of anxiety related to an intimate strangeness of the "home." However widespread, traditional therapies were marginalized and excluded in the institutional life of the postcolonial state, assigned to the position of an intractable irrational residue that could never claim the place of an interlocutor on an equal footing. The growth of Islamic movements had changed the terms of the relationship, occupying the public space, and directly challenging the authority of secular psychological sciences, and, indirectly, psychoanalysis. "Religion," and "Islam," had emerged as a problem for psychoanalysis, in Morocco as in other parts of the Middle East. This was at once an internal response to the spiritual revolution brought about by the Islamic Revival, and an effect of the international "war on terror." International psychoanalytic associations, especially the French based, had come to the Maghreb at the invitation of the local analytic community, for internal reasons—to meet a need for training, supervision, accreditation, and funding. But they had also come responding to concerns about the growing role of Islam in Europe among second- and third-generation French citizens of North African descent, and among the newly arrived often-undocumented migrants and refugees. By supporting Maghrebi psychoanalysis, they aimed at promoting a subject immunized from the call of political Islam.[7] French Cultural Centers, a branch of the French diplomatic mission, sponsored lectures, conferences, and seminars, and local analysts and psychotherapists had been called in to participate, including the members of this group. Psychoanalysis was being summoned as a pedagogical rampart in the age of political religion, to promote what was described as more tolerant, critical, and open Islam.[8]

Three successive conferences organized by the International Lacanian Association in Paris, Beirut, and Fes (in 2002, 2004, and 2005), and with the participation of an international group of psychoanalysts from the Middle East, the Maghreb, and France, had overseen the creation of the *Congrès international des psychanalystes de langue arabe* (International Congress of Psychoanalysts in the Arabic Language). The Beirut conference, which had been its founding event, was titled *"La psyché (al-nafs) dans la culture arabe et son rapport à la psychanalyse"* (The Psyche/*al-nafs* in Arab Culture and Its Relationship to Psychoanalysis). The conference had focused on the question of the "transmission" of Freudian psychoanalysis in the Maghreb and the Middle East, and on the obstacles to its implantation, which in the opening statement were attributed to three factors: the central place of Islam and the role of the divine law as fundamental tenet; the weakness of the nuclear family vis-à-vis the persistence of extended family networks and lingering tribal affiliation; and the ubiquitous presence of authoritarian forms of government. Psychoanalysts from Lebanon, recalling the terror of the civil war, and from Egypt, reflecting on state terror, spoke of how authoritarian regimes reduced people to a state of inner fear that halted "thinking" (in the psychoanalytic sense of unconscious activity), and inhibited the Freudian technique of free association, which is pivotal to the cure. In connecting the "psyche" to the *"nafs,"* the conference also asked the question of the relationship between the *nafs*/psyche/soul, in the Qur'an and in Islamic philosophy, and the unconscious in psychoanalysis. In the papers that were published from the conference there is evidence of a debate: some (among the conveners) argued the case of a fundamental incompatibility between the subject of the unconscious as intended by

Freud and Lacan, and the subject in Islam; and this is because in Islam, it was argued, the subject is founded in divine self-sufficiency and finds its fulfillment in God. As such, it doesn't ever confront the fundamental groundlessness from which emerges modern subjectivity as conceived by Descartes. The Muslim subject, as Adnan Houballah put it, had no use for psychoanalysis.

Others, such as the Egyptian psychoanalyst Hussein Abdel Qader, argued on the contrary for a structural parallel and a fundamental commensurability between psychoanalysis and Islam. The early history of psychoanalysis in Egypt, and the translation of the concept of the unconscious in terms drawns from Islamic spirituality, were a witness to this fact.[9] "It is wrong to say that religion is an obstacle," Abdel Qader writes, continuing in a tone evocative of religious admonition: "we need to understand our unconscious, for otherwise our phantasms will lead us into error." The psychoanalytic unconscious, he suggests, is an architecture of the "unknown," and its knowledge, the knowledge of an unknown-known, is comparable to a religious knowledge of the divine: "the discourse of every religion requires knowledge of an unknown place. The construction of the unconscious is not separate from religious knowledge."[10]

Hussein Abdel Qader's powerful point was lost, in a certain way, in the 2005 Fes symposium, which furthered the debate on psychoanalysis and Islam with a focus on religion and politics, and was more specifically aimed at identifying *within* the traditions of the three monotheisms arguments capable of countering the growing hegemony of "religious fundamentalism" (*l'intégrisme*), and its grounding in political theology. Entitled "*Les trois monothéisms: Après Maïmonide, Ibn Rushd, Saint Thomas. Ce qu'ils ont aujourd'hui en commun*" (The Three Monotheisms: After Maimonides, Ibn Rushd, and Aquinas, What They Have in Common Today), it had gathered, along with psychoanalysts, important names in the study of Islamic theology and historiography (such as Mohammed Arkoun), as well as specialists in Islamic philosophy, Muslim Aristotelianism, and Scholasticism.

In his comments Charles Mellman (then president of the International Lacanian Association) spoke of the psychoanalytic commitment to reject all "conformisms," and of "the right to a singular existence," as the foundation of the Freudian and Lacanian theory of the subject of desire. For true speech, what Lacan had called *parole*, as several of the participants proposed, was today suffocated by the passions of faith, by the mimetic impulse of religious communitarians, and the authority of religious interpretation performed with a "literalist" bias, as a source of religious intolerance and potential violence. In contrast, as it was argued in the platform of the conference, Ibn Rushd (Averroës), Maimonides, and Aquinas (twelfth and thirteenth centuries), respectively a Muslim, a Jewish, and a Christian philosopher and theologian, had attempted to reread the sacred texts in the light of reason, and with the help of Aristotelian logics, and had thereby indicated the path for the work of a rational hermeneutics, carved in a space of human agency autonomous from the interference of Divine Truth. But that interfaith effort had been brought to an end by the ruse of political power, seeking to preserve its divisive principle of authority. The conference proposed to reflect on the memory of that effort, and that defeat, as an opportunity for growth:

> In remembrance of that defeat (*avec la mémoire de cet échec*) the International Lacanian association elects to celebrate the legacy of ancient and medieval logic, not in order to commemorate them with a statement of good intentions, but instead to renew them by approaching them with the novel tools brought to us by Freud and Lacan. By returning its crucial place to speech (*parole*), and therefore to the primacy of the Other (*l'altérité*), Freud and Lacan made an important contribution to the secularization of the field of belief, all the while analyzing it scientifically: in other words, without making any recourse to passion (*sans recours à la passion*).[11]

There was a tension internal to the formulation and the reception of the platform of the symposium. For some (Charles Melmann, and historian and theologian Mohammed Arkoun in particular, and the International Lacanian Association in general), the question of reason and faith related to an international debate on religious resurgence with the deployment of well-known arguments—including a replica of the arguments of the Stasi commission for *laïcité* brought across the Mediterranean. For others, and in particular for the Moroccan participants (several psychoanalysts from this Rabat group, a political sociologist, as a scholar of religious texts versed in the study of Sufism), the question of the conference resonated as a call for reflection on something that implicated them directly, in their clinical practice and their attempts to make sense of some of the transformations and collective questioning that characterize the present moment in Morocco, and the reality of the Islamic Revival. For them, there was as an authentic engagement with the problematic of theological reasoning where this encounters human subjectivity. In this perspective, Fouad Benchekroun presented on the need to ponder anew the status of prophecy in the Qur'an, in the speech of patients, through a reflection on psychosis, and in the context of Lacanian psychoanalysis. His presentation proposed that the present historical moment requires that we move beyond the Lacanian theory of intersubjectivity, and towards the last Lacan, who in his seminar on James Joyce understood writing beyond recognition as what he called a *"sinthome"*—a makeshift connection in a symbolic fabric when all connections are broken. Prophecy, he proposed, might be that term connecting the impossible, the possibility of health at the threshold of madness, when the symbolic order is in ruin: "prophecy is health" (paraphrasing Deleuze).[12] Farid Merini, a psychoanalyst and psychiatrist in Rabat, addressed the problematic of "symbolic transmission" asking what a "tradition-transmission" might be in relation to a theological reference, and reflected on the interpellation of one of his patients, an obsessional neurotic, who complained to be afflicted by *al-waswās*—an insistent whispering in the ear, of demonic origin—and who had confronted him by saying "you know, too, that *al-waswās* is mentioned in the Qur'an," raising for the psychoanalyst the enigma of the psychoanalysts' own place in the transmission of his own religious tradition.

It is impossible to raise the question of psychoanalysis and Islam today, of the commensurability or possible translation of concepts and practices, in philosophical or theological terms, without registering the political charge of the field within which the question has emerged, and without posing, at the same time, the problem of psychoanalysis's reflection on its own politics.

All of this points to the need for a sustained theoretical reflection on the instantiation of subjectivity in contemporary Islam—for it is in the field of theological argumentation and spiritual practice that questions of being, destruction, truth, madness, and ethics are today raised for many in the Muslim world; and if one cares to listen, it is there that some core preoccupations of a psychoanalytic approach, in the Freudian and Lacanian legacy, are today being encountered. But opening up to this possibility requires admitting a modern subject constituted in response to a diving address, thinking the heteronomy of subjectivity in genera, as founded by a law originating in the Other. It entails exploring the homology and interconnected history of the psyche and the *nafs*, reflecting on the lacunary writing of the Other—through its "signs," symbols, and symptoms—of which one formulation is the unconscious in psychoanalysis. In a way, this is what Hussein Abdel Qader had suggested in his presentation at the Beirut conference, and several of the early Arab psychoanalysts he mentioned had attempted to do, by looking for "another scene" of the Freudian unconscious in the vocabulary of Sufism and in particular, as the Egyptian psychoanalyst Yusuf Murad had done in the 1940s, in the metaphysics of Ibn ʿArabi. If the unconscious is "un-knowledge" (*lā shuʿūr*), the term used by Ibn ʿArabi for the paradoxical knowledge of the soul, and subjectivity is a fundamental relation to that unknowledge, then psychoanalytic knowledge is crucially implicated with Islam and the world of the soul. Omnia El Shakry has shown this much in her historical and philosophical account of the "Arabic Freud," and the "other scene of the unconscious" in its generative Egyptian encounter with Sufi metaphysics in the writings and practice of Abu al-Wafa al-Ghunaymi al-Taftazani, a shaykh of the Ghunaymiyya Khalwatiyya Sufi order and later professor of Islamic philosophy in Cairo, with the psychoanalyst Yusuf Murad and their joined effort in the 1940s at the *Majallat ʿilm al-nafs, Journal of Psychology* (literally "the knowledge of the soul").[13]

Ebrahim Moosa gives a definition of heteronomous subjectivity in his book on al-Ghazali, one that interfaces with some of my considerations here:

> To comprehend the ethical subject is to grasp how the self/soul becomes the addressee of divine discourse. (. . .) The self is an ethical subject related to actions rather than pure intentions. . . . It is a locus of responsibility and a space of transformation . . . [The] Other is encountered at two levels: at the level of an intersubjectivity with other human beings in history, and at the level of a transcendental intersubjectivity in relationship to God, often expressed as *ḥuqūq Allāh,* the duty toward God.
>
> Ghazalian intersubjectivity thus could not loosen the existential axis from the transcendental axis. The divine element is always present and never suspended.[14]

This is a possibility that is a priori excluded (if with a few exceptions) in much contemporary psychoanalytic writing about Islam, where the subject of psychoanalysis is posed as necessarily secular—a presupposition that I understand as contrary to Lacan's own thought. Adnan Houballah, one of the conveners of the Beirut conference and a founder of the Société libanaise de psychanalyse, as well as of the Arab Center of Psychopathological and Psychoanalytic Studies, and a former analisand of Lacan, is an analyst who dedicated much of his life to understanding violence and trauma in the context of the Lebanese civil war. His considerations are grounded in his own clinc, experience, and losses, and in a commitment to think the Freudian and Lacanian project in Arabic and in Muslim cultures. He reflects on what he characterizes as "Islamic subjectivity" (*la subjectivité islamique*), the ambivalent place of the feminine gender, at once the sacred and the abject, and the specific form that the Oedipus complex takes in a context where the father and God are superimposed. It is religion that "takes on the task of engendering the Muslim subject through symbolic castration," and does so explicitly and consciously, without any sense of guilt: "as long as the Muslim subject respects the rules and has unwavering faith, his/her relation to the world is entirely mediated by religion." For Houballah this is the source of the problem: psychoanalysis interferes and clashes with the place of the sacred in Islam. It cannot operate in the realm of certainty; it must be a free exploration of desire:

> This doctrine [psychoanalysis, *taḥlil al-nafsi*], when it appeals to the split of the subject—the "parlêtre" (speaking-being, being in language)—runs the risk of colliding with the religious belief in being, entering into a rivalry with religion itself. Because religion claims the last word on all interpretation of myth, taboos, and the social prohibitions. Religion generates meaning but doesn't accept any intruder in its domain. How to discern between divine knowledge and the knowledge of the unconscious, as long as the *nafs*, the psyche, has not been subjectivized, secularized?[15]

In part 3 of this book I explore how this confusion of the *nafs*/psyche/soul might precisely be enriching and generative.

In his 2008 work entitled *Pourquoi le monde arabe n'est pas libre* (Why the Arab World Is Not Free), Moustapha Safouan, a prominent Egyptian psychoanalyst, prolific writer, translator of Freud's *Interpretations of Dreams* into Arabic, interlocutor of Lacan, and a founding members of the Association of Arab Psychoanalysis, suggested that the responsibility of Arab psychoanalysts today is the political one of addressing the subjugation of being, working against the terror of states and of empire, both colonial and postcolonial. Through their regimes of domination and their perverse organization of enjoyment, state terror disables the work of desire for the subject, and cripples the possibility of action, thinking, and critique, falsifying the nature of speech (*parole*) as fundamental intersubjective engagement.[16]

> The profound fear of the people, a fear of the Leviathan which is our state, a fear that goes back thousands of years, and that is the most malignant vice of the soul . . . [a fear] that has corrupted the very function of speech (*parole*) in our societies.[17]

Continuing a line of thought begun in some of his earlier writings, Safouan argues that voluntary servitude and the disabling of *parole* are not related to Islam understood as the revealed message of the Qur'an. They have to do with the coopting of that message by worldly state apparatuses. Oppression is the illegitimate rule of worldly sovereigns, who put their own person in the place of God, a place no human being can ever occupy as such: "God is by definition the being for whom Lacan's assertion applies that every identification is an identification to a signifier."

There is much in Safouan's line of argument that one could contest: from his discussion of vernacular language as an epiphany of the people, to his unproblematic embrace of the concept of democracy; from his idea of a necessary disjunction of the theological and the political in Islam, to his telescoping of history, which conflates realities as incommensurable as the Umayyad empire (650–748) and the colonial and postcolonial Middle Eastern states.

Here, however, I want to follow the trace of his thinking on the responsibility of psychoanalysis—the sense in which this addresses the questions raised at that evening meeting in Rabat. In the last chapter of *Pourquoi le monde arabe n'est pas libre,*[18] which takes the risk of writing against the grain of much psychoanalytic ink on contemporary Islam, Safouan discusses the questions raised by the Muslim Brothers in Egypt, and by Hamas and Hezbollah in Palestine and Lebanon. He suggests that, however complicated and fraught any assessment of the terrain might be, it would be an error to comprehend these realities as antidemocratic formations, becoming deaf to the fact that these movements are attempts at a resymbolization, at moving against the subjugation of the subject. They reinstitute forms of sociality within which a novel circulation of desire may become possible, with the emergence of a *parole* that may "interrupt" the tyranny of the state, and not just reinscribe the subjugation of being. (Three years later the Middle Eastern uprisings had been precisely that interruption.)

If there is a responsibility of psychoanalysis at this time in history, I would argue alongside Safouan, it is that of a political critique, and of the exigency of a particular stance, which Lacan named ethical—the pursuit of lucidity (*détromper*, un-luring) and of a movement across the limit that he pondered through the figure of tragedy. It is the responsibility to remain mindful of the "pole of desire," and *not* work—as Lacan put it—in *"le service des biens"* (the service of goods) in their moral or perverse configuration; be those of democracy or the universal value of human rights, or their perverse reversal in the enjoyment of the tyrant and those who exist in his shadow, or even the "good" of psychoanalysis itself, refusing to become a discourse of comfortable complacency. In Lacan's words: "To make oneself the guarantor that the subject might in some way be able to find happiness even in analysis is a form of fraud. There is no reason why we should make ourselves the guarantors of the bourgeois dream."[19] And inasmuch as, for Lacan, remaining mindful of the pole of desire is also, necessarily, a matter of encountering the limit, risking to venture beyond the economy of self-preservation, where an angle of visibility can be attained from the living contemplation of one's own disappearance, one could say that a psychoanalytic ethic necessarily encounters the limit of any psychoanalytic institution that has not subjected itself to a radical critique, in the realization of its historical contingency.

Safouan's intervention runs counter to discussions, often originating in France, that relate the question of contemporary Islam to a debate on religion and violence vis-à-vis what is understood as a crisis of the symbolic in late modernity, a crisis that many psychoanalysts locate in the "new psychic economies" centered on narcissism. The new psychic economies are understood as a generalized regime of boundless (deadly) enjoyment in the context of globalization, where the paradigm of addiction captures the new limit-forms of the subject. In this reading, at issue historically is the vanishing of the subject in an excess of proximity with the impossible Thing, origin and termination of the drives, in a world in which the immediacy of enjoyment (*jouissance*) saturates all demand, fills all lack, and annihilates the circulation of desire.[20] This unleashes the destructive work of the death drive, no longer kept at bay by the symbolic detours of the psychic economy of self-preservation, what Freud called the pleasure principle.

(This is, however, not the only possible reading of the "new psychic economies" in the wake of the Lacanian thought of the Thing and the death drive. In several sections of this book I implicitly engage approaches of primary narcissism and melancholy, attempting to think the question differently, and in a close engagement with the Lacanian idea of the emergence of form at the limit of destruction.)[21]

When applied to the specific realities and history of Middle Eastern societies, the picture is further qualified in terms of the traumas of a "failed" modernity and a "savage modernization" that have rendered the subject vulnerable to the fascination of authoritarian projects of religion and ethnonationalism, and to an even worse threat of destruction: the suicidal propensity of the system as such.[22]

This perspective is conceptually elaborated, as well as politically exemplified, in Fethi Benslama's *La psychanalyse à l'épreuve de l'Islam*, where the Islamic Revival is discussed as a "torment of the origin," and a traumatic response to the despair of the people (*le désespoir des masses*). Benslama's approach differs significantly from other readings of the relation between psychoanalysis and religion, and psychoanalysis and Islam specifically. Following the trace of Freud's last writings on religion, identification, and culture, he reflects on the crisis of culture (*Kulturarbeit*), its inability to provide articulation and shelter at a time of violent and sudden historical transformation in the Middle East, between the brutal violence of the colonial system, and the ravages of postcolonial modernization. He introduces some terms, *"dépropriation"* (at once dispossession and cleansing) and *"révocation subjective"* (subjective revocation), to describe the condition of exposure of a being deprived of protection and shelter, forced to fold back upon itself, to retreat into a phantasmatic original identity, a (psychotic) process that, he argues, anticipates the shapes of a genocidal drive. For Benslama, religion and Islam are not the problem, the *nafs*-psyche doesn't need secularizing. The opposite is true: it is the failure of religion as religion, its undoing under the pressure of the brutal dismantling of the structures of society in the colonial and postcolonial period, from education to the economy to language, that unleashes hallucinatory forms of despair, a despair experienced as decay of the physical body, and as the regurgitation of hollow identity: "the despair to be oneself" (Kierkegaard). For he sees religion, and the Islamic religion in its classical liturgy, as "sublimation," a necessary illusion, as Freud called it, which allows for the drawing of a border, a way of containing destruction, "encircling" the origin and the archaic Thing—as Lacan says in *The Ethics of Psychoanalysis*.[23] Religion, including Islam in its precolonial forms, is a foundation of culture. When religion "decomposes," the symbolic forms of culture fail, and a sacrificial logic takes their stead. Benslama visualizes this moment at the end of the Algerian war, after the million dead, the torture, the blood shed, when at the dawn of independent Algeria, speaking of the efforts of modernization in the new country, the president compared the flowing of Algerian oil and its refineries to the blood of martyrs. Such hallucinatory retreat into a carnal reality is what Benslama calls the "torment of the origin."

The torment of the origin invokes the "torment of the grave" (*ʿadhāb al-qabr*) in Qurʾanic eschatology, and might be understood in the double sense of the torment of reckoning to which the soul is subjected immediately after death, and the agony of the Muslim subject, who is today tormented by the traumatic shadow of its "depropriation"—the Islamic "Thing." The Islamic Thing is here the murderous superego of a tradition, when this tradition has undergone irreparable trauma and aspires to be fused to its origin in a literal "return." The problem for Benslama is not

Islam but the Islamic Revival, which he traces in the writings of the Egyptians Hassan al-Banna and Sayyid Qutb, as the call for a literal "return" to the Islam of the Qur'an and the Prophet.

Such "return," he claims, is delusional—psychotic and hallucinatory, in the psychopathological sense of the term. Psychosis is registered by a "political incest," which "abrogates" the origin in the delusional form of a return to revelation: "The delusional return gives itself as a journey backwards in time, all the way to a reinvagination where metaphor retreats, prior to the form of the origin. The return here is not traction, but re-traction into the formless, where the function of the Imaginary collapses, making the Origin appear as raw flesh, as a collective organ, a mouth open on a bottomless political anguish."[24]

In this psychotic folding of time, intersubjectivity dissolves, and in its stead appears the hallucination of a fragmented body, a nonsymbolic corporeality, as an organic resurgence of the collectivity as glued to the Origin. It is a body tormented by violence, Benslama says, the violence of a *Deus absconditus*, which has abandoned his creatures and lost all transcendence, becoming the agent of destruction, and sucking the life-world into the crater of the Origin. Evil and hatred are no longer associated with the problematic of hetero-aggression. Hatred, Benslama says, should in the context of "Islamism" be located at a more fundamental level, as a hatred of being, a hatred of life itself, including one's own. This is why, for Benslama, suicide bombing is the ultimate realization of this logic of annihilation; it is the system blowing itself up.[25]

In the end, the question of psychoanalysis's reflection on its politics translates in Benslama's text into a specific political position, one that participates in the discursive construction of contemporary Islam as a phobic object. This is authorized by a diagnostic act that appears to dwell unreflexive, a political position colored by the glimmering horror of an emergent Thing: "Like a person who had been artificially put to sleep, Islam awoke abruptly, disfiguring the world in its sleepwalking state." It is a monstrous awakening.[26]

Benslama's argument relies on a certain reading of Lacan's *Ethics of Psychoanalysis*—a reading that I question here. In interpreting sacrifice and suicide bombing as the realization of the auto-da-fé of the Symbolic, he overlooks the ironic use of the concept of evil and destruction in Lacan's discussion of ethics. Lacan introduces the question of evil as a necessary radical heterogeneity, a revealing element (an "anamorphosis") vis-à-vis the discourse on the good. He turns to the theology of evil to highlight the originality of Freud's gesture of moving "beyond" the Aristotelian tradition of the good and the utilitarian notion of an economy of good(s). That beyond is the death drive, understood, at one level, as the theological problem of evil. Lacan's move, however, should not be understood as a negative philosophy. In part 3 of this book I attempt to trace a different heterogeneity of evil, that of the Islamic figuration of Shayṭān, in the discourse of a Moroccan Imam and Qur'anic healer. For the Imam, in his ethical reflections and his kinesthetic practice of healing in the space of demonic possession, evil is an ongoing ontological challenge—one that opens a space of life, as the always-precarious possibility of a vulnerable being.

Benslama pursues the question of sacrifice in reading Ibn ʿArabi's commentary on the Qur'anic story of Ibrahim and his son. We find there an appreciation of the "other scene of the unconscious" in Islam, through his subtle discussion of the nature of interpretation at the border of the unconscious and the divine. Ibrahim has a dream, but has no consciousness of the dream's meaning (*"lā yashūr"*). From his unconsciousness springs an interpretation, an interpretation that is not a deciphering but an "epiphany," an imaginal event, and the ram substitutes for the child. The Islamic tradition of the Imaginal has a family resemblance to the psychoanalytic practice of free association and symbolic interpretation, where the "forms" or symbols are not representations but instead manifestations. Benslama introduces Ibn ʿArabi's concept of the Imaginal, the "imaginative presence" (*ḥadrat al-khayāl*) as the emergence of interpretation from the depth of unconsciousness or unknowing: "not presence to the imagination, but the presence of the imagination as essence of the absence that is the desire of the Other." Following Ibn ʿArabi, he comments that there is "a god lying in his [Ibrahim's] unconsciousness."[27] This is Benslama's remarkable insight, at odds with so much psychoanalytic ink about Islam; an insight at once into Islam and psychoanalysis, opening to a radical reflection on the nature of a psychoanalytic interpretation as "imaginal event."

He cites Ibn ʿArabi: "The manifestation of forms in the mode of imaginative presence (epiphany) requires another science to comprehend what God intended with this form . . . To interpret is to transpose the perceived form to another order."[28] Yet, rather than fully elaborating on the importance of this insight, Benslama moves to subsume the lesson of Ibn ʿArabi's reading to his own political argument in the book, juxtaposing those who can interpret against those who take the imaginative presence at face value; those who "sacrifice through the form of the son," and those who "sacrifice the son." The second are predictably the Islamists, literalist sacrificers and suicide bombers. Yet, one can ask, aren't Ibn ʿArabi and Lacan suggesting that we are all somewhat (some more, some less) in the position of

Ibrahim? Shouldn't that "unknowing" contain a caveat for the psychoanalyst as well? Shouldn't it warrant a lacunary, rather than diagnostic, mode of relation of the psychoanalyst with his or her world?

For the members of the Rabat seminar, the interpellation of religious faith is a call for reflection on something that implicates them directly, in their clinical practice, as an authentic engagement with the problematic of theological reasoning in the field of subjectivity. In their discussions, this reflection is central for registering the experience of madness, in the transference and in analytic theory, as well as for cultivating an ethical attitude in which one risks one's concepts, and oneself, in the opening to other traditions—welcoming, in the process, the transmutations of psychoanalytic knowledge.[29]

In a sense that I suggest is consistent with the inspiration of Lacanian thinking and practice, I treat psychoanalysis in this work as one but not the only possible discourse, one developed at the margins of European modernity, from the debris of minor or obliterated traditions, and in the form of a countermove.[30] Freud's and Lacan's concerns with the questions of being, destruction, madness, and death are not psychoanalysis's only lot. If we take the psychoanalytic tradition as a critical opening to these questions, we see how it would encounter other vocabularies of being, alterity, and loss. At the same time, a psychoanalysis open to these questions is also one open (as Freud was) to the possibility of its own *remise en question* by the other, by the event of encounter; when, as well, the encounter touches at the limit of the intolerable, and makes appear the disquieting shapes of the Thing. Only in this way can psychoanalysis remain capable of producing countervisions and countermoves.

In his 1945 article "Le temps logique," written in critical dialogue with the problem of epistemology in experimental science, Lacan discusses the question of understanding with reference to the experience of time. He addresses this through the positing of a logical riddle, which he demonstrates to be insoluble from the standpoint of classical logics. Outlining the unfolding of a different solution, he introduces the factor of time, and distinguishes "a time for comprehending" (*le temps de comprendre*) from the advent of resolution and utterance, which he calls "the moment of concluding" (*le moment de conclure*). Understanding, for Lacan, is inclusive of both registers. It is not just the fact of "comprehending" the other—assimilating it into a preexisting discourse or configuration of the self. It requires openness to alterity, a radical discontinuity of experience. The temporality of understanding, in this complex sense, is not linear, and cannot be reckoned within the categories of classical logic. It a discontinuous space-time of structural positioning in relation to the Other; imaginary identifications, and hesitations, which lead to the "leap" of performative affirmation: "the moment of concluding." Apprehending the possibility of different life-worlds calls for the conceptualization of a discontinuity, incommensurability, and a topological fold that inscribes the "affirmative" dimension of subjectivity in the radical risk of alterity.[31]

A temporality of understanding in the complex field of Islam today cannot spare the work of engaging the risk of alterity. It is opened by the anthropological realization of the contingency and limits of one's conceptual tools in approaching what is perceived as the unfamiliarity of other forms of life: whether these be expressed in coherent discursive form, as with revivalist Islamic pedagogies making a claim for a collective new life,[32] or instead in the form of the fragment—the fragmented, painful, and sometimes original ways of inhabiting a world where none of the available vocabularies can be fully inhabited, even when they are invoked, and the attempt at reconstruction takes the form of a solitary self-creation, in a space of destruction which is also, sometimes, self-destruction.

It is from this perspective that the philosophical ethnography that follows might offer, as a reply to Benslama, the elements of a different reading of (and a different relation to) a set of practices that seek not a "return to the origin," much less a delusional one, but instead aim at addressing the predicament of feeling and thinking in a context of social, political, and spiritual crisis, and do so through the confrontation with human vulnerability and unreason, through a concrete ethical engagement in the world, and through the task of critique.

PART II

The Passage: Imagination, Alienation

FIVE

Taʿbīr: Figuration and the "Torment of Life"

> [We] must not think of this world-house as the simple reflection of a tranquil cosmology. For the mistress of the house is the most fearsome of all beasts—the serpent.
>
> —Aby Warburg, "A Lecture on Serpent Ritual"

In this section I engage with Ilyas's paintings and his life, as well as the life of Samia, his companion, and their bond in the surroundings of illness. I follow the path our conversations took, tracking their voices, the way their voices intertwined with my voice, as well as the insistence of the paintings themselves—the force of a vocabulary of images that emerged as an "imaginal presentation" (*ḥadrat al-khayāl*), and became with time almost a visual syntax, raising for us questions concerning madness, traumatic history, and divine disclosure, in our confrontation with the paintings themselves.

I reflect on the hermeneutic and ontological status of those images, and their agentive force in Ilyas's and Samia's lives; this at once in the conceptual terms that Ilyas brought to our conversation, based on his inventive inhabiting of an Islamic tradition of the imagination, the "operation of form" and its effects on the soul, and in terms of a parallel phenomenological and psychoanalytic approach to the image and the unconscious in the thought of Binswanger, Warburg, and Lacan, who could be said to be distant heirs in the West of a problematic of the imagination and form as affective impression, ontological challenge, and prophetic experience.

Figure 1. *Thuʿbān huwa l-marḍ dyāl shakhs* [the snake is the illness of a person], 2005.

Introduction to the Paintings

We are sitting on the floor in the empty entranceway of Ilyas's apartment, two rooms on the roof of a building in this low-income neighborhood in Rabat. Only one room, in fact, because the dividing wall has been removed. The floor is made of old decorated tiles, beige, brown, and black, reminiscent of buildings that date back to the colonial period.

This is my second time here. It was Samia who first mentioned Ilyas's paintings to me, who brought me to this place one day when he wasn't home, and asked that I come back to meet with him. The wall paintings had come up towards the end of a long conversation about her life, the abandonment that had colored her childhood, and the encounter with Ilyas, who had cared for her and loved her. She wanted to ask me something, she said, and went on to mention Ilyas's *maraḍ nafsanī*, his "mental malady," which in Arabic resonates with the sense of a malady of the soul. She spoke of their separation, and his mural paintings. She described his paintings of the serpent and the mermaids, and offered an interpretation of their meaning in his illness and his life. Would I go with her to his place, look at the paintings, and meet him? I would find them interesting. But we had to go quickly; he had already started to whitewash his images, as he always did at the end of an episode. She missed him and was attentive to each sign of his recovery, even though she realized she could not go back, at least for some time.

The second time we went Ilyas was at home, waiting for us. What was to be an afternoon's visit turned into a conversation that spanned seven years and is still ongoing.

The neighborhood where Ilyas lives is one of the oldest informal extensions of the city of Rabat, built in the 1960s on the side of argillous and barren hills and overlooking swampy flatlands, built partly as shantytowns that were consolidated with durable materials, in keeping with the layout of the old settlements. For many living here, there is a history of migration from the rural hinterlands, people leaving villages in periods of drought, or just to seek work and a new life in the city; families have been dismembered and reassembled. There is extreme, sometimes complete unemployment, and an absence of most services and infrastructures, a tangible retreat of the state from any form of collective care; and, on the other hand, the countervailing presence of an Islamic ethos reflected in neighborhood community organizations. Today, a growing sub-Saharan population is

Figure 2. Roofs.

impermanently settled in the neighborhood as well, treated by some with hospitality and solidarity, rejected by others in often violent forms of racialized exclusion and growing explicit racism. These are young men and women hoping to make the crossing to Europe, and parked here in indeterminate waiting, caught in a suspended journey between two continents, just as are many Moroccan youth from this same and many other neighborhoods longing to make (and oftentime risking) that journey.[1]

To get to Ilyas's rooftop one has to walk through densely populated streets, a long descent amidst street markets and vendors. His immediate neighborhood begins toward the end of the plateau, as the street falls into a ravine overlooking the valley below. Side streets are numbered 1 to 50, as in a *lotissement* that was never completed. A metal door among others opens onto narrow stairs leading the visitor to the third floor, on the roof, where Ilyas's apartment is located.

The first time I walked up those stairs I was warned by a sign at the turn of the last ramp: written in French, capital letters, and spilling red paint, it said: "ILYAS DANGER."

Inside the apartment, on the back wall of the sleeping area, an immense fresco comes to the fore (fig. 1), featuring a gigantic snake, painted in dark blue, black, and teal colors. The snake has horns like a dragon, scales like a snake or a fish, and brandishes a sword; it is adjoined by an Arabic inscription, an injunction and a warning, which reads, *Lā ghāliba illā llāh* ("No one is victorious except God"). Other prominent iconographic elements include three crosses drawn in the style of a Christian crucifixion, a disconnected arm holding a key with chains, the recurrent motif of an eye, and surrounding water and waves: the sea.

The fresco occupies the entire surface of the wall, and dominates the scene from every angle. Surging from the depth of another scene, visually it claims the space of the home. Foreground and background are blurred, so as to make the Serpent seem actually to protrude out of the wall, spilling into the space of ordinary life. The feeling is that of being surrounded, abducted into an otherworldly scene, which is here, in the midst of this world. Under the gaze of the snake, the house ceases to be a habitation for the living. The scene is not for our eyes; yet we are here in its midst.

The place has been empty of all objects since the onset of his illness. There is no electricity or utensils or any other sign of habitation, save the wooden banquette where he sleeps, under the painting, and the clothes hanging from a hook on the wall.

The apartment had once been their marital home, his and Samia's, and used to be furnished with the traditional sofas and other items Samia's family had brought in at their wedding as her dowry. But since the birth of their daughter in 2003, and the onset of her illness, her illness that intertwined and overlapped with his, Samia no longer lived there. A psychiatrist (the first one she visited, accompanied by one of her brothers) advised that she be taken away from her husband, back to her own family, and at the time we met, she was living with her daughter at her mother's place, sharing the space with her two brothers and their families. Upon her departure Ilyas had lived here alone. Now, after two years, he was emerging from his illness (the words he uses are *ḥāla*, "state," altered state, condition, or *maraḍ*, "illness"). In the past, and through two of what he describes as his major episodes—the first at the death of his mother, the second at the birth of their daughter—he neither sought a psychiatrist nor was he ever hospitalized. In general, throughout his life and the recurrence of his symptoms he stayed away from all forms of diagnosis, and the institutional and discursive sites of Western medical science. He also never sought the care of a Qurʾanic healer. Instead, during his episodes, which in their acute phase lasted several months, he took to the streets and "traveled" from city to city, as he said, without aim, wasted (*ḍaʿī*), obeying an urge to move restlessly. He lived like a wandering soul, homeless, sleeping outdoors. This was followed by a period of complete melancholic seclusion, until his "state" receded on its own: "I emerge from the *ḥāla* just like that, without realizing it until it is past, without any consciousness of how and why" (*bi-lā man shaʿr*).

This last time around, towards the end of his restlessness, Samia took him to the hospital to see her doctor, a young psychiatrist in whose presence she felt comfortable and safe. She asked this doctor to find a way to bring her husband to the hospital. The psychiatrist wrote Ilyas a note, asking him to accompany Samia on their next consultation. Ilyas complied, but without any investment, only because she had asked him. This happened when Ilyas's condition had begun to recede, and he was left sunken into a melancholic state, unable to otherwise leave the house or even speak. Her psychiatrist prescribed a tricyclic antidepressant for him, and the medication helped him to get back into a rhythm of life. He took it for two months, and then stopped, and started working at a vegetable market in the neighborhood. This was around the time that we met.

Their families, as is common for most residents in their neighborhood, were originally from rural areas, but had migrated to the city when their children were young. Ilyas was born in a small Berber-speaking town in the foothills of the Atlas Mountains, surrounded by olive and almond orchards. Samia's family was originally from the plains of Chaouia, where hamlets surrounded by thorny hedges interrupt the immensity of wheat fields.

When I asked Ilyas about his hometown, he told me that his parents migrated north when he was born and never went back; Samia, on the other hand, returned regularly to the ancestral village, where her mother still had a home. Ilyas rarely talked about his immediate family. Since childhood, he had both an inclination to withdraw into himself and a passion for drawing, painting, and making things—miniature objects decorated with great care. Samia was marked by the early desertion of her family, their "abandonment," which she felt as an unbearable and crushing weight throughout her adult life, and at moments literally as a physical symptom. Unlike Ilyas, who had almost no exposure to psychiatry (his specific mode of withdrawal allowed him to elude the medical gaze, and to be indifferent to institutional recognition), Samia was in treatment as an outpatient at the psychiatric hospital (the same hospital I discuss earlier in part 1) and had herself asked for a psychiatrist. Their opposite relationships to psychiatry also marked their approach to others, and to each other especially. She had a desire for care. "What do you want?" I once asked. She smiled, as if surprised by the boldness of her own reply: "I want love" (*bghit l-ḥnān*, in the sense of affection). And Ilyas had cared for her as no one had before. As Samia put it once, despite their sharp differences they had something in common: they were both shy, didn't like certain foods, or going to certain places, the public bath (*ḥammām*), for instance; or, as Ilyas said, they had in common a sensibility. She was an intercessor of his coming into the world; he shielded her from the devastating force of her memory.

Only when he is ill does Ilyas paint the shapes that take form in what he calls his "unconscious imaginings"—his visions *bi-lā shu'ūr*, "without or inaccessible to conscious perception." And these "forms" or "shapes" (*ashkāl*), he says, are "expressive" (*ta'bīrī*), or "symbolic" (*ramzī*): they do not correspond to the forms existing in the external world, but carry the shapes of a mythical world, inhabited by monsters and nonhuman creatures, a theater of violent struggles and scenes of torture. They are manifestations, apparitions, rather than representations of the external world. At once hallucination and vision. Messages from another world, or, more accurately, witnesses of a journey into the intimate alterity of this world.

Bi-lā shu'ūr is a term that keeps returning in our conversation and takes in Ilyas's discourse the status of a concept. From the verb *sha'ara*, to be conscious, to be aware, in the sense of an intuitive understanding (*shi'r* means to compose poetry), Ilyas's use of the phrase resonates at once with the theological question of divine disclosure and the human (in)capacity to acquire knowledge of *al-ghayb*, the realm of the nonmanifest; and with *lā shu'ūr* in the sense of the unconscious, the realm of passions and concealed meanings, as in the psychoanalytic concept of the unconscious (*al-lā shu'ūr*).[2] We will see how the two dimensions are related in Ilyas's account.

To an eye attuned to Islamic ethical and eschatological themes, and reinforced by the inscription invoking the sovereignty of God, the snake fresco is evocative of the Qur'anic scene of *'adhāb al-qabr*, the "torment of the grave." This is the event of the soul's being subjected to trials and questioning by the angels in the immediate aftermath of death and to bodily torments from which no one will be spared. In classical narratives, such as those of al-Tirmidhi and al-Ghazali,[3] torments are visualized in the form of scorpions and snakes. It is a scene of great emotional intensity, reiterated in the eschatological tones of homiletic literature, in moral storytelling, and today vividly present for many in the affective texture of everyday life through contemporary forms of pious exhortations, in printed pamphlets and the visual media.[4] And yet Ilyas was hesitant when I inquired

Figure 3.

about the possible kinship of the snake on the wall with the bestiary of *'adhāb al-qabr*. Samia challenged him. She even remembered that once Ilyas brought home a small book on the aftermath of death and the "torment of the grave," with the picture of a snake on the cover.

To qualify his own hesitation, Ilyas explained that the two images were discrepant, and visibly so in iconographic terms: the snake of the torment of the grave was usually drawn in the shape of a cobra, while his own snake was "changed" or "altered" (*mbeddel*): it had horns, like a dragon or a dinosaur. Ilyas's snake straddles the borders of a recognizable symbol within a cultural or a religious tradition. Its emergence undoes the coherence of the cosmos, disconnects the faithful, and sets him adrift from the community of trust in which he can belong. Beyond its recognizable traits, serpent or dragon, it signals the advent of an irreducible Other. Something in it makes its apparition impossible to share within a given discourse, even an eschatological narrative. Its emergence is the materialization of the danger that is announced at the entrance of the home: "ILYAS DANGER." Something so proximate as to be indistinguishable from him, and comparable perhaps to that strange and impalpable yet material being, elusive yet overwhelmingly present, that Maupassant called "the Horla": "Je sens bien que je suis couché et que je dors . . . je le sens et je le sais . . . et je sais aussi que quelqu'un s'approche de moi, me regarde, me palpe, monte sur mon lit, s'agenouille sur ma poitrine, me prend le cou entre ses mains et serre . . . serre . . . de tout sa force pour m'étrangler."[5]

And yet the serpent on the wall did evoke the Qur'anic vision of the grave, and the terror and pain of the faithful soul in the trial of illness. Ilyas shared this with me only much later, as we looked at a photograph of the painting, which by then had long been erased from the wall. "The snake is the illness of a person (*thu'bān huwa l-marḍ dyāl shakhṣ*). And the illness too is a torment (*'adhāb*), a divine trial (like the trial of the grave). So much pain and torture a human being is made to endure, by the illness!" But it was only several years later, when I had already written a version of this text and was discussing it with him, that Ilyas clarified what the painting of the serpent actually did for him. He looked at Samia and me with an intriguing smile, he seemed amused, remembering our conversations. "The serpent was frightening for you two . . . but it wasn't for me!" He explained that at the time of his illness he had not been able to sleep for months, moving about restlessly, anxiously, aimlessly. When he finally returned home he was crushed by an overwhelming torment. Then the painting materialized. It appeared. He "threw" the image on the wall without any consciousness of what he was doing; and the gaze of the image gave him sanctuary. In the shade of the serpent he could finally sleep.

Two Approaches to Illness

When we first met, Ilyas was thirty-nine and emerging from a psychotic episode that had lasted more than two years. He had lived the previous months in despondent seclusion, at one with the walls of his home and the paintings on those walls. Now he was slowly returning to the world of relationships. Samia was herself afflicted by a condition that reduced her to apathy, and at times gave way to a delusional state. In her late twenties, she was tormented by physical pain, especially in her joints, and by a crushing weight on her chest. Ilyas and Samia had been married four years: at the birth of their daughter, who was now three, they had fallen ill, each in their way. For Ilyas it was the third time. He had known madness before, had been ill in the past, in a similar and even in a more acute way. For Samia it was the first time; it was also her first encounter with Ilyas's psychosis.

Their perceptions of illness differed one from the other, as did their experiences of being ill. Samia saw her illness as the sedimentation of the story of her life. She reckoned the psychic crisis, paradoxically, as both a release and a coming of age. She explained: "the illness made me aware; it is as if there was a knot in me, and it was blasted open" (*w'anī l-mrḍ; bḥal ila kent fīyya waḥd l-'uqda u tfarga't*). She had chosen a charged term, *w'ani*: *al-wa'ī* is awareness, consciousness, and hence responsibility, in the sense of awakening. In a vocabulary common to many spiritual narratives of transformation by illness, from al-Ghazali's twelfth-century autobiographical account of the illness that tied a knot in his tongue to innumerable vernacular Moroccan hagiographies, Samia suggested that the illness had been the spiritual crisis that caused her to grow. After her illness she had donned the headscarf and started to pray regularly. She meant that she had embraced the path of God with invested awareness, but also that for most of her life she had been unaware, bound to early childhood by the trauma of abandonment.

But for Ilyas, madness could not be integrated into a life story that might make it intelligible. Madness meant being seized and becoming undone, delivered into an Outside where the "I" ceases to exist. Remembering it was at best the avowal of a chasm and a lapse. The Serpent on the wall was the memory, the imprint, of such undoing and being seized. Yet the *ashkāl* (forms, shapes) of the pictorial composition—what he also described as *'ibāra* or *ramz* (expressions, symbols, ciphers)—opened for Ilyas a space that could become the stage of a confrontation in which his very existence was at stake. In our conversation he conceptualized such an emergence as the operation of *ta'bīr* (expression, visualization—literally "crossing over," "traversing," as discussed briefly in the introduction and developed further here below). There, in the interval opened by the image, in the confrontation with the painting, and in his own being-with the Serpent, Ilyas could become the *sujet de sa folie* ("the subject of his madness"). It is a phrase and a concept I borrow from Gladys Swain, who in her rereading of the history of early psychiatry argued that a dialogue with unreason is possible if one can appreciate the "spacing" of the subject with her or his own madness (*"les modes de différence du sujet d'avec sa folie"*), or in other words "the interval (*écart*) that separates the eclipse of the subject from its abolition." In that interval, a consciousness lingers, or is born, side by side with or even from within delusion. There, in that interval, lies the possibility of relation: for the mad with the singularity of their symptom; for each of us, with unreason.[6]

It is here impossible not to look back at Hans Prinzhorn's *Bildnerei der Geisteskranken* (literally, "the imagery of the mentally ill"), published in 1922 and based on the study of a vast collection of artworks gathered at the Heidelberg psychiatric hospital where Prinzhorn was a psychiatrist and art historian.[7] Moving away from the common practice of treating the artwork of schizophrenics as mute indexes of pathological states, automatic response to an inner necessity, Prinzhorn stressed the artistic value and the formal qualities of the works that he collected from patients, and considered them aesthetically comparable to the works of well-known artists. What made them comparable, he argued, was the universal presence of an "expressive urge" (*Gestaltung*), a primary "formative power" that he saw as latent in each of us as a configurational attitude, and is realized by some, the artists, in its highest form. Therein lay for Prinzhorn a fundamental formal communicability of the artwork. It is well known that Prinzhorn's collection was influential in the development of European modern art, from Expressionism to Surrealism and abstract art, and led the way to, among others, Jean Debuffet's artistic movement of "art brut" ("raw" or outsider art). Yet, and despite the controversy that colored the afterlife of his book, which concerned its political and aesthetic instrumentality,[8] it is clear from reading *Bildnerei der Geisteskranken* that Prinzhorn was mindful of the mental pain from which the works in his collection were born, their artistic value notwithstanding; terrifying internal upheavals, with stakes of life and death. In the words of Inge Jádi, psychiatrist and curator, "every artistic activity on the patient's part is an act that creates meaning as a way of countering the existence-threatening erosion of meaning by the psychosis."[9] Prinzhorn paid attention to the way in the internment of the asylum that patients invested objects, and the surrounding physical space, as an extension of their body. In his discussion of particular works he traced the unraveling of symbolic forms, cultural and often religious, and their congealing in autistic hermetic lexicons, which at times, he argued, could become a support for healing, at other times were a just a site of solipsistic and mannerist repetition.[10]

Ilyas's fresco of the Serpent and the other images on his walls register a similar unraveling of symbolic forms, and a similar congealing in seemingly autistic poetic and hermetic lexicons. Yet, and in this way differently than in Prinzhorn's analysis, Ilyas's paintings imply a paradoxical kind of sharing, in the context of his relationship with Samia, and in the figural logic of the images themselves. There, I suggest, in the interval "between the eclipse of the subject and its abolition" (Swain's concept; an interval Ilyas designates, in his own analysis of things, as *ramz* or *ʿibāra*), something happens that renders a transformation possible.

The Mermaid

Several other wall paintings, of smaller size, populate the walls. The shape of a woman-fish (*ʿarūsat al-baḥr*, "the bride of the sea") or mermaid, in blue and gold, is enclosed within a painted frame. It has scales, like the snake, and at the place of the head there is a white spot. It is the place (Samia will explain later) where a picture has been scratched off the wall, the photograph of a woman important in Ilyas's life. Uncanny meeting of the mythical and the biographical. A North African mythical image of watery metamorphoses, sexual desire, temptation, pleasure, and demonic intercourse, the mermaid is recurrent on the walls in a multiplicity of forms and versions. It is a cipher of enjoyment and capture, one that for a long time remained silent in our conversation, a silent place, as well, due to our tacit agreement to keep it off limits. For the mermaid holds the key to a dimension of the snake that partakes of its traumatic insistence, and its painful and ecstatic corporeality. Years later I asked Ilyas what the mermaid was for him. He answers in French: "*la femme perdue.*" The woman one has lost.

It is well known that according to vernacular culture and the esoteric knowledge of magic, jinn take pleasure in water, and dwell in pools, and in the ocean. One jinn in particular, Lalla ʿAisha Baḥriyya, Lady ʿAisha of the Sea, is a she-demon to whom many sites and grottos by the ocean are dedicated along the coast of northern Morocco. To any viewer familiar with the mythological repertoire of vernacular demonology, the mermaid and the

Figure 4. *ʿArūsat al-baḥr* [the bride of the sea], 2005.

water motif recurrent in Ilyas's paintings are suggestive of an environment haunted by jinn. The Serpent as well. However, for Ilyas things are more complex.

A dimension of the demonic is present and active in his paintings, and he alludes to this sometimes indirectly, as people do who allude to the jinn. As when he makes a passing reference to Abbès Saladi—a Moroccan painter who was celebrated as a great artist only after his death, who lived and died in poverty and spent the last years of his life in and out of the psychiatric hospital. "Saladi is a painter of jinn (*kayrsem l-jinn*)," Ilyas said. He had seen reproductions of Saladi's works and had noticed the resemblance between Saladi's figures and his own—the woman-fish in particular, with her elongated forms, resembled Saladi's birds, his women-birds.[11] And there were Samia's comments: her noting that when Ilyas was ill he saw the mermaids come alive at night; they would step down from the wall and dance for him: "they must have been *jinniyāt* (female jinn)."

Yet the reference to the jinn remains oblique, as to his "metamorphosis" during his episodes of madness. I respected this omission, the veil cast on the immediate nature of his experience. At the center of our conversations were the paintings, not his psychosis as such, but I came to know that two major episodes lasted for several months, during which for some time he was (in Samia's words) "changed." The character and theme of his transformation are relevant in connection with the painting. During those times, at least in the course of the latest episode, Ilyas's world was organized by a Christian theme. He has no recollection of this now, and listens to Samia's reevocations of his *ḥāla* ("state"). She tells of how he would prefer speaking in French like a *Naṣrānī* (Nazarene), how she could not understand him, and how he would wear the crucifix, multiple crosses, on his neck and body. A Christian theme is also a French theme; in Morocco there is no Arab Christian community and *Naṣrānī* unambiguously means French, European, immediately evoking a colonial history. The apocalyptic imagery of the painting of the snake, its torments and its passion, in both Muslim and Christian iconology, is intimately related to this history of conquest. The scene of madness is haunted by the ghost of colonial (Christian) history.

Alongside the mermaid are traditional Moroccan decorative motifs found in *zellij* (mosaic-work) and painted woodwork. Prior to the last episode of his illness, Ilyas had worked as a painter-decorator on woodcarvings in the traditional style (*naqsh*), and his paintings and technique draw inspiration from that. But his relation to painting is older than his craft; his love for painting started the moment he learned to write and draw in elementary school. It was his *hawāya*, he says, his hobby or passion.

When I ask him—and I asked him many times over the course of the years we talked, through his different states and in different phases of his life and mine (from 2005 to 2015, when I wrote the last version of this section)—Ilyas insists that there is no direct relation between his attraction to painting and his mental illness. He never stops painting: it is "what" he paints that undergoes a mutation. When he is not ill, he paints "ordinary things," realistic scenes, landscapes, or traditional geometric motifs. He shows me a painting of an old walled neighborhood in Rabat, viewed from the sea. That scene represents, he says, what he saw everyday when he used to work in that neighborhood as a craftsman, before he became ill. In fact, it is not a realistic picture: houses are drawn as if they rest on clouds, and colors are glaringly juxtaposed (pinks and intense blues). But it is a peaceful image, as he himself points out, and it bears no resemblance to the fresco and to the other wall paintings that are facing us, those addressing us now.

Luḥāt lli fīhim ḥāla: *Paintings of a "State"*

Those paintings are made in an altered, pathological, state. They "are pictures that contain a state" (*luḥāt lli fīhim ḥāla*), he says. *Ḥāla* is the common nonmedical term for psychopathological state; it is used in the context of mental illness as well as of jinn cures, where it designates the event of possession, or more specifically the event of the manifestation of the Invisible. From the verbal root *ḥ-w-l*, *ḥāla* is a semantheme of time and being; it conjures change and transformation, movement, and passage between states. In a dictionary description:

> *ḥāla*: the state, condition, or case, of a thing (considered as subject to change); or the quality, or manner of being, and state, or condition, of a man, in respect of good or evil; or the particular case, or predicament, of a man &c., in respect of changing events, in the soul and the body and the acquisitions; and in the conventional language of the logicians, a fleeting, or quickly-transient, quality, such as accidental heat and cold and moisture and dryness; anything changing; the time in which one is; (the present time;) the end of the past and the beginning of the future; (. . .) the changes, or vicissitudes, of time or fortune.

Hence the saying *lā ḥawla wa lā quwwa illā billāh* (no strength nor power but in God). One of the same verbal root's forms (*ḥā'ila*) designates the fact of being transmuting, changing in color, or becoming other.[12] The related term *ḥāl* designates a nonpathological altered state in Sufi-inspired practices. In this sense it is related to the term *wajd* (presence, presencing), which in the context of liturgy and ritual refers to trance.[13]

Luḥa lli fīhā ḥāla has for Ilyas the status of a concept. It designates a particular kind of efficacious image, a "pathological" image, which can become an agent of transformation. The "picture that contains a state" is an image that stores affect, the memory of a disappearance. At the same time, by its existence, it constitutes an imaginal barrier. It opens an interval that also functions as a bridge to another modality of being where a kind of witnessing becomes possible. This has direct resonance within an Islamic tradition of the image that is directly implied by Ilyas's choice of terms. The efficacious character of his images, and more generally of the operation that he calls *taʿbīr* (expression, visualization) can be related to the ontological intercession of images in the space of the limit that Muhyi al-Din Ibn ʿArabi (d. AH 638/1240 CE) had called *barzakh*: an imaginal border that joins by separating, such as an isthmus or a bridge, and that is the site of a passage for bodies and spirits; a partition, a screen, between two modalities of being, spiritual and corporeal, widening and delimiting, this world and the other; the site where the impossible can manifest itself in concrete form.

In this sense the *barzakh* of Ilyas's pictures is a visionary geography that rests at once in the material world of experience, in its historical reality, and on the autonomous ontological status of the images themselves. Ibn ʿArabi draws a distinction between the "contiguous imagination" (*al-khayāl al-muttaṣil*) as a faculty of the soul, whose existence is connected to the viewing subject, and the "discontiguous imagination" (*al-khayāl al-munfaṣil*), whose existence is independent of the viewer. The realm of the autonomous imagination is *ʿālam al-mithāl*, the intermediate world of images, where divine presence manifests itself in concrete form. This is what Ibn ʿArabi captures through the simile of the shadow: the cosmos as God's shadow.[14] Discontiguous imagination cannot be the object of representation and thought; it can be accessed only in the mode of "witnessing" (*mushāhada*). The path to knowledge, in that sense, is a honing of the capacity for witnessing. Even though the analogy is only partly granted, it could be said that Ilyas's imaginal visions (his pictures that contain a "state") are a form of "witnessing" in the eclipse of human presence. Once the *ḥāla* recedes, Ilyas says, the paintings that contain a "state" become unbearable, like a burning exposure. And this is why they must be covered over by a thick layer of white paint.

On another wall is the fresco of a loggia, decorated columns separating window openings in a traditional Morocccan-style veranda—an internal arcade with a balcony that seems to open to a courtyard, but depicted here as if belonging to a parallel reality. The fresco is half covered over with whitewash, for Ilyas started erasing, or more precisely covering up and withdrawing from visibility, the "shapes" (*ashkāl*) that materialized from the midst of his *ḥāla*. When I first visited the apartment with Samia, I saw other paintings that have now disappeared under a thick layer of white

Figure 5. Whitewashing (c. 2005)

paint. The mermaids were the first to go. In the space of two weeks they were all gone. (The wall paintings now exist only in the photographs, later digitized and printed, I took that day and during the week when Ilyas was whitewashing his walls.)

Tree of Life, Tree of Death

On the front door of the house, turned outward and addressing the visitor, there was another painting, one that, along with the fresco of the snake, would become important in our conversation as well as in the unfolding of their relationship—the bond that ties Samia and Ilyas.

The door painting shows a tree with two human personages, reminiscent of the Qur'anic story of Adam and Eve (Arabic Ḥawwa') and their expulsion from the Garden. "It's the two of us," Samia told me the first time we walked through the door. Painted in red, black, different shades of green, and energetic strokes of color, the tree is heavy with fruits. A roughly sketched human figure stretches an arm upward to pick a fruit that lies beyond its reach. It is a posture of disablement and despair. Another figure, with its back turned to the other, offers an empty hand to the viewer. Stretching out one's hand, Ilyas says, is the gesture of the beggar.

Later he explained the circumstances in which the painting had come

Figure 6. *Shajarat al-ḥayāt* [the tree of life], the front door of Ilyas's place, now in my apartment, c. 2005.

into being. He was trapped in his illness, unable to provide for the necessities of their life. The painting shows Samia hungry and unable to reach, and himself, his back turned, empty-handed. He calls this image *Shajarat al-ḥayāt* ("the tree of life").

One afternoon in 2005, while completing the whitewashing of his home and getting ready to brush over the two personages and the tree, Ilyas asked me whether I would like to have the door he had painted them on, so that I could keep and care for it at my place. By then we had had many conversation about these images, his visions, his *ḥāla*, and his paintings. He was ambivalent about destroying the door—it "stored" the cipher of his relationship and life with Samia—but he knew that he could not start living again in a space populated by these witnesses to the world of his illness, traces of a burning exposure. He needed a new door. I proposed to buy it, but he said that such paintings (paintings that contain a *ḥāla*) could not be sold. We arranged for a small three-wheeler truck to transport the door to my place, where it still is today, "on consignment," or rather as an *amāna* (something entrusted to a temporary caretaker).

Four years later, in 2009, at a time marked by the threat of relapse, the "tree of life" reappeared as a dead tree drawn in the style of the illustration of a children's book. In this new version their little girl was included in the

Figure 7. "And we are separating, each departing on our own way," 2009.

Figure 8. *Masjūn fī-l-ḥayāt* [Imprisoned in life], 2010.

picture. She was departing with her mother, in a direction opposite to her father's: faceless black silhouettes walking on snow against a frozen sun setting in an apocalyptic purple sky. Ilyas's gloss: "The tree is dead, and we are separating, each going our own way."

Ilyas's tree is a faithful mirror of the state of the soul, of the rhythm of life and its extinction. It alludes to many trees in Maghrebi oral culture, where the succession of seasons and the catastrophic consequences of drought convey the tangible proximity of the experience of death.[15]

It is in this sense that the tree appears in a painting from 2010 that Ilyas names *Masjūn fī-l-ḥayāt* ("imprisoned in life"). In this canvas the self is portrayed in tones of dark green and gray as a man in the posture of despair, imprisoned in a cell, and grasping a dead tree with one hand. The tree is miniaturized and out of context in the scene, and here fully reveals its iterative character as an emblem. It is a citation from an archive of previous images that "contain a *ḥāla*," the personal archive that Ilyas shares with Samia. We can recognize in it a "formula of pathos" (*pathoformal*) in the sense proposed by the German art historian Aby Warburg,[16] a parallel I discuss at more length below. To cite such an efficacious image amounts to summoning the affective history that is condensed in its form. "Dead tree with sitting man" is the composite figure of a life shrinking. An encrypted image

Figure 9. *Her illness, and his sorrow. Each locked into their incommunicable world*, 2009.

Figure 10. *Her snake and his despair*, 2009.

or a cipher, the "tree" is a citation and a knot, a rhyme, of sorts, in the poem of Ilyas's and Samia's lives.[17]

In fact the entire set of small paintings Ilyas made in 2009 and 2010 during a time of crisis and relapse attests to the poetic, "symptomatic," and efficacious character of this vocabulary of figures.

At that time Samia was again prey to a spell of her illness, and Ilyas became prostrated, drifting into the growing estrangement of an incipient "state" (*ḥāla*). The serpent and the other figures that I had photographed in 2005 were reactivated, at once a memory of illness, a commemoration, and a remedy.

The tree, the snake, the cross, the eye, the chain, and the sea: they are the elements of an imaginal lexicon born urgently and at a time of crisis. Visual forms charged with pathos ("pictures that contain a *ḥāla*") engage in a work of their own, a silent writing of the disaster, at once wounding and repair.

A small painting from 2009 tells the story of his despair through the visual vocabulary of the snake, the "torment of life." Ilyas explains: "You see, the snake is female now (*unthā*). Now it is *her snake,* and he is drowning, he wants to die, the cross is his suicide." The center scene is enclosed within the shape of a nonhuman eye, in whose presence the self drowns and life recedes. It is a story in pictures that visualizes Ilyas's torment as seen by that impersonal gaze outside: the home on fire, the self kneeling (the posture of melancholy—note the small figure kneeling inside the burning house), the cross with a bleeding heart, and a masculine figure drowning in the ocean. The enframing eye points to the emergence of another gaze, the gaze of the *ḥāla*. It is a gaze colonized by the Serpent, here a female snake. In the lower section of the painting, there is an empty nest and two severed arms and hands. A bipolar image: one hand holds a snake; the other, a bouquet of flowers. "It is the empty nest of our family," Samia explains in a matter-of-fact tone, "The hand brings flowers, that is *his* love (*l-ḥanān*)." "And my hand is bringing poison in return!" Samia adds, laughing.

I am reminded of "psychoanalysis lithographica," and of the clinical work of Nicolas Abraham and Maria Torok on the gray zones of meaning they called "anasemia," where proliferate "cryptic" symbols that are excluded from representation and thinking, even of an unconscious sort. Anasemic symbols elude the kind of elaboration Freud had attempted to map through the dream-work. Such a symbol, write Abraham and Torok, is the result of "an exceptional work of crisis." It is "the symbol of what cannot be symbolized."[18] The cryptic symbol (symptom, image, stereotyped phrase or gesture) is, in their reading, the cipher of a secret haunting and of an impossible mourning, a failed mourning, one passed on across generations as a traumatic transmission. A corpse is left unburied in a psychic crypt, unbeknownst to and beyond the reach of the subject, and a secret enjoyment is obtained through the deployment of a secret lexicon (we may think of the mermaids). Anasemic constellations are rebuses without a key, ciphers of unknown wounds that seize the body and mortgage the future, sealing the melancholic fate of persons and collectivities.

The Images, between Samia and Ilyas

As Samia was explaining and asking questions about the images, I realized that the wall paintings in the apartment, the very paintings that had taken over their home and had forced her to leave, were hers just as much as they were his. Not because they were the product of a shared delusion, a *folie à deux*, but because they had become the ground of an encounter.

Samia had been talking with me for two long days, first at a park of eucalyptus trees (she longed for open spaces), then at her mother's home, and finally in Ilyas's apartment. She is the older sister from a different father of a young man I had gotten to know in the context of my work on undocumented migration to Europe. Her younger brother suggested that I meet with her because he knew that I spent time speaking with people at the psychiatric hospital and he thought I might know how to talk with her; also, perhaps, so that I might have a deeper understanding of his own life.

Samia told me the story of her childhood, spent in an orphanage (*khayriyya*) where her mother had left her when she remarried after her father's death, "so that she could go to school," an orphanage where she was both forgotten and where she says she came to develop a deep mistrust of adults and an incurable feeling of emptiness, of the vacancy of life (*faghar*); she told me of her return to her mother's home after many years, when it was too late for her to reconnect. She refers to this story as the story of her *ṣadma*—a term that means to be stricken, and is the psychological/medical term that translates trauma in Arabic. This trauma, this violence (she also speaks of *ʿunf*, violence), is for her at the origin of her illness, and of her relation with her family, fraught with ambivalence, resentment, and a paradoxical longing. Samia tries her best to be devout, to be fair in her exchanges with others and fulfill her responsibility to the words of God; this, not just because of her illness, even though her illness caused her to experience the terror of ultimate solitude. Prayer had become her sole source of pleasure, and she could better relate to her condition by accepting it as a trial from God, a *miḥna* and *balāʾ*, a testing rather than an illness that would shame her.

> Illness is from God, it is not from them [other people's harmful intervention, as in sorcery, or the jinns], it is not caused by humans. God gives you the illness and tests you by it, whether you can endure suffering in patience (*ṣabr*), or rebel instead. Why do families want to hide sickness? There is nothing to hide, illness is sent by God.

She continues:

> Now I know my illness (*kanʿarf marḍī*). I lived it for three years already, and it is not a small thing. At the beginning it was hard. I was screaming, going out in the street at night . . . My illness is hard, harder than his (Ilyas's); at least he's a man, a male, I am a woman, a female. When I started going out in the street my brother couldn't stand it. My mother would tell him: "You know that Samia is ill." I went out in the street and people, the neighbors, brought me a sheepskin to sit on. And still today, when I am sick and I begin to feel better, the neighbors come to see me, they ask "How are you?" Why would I be ashamed? God gave me this illness; I live with it, walk through it, until God one day may deliver me from it. If you are afraid of the gaze of others, if you are ashamed, you go crazy. One must commit oneself to God. My intention is pure (*anā niyyatī ṣāfiya*).

In those first conversations Samia spoke of her vulnerability, of the wound that kept reactivating itself, carrying the trace of former losses. When this happened, everything changed around her, she felt "as if the world were collapsing on me" (*bḥal ila kull shī kaythattam ʿaliyya*). She felt a weight on her chest that no medicine for the lungs could relieve, a sense of oppression, her tongue becoming so heavy that she could no longer speak; her perception of people and of her surroundings became altered: being full of mistrust and hostility she could no longer relate, and sometimes when her energy came back she erupted, ranting and striking, in an incontrollable fury. "My condition (*ḥālati*) is such, when I lose someone I am attached to, I transform, I become another" (*anā l-ḥāla diyālī haka, melly kanfaqd shī waḥid ʿazīz ʿliya kantghiyyir*).

ʿArfti shahl mrḍt f-Ilyas? "Do you know how sick I got over Ilyas?" And she went on to tell me of her engagement to him, her marriage, their relationship, and then his illness. When she got married to him, she said, she felt that she entered childhood for the first time, because of the love (*ḥanān*) he gave her. She described how he would bring her little presents when she was pregnant, and how he withdrew from her when she had their baby, and when he started withdrawing (she didn't know about his illness then) she felt such emptiness, when he went out at night and wouldn't come back until daybreak. She spoke of his family, and the way they kept the secret of his illness. When he started "transforming" they told her to hide her gold, her good plates; she didn't understand why. Then she understood. He had turned into a dreadful apparition. But by then she was ill herself.

The Expressive and the Imaginal: Ilyas and Samia on the Border of Madness

Perhaps the continuing conversation between the three of us over the course of years is in some way responsible for the formal elaboration of Ilyas's visual vocabulary and its affective investment, and ultimately with its deployment as an imaginal border in the paintings that Ilyas describes as "pictures that contain a *ḥāla*." It is that imaginal border that curbs the invasive strangeness of the experience of madness.

Our relationship started because of Samia's desire to show me the mural paintings and take me to Ilyas's home, and (by way of a conversation with me and though the intermediary of his paintings) to reconnect with him, in his home (their former home), as he was returning from his journey into madness. Her request opened a circulation, a gift of forms and attention in the *barzakh* of a deathly image. An ambiguous request, comparable perhaps to the craving for grapes she once expressed during her pregnancy in the cold of winter, and that had prompted Ilyas to paint a cluster of grapes for her. She will remember that gift of an image as the supreme expression of love. The repertoire of images returns each time that things become too strange, announcing the presentment of relapse. They punctuate Ilyas's and Samia's lives as the efficacious ciphers of their story, and during the years that I have known them, the forms have effectively contained relapse into severe illness and kept it at bay. The entrusted loan (*amāna*) of the Tree of Life—the door—is most likely another "bead" in the flow of that exchange.

I resist casting the story in a solely relational frame, for I think that the unbearable, mad, and visionary dimension of the painting of the Snake must be appreciated as such. Yet I realize the way in which our lives, our desires, and a certain unbearable, singular for each of us, came to be woven around the paintings, in the proximity of a radical existential and theological risk that for Ilyas was visualized by the Serpent.

Ashkāl: Figuring the Unconscious

2005. In the dimming afternoon light we are talking in the shadow of the Serpent. Ilyas speaks slowly and in a soft voice, addressing us, Samia and myself. He is explicating the "shapes" or "figures" (*ashkāl*)[19] in terms of what could be called a symbolic lexicon: the Serpent, the Sword, the Key, the Writing, the Cross, the Sea Creatures. . . .

Each time, after an episode of illness, Ilyas covers up his frescos with a coat of whitewash. Once he emerges from the *ḥāla*, he says, "I can't bear to see them" ("*manqdarsh nshufhum*"), which is why they must be covered, withdrawn from the realm of the visible. They are born under the pressure of catastrophic internal events that threaten his existence and are a "concretization," a materialization of this radical state of exposure. The images stage themselves, he says, in unconsciousness, like a corrugation on the face of the earth during an earthquake. They are an effect of "the things that were agitating inside me" ("*dak shī lli kaytharrek fīyya*"). As far as he can remember, he feels an urge and a mounting tension ("*kantzeyyer*") before painting, and a sense of relief afterward, as though he has shed a heavy load.

It is getting dark. We are looking at these images in a narrow interim, just prior to their disappearance. I am still taking photos of the paintings and Ilyas lights a candle for me to see where to orient the camera. Samia asks questions based on her intimate familiarity with the images, which are so important in the story of their life together. Ilyas explains. Samia interrupts, to provide a context or fill a gap in his words.

The way Ilyas narrates the painting now differs from when, in his words, he "put down" or "throws" his state, being, illness "in the picture" (*kanḥattu f-ṣūra*). Now in the aftermath of that event he is better able to recognize the shapes (*ashkāl*), the figures (*ʿibārāt*), and the way they function allegorically—their "ciphers" (*ramz*)—in the mode of a textual reading, and in terms of a "symbolic" lexicon of figures that accompany himself and Samia in their lives. Ilyas emphasizes the gap; for him there is a radical discontinuity between the person who is speaking today and the one who painted on the wall. He smiles—and his mercurial smile betrays a glimpse of what might have been. He emphasizes the rift, the inadequacy of his account. He was not the same person then; he painted "without consciousness," driven by a powerful urge, and the shapes (*ashkāl*) emerged ready-made from the inner upheaval:

> The painting happens outside of consciousness (*bi-lā shuʿūr*), it comes without a plan, chaotically, impulsively. I paint what is inside, all that is agitating inside (*kaytḥarrek*).

He says *"nḥatthum f-ṣwra"*: "I put them down in the picture," as one downloads a heavy current. He was not there to compose the painting, it came out already composed, "like something that was already there, present," he said. He smiles, "The unconscious too works on its own (*bi-lā shuʿūr hetta huwa kaykhaddem*)!"

There existed a whole world in there, *live*, powerful forces, in those colors and shapes. Again he smiles. Have they really withdrawn? But he jokes, the Serpent "is confined to the wall now (*ḥddu l-ḥayt deba*) . . . ! And in a few days, when I'm done whitewashing, it will disappear altogether! . . . I no longer have the snake here (*mabqash ʿandi lfaʿ hna*)," pointing to his head.

But yes, the paintings are "his," in the sense in which "his" life, as also our life, is a collection of a multiplicity of states and chapters, and in some of those, under the pressure of a pain he no longer remembers (a torment encoded in the snake on the wall), he inhabits another "consciousness" or another mode of existence, which from the standpoint of what he calls an "ordinary person" (*insān ʿādī*), and of himself in his ordinary state, can only be described as unconsciousness or delusion. Such is what from the outside, and in its aftermath, Ilyas describes as his illness. At no point in our conversation does he present his experience as anything other than a mental illness; in the aftermath of his episode, at least, he claims for himself neither the aura of the Sufi mystic or the inspired visionary (*majdhūb*, from *jadhba*, trance), nor does he see himself as a person haunted by the jinn. But in our conversations he is clearly interested in the metaphysics of creation associated with his experience of "states," as an unconscious production and a sort of automatic writing, of something that is both "inside" and elsewhere, in another modality of existence.

Ilyas makes a clear analytic distinction between his *ḥāla* ("state") and what he calls "ordinary life" (*ḥayāt ʿādiyya*). In his ordinary life, when he is not ill, he is better adjusted to the practical requirements of this world, but has no access to the experiences and heightened visionary awareness of "states"—states in which, however, his worldly self is obliterated. The different styles of his paintings, when he is "ordinary" (*ʿādī*) and when in a "state" (*ḥāla*), attest to the discontinuity of his experience, as does the inability to reach, in his "ordinary" mode, the aesthetic pathos and formal complexity of his paintings of "states." Yet neither he nor Samia, Ilyas says, can never really be considered "ordinary persons." They have what he calls *ḥissa nafsiyya*, a special psychic/spiritual sensibility, which is not ordinary, and makes them permeable and sensitive to the world. Samia too. This sensibility is something artists share with the mad, he elaborates, assigning both to an exilic position, given to an Outside.

> The artist (*l-fannān*) may seem to people like a mad person (*ḥmaq*). An ordinary person (*insān ʿādī*) will not look [at a painting] and understand it; he will not value and respect the artwork. While instead, the painting is an expression, a coming to form. The artist has thoughts (*afkār*), and his thoughts are those lines (*khuṭūṭ*), those curves, those colors; they contain thinking and visual meaning (*ʿandhum āfkār u ʿandhum maʿānī*). In the past, and even more than now, ordinary, normal people didn't attribute any value (*qīma*) to works in the plastic arts (*lawḥāt shikiliyyīn*).

In its aftermath, the fresco of the Snake can only be read—by a witness who is no longer in the event—as is the text of a dream upon awakening.[20] Yet any simple notion of hermeneutic deciphering or symbolic interpretation fails to appreciate the nature of those images, their persistent energetic quality as "emergent" forces.[21] Its status as an image is what Ibn ʿArabi calls an "imaginal presentation." It is a "shape" that makes visible, in a sensible form, in Ilyas's words, "the form of a human being imprisoned in life" (*bḥal shkil masjūn, shī insān masjūn fī l-ḥayāt*). A form that is also, by the same turn, an effective manifestation of the power of God.

Understanding Ilyas's explanation of the figural logic of the paintings calls for a different philosophy of the image, one that is not confined to a concern with representation, but instead is capable of grasping the image's fundamental relationship with divine self-disclosure. Only from this angle is it possible to apprehend how for Ilyas the painting of the Serpent can become the transformative stage of an actual confrontation where the coordinates of the subject's position in the world can be reordered through a passage through madness.

Reading the Mural Together: Visual Meaning and Divine Admonishment (*Maʿānī* and *ʿIbar*)

> If we want to explicate the painting (*l-lawḥa*), there is the Serpent (*thuʿbān*, *lfaʿ*), it is the torment of life (*humūm l-ḥayāt*): life when it is hard, when it is painful, is like a Serpent. It is poisonous. As for the sword (*sayf*), the Sword is

> the force that conquers all things: next to the sword he [referring to himself, the painter] wrote in Arabic *Lā ghāliba illā llāh* ("No one is victorious except God"), because God, praise and glory on him, only God is sovereign on all things. For all that happens in the life of creatures, all that human beings (*insān*) suffer and endure, their successes and their failures, it happens with the permission of God. However much a person wants or likes something, what happens is because God allows it to happen. And over there [pointing to the right side of the painting] there is a key; it is the figure of imprisonment (*shakl al-sajn*), the form of a human being imprisoned in life (*ṣārut bḥal shakl masjūn, insān masjūn fī l-ḥayāt*); because the life of a person without works (*aʿmāl*), without aim and without fulfillment, is the life of a person in prison. This much is made visible, expressed, in the painting (*dak shī llī fīhā diyāl taʿbīr*).

For Ilyas, four figures recapitulate the scene: the Serpent, which is the torment of life; the Sword, an image of the divine power that conquers, punishes, and saves (but also, Ilyas will say, the Sword is *jihād*, "effort," and *ḥarb*, "war," with the illness and with the hardship of our times: (*l-jihād wa l-ḥarb maʿa l-marḍ wa l-waqt*); the Writing (*kitāba*) that proclaims God's sovereignty in all things and reminds humans of their vulnerability; and the Key and the chains that evoke the prison of life. The figures, once again, are not symbols in the conventional sense of representations that stand for other things, whether objects or ideas. Their nature is imaginal: they are presentations, at once a screen and a bridge to what they make visible. They have "meaning" (*maʿnā*), Ilyas says. "Meaning" is essential reality in the invisible world (*ʿālam al-malakūt*), the world of angelic intelligence and divine reality, which is given sensory form by the imagination.[22] Such is the force of the operation of expression, what Ilyas calls *taʿbīr*. The emphasis is on the torment of the soul/self, a state of things that, Ilyas suggests, is the outcome of a specific historical condition, that of a society built on dispossession and where human beings are abandoned to wander and waste away (*ḍaʿī*). "Empty-handed," as in the painting of the tree. The snake, the illness, is not just an existential condition and a theological dilemma: it is also that very historical prison. The writing *Lā ghāliba illā llāh* ("No one is victorious except God") has the status of a divine utterance, injunction of a divine law. In the physical, metaphysical, and moral scene of the illness—the illness as a struggle of the soul, exposed to the double risk of madness and damnation—the injunction of divine writing has illocutionary force.

I ask Ilyas whether the key in the painting may be able to open the prison of life.

"The key doesn't exist (*makainsh*)," Ilyas responds vehemently. "Look, the painter drew a circle around the key, a frame, to show that the key is unattainable." Then, shifting to the first person: "I can't reach it (*manwaslush*)."

The key and the sword belong to a different order: not the order of the snake, the illness, the vulnerable human, but that of God's self-sufficiency.

Samia interrupts, asking about the three crosses on top of the painting, between or beyond the horns of the serpent; a taller cross at the center, two smaller crosses to either side, reminiscent of crucifixion in Christian iconography.

"The cross is death" (*ṣalīb huwa l-mawt*), Ilyas replies peremptorily.

I ask him why he represents death by the cross of the Christians (*Naṣārā*, Nazarenes, which in Morocco simply means "the French" and by extension Europeans).

"When you are mentally ill (*marīḍ nafsānī*)," he says, "there are times when you think that there is no exit; there is no cure, no medicine, no end to the torment. All you can think of is suicide (*intihār*). It is suicide that I concretely visualized with the cross."

Samia insists: "Why does he [the painter, namely Ilyas in his other state] use the Christian cross to visualize suicide?"

"In the Muslim cemetery," he replies, "death is hard to visualize, there are only two stones [at the head and the feet of the dead]. The cross instead is a clear visual image (*ṣalīb bayyin fī ṣūra)*, the image is visible in the cross." It is the question of an object's propensity to become an emblem. Yet as I write this, I am thinking that Ilyas's statement is also open to another reading: that of not having a place for his "image" in the cemetery of the Muslims.

I ask Ilyas whether the painting of the snake is not also a protection for him—I mention the Sword. He denies this. He says that the Sword (*sayf*) does not exist on the same plane as the other images: "the Sword doesn't follow [the logic of] the illness, the logic of the Serpent, it is not part of the scene of the illness, it follows [the logic of] Divine power (*ṭabaʿ quwwa ilāhiyya*). The power of God can free you from illness, if God wills, God the highest has the power to heal you."

Samia intervenes; she tells how when Ilyas falls ill—during an episode—he carries a wooden sword all the time. She turns to Ilyas, *"Do you remember that?*" He seems dubious, and replies that at those times he is out of his senses (*ḥawāss*), he loses touch with reality. Samia is saddened as she remembers, "You were out of your senses, but I was with you and saw you." She goes on to explain that Ilyas "transforms" (*kaytghiyyer*) when he falls ill, "he becomes someone else" (*kaywlli wāḥid ākhar*); not another personality, but an uncanny creature (*waḥsh*): "When he's ill, he doesn't know anyone, doesn't care about anyone, he's like that snake on the wall! He becomes like that painting he painted on the wall! He no longer listens, no longer hears, despite the fact that he talks so much and so fast. And he speaks French, and transforms into a Christian, a European.[23] Talking with him is like talking to the wall. He becomes yellow (pale, *ṣafār*) like a corpse, and wanders the streets in strange attire." She says this with neither resentment nor the pleading tone family members in the hospital emergency room often use to convince psychiatrists of the reality of their spouse's or children's mental illness and in that way gain validation of their own painful experience.

"I love Ilyas (*anā kanbghī Ilyās*), if I didn't love him I would have divorced him. I love Ilyas because of the gentle way he treats me, his gentle character. But [addressing him] we are not living in a desert island, just you and me: there are our families, our neighbors . . . And all that is full of problems."

She says this with acceptance. This is their life, and she accepts it. But the acceptance that this love makes possible does not have a place in everyday life, where relationships, allegiances, and entanglements carve doubt and the hollowing work of fear and mistrust. Her brothers, for instance, kept fighting with Ilyas when he became ill, and eventually rejected him. They didn't understand that he was mentally ill:

> Because we lived through great hardship (*mashākil kabīr*). He was ill, he would go out, wander the streets, and he was mad. [Turning to me:] Do you have an idea of what madness is? Madness (*ḥumq*)! My brothers couldn't accept his behavior; they thought he acted intentionally, they had no understanding of a mental illness (*ḥāla nafsiyya*), had never read anything about it.

Only her older brother, she added, her brother from the same father and mother, understood. He told the others: "Stay away from Ilyas, leave him alone, he's ill (*marīḍ*)."

Taʿbīr: Imagination of the Real

"Do you see the serpent actually appearing in front of your eyes?" I ask.

"It is a *ramz*, it is not real (*haqīqī*, in the sense of material reality)," Ilyas replies. He pauses, then qualifies his statement: "The snake allows me to visualize, to express; its nature is *taʿbīrī* (*deba l-ḥansh kanʿabbar bih, huwa taʿbīrī*)."

The concept of *ramz* and the operation of *taʿbīr* are central to what Ilyas sees as the relation between the figures (*ashkāl*) and what they make visible. *Ramz* means sign, cipher, symbol, or emblem, pointing to a secret at the core of a symbolic relationship, to something that will remain hidden, beyond the ordinary reality that can be perceived by the senses—call it a "signature." On the other hand (and as briefly discussed in the introduction), *taʿbīr* is a noun from the verbal form *ʿabara*, meaning to cross over, to traverse, as between two shores of a river, from one mode of existence to another; to interpret a dream; to be taught a lesson, to admonish, to give an example. *ʿIbāra* means expression, concrete manifestation, sign, passage, and interpretation.[24] *Taʿbīrī*, the adjectival form of *taʿbīr*, might then be translated as the "expressive" or "figural," in the sense of an example that makes something manifest. Yet this something can be expressed only through an example (an example that is here an image) by way of a bridge or a crossing, and as such marks an inadequacy, a disjunctive encounter of the visible and the invisible.

What is at issue here is the paradoxical connection between the two lapsed modes of Ilyas's relation to the image: on one hand, the serpent as an immediate experience in his *ḥāla* ("state"), an experience that amounts to a shattering of the personal world; on the other, the "symbolic" reading of the painting in the aftermath, as a landscape of allegorical writing and ciphers. Ilyas's recourse to the concept of *taʿbīr* is illuminated by the double-edged nature of its semantic constellation, which conveys the immediacy of expression even as it also gestures to the indirect nature of allegory and the ethical dimension of the lesson: the "example" (*al-ʿibra*, pl. *ʿibar*) that is the image of the Serpent and that becomes an admonition for those who can see it.[25] The *ʿibra* speaks of the example that makes one ponder one's own life, a process that changes one.

Ilyas also refers to the painting as *ṣūra* ("image") and often also as *lawḥa* (the "tablet" on which something becomes visible). In the classical tradition of the image, *ṣūra* is the imprint of form, and the verbal form *taṣawwur* (from the same root) is a faculty of the soul, the "formative faculty" or retentive imagination, related but not identical to the cosmic imagination (*takhayyul*, from *khayāl*, imagination). Understanding what Ilyas means by *ramz* and *ta'bīr* requires considering the place of expression, manifestation, and form within an Islamic metaphysics of the image and its relation to the soul and the cosmos in both medical and metaphysical terms; a metaphysics in which images are not representations but concrete events and "subtle" realities, in the macrocosm and the microcosm. Ilyas does not refer explicitly to this tradition of knowledge, but his terminology and his way of describing his pictorial practice in the space of illness testify to it.

It is useful to here recall Ibn 'Arabi's discussion of the shadow, earlier discussed in the introduction. According to Ibn 'Arabi the world is God's shadow, related to God as the shadow is related to the person: at once intimately connected and distant, at once the same and other. "Imagination" is the realm of God's shadow, and interpretation is the necessary work of discerning the divine self-disclosure. *Ta'bīr* is the imaginative bridge that spans such intimacy and distance. It is the hinge that separates (and joins) the realm of the visible and experienceable (*al-ẓāhir*) from that which is concealed from ordinary perception (*al-bāṭin*) and points to the mystery of divine reality (*al-ghayb*).

As formulated by Ibn Sina, the eleventh-century Muslim Aristotelian, physician, and explorer of the visionary imagination, the question is that of the relation between the imagination as "formative faculty" and the imagination as "visionary activity" of the soul. If the imagination as formative faculty is in the Aristotelian tradition the imprint of external reality on the human soul, which generates forms as molds stored in memory, the imagination as visionary activity (*al-mutakhayyila*) is the capacity of the soul to detach itself from the sensory experience of the external world, to become capable of knowing supra-sensible realities that are beyond human faculties but nonetheless appear in the form of imaginal "semblances" (*al-ashbāh al-mithāliyya*). In this visionary or active mode the soul forgets external objects and instead encounters or "remembers" another reality to which it thereby gives sensible form: a nonphenomenal form carried by the "imprint," the trace that, as such, becomes a site of manifestation. The sensible forms of the "semblances" (*mithāl*) are images, manifestations of nonhuman realities mirrored by the soul in its visionary activity. According to Ibn Sina (as well as, in differing respects, for Ibn 'Arabi and al-Ghazali), it is precisely here that the capacity for witnessing the truth of Being resides.

We could understand Ilyas's conceptualization of his "figures" (*ashkāl*) —the serpent, the sea, the cross, the chain, the key in the "pictures that contain a state"—and of the operation of *taʿbīr* in terms of Ibn ʿArabi's discussion of imaginalization, the clothing of spiritual meanings in substrata:

> Imagination is the widest known thing. Yet in spite of this tremendous wideness by which it exercises its properties over all things, it is incapable of receiving meanings (*maʿnā*) disengaged from substrata as they are in themselves. That is why it sees knowledge in the form of milk, honey, wine, and pearls. It sees Islam in the form of a dome or a pillar. It sees the Qur'an in the form of butter and honey. It sees religion in the form of a cord. It sees the Real in the form of a human being or a light.[26]

In a perhaps related sense, Abbès Saladi (the Moroccan artist whom Ilyas described as a "painter of jinn"), in an interview just before his death, described the recurring iconographic lexicon in his paintings, his own *taʿbīr*, in the following terms: "Take for instance the dome, the candle, the eye. They are elements imbued with a sacred meaning that I perceive. This is why they are repeated in all of my works."[27]

But it is not just a matter of referring concepts back to their historical or cultural environments. I want to take them into account for what they can elucidate, for the worlds they make possible, within and in spite of the gap of translation. To ask about the status of the images in Ilyas's painting amounts to asking about their activity, agency, and effectiveness, their relation to trauma and psychosis, their bearing on the possibility of being, and (stressed in Ilyas's own reading) their relation to the manifestation of a divine gaze. These are questions that in modern times, and as an archive that shaped my way of thinking about madness and imagination, have been pursued by Aby Warburg, by Ludwig Binswanger, and by Jacques Lacan in his later works.

For Ilyas, painting is a stage where a noetic Real, unapproachable at such, comes to the fore in an arrangement of figures. The figures do not exist in a relationship of correspondence with external objects, and are not just the elements of a visual language. Borrowing an analytic distinction from Lacan, we may say that the objects that show in Ilyas's painting do not belong to the order of the German word *Sache*, but to an altogether different order, that of the German word *Ding*. An object in the sense of *Sache* is an object of value in the human world, which exists in language and in a set of preexistent social and legal relations. A thing in the sense of *Ding* is instead beyond relationship and meaning, and beyond human life—it is, Lacan says, *"le secret véritable,"* the locus of a true secret. This other thing, *Ding*, is charged with affect, and with an urge, a pressure and insistence, to which Lacan attributes a destinal character.[28] A thing that carries the quality of *Ding* participates in the secret. Its circulation, from "thing" to "thing," belongs to the order of the drive itself. We can say that the signs Ilyas calls *ʿibārī* and *ramzī*, his images, carry this quality of *Ding*.

The snake is not, or not only, an apparition or perceptual hallucination (that was my psychiatric question to Ilyas), but it is also, at the same time, not simply a metaphor of the illness. It imaginalizes the illness of being, the torment of life, and as such becomes the stage of a direct confrontation in which Ilyas's existence is at stake. Dense with eschatological themes, the painting stages a struggle with harm, with the serpent, with forces in the self/soul and in the world that are materialized in the symptoms which hurl Ilyas into a *ḥāla*. On that stage of life and death there is a literal wrestling with history—Ilyas's singular history and a collective history of oppression and violence. In the scene of that struggle, *in the painting*, the sovereignty of God is rendered visible at once as a presence and an unattainable limit, a command and an appeal.

Henri Corbin introduced the term "imaginal" (used at once as an adjective and a noun) as the translation of a family of concepts related to the Arabic and Persian notion of *mithāl* (image and semblance, example, vision, witnessing) in the Muslim encounter with Platonic and Scholastic traditions. His term "imaginal" points to a conception of the imagination as an organ of active perception and of cognition of suprasensory realities. In his reflections on the image, Corbin bridges the European traditions of the *mundus imaginabilis* and the Islamic concept of *ʿālam al-mithāl*, "the world of the image or semblance," an intermediate realm of "subtle bodies," where witnessing the divine in the form of the image becomes possible to a certain degree. The imaginal world is ontologically real: in this conception the imagination is a privileged locus of experience, transformation, and relation; not illusion and error, but the site of true knowledge. Dreaming is an experience all share that opens onto the imaginal; and the veridical nature of visionary dreams, bearer of otherworldly knowledge, attests to the reality of the imagination. Imaginal experiences are more real than concrete experiences in flesh and blood; yet they also share something with sensory experiences, as they cannot take place, at least at first, without the mediation of the senses.

It is with a preoccupation akin to Corbin's that Agamben wrote of the "destruction of experience" associated with the decline of the *mundus imag-*

inabilis in early modern European culture. For, as he puts it, in antiquity and medieval culture Imagination occupied the place of experience, intermediary between the senses and the intellect. The image or the phantasm were not the product of a subjective cogitation, but were instead the site of an encounter, of the coincidence of subject and object, which in the image could meet and be realized. The realization of experience, the confrontation of experience, was the image itself: "As the intermediary between the senses and the intellect, enabling, in phantasy, the union between the sensible form and the potential intellect, imagination occupies in ancient and medieval culture exactly the same role that our culture assigns to experience. Far from being something unreal, the *mundus imaginabilis* has its full reality between the *mundus sensibilis* and the *mundus intellegibilis*, and is, indeed, the condition of their communication—that is to say, of knowledge."[29]

Agamben traces the historical transformation of the relationship of imagination and experience, from the Scholastic *mundus imaginabilis* and its relation to the soul and the passions, all the way to the expulsion of the Imagination to the no-man's-land of illusion and error in what Foucault called the Classical Age (and its inscription, as Foucault had written, into the history of medicine as a primary cause of dementia and delusion).[30] There is no nostalgia in Agamben's reading, which (in this sense unlike Corbin's sense of regret) stresses instead that from the destruction of experience new forms of experience may be born, provided that "destruction" is assumed as such, made visible, and in that way paradoxically experienced. (It is perhaps in this sense that the Iraqi artist Jalal Toufic does not allow the viewer to hear the soundtrack by oud virtuoso Mounir Bachir in a video on the Lebanese civil war: for only that absent-presence, that silence associated with a name, can make visible and heard the fundamental inability to experience, and hence to hear the voice of an artistic tradition that in the aftermath of collective violence remains suspended and cannot be passed on.)[31]

In his committed plea for the Imaginal, and the reality of the active Imagination, Corbin draws a sharp distinction between the function of the Imaginary as locus of representation, fantasy, unreality, and illusion, and the realm of the Imaginal, where the manifestation of forms or semblances is fundamentally anchored in a relationship with truth, the reality of God and the cosmos, and the witnessing of the divine. In this sense Corbin is quick to denounce any blurring of the "imaginal" and the "imaginary": the imaginary, he says, as the realm of imagination and fantasy described by modern philosophers since Descartes and Kant, and today celebrated by the media and television ("our civilization of the image") marks de facto the extinction of the active imagination. Modern imagination, he argues, having severed any dimension of witnessing the Real, has become the domain of unreality, illusions, and whims rather comparable to the delusions of the mad and the schizophrenics.

This sharp distinction is in part what I am attempting to blur here, following the suggestion of Ilyas's story itself. It is not that Ilyas is not ill: he himself names the illness, even though he never sees it from the point of view of psychiatry. The question is, rather, if one is to engage with the concept of the imaginal authentically, What is the status of visions and psychotic states? And what is the efficacy of *ta'bīr*, the operation of figuration, or as I called it above, "the interval of the image," in the lives of Ilyas and Samia?

My argument is that the enigmatic address of the Other, which is cited in the painting in the form of the Writing of God's Power, is present, as well, in the work of the images, and in the operation of *ta'bīr*.

Struggle with the Monster: Imagination and Psychotic Existence

Aby Warburg was for a time an inpatient in Ludwig Binswanger's psychiatric clinic at Kreuzlingen in Switzerland.[32] Binswanger's therapeutic relationship with Warburg, in the acute phases of the madness that shattered the life of the art historian between 1921 and 1924, became a dialogue that transformed both the patient and his therapist. For Warburg, it opened up a possibility of existence and some form of healing through a confrontation with what he called the "catastrophe of being." Warburg called this experience of madness his "struggle with the monster," by analogy with the ritual and mythical struggle with the serpent he had observed among Hopi Indians twenty years before. This was evocative of his idea of "*Pathosformeln*" (formulae of pathos), literally formulae by which the powerful contradictory forces he had seen throughout his life as the tragic core of artistic and cultural experience were contracted and transmitted into iconographic forms. For both the patient and the psychiatrist, and in their dialogue through the most acute phases of Warburg's psychosis, there emerged the new ground of a "construction within madness"[33] that could produce novel analytic insights.

I read Binswanger alongside Freud and Lacan on the question of how to apprehend a life, and how to consider psychopathological and psychotic experience. For each, in discrepant but related ways, the question is rooted in the vicissitudes, challenges, and uncertainties of clinical practice, and in an encounter with psychosis in the concrete reality of the hospital. For each, that practice engenders a reflection on truth, desire, and destruction that transcends the context of psychopathology, and yet originates in the neighborhood of madness and in an ethical engagement with it.

In Binswanger's approach (as also in psychoanalysis), the psychopathological symptom is not the sign of a recognizable psychiatric disorder, but the index of a transformation of the soul: "For indeed the symptom (e.g., the flight of ideas, psychomotor inhibition, neologism, stereotypy, etc.), proves to be the expression of a spreading change of the soul, a change of the total form of existence and the total style of life."[34] This does not mean that Binswanger does not make use of diagnostic concepts: his analytic descriptions of mania, depression, melancholy, and what he called schizophrenia are prominent in and across his clinical case histories and are associated with the names of Ellen West, Lola Voss, Ilse, Cecile Munch, and Doctor Anbuhl.[35] Yet, rather than naming manic depression and schizophrenia disease entities, they are better described in his view as "styles" or "modes," in a poetic or musical sense, that capture and structure the rhythm and modulation of an experience.

Deeply influenced by Heidegger and in dialogue with Freud, Binswanger attempted to relate the philosophy of being to the experience of psychopathology and the estrangement and uncanny this entails, seeking to grasp psychosis as a form of life.[36] For Binswanger, dreams, delusions, and other imaginary forms, as well as the very shape of everyday life, are "poetic," in the sense that they are formal articulations immanent to a particular life. They register the expansion or shrinking of existence, its rising and falling, its opening up or its imprisonment.

"The nature of poetic similes," Binswanger writes in *Dream and Existence*, "lies in the deepest roots of our existence [*Existenz*] where the living, spiritual form, and the living, spiritual content are still bound together. When in a bitter disappointment 'we fall from the clouds', then we *actually* do fall . . . Until we can again find a new, firm standing position in the world our own Dasein moves within the meaning matrix of stumbling, sinking, and falling."[37]

For Binswanger imagination partakes of what he calls the "life function," which expresses the "thrownness" of being in the world (*Umwelt*, prior to or beyond its subjectivation), divested of all individuality and qualifications. In dreaming, a key dimension of imagination, existence as such comes to the fore and gives itself from the outside. As Foucault notes in his introduction to Binswanger's text, "in dreaming consciousness sleeps but existence awakens."[38] Awakening can take place only beyond the personal subject: the subject of the dream is not the dreamer but the dream itself—the world in its manifestation. And this is why Foucault can state that dreaming is not "another way of experiencing another world," but "the radical way of experiencing one's own world."[39] In this, Binswanger is for Foucault the heir of a tradition of the imagination as impersonal world-creating process, which in the West he traces back to Aristotle, Plotinus, Spinoza, and the mystics (and in a certain way to psychoanalysis). This is an insight central, as we have seen, to the Islamic tradition of dreaming and the Imagination, which reverberates in Ilyas's story and his painting.

For Binswanger, delusions share the same quality as dreams in that they are imaginary experiences registering movements of being. For this reason, Binswanger says (against Freud), the manifest content of dreams, the dream as visionary experience, should be appreciated in its own right, as an expression of the impersonal "life-function,"[40] and not just for the fact it gives access to unconscious dream-thoughts. The same applies to delusional states: dreams and delusions show the contours of a form of life. They are poems of existence. Delusions are not merely driftings of thought or disturbances of the faculty of judgment: they are manifestations of being, and register its falling, its entering zones of crepuscule, of paralysis; they trace the outline of its contortions and its lapses.

Binswanger writes how in dreams "existence" is visualized pictorially, materialized into an image, as in the "bird dreams," where vision of a falling wounded bird condenses the wounded existence of the subject into an image. This visualization becomes an anchor to the world in moments of vacillation and despair. "Something in me, a part of me," Binswanger writes, "has become a wounded bird of prey."[41] Or as in the cosmic or "oceanic" dreams of dissolution of the body and being: "I found myself in a wondrously different world, in a great ocean where I floated formlessly. From afar I saw the earth and the stars and I felt tremendously free and light, together with an extraordinary sense of power."[42] This aloofness signals for Binswanger a loss of connection to the world, the unbinding of existence sucked into nonbeing.

The structural continuity of delusion and dream does not imply that for Binswanger psychosis is not a pathological experience. And even though the very notions of the "falling" and "rising" have led Binswanger to explore the instability and porosity of the normal and the pathological—in the realm of art, for instance—there is no attempt to dilute the illness of being (the "psychopathological," which Binswanger writes in inverted commas to index that this term belongs to a universe of discourse foreign to the language of *Daseinanalyse*). In several of his case studies (in particular, that of Ellen West), Binswanger suggests that existence is caught in an oscillation between "ascension" into an ethereal world, the "whirling of the flight of ideas," and the "sinking" into the earth and the underground; between the vertical flight of the bird and the horizontal crawling of the earth worm. The sky and the sinking ground are not metaphors; they participate in the materiality of the cosmos and its physical elements. In these configurations of shrinking existence the dimension of "encounter" fades away (the *Mitwelt*, the world-with, and *Eigenwelt*, the internalized awareness of being-with-others).[43] And with it the world itself withdraws, because the world exists as a web of relations and connectedness: "The freedom of letting 'world' occur is replaced by the unfreedom of being overwhelmed by a certain 'world design.'"[44]

For today's humanistic sensibility, raised in the disavowal of the "scandal" of madness, Binswanger's existential approach to the psychotic being-in-the-world may seem harsh and devoid of empathy. And yet, Binswanger says, it is precisely that appreciation of illness as such, the pondering of shrinking existence, and the willingness to listen to it, that is crucial in the therapeutic encounter. It is the willingness to enter the story, in its risings and fallings, to engage with its images, its poetry, and the materiality of a "world design," which paradoxically makes possible a certain sharing, the apprehension of the singular trajectory of a life, and the willingness to engage with its world of shattered forms. In this sense, as pointed out recently by Georges Didi-Huberman, but crucially posed by Freud and Lacan, the "symptom" is not the sign of an illness but a fundamental structure of experience; illness and hence the symptom are "a total vital fact."

The Serpent and the Dynamogram

> For Warburg, the attitude of artists toward images inherited from tradition was therefore conceivable in terms neither of aesthetic choice nor of neutral reception; rather, for him it is a matter of a confrontation—which is lethal or vitalizing, depending on the situation—with the tremendous energies stored in images, which in themselves had the potential either to make man regress into sterile subjection or to direct him on his path toward salvation and knowledge. For Warburg, this was true not only for artists [. . .], but also for historians and scholars, whom he conceives of as extremely sensitive seismographs responding to distant earthquakes, or as "necromancers" who consciously evoke the specters threatening them.
>
> —Giorgio Agamben[45]

Warburg traveled to New Mexico in 1895–96, seeking to follow the affective life of forms outside of the Greek-European civilization, and their insistence, or what he called their after-life (*Nachleben*, survival or posthumous life) in the wake of cultural marginalization and repeated violent obliteration—under conditions of colonial domination, cultural hegemony, and technological modernity. As becomes clear in his later writings, he also sought to explore the way that forms and their multiple inscriptions and reinscriptions—and the question of form as such—express core human conundrums and existential questionings in the midst of and across different traditions: "I shall be content if in the pictures of the daily life and festive activities of the Pueblo Indians I have proved to you that their masked dances are not a game, but the heathen's answer to torturing questions on the why and the wherefore of things."[46]

He did not return to the Pueblo Indian materials until 1923, when he prepared a lecture to present to an audience of patients and medical staff at Ludwig Binswanger's psychiatric clinic in Kreuzlingen, where he had been residing as an inpatient. He was slowly emerging from the illness that had shattered him for over two years. The psychotic phase had been acute: his body in restless "contortions," accompanied by his feeling of being persecuted, tormented, and tortured. Binswanger, his psychiatrist, writes that in his room in the locked ward, Warburg used to endure the torment of the nights talking to moths and butterflies, his "small living souls," the only companions by whom he felt understood and to whom he could tell the story of his illness.

Warburg's lecture was meant to demonstrate to his audience his capacity to think, emerging from the depths of madness, sloughing his skin, like a snake, and returning to his scholarly work. In this sense "A Lecture on Serpent Ritual" marked the beginning of a return. Warburg spoke as much of Hopi kachina mask rituals and of the serpent ritual, as of his own struggle with the "monster" and the uncanny knowledge that was borne of folly, the monster that could never be completely defeated. In revisiting the serpent ritual twenty-eight years later he asked what healing is, and in what mysterious and entangled ways life and death, destruction and creation, are connected in the being of illness and at the innermost core of existence; and of how the symptom, the illness, in the very singularity of its expression participates in the imaginal migration of forms, and hence, in the shared dimension of collective memory.

Among the Hopi in 1895 Warburg had taken photographs of rituals and structures, buildings and the natural environment. His pictures of canyons and rock formations show the writing of time on the landscape, an impersonal memory of shapes at the intersection of the living and the inorganic. He was particularly interested in what he called the serpent ritual (a water rite, in a region marked by perennial drought), which staged the "schizoid nature" of destructive and healing powers, in a struggle that grasped the core sense of existence, and that Warburg referred to as a "dialectic of the Monster." His question among the Hopi, but also his question in general, had to do with the violence of colonization that had obliterated a culture, a world of symbols and a mode of life, and superimposed on it a new life: "modern life," and technological rule, which has no space or time for serpent rituals. He sought to understand the status of "pagan" survivals in the aftermath of Spanish-Catholic colonization, and American recolonization. But the question also had to do with the "interval" of symbolic thought itself. What was the nature of obliteration, survival, and regeneration? What was the relation of catastrophe to emergence, to the insistence of a trace, and to the work of a social memory, transmission and creation? What was the historical and ethical lesson of images, and of the "interval," the "distance," "intercession," introduced by the symbolic mode of thought?

Among the Hopi, Warburg found what he understood as an originary form of such schisms in the unresolved bipolarity of conflicting characters and affects intrinsic to the "symbolic" mode of expression proper to this cultural tradition, and associated with the image and with the heraldic emblem—an intermediary stage between realistic representation and script, image and sign. In that mode, the tragic quality of existence could be seized in the emblematic space of a rite.

An enactment of the fundamental bipolarity of existence at the limit of creation and annihilation, the serpent ritual was also a theater for the work of the "symbolic" itself: what Warburg called the "interval" (*Zwischenraum*), "a kind of no-man's-land at the center of the human."[47] The "symbol" was itself bipolar: the intercessor and the "monster" were intimately connected as the death/poison/folly at the heart of being. The one was never at rest in the other, and the capacity to "see" their co-presence was for Warburg both the ethical lesson and the specific therapeutics of images. This is why the serpent, poison and antidote, monster and symbol "grafted onto one stem," remained for him a central and exemplary image, all the way to the psychiatric clinic and his own experience of madness.

In the written version of the lecture, published after his death, Warburg apologizes for the inadequacy of his recollections of a journey made many years before. Yet, he adds, "I do so in the hope that the direct evidence of the pictures may carry you beyond my words." Images encoded a powerful syntax of symbols, the energetic image-signs he had been seeking and studying, in the live performances of Hopi rituals and in their iconography: affective "evidence" of other lives and worlds in the mode of an *agentive trace*, which has the power to carry us beyond our language, consciousness, and knowledge, and "remember" in us. The realm of the visible bears the mark of a forgotten memory. It is a memory of forms, but also an emergence of form[48] in the mode of *Nachleben*, survival or afterlife, and in the aftermath of disaster: the Spanish-Christian conquest, the bulldozers of American modernity, electricity, railroads, and the school system, the spread of alcoholism and suicide among the Indians. And for Warburg himself, there was the destruction of World War I, the experience of the trenches, which kept coming back in the form of deliria, the catastrophe of language and writing during his illness, the resurfacing of the shape of the serpent in his scrapbooks and his diary, sinuous lines with an arrow: the trenches, the snake-lightening, and the collective history and tragedy of a culture, of which his illness as well as his research were the seismographs.

The "direct evidence of the pictures" had to do with the *force* of images, their "biological necessity" and their potentiality as imprints or forms, active as such, and bearers of social memory. As Agamben points out in his reflection on Warburg's "symbols," which Warburg sometimes called "dynamograms," the social memory stored and transmitted was not folded into the past as the archival record of what had already happened, but projected onto the future as the enigmatic cipher of a confrontation that, depending on the situation, could be either "lethal or vitalizing."[49]

Pathosformeln—literally formulae of pathos—was both direct and indirect. It conveyed pathos, a set of affects, and a force; but encoded into an emblem, constructed as a heterogeneous and contradictory composition of signs to decipher. Image and inscription were "both grafted onto one stem," and their effectiveness had as much to do with the one as with the other.

Back in 1896 Warburg had collected photographs and oral accounts, and had traced the persistence and insistence of the serpent symbol in the drawings and imagination of the contemporary Indians he met. It was the serpent that was at the center of their ritual marked by juggling with poisonous reptiles, *as well* as the "lightning-snake" painted on Hopi vases and vessels (a sinuous line with an arrow, at once snake, lightning, and cosmological inscription): "A drawing that I acquired from an Indian (pl. 44b) proves that what appears as a purely decorative ornament must in fact be interpreted symbolically. One of the basic elements of cosmological imagery—the universe conceived in the form of a house—is united in this drawing with an irrational animal conception, a serpent, which appears as an enigmatic and awe inspiring demon," pointing to the fact that the cosmos itself, in its very order, and the home as ground and locus of belonging, was haunted, endangered, and perhaps even made possible, by the looming and encompassing co-presence of the Serpent: "[we] must not think of this world-house as the simple reflection of a tranquil cosmology. For the mistress of the house is the most fearsome of all beasts—the serpent."[50]

Images, "symbols," which Warburg takes in the late Medieval and Renaissance sense of heraldic emblems, are operators of distance: they are "intervals," at once the rift and the bridge, presence and absence, vitality and inert materiality. Intercessors, they create "spaces for devotion and scope for reason." The ethical nature and healing power of symbols/images resides for Warburg in this bipolar vocation, capable of being at once flesh and spirit, trace/writing and live presence, future and past. This bipolarity is dramatized in a segment of the serpent ritual, when live snakes captured in the desert are thrown into a sand drawing of the snake-lightning symbol; the drawing is obliterated and the snake is covered with sand, the sand of the image, in a spiral movement from image to living creature and from living creature to image, whereby the image is "vitalized," and the living reptile is turned into an emblem staging an exchange of life and death, presence and absence, proximity and infinite distance, future and remote past. The capacity to inhabit and grasp this double movement is for Warburg the presupposition of any possible cure. It is a cure that acknowledges and engages with a dimension of the incurable, and that is healing not just for an individual but for a collectivity, even for the "civilization" of which the person, the symptom, the artist, and the historian or anthropologists are witnesses. In Warburg's words, they are "extremely sensitive seismographs responding to distant earthquakes, or necromancers" who consciously evoke the specters threatening them.

Ilyas is one such seismographer. His repertoire of figures associated with his illness, as well as his own analysis of the nature and work of the images in the "paintings that contain a *ḥāla*" (through the concepts of *ashkāl*, *taʿbīr*, and *ramz*), bear some resemblance to Warburg's dynamograms: forms charged with contradictory and nonpolarized energies, which bridge without resolving incommensurable times, states, and qualities. Stylized figures as well as "affective signs," they are active operators of transformation and unconscious transmission. As Warburg himself experienced in the psychotic illness that afflicted him for the later part of his life, such images and signs are powerful forms that "emerge" in the dissolution of the subject out of the ruins of representation and culture, written in the "contortions" of delusional experience.

"The Hand by Which He Seizes": Melancholia and Transformation

> The normal process of life contains moments as bad as any of those which insane melancholy is filled with, moments in which radical evil gets its innings and takes its solid turns. The lunatic's visions of horror are all drawn from the material of daily fact. . . . To believe in the carnivorous reptiles of geological times is hard for our imagination, they seem too much like mere museums specimens. . . . Crocodiles and rattlesnakes and pythons are at this moment vessels of life as real as we are.
>
> —William James[51]

Samia describes the snake as a *waḥsh* (monster, beast), a dreadful apparition that is a visualization and manifestation of Ilyas's madness. It is a surfacing of the serpent as "the most fearful of all beasts," as Warburg says of the Hopi symbol of the serpent, a beast located in the intimacy of the home. Ilyas listens and does not disagree. Samia is a witness in the lapses of his life. The Serpent, he knows, "is the torment of life."

Yet, as I look at it, I see a figure at once pained and gentle, a wounded creature, whose bodily features recall some of the other drawings on the walls, hybrid feminine images of maritime inspiration, with their flexing fish bodies and their skin covered by scales. The small head, the elongated eye, the closed mouth, connote vulnerability, and a melancholic beauty. The composition winds, curves, and folds into itself as if protecting a life, or a gaze within. Is it a gaze the painting seeks to shelter, or is it a harmful gaze? "The eye in the picture gazes at all life around," Ilyas says. But from outside of life. It is the gaze of things, the gaze of death looking back at us humans.[52] The eye (*ʿayn*) is important motif in Maghribi iconography: source, origin, letter of the alphabet, predatory violence of and protection against the gaze—of the evil eye (*ʿayn*).

We are looking at the painting: but the painting is looking at us from the infinite distance of its nonhuman eye.

There is abandonment in the shapes, a sense of life shrinking. The only two elements in the composition that are fixed and formally heterogeneous to the scene are the calligraphic inscription of God's power, *Lā ghāliba illā llāh* ("No one is victorious except God"), on the left side, and the key and chains on the right side. The space of the key is isolated, as if selected out of the picture. And in fact Ilyas asserts that both the writing and the key "don't follow the logic of the illness, of the Snake, but follow instead the logic of Divine Power."

While the picture is entirely full (Ilyas said that he filled it with the waves, the clouds, and the smoke), the space of the key is empty, and carefully drawn in its contours. The arm that holds the key appears as if brandishing a weapon. And there are the two little arms, the arm that holds the sword but cannot strike (the sword cannot protect him from the illness, it is God's instrument and is subjected to God's will) and the arm that strives to grab the key but cannot reach it—echo, on the front door of the house, of an arm too short to grab a fruit it cannot reach. Arms that cannot reach, that cannot strike—on the door—an empty hand, unable to provide, all are scenes of disablement. But there is more: the second arm can be seen in a reflexive movement of striking the snake. Where the arm is attached to the body of the snake there is a wound, and the mark of bleeding. The snake-torturer, imaginal presentation of madness, is also a victim of torture. We can see, with the intercession of Warburg's reflections on the serpent ritual as a "dialectic of the monster," that Ilyas's snake is a "bipolar" image, staging a never-resolved theater of destruction and healing. A mythological image of terror, and a visualization of the Illness, the snake is also the self, the soul (*al-nafs, al-rūḥ*) in agony under attack, exposed, wounded, and tortured, and experiencing pleasure at the same time.

The place of God in the picture, marked by the writing and the key, should be reflected upon. The "writing" is the inscription of a Qurʾanic utterance, a recitation that is also a divine "interruption" and command. In his "unconsciousness" (*bi-lā shuʿūr*) the painter knows that the ultimate appeal is in God. But there is no salvation. The serpent and the Qurʾanic writing are not the elements and the theme of his delusion (as might be suggested in the language of psychiatry), but the terrain and the weapons of a confrontation. The struggle happens when Ilyas's faculties of sensory perception are eclipsed and when, as Binswanger puts it, existence is exposed, beyond all personal life. It happens on an imaginal stage that is also the stage of the soul (*nafs*), and which resembles the dramaturgy of the Qurʾanic cure called *al-ruqya*, a liturgy where the religious therapist recites the Qurʾan over the body of the afflicted struck by an illness of demonic origin. The divine utterance intervenes or descends as an incision that interrupts, and opens the space of a struggle. In that struggle, the jinn and the soul (*nafs*) keep exchanging places, and alternatingly the one and the other are tortured in the always-vulnerable perspective of deliverance.[53] This is not to say that the confrontation in Ilyas's painting can be translated into a ritual of de-possession, one that he never had wanted to seek; but that, as I will show in part three of the book, the ritual of de-possession itself opens onto an imaginal space where the question of being, madness, and divine interruption takes center stage.

We should take a step back and ponder Ilyas's visualization of the self in despair in the temptation of suicide and in the agony of death. Three crosses, staging the scene of the crucifixion of Christ, cast the painting in a sacrificial mode. But why the Christian reference, while the Islamic tradition, all the way to popular ritual practices, has its own repertoire of sacrificial and martyrological images?

"The French-Christian cemetery" (*rawḍa diyāl naṣārā*), Samia said in explaining the painting. She went on to say that when Ilyas is ill he is "colonized by the insignia of the Christians" (*mustaʿmar bi ʿalāmat al-naṣārā*), and he speaks mostly in French—a language he never spoke with me, even though I am European. The place of the cross in the painting and the Christian imaginary are even more salient when one notes that the Serpent—an Islamic figure of an impious death and of the torment of the grave—is also a visionary citation of Saint John's Apocalypse, of the final combat with the Beast and the multiple monstrous beings of the Apocalypse: the red Dragon, its combat with the Woman and with the Archangel Michael ("And there happened a battle in the sky: Michael and his angels against the dragon, and the dragon stroke back . . . and he was crashed, the dragon, the great, the ancient serpent called devil and Satan, the one who drives to ruin the inhabited earth"), the Beast of the earth and the Beast of the sea ("I have seen another Beast coming out of the earth: it has horns like a lamb and roars like a dragon").[54] Here again, as in the case of the snake in the painting, the Christian reference is double: an image of damnation, in which the Christian self is damned; and an image of salvation, where the dragon is killed by the angel.

From the perspective of the inscription *Lā ghāliba illā llāh* ("No one is victorious except God"), the painting is a scene of damnation. The self in despair has repudiated Islam: he is an impious soul, a hypocrite, or a denying disbeliever (*kāfir*). (While strictly speaking Christians are not *kuffār* [sing. *kāfir*], in the popular imagination they are perceived as such. In Morocco there are no Christians of the Eastern churches, and Christian only means European, associated with the former colonizer.) And suicide is forbidden in Islam, because the lifespan of creatures is determined by God.[55] The self-in-despair loses all hope of salvation, for it has already strayed out of the path of God. The sword in the painting cannot fight the illness because the hand that holds it is not authorized by God.

From that perspective the painting stages the eschatological scene of the torture of the grave (*ʿadhāb al-qabr*), where serpents and scorpions torment the body of the impious immediately after death. The snake evokes then a family of snakes in the apocalyptic bestiaries of popular books on death and its aftermath, in the classical genre of a theological literature on death, which finds its roots in early commentaries on the Qurʾan and the hadith, systematized by among others the texts of Abu Hamid al-Ghazali (d. AH 505/1111 CE) and Abu Abdullah al-Qurtubi (d. AH 671/1273 CE), a genre that extends all the way to the contemporary booklet by the Egyptian Shaykh ʿAli Ahmad Tahtawi, *Aḥwāl al-qubūr* ("Terrors of the Graves").

The cartoonish cobra on the cover of Tahtawi's book (perhaps the booklet Ilyas brought home one day) has a mouth drawn open, throwing fire, crushing the body of the damned, and pushing it underground. The text itself, popularizing al-Ghazali's meditative exposition of death and the afterlife, is divided into three sections: the state of the person in the world prior to the "taking of the soul (*rūḥ*)" (at the moment of death); the state at the moment of death (the taking of the *rūḥ*); and the state after death when awaiting Judgment. Sayings of the Prophet (hadiths) are cited to describe the blessed death of the pious, who are not fearful of passing because death in this world will awaken the vision of God, and the cursed death of the impious, those who refuse to die and who will be tortured in the tomb. At once inflicting torture and being tortured, the snake in Ilyas's painting is also the soul subjected to the torment of the grave.

Tahtawi's booklet cites a famous hadith, transmitted by *Ṣaḥīḥ al-Bukhārī* and multiple others, and originally attributed to Abu Hurayra, which describes the empowerment of the self as a divine empowerment, the fact of one's hand becoming the hand of God, and the impairment of the self as form of "divine disabling":

> The Prophet said that God said:
>
>> The one who seeks my protection, I authorize him to go to war. And my slave can become closer to me by practicing the things that I prefer, rather than those that I order him to do. And if he keeps coming close to me with his prayer, I start loving him. And when I love him, I become the ear by which he hears, the sight by which he sees, the hand by which he seizes and can overpower the enemy (*yabtushu*), the foot by which he walks.[56]

The same impairment of the hand, and inability to reach salvation, is found in the painting of the tree, on the door of Ilyas and Samia's house.

He painted this picture during the time when Samia's brothers and family were accusing him of not providing for her, he said, of being inactive and worthless. Ilyas is the figure on the left: "my hand is empty" (*yddī fārigh*). Samia is the figure to the right, who attempts to grab an apple from the tree but cannot reach. She is moved by this interpretation, about the apple and the empty hand. Why hasn't he told her earlier, this would have explained so many things. He couldn't have told her; it was too hurtful. She says it wouldn't have been hurtful; what was hurtful was his silence, his absences, and the fact that he spoke with her brothers about her, but not directly to her. Around the paintings they both stage their delicate work of repair.[57]

From: stefania pandolfo

Date: Sat, Aug 1, 2009 at 7:04 PM

Subject: (no subject)

I came back yesterday and went to see Ilyas this afternoon. He had called me to say that he had completed a painting of the neighborhood on the canvas I had given him before I left. But when I called this morning and Samia answered the phone I knew that she wasn't well: *muʿaṣṣba*, she said. She was surprised that I could hear that in her voice.

As soon as I arrived she started crying, her mother was there, then left. She was angry at Ilyas, who was silent and sad, and took me to the kitchen where he was making tea to show me three paintings he had made recently—from the "torment" of these past few days, he said. I attach the pictures. The first is the pink one, with two eggs, so to speak, with him and her. She is shown as a baby—gone back to be an infant, he said, with all the ghosts and phantasms (*wahm*) she was tormented by when she was a child. Snakes and scorpions express the imaginations of harm, the things that terrified her. In the other egg, black, the silhouette of a man chain-smoking, lost on a planet where there is only solitude and anguish (reminded me of *Le Petit prince* of Saint-Exupéry). They can't communicate, their worlds don't intersect. In a second painting he represented her madness, and his despair, his own drowning. Her madness is represented by a snake, with a feminine face. The theme of the snake keeps returning. In the center, a cross (always a cross, symbol of his death, his suicide, always expressed by him in Christian terms), and his broken heart. A third painting rehearses again the theme of the tree of life. It is the same tree as in the painting on the door he gave me. Now, he said, the tree of life has died, it is only dead wood, and they are parting, splitting up in opposite directions. After a while, I asked their little girl to go play outside, and invited them to talk, with me, and with each other. It was strange, but also possible. In whatever strange overlapping of worlds, I was a witness to their story. I thought to myself that perhaps I should go. But I stayed. A strange conversation. As if feelings were simply exposed. As if I was literally part of the story, or I was their archive, and could, should, speak back. Samia was on the way to an episode. Her eyes were circled by lack of sleep. Ilyas took me aside and said that now that she was ill, he was in her eyes the source of everything harmful, and he couldn't stand it anymore.

So I asked her why she was so angry at Ilyas. I was thinking about their story, and the way I wrote their story as a story of love in the surroundings of the incommensurable Real of their experience of madness. I knew, even in the past, that there must have been times when anger took the place of love, and that too must be heard. Today it was a day of anger. She wanted him to take responsibility for his wife and his daughter, to go to work, to make some money so that she might be able to buy her medications. He responded that he does work, that he does buy her medications, but that sometimes he has no money, and that he cannot find work. She yelled her resentment at his paintings, the painting she usually likes so much. She said, "At least he can paint, he is sick, he paints, he expresses (*key'abbar*), and feels better, while I have nothing, and have to swallow everything inside, harbor everything inside, and it kills me."

At some point I intervened. I told her that Ilyas, as she herself had always told me, was a different kind of person. He was spiritual (*rūḥānī*), visionary but also kind. He was hurt by what she was saying, even though he said that he knew that she spoke like this when she was sick. He said very often she couldn't get up, and when he came home from work there was nothing to eat, and he had to go back to work on an empty stomach. We talked about the deeper things. Her abandonment as a child. When she falls prey to this "state" (*ḥāla*), she goes back to that moment in her life—the thing Ilyas painted in her image—and becomes resentful, angry, demands love and also pushes it away. She cried, and screamed that yes, he had changed, at the beginning he was love (*l-ḥanān*). Once she was pregnant and wanted grapes, and he couldn't find grapes, and so he made a painting of grapes for her!

It turned out that she had not taken her meds for a while, the antidepressant and the antipsychotic. She cried and Ilyas felt, he said, that he was sinking, that their paths were parting, that he was himself sliding into madness because of the way she was. Finally she collapsed, lay down, and her anger gave way in to an immense vulnerability. And he took her in his arms, and held her there for a long time, while she fell asleep in his arms.

Ilyas then walked me to the road outside, outside of the neighborhood, where it is possible to find public transportation. It was past 8 p.m., everyone was out. We saw many sub-Saharan African youth, many more than in the past; they had come across the Sahara, and many more had not survived in the passage; they were in transit to Europe, but stuck here forever now, mixing with people in the neighborhood, and with the Moroccan youth who, like them, are consumed by a longing and resolution to migrate.

Coda: August 2012

In August 2012 I asked Ilyas whether he would give me permission to publish the photographs of his mural paintings in this book; the photographs I had taken, with his and Samia's help, back in 2005, and before he whitewashed the walls of his apartment and covered the murals over. There were also other photographs, of other paintings, on cardboard or plywood; the series of small paintings that he had made in 2009 and 2010, including the melancholy self-portrait he called "imprisoned in life." And there were the photographs of the painting of the Tree of Life (*shajarat al-ḥayāt*) on the door that he had given me in consignment, back in 2005. And the paintings of the she-snake, which Samia asked me to keep, with the Tree and the door, on her behalf but not too far away, in Rabat, not in the US. Although she preferred not to have those images of their illness and healing in the house, she wanted them kept within reach.

Ilyas replied that he had no objection to publishing the photographs, which now remained the only visible record of his most beautiful and expressive paintings. I explained that it wouldn't be for an art book, even though I hoped that the images would someday appear in such a book; that they would be published in a book titled "Knot of the Soul," I said in Arabic, *'uqdat al-nafs*, a book that was my attempt to reflect on the lives and ties that people weave in the proximity of madness.

I told them that I would try to rely on the paintings themselves to tell their story. I said that I would try to show how over the years and until today the paintings had been for them not just the stage of encountering their illnesses, but also a kind of cure (*'ilāj*).

Ilyas's response was that he hoped their story might offer hope or some kind of insight to those others who might recognize their own troubles in their story and in my book, and that his paintings might open a path for someone in their own struggles with troubles of the soul. Samia on the other hand reminded me that the paintings, and also their power to cure, bore witness to a story of love.

SIX

The Burning

When you recall the Departed, count yourself as one of them.

—al-Ghazali

More real than your waking but not real enough, your journey carries you through an illucid world—the stranger leading you and does not know which way to go. No longer in the land of the living, but in the midst of a memory, what you inhabit is coming out of another time entirely, a future awaited and made possible by what takes you inward, moving, moment by moment, towards the tomb.

—David Marriott, "Only Sleeping"[1]

Mghāmar b l-ḥayāt: Migration, Transgression, the Limit of Heresy and that of Life

We are discussing the question of risk—the risk to one's life, in the crossing—the sense of one's death, if one dies, and the moral conundrum this produces. The three of us, sitting in a public park under the old eucalyptus trees that date back to the colonial period. Coming out of the neighborhoods to places where "nature" (*ṭabīʿa*), as they say, gives a sense of space, has become one of the rites of our encounters.

Eucalyptuses are not native to the Maghreb. The French brought them to facilitate the forced settlement of populations and the creation of agrarian lands. Everywhere they are, alongside the pleasure of their shade and fragrance, they carry that silent memory of abuse.[2] We sit at the table of an outdoor café that today is closed, in the shade of the eucalyptus trees. As much as these youths like this park, they are reluctant to mix with people walking and exercising, families picnicking, while they are reflecting on the forms of alienation that infiltrate their lives. "The day has eyes and the night has ears," Kamal warned me once, one of the first times we met.

Kamal and Jawad are forcefully disagreeing on the meaning and moral evaluation of the attempt at migration (*muḥāwala*, "attempt" or "endeavor"), a "crossing" Kamal has singlemindedly if unsuccessfully pursued for a long time. A theological dispute unfolds about the status and nature of death in the "attempt" at illegal migration, universally known as *l-ḥarg*, the "burning," and of what they call *l-qanṭ* (classical Arabic, *al-qanaṭ*), the condition of "despair"—the temptation to do away with life, the loss of all hope, in the religious sense, as well as, in the vernacular sense, a feeling of oppression, apathy, absence of horizon.

JAWAD:[3] Just look at how many people die each day in the boats (*lancia*, the boats that attempt to cross illegally to Spain from the Moroccan shore). Each day the news tells you how many, shows you the images. You could be one of them, your life wasted (*mshiti mdiʿ*). We say that the person who is risking the crossing is putting his life in danger (*mkhāṭar b-ḥayātuh*), that is, he embarks on a mortal journey—gambling with his life (*mghāmar b-ḥayātuh*). Each day, when you look at the news, you think that you could be one of those corpses floating on the water. There is no exit. They find themselves against a wall, have no perspective here, no exit, and when they get there, if they do arrive, have the problem of the papers and all that, no exit there.

STEFANIA: Against a wall, for them there is no landing and no return. Do they know this when they decide to go?

KAMAL: Those who decide to go know kids over there, for the most part they have a *damen*, a "guarantor," a protection, someone on the other side who gives them a map of the situation, tells them what to expect. But in truth one who decides to leave is *ḥayr*, beside himself, furious, bewildered, and his feelings are flooded by exasperation with the present conditions of life. He's in a rage: blood has gone up his head, and doesn't care whether he will die (*ḥayr, ṭalaʿ lu ddim f-rras, maʿandu gharad wash ghadi ymut*).

JAWAD: The one who has no protection and still wants to get across will either die or ruin his life. Of a hundred that go, ninety will die; ten will survive and fall into the hands of the Spanish police.

STEFANIA: How does one understand death in the crossing according to the teachings of Islam?

JAWAD: It is a suicide (*intihār*).

KAMAL: Why suicide? I disagree with you brother, it is not a suicide . . .

JAWAD: You go gambling with your life (*ghadi mghāmar b rasek*), in other words, you have chosen to die, in full awareness (*katdir f-belek ghadi tmut*). The one who died at sea, we say, he's taking a gamble with his life (*mghāmar b-ḥayātuh*). Either he will live or he will die, and if he died, he had already chosen death, without waiting for the time appointed (*met b-lā khaṭar*). He throws himself into an illusion, that's what we call rushing off into the forbidden (*kaysimma dfa` rasu f-l-ḥarām*).

KAMAL: What else could he do?

JAWAD: This is the problem, this is what happened to you and caused you [Kamal] to burn (*hadi hiyya l-mushkila llī ja'ala lak ḥatta ḥargti*).

KAMAL: What else could you do, become a thief (*sraq*)?

The theological turn of our discussion is not a surprise. Since the earliest conversations about migration and "burning" I realized that as soon as the question of the decision to migrate is raised, one finds oneself speaking in several registers at once: the narrative conventions are blurred. There is first the project of migration as a concrete reality of "this" world, an individual and political response to a situation of closure and alienation and injustice, a departure from a nonlife towards the horizon of a life that might enable a claim to symbolic recognition.

This worldly sense opens to the larger imagining of the migratory project as a venture, a dangerous journey. It is the necessary risk to take if one is to cross over to the other side (of the Mediterranean), with all that this entails; the anticipation and fear, but also the skills, knowledge, sheer ability, and not last, the fascination and excitement. This is the sense reckoned by the concept of *al-riḥla*, which could be translated as a journey, as moving in space, and which defines a whole genre in classical Arab geography and travel narratives that are also, often, tales of marvelous encounters with the unknown and the uncanny (*al-gharīb*). Awareness of a mortal risk in this endeavor is conveyed by the generalized use, in the language of Burning, of the verb *ghāmura* (in the fragment above, *ghadi mghāmar bi rāsak*, you go gambling with your life), "embarking on a hazardous adventure," risking one's life, connoting the potentiality of a destructive outcome.

Both senses of worldly travel are intimately connected to a theological and moral dimension of "departing": the fact of severing familial ties, exiting, choosing exile, or crossing to another world. It is the meaning mobilized by the concept of *hijra* as discussed in the Qur'an and in the hadith, even through its modernist interpretations. *Hijra*, literally the fact of "abandoning" or "severing the ties,"[4] is a foundational concept in Islam. It sets the conditions of a specific ethics, no longer based on genealogical attachment but instead upon a community to come.[5]

Migration—which is increasingly understood as the compelling yet often unrealizable project of an undocumented crossing to Europe—has profoundly changed its connotation since the closure of European borders in the last two decades. One says *kanriski*, "I'm taking the risk," in a mix of Arabic and French, to signify the clandestine departure, hidden in the bottom of a truck, or by hazardous sea passage; a departure that is also called *l-ḥarg*, "the Burning" (from the verb *ḥaraqa*, "to burn"). In the metaphor and the discourse of *l-ḥarg*, incineration, burning, transgression (in the sense that one also says *ḥargt l-feu rouge*, I "burned," that is, went through, a red light)—clandestine migration, which in standard Arabic and by the media is called "secret migration" (*ḥijra sirriyya*)—and in the stories of the *ḥarraga* with whom I spoke, there is reference made to a heterogeneous configuration relating to the figure of a "burned" life—a life without name, and without legitimacy; a life of enclosure in physical, genealogical, and cultural spaces perceived as uninhabitable; and the search for a horizon in the practices of self-creation and experimentation, drawing on an imaginary of the elsewhere and of exile.

The use of language is itself affected: Kamal, Jawad, and the others speak Arabic with a Moroccan accent, but their preferred idiom is a form of standard Arabic that is increasingly a lingua franca for those who speak with a larger Arabic audience in mind. From our first encounters our conversations unfolded in a shifting realm between geography and theology, between a disenchanted sociopolitical description of exclusion and a moral account of banishment and transgression; between the violation of the law of states (by the illicit trespassing of frontiers) and that of the law of God; between a mode of personal narrative and one of moral admonition; between life and death, this world and the other.

The shifting realm of our conversations is also voicing a hesitation between orthodoxy and heresy, belief and unbelief, in the account of personal lives, as in the turn of theological discussions. By attempting to inhabit this rift, and by elaborating a way of "remembering death" in their everyday life experience, the youths with whom I talked carve a possible space of critique by drawing on vocabularies and looking for answers in the Islamic tradition. I trace the way their accounts open to an eschatological elsewhere, which is not a closed hermeneutic horizon but an open imaginal space.[6] I see there the work of a creative imagination, with and against the limits of one's cultural universe.[7]

The predicament of migration and "burning" took on a new urgency in the wake of the "suicide" bombings of May 16, 2003,[8] in Casablanca, which brought to the forefront of the Moroccan public debate, for better or for worse, a situation of social and political exclusion, the existence of vast zones of nonrights and social abandonment, the lack of horizon and the rage that characterize the condition of the youth and are expressed in the attempt at migration, as well as, as at the time was increasingly argued in the press, in the turn to political Islam. In the days immediately following the events in Casablanca, an association was hammered firm in public discourse between underserved urban areas, shantytowns, Islamic radicalism, and international terrorism.[9] Journalists interviewing relatives and neighbors of the "kamikaze" at "Kamikaze-city," as shantytowns were dubbed in the press, found themselves unwittingly contributing to the criminalization of the urban poor, which was accompanied by a call for urban reform but most fundamentally translated into a period of massive police repression.[10]

A few days after the events in Casablanca I was able to meet with Kamal. We went to the green area around the university, it was mid-May, the sun was hot, but Kamal was wearing a heavy coat. He was sick, he told me, because of something that happened in the neighborhood, the murder of a young man who years before had attacked him with a knife. Kamal had never forgotten, and the hurt was never appeased. But now when he heard the news of the other youth's death the memory, and the paradoxical pain of seeing the other's death, came back all at once. He was sick to the point of not being able to speak or go to the funeral. This coincided with the events in Casablanca, and then the police raids in low-income neighborhoods, including his own. "Casablanca is too raw to discuss," he told me. But when were driving back we passed by one of the oversized posters that populated the public space since the Casablanca events: A hand of Fatima, red on white background, with the written intimation, in colloquial Arabic and French, "Don't Touch My Country." "It is as if this is their country, and neighborhoods like ours are the enemy . . ."

Kamal and Jawad come from the same neighborhood, the same as Ilyas and Samia, a former shantytown in the near periphery of Rabat, one of the neighborhoods that gathered population from the early rural exodus of the 1960s and '70s. They refer to it as *l-huma*, our neighborhood, a term that conveys a sense of physical belonging that can turn into ambivalent rejection but cannot be anodyne. A landscape made of informal housing settlements often without infrastructure, unfinished cement buildings that will perhaps never be finished and are inhabited as such, large avenues bordered by *terrains vagues* where children play and people gather in the afternoon.

Downhill from the neighborhood is a swampy area bordering the freeway to Tangiers, the gateway to Europe, and an industrial zone with textile factories that get commissions from European companies (the *sharikāt*) and employ an underpaid, noncontractual, mainly female labor force drawn from the surrounding areas. Each day long-distance trucks for international transport come to load and unload, and each day youths from the neighborhood hope to make an "attempt" (*muḥāwala*), as they call it, by hiding in the trucks all the way across the Spanish border.[11]

Neighborhoods such as these, which according to official estimates make up about 30 percent of housing in urban areas,[12] came under the scrutiny of state security forces as well as to the attention of the national and international press after the 2003 Casablanca bombings. The perpetrators of the bombings were youths from the shantytown of Sidi Moumen, within the larger perimeter of the city of Casablanca. Shantytowns, according to the same official estimates, represent about 10 percent of the urban housing stock. Both forms belong to the so-called informal housing sector that has plagued Moroccan cities since the beginning of the twentieth century. (The first *bidonville*—the local French appellation for these makeshift dwellings built with scraps of can metal collected from waste—was created by Moroccan construction workers brought to Casablanca by the French colonial administration to build the modern European part of the city.)

For more than three decades, and well after World War II, the French colonial authorities never considered that the housing needs of Moroccans might become a political liability, and a housing policy was initiated only in 1949, as a response to the rise of the independence movement. Such a policy primarily consisted of relocating shantytown dwellers to new sites where they were provided with small lots (400 to 600 sq. ft.) unevenly equipped with sewers, electricity, and running water. This policy resulted in the implementation of a vast housing program, which was carried on after Independence (1956), but came to a halt by 1967. With a change in the political orientation of the country, and with new economic priorities, the necessary financial subsidies were no longer available. It is then that the turn to informality began. A decision was made to allow the housing sector, or at least the portion supplied through state subsidies, to go informal, a fact that immediately translated into the growth of a large sector averaging between 25 and 30 percent of the national housing market. Even more impressive was the development of the informal sector in cities such as Sale, where it was estimated to reach 90 percent of the annual housing production.[13]

Despite the implicit social contract presupposed in such use of urban space, the recent history of Morocco has been punctuated by the recurring eruption of violence originating from dispossessed neighborhoods. In Casablanca, Marrakesh, Fes, and Nador insurrections broke out in 1981 (known as "the bread riots") and in 1984.[14] Protest was suppressed with great violence by the state, resulting in thousands of casualties.

The May 2003 bombings in Casablanca brought to the fore of public discourse the recurring political question of urban social exclusion and violence. And again suppression and hundreds of arrests, side by side with techniques of city planning, were put to work. A new housing program called "Villes sans bidonvilles" (cities without shantytowns) was devised, according to which shantytowns throughout the country were to be eradicated by 2010.

At the time of the 2003 Casablanca events I was doing fieldwork in Rabat. The political moment—it was also the time of the Iraq invasion—necessarily affected my research and the conversations I had. It also affected how I thought of writing: I hesitated between the responsibility I felt to convey the experiences and thoughts that were entrusted to me by my interlocutors, and the concern that those same experiences and thoughts might reinforce the common figures of public debate, feeding the phantasm of an official discourse on violence. Later, as I was writing, I realized that the conversations I had indexed a completely different set of realities and conceptual possibilities from those represented in public discourse. They demonstrated the presence of debate, in the strongest sense of "argumentation," unfolding within the terms of a religious reasoning that was both creative and experimental. They suggested the forms of a lucid reflection on despair, dispossession, and depersonalization, as well as on the possibility and risk of those states, in an existential and a theological sense. And they were furrowed by questions insistently asked, in the lives of my interlocutors, about the meaning of it all.

Kamal is twenty-six. The first time we met he told me, as if to recapitulate his existential posture in a visual image, how he spent most nights on the hill overlooking the neighborhood and the textile factories, gazing at the freeway with his binoculars. He jokes about his posture as a night creature, one he shares with his close friends, each of whom had withdrawn from social life in the neighborhood and as much as possible from interaction with their family. After five years of waiting and attempting, he has perhaps lost faith in the possibility of actually getting across the border. Yet his position, as that of many others, remains one of self-imposed exile—a "refusal" born of disillusionment, and of a lucid assessment of political realities. If only by a wish or aspiration, he refuses to participate in the "conviviality" of power relations—the blurring of "eating" and "being eaten" at the same table, in a mode of psychopolitical domination wherein symbolic recognition takes the form of voluntary servitude.[15]

Kamal is unmarried, went to school until about age fifteen, and after several failed efforts (he once worked at one of the factories as an office clerk, and later unloading trucks) gave up on finding a job in Morocco and determined to leave at all costs. He introduced me to Jawad as his counterpoint, someone who had instead chosen to stay. Jawad remained in school longer, almost reaching the baccalaureate, but lost his father to illness at the age of sixteen and was led out of school by lack of support. No one in his family helped him. He shares with Kamal a critical awareness of exclusion and injustice, of abusive power relations, and of the reality of social abandonment, but has a different approach to life that relies, to a certain extent, on his understanding of Islam in terms of the virtue of patience. He is married and has a young daughter, does not have a permanent job, but each day sets out to seek temporary employment as a car mechanic, while on weekends he plays the violin at weddings and other social events. He is aware that in religious reformist circles *shaʿbī* (popular) music is considered impious—but he is not disturbed by this judgment, which he considers too rigid. By contrast, he is inflexible on the question of risking one's life in the migratory attempt. In his view putting one's life at risk is a religious transgression (*maʿṣiyya*), a sin. Suicide (*al-intiḥār*) is prohibited in Islam; both the actual act of killing oneself, as well as just "hoping for death" (*tamannā al-mawt*).[16] In this sense, Jawad argues, the Burning is an ultimate rebellion against God, equivalent, he argues, to an act of apostasy (*shirk*, denying the oneness of God). Because the person who gambles with life doesn't wait for the time chosen by God, and pursues his or her own cause of death, what Jawad glosses as an "improper" death. In his view, there is value in the fact of living as such, however unbearable its present condition; not because human life is inviolable, but because no one has access to the knowledge of God and it is God who gives and takes life.

Kamal disagrees. He counters that, for someone like himself, the attempt at crossing to Europe and the risk of death this entails are not a challenge to God, but an ethical struggle for a better life. He argues this in terms of injustice, the notion of a life that has lost all value, that has been humiliated and degraded, and in terms of the Islamic ethical concept of *jihād al-nafs*, the "effort" of the self, the "struggle," against one's worldly desires and towards a possible future in a situation in which all paths are barred. Jawad argues for patience, the virtue of *al-ṣabr*; Kamal expresses and seeks to justify impatience as a moral struggle on the part of the self, as a religiously granted exception in a time of oppression.

Jawad is referring to the theological and ethical question of the limit of human freedom in despair. In different ways both Ibn Miskawayh (d. AH 421/1030 CE) and al-Ghazali discuss the importance of containing anger and learning to lead a balanced life, both through self-discipline and prayer, and through trust in the mercy of God (*rajā'*). In particular Ibn Miskawayh raises the issue of "false virtues," maladies of the soul that model themselves on virtues while instead perverting their nature. True courage, he writes, is the opposite of taking unnecessary risks with one's life, even in battle. More courage is required to face the agony of death in one's bed, when death comes at its appointed time, than to expose oneself to an enemy strike in misplaced acts of courage.[17] Jawad has not read Miskawayh; he might have been introduced to al-Ghazali's ideas in school, or in the booklets that circulate as a popular religious pedagogical literature, through cassette tapes of sermons, and television and radio programs that host lectures on Islam and daily question-and-answer sessions with *mufti*s and scholars. Jawad's pronouncements, however, are also deeply rooted in the popular religious imagination, which is the terrain upon and against which further elaborations have developed. The virtue of patience and endurance, the recognition of the unfathomable knowledge of God and a structural blindness of the faithful, the value of leading a balanced existence, without giving in to anger and to the influence of unrestrained passions, are present in the vernacular as much as the literate understanding of what a good life might be.

But Kamal disagrees; he appeals to the appropriateness of the emotional surge, a passionate unrest, in the present situation (the feeling of being in *ḥayr*, fury, exasperation—a condition that shares a familiarity with anger and trance and overwhelming confusion), and to the legitimacy of the "effort," which is also a struggle for life in a situation in which life is unlivable and a change of conditions is called for. He opposes the attempt at migration to the available alternative of losing moral integrity (becoming a thief); and in the Qur'an it is clearly stated that the oppressed has an obligation to migrate rather than risk losing moral integrity or faith. Finally, he introduces the pivotal concept of "despair," both in the existential and in the theological sense.

As becomes clear in the exchange below, Kamal's position is complex. In one sense, it is reminiscent of certain currents of the contemporary Islamic Revival in Morocco and elsewhere, which establish a close relationship between a denunciation of social injustice, of alienation and marginalization, and the ethical-theological project of living in the ways of God (*fī sabīl allāh*)—if necessary, by choosing exile or engaging in rebellion. The writings of the Egyptian Sayyid Qutb and the Iranian Ali Shariati in particular set forth the notion of individual agency and responsibility in the struggle, which is *at once* a struggle for this world and the other, and which may result in death, a death that can be understood as martyrdom. Perhaps most prominently, in Kamal's position can be heard the intellectual influence of Shaykh Abdessalam Yassine, founder of the Moroccan movement *al-ʿAdl wa al-iḥsān* (generally translated as "Justice and Spirituality"),[18] which has an important grassroots constituency. In his writings as in his teaching, Shaykh Yassine offered an original synthesis of, on the one hand, Sufi affective and prophetic registers, visionary experiences, and pedagogical practices, with, on the other hand, the contemporary concerns and political critique characteristic of modernist and revolutionary Islamic Revival, all the while explicitly drawing inspiration from the work and life of al-Ghazali.[19]

It should be noted, however, that the link between social critique and eschatological concerns as such is not unique to the Islamic Revival over our past century. It holds an important place in classical Islam from the formative period and persists in a continuous way in vernacular practice. It is associated with the Qur'anic imperative, so variously understood, of *al-amr bi-l-maʿrūf wa l-nahī ʿan al-munkar* (advocating good and denouncing evil), which, at least in the hagiographic recollection, has opposed the "fury" of contestation in the name of God's way to the unjust domination of rulers.[20]

In another sense, however, Kamal's position is yet more complex. He reflects, debates, and explores possibilities and the limits of his thought, in the laboratory of his own life. And in that searching, which as such has an experimental character, he finds himself confronting the limits of belonging, as well as the limits of faith.

Jawad reiterates his point.

JAWAD: He pushes to a limit [while it is God who sets the limits in his law], he may live or he may die, he may succeed and reach his goal, as he may die (*kayt ʿaṭe waḥed l-ḥadd, imma ghadi iḥya imma imūt*).

STEFANIA: Why is this wrong?

JAWAD: Because he sets a "limit" to his life on the base of this alternative, he gambles with his life: he'll succeed in getting where he may find work, or he will die. On the other hand if he had stayed home he might have eventually found work, and in any case he would be still alive: for life as such is a "work," and as long as you are alive you have "work" ahead of you [in the moral sense of doing good works] (*ma haddak 'aysh 'andak waḥed l'amal*).

KAMAL: I disagree.

JAWAD: I said it's a suicide!

KAMAL: No! It is not a suicide. We speak of suicide when a person can't stand it anymore, blood goes up his head, he's furious, and he throws his life off; but here you have someone who is striving to find a way to live, to make a life for himself, feed his brothers and sisters, and send money to his parents, so that they may have a life and find some strength, a way out this wretched existence: it is not suicide! I can't agree!

JAWAD: I'll explain it to you with a different example. If he dies, if he drowned, his family won't find out, they think he made it to Spain. I know kids (*ddreri*) who want to flee to Spain and take their cell phone to call their family when they arrive. Then they get in the boat, and the boat capsizes and they all die [because, he explains, the dealer doesn't care, the boats are old and not maintained]. They all die. For the most part, those who die don't die at their own time (*makiymutush 'ala khatarhum*).

I ask at this point what they mean by *l-mawt blā khaṭar*, a death that is not one's own, the death of a person who doesn't take the time to die.

Together, Kamal and Jawad reply with another example: the death of a taxi driver in Rabat, who after taking a passenger to his destination died at the wheel of his car. However suddenly he died, *ʿalā khaṭru*, they explain, he did so at his proper time, that is, at the time chosen by God (*'alā khaṭar allāh*), he met his term (*lahg l-ʿājil diyālu*).

Jawad notes, "But there are those who can't wait to die that way, the death assigned. He is his own cause of death (*kayqtil rāsu b rrāsu*); his death is a transgression, a sin, a rebellion against God (*ma'ṣiyya*). He disobeys, and doesn't wait for the time appointed; for example, he hangs himself. If he drowns at sea, or dies asphyxiated in a truck, he creates his own cause of death, and a person who died having created their own cause of death is like a person who doesn't recognize *tawhīd*, the oneness of God (*bḥal ilā shirk bi-llāh*). That person is an apostate; he is equivalent to an unbeliever."

Jawad raises the question of transgression in terms of *shirk* (heresy, literally idolatry) and *kufr* (unbelief). I will come back to this important point, for what is implied in Jawad's indictment, as also in Kamal's reply, is that the "risk," to one's life in migration and to one's soul in the fury of despair, is also that of losing faith.

Kamal does not join in condemnation, understanding from his own experience how the life of a person can withdraw, shrink away, all the way to seeking death. He has friends who committed suicide. A couple of days before this conversation he told me about a close friend who hanged himself in his room, and when they found him his face was so white, he said, and translucent, as if all the blood had come out of his body. Kamal sees this as surrender, a form of madness that slowly took over their lives, and from which he doesn't consider himself immune. He gives a definition of despair:

KAMAL: We say of a person, *qanṭ*—that person fell into despair (*qnaṭ*). A human being, when he falls into despair, all doors close up for him, and he can no longer see or distinguish anything (*mabqa ybeyinlih walu*—with a connotation of having no horizon), and abandons himself to drugs. That's it. He has reached a limit (*laḥg waḥed l-ḥadd*). His mind is full; he sees only one thing, hanging himself. In the end, his soul (*rūḥ*) doesn't stay in place, is no longer there, his *rūḥ*, he sent it off with the drugs (*l-muhim, rrūḥ diyālu makatbqash, rūḥ diyālu rah seddrha b ll hashish*) . . . And as for what is on his mind, only one thing: death.

JAWAD: This is what we call suicide.

KAMAL: This is despair (*l-qanaṭ*). [Kamal is using the term as a theological concept, and explains:] Allah said, "Despair not of the Mercy of God: for God forgives all sins, He is all forgiving, most merciful" (Qur'an 39:53). If you feel desperate, if you have lost all hope, trust your hope in God, perform your prayers, and see how your life will change . . .

STEFANIA: But not all people have this kind of moral strength . . .

Kamal refers me to a tape of sermons, one he had previously mentioned as specifically addressing the malaise of the youth.[21] It is one of several tapes he gave me as an introduction to the way piety and theological preoccupations came to inform his existential and intellectual world, at least at one level. Each sermon is composed of examples drawn from daily life and presented in the mode of a moral allegory. The point is to show that in their involvement with worldly pleasures and gains, including Western-style music, drugs, and the pursuit of wealth through abusive work relations and corruption, young people are "dispossessed" (*al-muḥarramūn*, the title of the tape) from the way of God. (Examples of sudden impious deaths, intended to instill the fear of God in the faithful, and, on the other hand, of sudden "awakenings" to the path of God are at the center of argument.) At one level Kamal identifies with this lesson, which corresponds to an aspect of his life experience, when in a moment of straying and desperation he was able to find rest in prayer. He did not tell me the story of that period in his life—which he sees as formative of the person he is today and of his coming to a certain kind of consciousness (*l-waʿī*)—until he showed me the place where he used to spend the night with his friends; an open green area at the edge of built space, where they drank and did drugs, engaging in violent ganglike activities. He had lost all sense of and taste for life, gave himself up to drugs, what is colloquially called *l-qarqubi*, namely antipsychotic medications that one can buy in the street.[22] Drugs made him feel like a corpse, he says, took all sensitivity out of him, and this is why he took them. Despair is a critical figure in his discourse, and in the context of this account, itself structured as an "example," it is a turning point.

During that period one day a man approached him with an exhortation to join in prayer. Kamal did not listen. He did not want to fall into the proselytism of the *islamiyyīn* in his neighborhood, even though he respected the work they did to help people with charity and provide social services neglected by public institutions. He was apathetic in his depression. But the man came back and gave him an illustrated booklet showing the positions of prayer (*ṣalāt*). Kamal tried out of boredom, he says, as a sheer physical exercise, and started feeling better. He took on praying and attending a mosque, joined the community in their activities and in their outdoor retreats, where he was able to find again a sense of community, even just in the fact of performing tasks together—gathering firewood for cooking, peeling vegetables, practicing sports, performing communal prayer. He joined them for a while, until they opposed his decision to "burn" to Europe, and he couldn't renounce his project. He then separated from the group, and continued his search alone, or in the company of others with whom he shared the resolve to leave.

Jihād al-nafs: The Struggle

I push Kamal to elaborate his position that death in the "burning" attempt would not be a suicide. Is he suggesting that death in the *ḥarg* is comparable to death in war (*ḥarb, jihād*)? He nods and explains: "Yes, there is a resemblance; I mean war in the sense of being at war with your self (*ḥarb nafsak*). One struggles against the worldly desires of one's soul (*nafs*)." Kamal goes on to oppose the short-term desires of the *nafs*, in their whimsical immediacy, and the long-term hope that is represented by the migratory project. It is in this sense that death in the *ḥarg* may be compared with death in war:

> *L-ḥarg*, you want to go to find a way to support your family: this is the main idea, you want to help, they don't have anything, a single room for ten people, it is like being in prison, ten people in a single room. One has to do something with one's life; I will do something with my life. This can't be called suicide . . .

Migration, in other words, is a work that pleases God. Its pursuit is a *jihād*, a struggle on the path of God. And if death were to occur, it would be like death in a religiously authorized war, for which the faithful finds reward in the afterlife.

Kamal's appeal to the notion of war combines two different understandings of *jihād* that in current debates are seldom considered side by side, even though in classical literature they are shown to be closely related.[23]

On the one hand, *jihād* is a constant "war" with oneself against an internal enemy, impossible to eliminate, and in fact also necessary for life—a *jihād* that ends only at death. On the other, it is a war against an external enemy who represents a threat for the community of Muslims. While in the first sense of "self-war" Kamal's use of the concept is close to the classical understanding of ethical cultivation, the second sense situates the "enemy" as a form of oppression internal to the society—poverty, injustice, humiliation—stressing the struggle towards a change in historical condition. For Kamal the two meanings are closely related, and are both at play in the predicament of migration.

Jihād in the first sense is the effort to form and improve oneself, a work of poiesis in the tradition of ethics reformulated in the Islamic concept of *tahdhīb al-akhlāq*, the refinement of character. *Jihād al-nafs* is the shaping of character by developing its fortitude and by learning to restrain the *nafs*, embodied soul or "self," and its natural dispositions. In al-Ghazali's reading it is not so much a question of containing a demonic self as in a struggle between reason and passions, but rather—for those who so choose, for it is a question of "volition"—to re-create their character and natural dispositions in the direction of a life dedicated to God. "Were the traits of character not susceptible to change there would be no value in counsels, sermons and discipline, and the Prophet would not have said, Improve your character."[24]

Al-Ghazali understands this work of reshaping dispositions as an effort towards "deliverance" (the Arabic term is *najāt*), which could be translated as a practice of freedom. It is the deliverance of the self from the tyranny of appetites (*shahwa*) and the pursuit of pleasures (*raghba, ladhdha*) by refining the character and inculcating higher desires. Deliverance and awakening are made possible for al-Ghazali by the coming to awareness in the experience of death—what he calls the remembrance of death. The two aspects are intimately related, for the ethics of "deliverance" he sets forth through self-discipline (*riyāḍat*) and the meditation on death (*dhikr*) could not be understood without the "departure" from this world into the other, in the frequentation of death. Death, he writes, is the "spoiler of pleasures," a disturbance, interruption, that produces a sudden realization away from the numbness of everyday routine.[25] The possibility of justice and political critique in this world depends on the cultivation of that *regard éloigné*, a gaze that is not of this world. Only a vision of the hereafter, through the familiarization with death, and the patient work of remembering death every day, in anticipation, in fear, and in the vicarious pain of separation, can free the believer from the preoccupations and greed of the soul (*nafs*). In this sense it can be said that eschatology and ethics are closely related, at least in the thought of al-Ghazali. For some of these youths as well.[26]

Kamal explains:

> You struggle (*katḥarb nafsak*), you are at war with your self (*nafs*). Your *nafs* wants this and that and can't wait, and you resist, you attempt to restrain it, "attach it" (*katrbṭha*). The *nafs* can be understood with the example of a horse; if you don't restrain the horse with a bridle it wanders around, can't find its way. That wandering is *l-hawā*, the whimsies of our desire. God tells us that *l-hawā* follows the random whimsies of the self, wants to drink, smoke hashish, wants girls, wants to wander about in the streets. The *ḥarg* on the other hand, the desire to migrate, to "burn," is the precise opposite: you want to go in order to support your family, feed them, they are poor, don't have anything, live packed in a single room, a prison. In one's life a person has to do something. I will do something with my life, and this is not a suicide.

The implicit assumption in what Kamal is saying is that dying in the effort of a *jihād*—a struggle for a better life, the ultimate scope of migration—is not a suicide, but a death in the way of God, for which there is reward in the afterlife. Even though he may die in the endeavor, the "burner" of international frontiers will not, in his interpretation, burn in hell.

Jawad counters that there are no grounds to consider illegal migration a war. The illicit migrant seeks only to resolve a personal problem, to improve his life, obtain a material gain, while in a war one fights in the collective interest: "In a war you fight for your country, in the *ḥarg* you fight for a dream, an illusion."[27] Kamal puts an end to the debate: "We don't fight for an illusion, but for something that will find realization, God willing. You make the first step, God makes the next. It is not suicide."

Jawad's point is that a war must be authorized, and the project of illegal migration is far from being authorized as a collective endeavor. There is a long tradition of debate in Islamic jurisprudence about who is authorized to call for *jihād*, to declare someone to be apostate, or even simply to "condemn wrong", and what kind of consensus is required for such a claim. Kamal's approach suggests the possibility of authorizing oneself in a situation of exceptional hardship. Such self-authorization, from his friend's point of view, is a transgression and ultimately a sin. It is here that Kamal's position is closer to a modernist interpretation of the subject's responsibility, a responsibility that is at once towards this world *and* the other. For Kamal, who is giving a theologico-political reading of the situation from which he seeks to migrate, the "worldly benefit" to be gained in the endeavor is also, as he attempts to show, a spiritual struggle, as in the pedagogy of Shaykh Yassine and his movement.

Yet within the logic of Shaykh Yassine's movement today, self-authorization would not be an option. One would have to rather look in direction of the Iranian theologian Ali Shariati, who in explicit dialogue with Fanon and Sartre speaks of the emergence of a "new self" who has come to the awareness of injustice through despair, and can authorize himself or herself to think and act on the path of God for a change of condition. Shariati describes the characteristics of such a new self, in terms of awareness, sensitivity, boldness of thought, loftiness of spirit, and fortitude of the heart. They are the characteristics of the Ideal Man, "a man of *jihād* and *ijtihād*, of poetry and the sword, of solitude and commitment, of emotion and genius, of strength and love, of faith and knowledge. He is a man uniting all the dimensions of true humanity," who is not one-dimensional and alienated from his own self, but through submission to God has been summoned to rebellion against all forms of compulsion.

Yet Kamal is not the "ideal man" of Shariati. Despite his resorting to the vocabularies of selfhood and effort on the path of God, his approach, as well as that of his friends, is solitary and eclectic and fails to live up to the "absolute"—Shariati's condition for the realization of the new self.[28] However conscious of pain and horror, Kamal's posture is ironic. Each of these youths is engaged in a search, a solitary quest that is external to institutions, and of which the migratory project, and the willful habitation/violation of boundaries, is but a metonymic image.

As we closely follow the implications of Kamal's argument about the reciprocal relation of the "war" against the self, the "war against poverty and injustice" (*jihād al-faqr*), and the migratory project, we see the outline of a parallel between the "hope" of the desire for God and its eschatological realizations, and the long-term project of migrating to Europe. At this level, the personal and the collective registers, the private and the public, are intertwined. In both cases, the long-term horizon is made possible by the opening of a gap, a departure from one's "self" and one's attachments, or, to borrow Shariati's expression, a "migration from the self."

The Life-world of *l-Ḥrīg*

In my conversations with these youths I have tried to capture the state of mind of the *ḥarg*, its figures and vocabularies, as a specific modality of being in relation to death, transgression, and the struggle for life. In attempting to follow their discourse from within, and in terms of the figures they themselves deploy, I would like to draw attention to its reflexivity, in the modality of experiential narrative as well as of intellectual argumentation. From this perspective, I will now turn to a description of the conceptual and existential world that emerges from our conversations, focusing on a repertoire of concepts or figures: "despair" and the pursuit of "limits," the degradation of life, the confrontation with death, the thought of migration, the paradoxical coming to "consciousness," and the cultivation of an eschatological vision of the Last Day in the everyday.

In the structure of address—I am their interlocutor—there is a request for listening, and for the validation of an experience that does not otherwise have a title to recognition. They watch Moroccan and satellite TV (al-Jazeera and al-Arabiyya), which give much space to social and political reportage as well as roundtable debates on political and religious issues, and are familiar with the genre of the documentary and the mode of individual witnessing that throughout the world, and increasingly in the Arab world, is promoting a new style of testimonial authority. At some level, they seek to occupy the position of institutional "witness."[29] At another, however, they speak from a place that cannot be appropriated, and in terms of a question that is singular, and is the mark of their own painful quest. In this sense, they bear witness to the vulnerability of a life form, which is also personally felt as the risk of one's own extinction; and to the encounter with a drive to life, born in the confrontation with the limit of death.[30] In conversation with me they moved between different voices: the epic register of travel narrative, as a geographical exploration of limits; a mode of personal narrative with an implicit, and sometimes explicit, demand for a psychotherapeutic intervention (particularly in the context of traumatic experiences and relations with their families); and a mode of theological argumentation, from which they attempt to draw the elements of a possible reading. Inasmuch as the different "voices" are inseparable, overlapping, and developed in an internal counterpoint, I will not try to separate out the different registers, and will discuss them instead as they come up in the narrative accounts.

Al-Qanaṭ: Despair

At issue is a sense of a withdrawal of life, of life shrinking. It is as if by the aftershock of an impact, human beings have been ejected from the space of life—the blood drawn out their bodies, thrown into an Elsewhere that is also a different time, a temporality that is not of this world, and, at the same time, is the bodily record of a zone of exclusion. This is expressed through the concept of *al-qanaṭ*, or *qanaṭ al-dunyā*, despairing of the world, extreme boredom, depression that becomes despair, loss of all hope. Or with the image of the metaphysical soul (*rūḥ*), departing from the body, its "sending it off," or "migrating," into a space of death. It is what happens in dreams according to the Qur'anic and vernacular understanding of dreaming.[31] But in the uncanny doubling of melancholy it happens with drugs. Let's recall Kamal's definition:

> We say of a person, *qanṭ*—that person fell into despair (*qnaṭ*). A human being, when he falls into despair, all doors close up for him, and he can no longer see or distinguish anything, and abandons himself to drugs. That's it. He has reached a limit. His mind is full; he sees only one thing, hanging himself. In the end, his soul (*rūḥ*) doesn't stay in place, is no longer there, his soul, he sent it off with the drugs . . . And as for what is on his mind, only one thing: death.

Al-qanṭ (classical Arabic *al-qanaṭ*) is not despair as universal human experience, as such immediately accessible and translatable—even though it claims universality on its own account within a different tradition of ethics. We might relate it to Kierkegaard's analytics of despair, or William James's experience of melancholy;[32] but we must also take seriously the fact that in the usage of these youths, despair is a theological concept whose semantic configuration refers to the notion of "trial" of the believer.

In its vernacular usage in Moroccan Arabic, *l-qanṭ* is an image of imprisonment, lack of space, extreme boredom, and a cause of madness or suicide. When mentioned in this sense by a patient in the psychiatric emergency room, it is understood by psychiatrists as a sign of "depression" or "melancholy" (*ikti'āb*), which can take hold of a person and reduce her to a psychic and bodily quasi-death.

Despair's relation to madness and migration is a recurrent theme in our conversations, in an intertwining of medical, theological, and existential registers. Despair can lead to madness, losing a person's mind in the sense of *l-ḥumq*, madness without return, but also lead the believer astray, erring away from the path of God. The two senses are both distinct and related, inasmuch as madness has a theological connotation contiguous with a medical one, in the vernacular understanding of demonic intrusion as well as in the "jurisprudence of the soul" (see part 3).

The thought of migration is an antidote of despair. Kamal explains this to me with reference to his own malaise. He sees himself as "knotted" or traumatized (*mu'aqqad*) by an intimate wound, an essential vulnerability that exposes him to the risk of madness. This wound, which he traces to his early life within the family, is both the source of his vulnerability and of a certain vision; and it is at the origin of his desire to expatriate. The thought of the *ḥarg* (burning), he says, despite the risk of death, is for him an effort to seek health. He explains the relationship of clandestine migration to madness (*l-ḥarg u l-ḥumq*) by the vernacular etiology of the "black dot," the theory of a destructive potential in any one of us, which is kept at bay by leading a life of ethical "works." In his words:

> In the head of each human being there is a black dot (*nuqṭa kahla*). If you are active and involved in the things of life, if you practice the works that please God (*l-a'māl*), you succeed in forgetting its presence inside your head, and its potential of destruction remains unrealized, the black dot remains contained, like a cyst, and does not harm you. But if you are not doing anything, if you are not working, just waiting in boredom, you start feeling its presence, become obsessive, and it is as if a wind blew through that black dot inside your head, and shattered its content in a million fragments. The black dot turns then into dust, and you go mad, you are lost.

The risk of madness in despair is paralleled by a risk of doubting the foundation of faith, or even challenging God, entering heresy. Ibn Qayyim al-Jawziyya elaborates on this in his "Treatment of Calamity,"[33] stressing that "losing the reward of patience and submission is truly greater than the disaster." *L-qanṭ*, in this sense, is close to the classical theological notion of "losing hope" and "losing guidance," "straying" (*ḍalāl*), as the experience of feeling abandoned by God. The person in despair has thoughts of being abandoned by God. It is in this sense that despair shares in the semantic structure of the concept of *kufr*, usually translated as "unbelief," and the person in despair comes to inhabit a border, a region of normative instability: "he has reached a limit (*laḥag waḥed l-ḥadd*)." The advent of questioning, from the Prophet Muhammad's reported moment of confusion as to the nature of his revelation[34] to al-Ghazali's self-narration of a spiritual crisis,[35] both is foundational to the possibility of belief and represents an essential risk. "Who would despair of the mercy of his Lord save those who are astray in Error (*ḍāllūn*)?" (Qur'an 15:56). In the debate with which I opened this section, Jawad sensed such potential transgression in the words of Kamal, and in the spirit of what he understood as the law, appealed to the language of "sin" (*ma'ṣiyya*), and charged with heresy the position of the illegal expatriate, a burner of political and theological borders. Kamal himself, just as he was describing the experience of losing hope, an experience that is also his own, cited a Qur'anic exhortation not to fall prey to despair, not to forget the compassion of God—also, perhaps, for its performative force.

Despair is a trial, one of the trials of *fitna* to discern the quality, and truthfulness, of a person's faith. *Al-fitna* is a pivotal concept in the Qur'an, as also in the vernacular understanding. Reinterpreting a pre-Islamic notion of the immanence of harm and desire in the terms of a new ethics, *al-fitna* in the Qur'an is the "limit" or "trial" to ascertain the faith of the believer: "Every soul shall have a taste of death: and We test you by evil and by good by way of *fitna*, and to Us you must return" (Qur'an 21:35).

Falling into despair and dwelling in that state amounts to losing trust in God, losing "hope" (*rajā'*) in his compassion. Despair then is one of the "limits" that can transgress into apostasy or establish the truth of God's law. One aspect of this trial is "the ordeal of affliction and torture" (*fitna al-miḥna*), which subjects the faithful to suffering at the limit of the intolerable. It is comparable to a whispering of the devil in the ear (*waswās*), one of the widespread causes of madness: "the *fitna* of the heart is the *waswās* (*wa fitnat al-ṣadr al-waswās*), obsession and internal delusion."[36]

Despair marks the failure of the virtue of endurance (*al-ṣabr*). And yet in certain Sufi readings it is seen as a state, a station (*maqāma*) that is reached by the adept by way of a passage through a radical loss of self, which necessarily entails a risk of nonreturn.[37] According to the revolutionary eschatology of Ali Shariati, on the other hand, who reads the Qur'an and the hadith in light of Kierkegaard and Sartre, despair is the consciousness of injustice and suffering. Shariati sees a kernel of responsibility in despair, the responsibility of the oppressed (*maẓlūm*), who becomes a martyr in full awareness of his defeat in this world. In the debate with Jawad, Kamal's position pushes belief and personal-political engagement to a limit that is that of *fitna*—at the risk of impatience and arrogance, of overstepping the bounds (*ṭaghā*), by assuming the experience of despair as a coming to consciousness. Al-Ghazali himself points out that sadness (*al-ḥuzn*) is a state in which the soul is "softer," already distanced from the pleasures and ambitions of worldly attachments, hence more receptive to the work of remembrance of death, and therefore to the possibility of vision, awareness.[38]

The Slow Death

The meditation on despair as an existential and theological risk gives way to a reflection on depersonalization, and on the end of connectedness in what is described as an aftermath of social life, and of life tout court. The words that keep coming to describe the event of becoming a nonperson are *al-maḥgūr*, the wretched, humiliated, reduced to the status of scum; *al-maqhūr*, the one who is overpowered and vanquished, subjugated; and *al-maqmūʿ*, the one who is despised, valueless, subjected. These words lend image to the experience of what the youths call a "slow death" (*al-mawt al-baṭīʾ*), death by lack of place, a certain way of becoming a spirit (*rūḥ*) while still alive, a living dead, through the "shutting of all doors," the flattening of the horizon, metonymically embodied in the use of drugs, which "send off the soul," render the body insensitive, rigid like the limbs of a corpse:

> The slow death (*al-mawt al-baṭīʾ*) is the death of a person who is subjugated and vanquished: the one who dies in pain and hardship, who dies angry and resentful; the wretched, the one who is humiliated, and of the one who is despised and devalued, the one for whom life didn't open up its gates, the one who didn't encounter nice words, and who didn't experience the solidarity of people together (*al-nās mujmūʿīn*)! He doesn't find recognition, is despised, traumatized. That person dies, we say, a slow death, dies little by little, a sneaking death . . .

"And what killed him? He was killed by a psychic state, the state of the soul in which he is forced to live (*ḥāla nafsiyya*)."

And in this context there would be so much to say about the frequentation of death, suicide, illness, and violence, which engender a phantasmagoria of images, a world populated with spirits and regulated by the operations of magic, where the risk of the one who "gambles with his life" to cross over to Europe is also the risk of being "touched" by the jinns.

We leave here the domain of the ethical struggle, at least in the prescriptive sense, to enter *al-gharīb*: the uncanny, the strange, that which exceeds mundane reality. It is the encounter with the demonic (another dimension of *al-fitna*) as a pervasive dimension of everyday life, as well as an encounter with "harm" in the form of abandonment and oppression. At some level these youths situate themselves in that perspective. Yet their position is not one of affirmative moral denunciation: they are also existentially dwelling in a space of *fitna*. They are "standing on the cusp," in a precarious and uncomfortable position, fraught with ambivalence.[39] "Home," for them, has become *unheimlich*. "So many of us have been struck in the attempt at migration" (*tqasw*, touched, implicit by the jinn): in their interpretation it is this "having been touched," exposed to the realm and the operations of death by the hand of the jinns, that causes the unleashing of the death drive, and results for so many in suicide.

Their reflection on the *huma*—the neighborhood, but also the social community in which they were born, a sharing of assumptions and habits, rites, ways of being together, and which in its ideal representation would be based on a sense of closeness that persists—is aimed at showing that the space of familiarity is both unlivable and uncanny, "against nature." As Kamal puts it, there is no transmission of a desire to live. Not in any case in the unreconstructed places of genealogical belonging—the relation with fathers and mothers, with sisters and brothers. Fathers are represented as participating in the "crushing" of the self, by the performance of their own weakness, as well as by the exercise of an empty authority that does not correspond to a symbolic "support" (*ḍāmin*).

"You could have a university degree," says Jawad, elaborating on his sense of having been abandoned by his family at his father's death, "and in these neighborhoods several youths do have degrees, but if you don't have support when you need it, a person whom you can lean on, a guarantor, you will eventually surrender to drugs." This condition is characterized in their eyes by the fact of not having a "guarantor" (*ḍāmin*)—a father, very often in their stories, but also a principle of legality, at the local as well as the international level. "These kids who kill each other with knives and swords in our neighborhood at night, you may find that they are educated and even have university degrees: *ṭhagrw*, they have been crushed."

They tell me how the project of "burning" began, in school, when they were about fifteen, people had started crossing to Europe and would come back in the summer and tell stories, or there were just stories told about them, on the other side. They had left illegally, in the long-distance trucks that would come and go, load and unload at the textile factories down the hill from their neighborhood (*sharikāt diyāl export*). The idea started entering their minds like a whispering, an obsessive whispering in their ear (*waswās*), and they could no longer concentrate in school, "Our minds flew away with those distance tracks, our bodies were here, our being over there, we were *ḥayr*, beside ourselves, until we dropped out of school." For them, there were only exhausting jobs lifting heavy boxes and loading trucks. Until the day they were able to climb into a truck unseen and depart. Afternoons spent remembering those first "attempts" (*muḥāwala*) with me, the excitement and the fear, long descriptions of *r'muk* (Fr. *remorque*), the long-distance cargo trucks, in their technical and mechanical details: how the doors lock, how you elude control, what happens at the border with the customs police, how it feels to be in there, squeezed in the midst of piles of jeans in plastic bags, in the dark, with no oxygen, flattened against the walls and hardly breathing. And then, in most cases, the disappointment of being discovered, on the Spanish or the Moroccan side, being questioned and sent back, and often beaten up by the police (beatings on the legs, to break the bones, "so that we can't try again"). Kamal and his close friend Said made at least ten attempts. Said never made it to the other side; Kamal made it once, all the way to Algesiras, but when the police caught him in the street and addressed him in Spanish, he couldn't reply, and he was taken to the station and sent back. Only once did they try at sea. They speak about *l-ḥarg* openly, the attempts, the fact of taking risks to go across. In the stories of crossing there is an adventurous dimension that makes them feel alive, and creates a bond among those who live in this space of abandonment and self-exile. Other things are much harder to discuss: the sense of being crushed, the suicide of friends, the fear of becoming mad, the situation at home, with parents and siblings, the impossibility of relating to their fathers.

They describe the state of mind of the *ḥarg* in a language of addiction: burning flows in my veins like blood, I am addicted (*l-ḥarg keyjri f-l-ʿaruq bḥal ddim, anā mbli*); *mbli*, a term that is used for drugs, but also for being in love: I have lost all desire (*raghba*, desire, longing) for anything other than the Burning itself. And in terms of rage, oppression: *anā ḥayr*: I am beside myself (*ḥayra* is confusion, helplessness, extreme anguish); and by the image of an elsewhere that becomes an obsession, and produces a cleavage, a rift, somewhat comparable to what happens in dreams: "my body is here, my Being is over there [with a gesture of the hand, far away, over there, in Europe], as if with a constant whispering in my ear" (*ddahti hna, khaṭry lehe, bḥal l-wswās fīyya*).

L-Gharīb

"I got myself exposed/touched by the jinns because of Burning" (*anā qasit 'ala udd l-ḥarg*). Stories of encounters with the jinn are recurrent in our conversations. Because "Burning" requires nightly waiting in forsaken places or by the water, sites characteristically haunted by the jinn. But the exposure to "touching" and demonic possession has also to do with the emotional state of a person who is *ḥayr*, in a rage, or in the heat of despair. These stories are accounts of events of being seized into a space of death for those who are vulnerable and will end up losing their minds or committing suicide; they are told as cautionary tales, but also offered as factual reports on a state of things, indexes of the withdrawal of life. But there are other narratives in which the person stands up to the jinns and tests the fortitude of his or her will. The "burner" is represented as cultivating the volition and skills of a healer, who develops the interior strength to encounter the demonic without being seized. As Said tells of his encounter with a feminine presence one night that he was "risking," he is narrating such a story:

> One night at Aswak Assalam [a supermarket in Rabat] we were "risking" (*kanriskiw*), just by the freeway, there is a thicket, these are haunted woods (*ghāba mskuna*). And a girl went by, she was beautiful, wore a long white dress, and was all covered with gold, and we were sitting there, waiting [waiting to see whether they could climb inside a cargo truck]. I got up, wanted to check out her beauty from close up, verify her true being [jinn or human], and my friends held me down. I am not afraid of Them, even if they materialize right here in front of me. If you are afraid of them, they strike you. I am checking her out carefully, she is walking very slowly, I check her feet, she has camel feet—They don't have feet like us humans. The other kids were hiding or calling for help, I kept looking at her, and our gaze met, my eye met her eye, she made a sign and I replied with a sign, she turned her face around, started walking very slowly, and I followed her, she put some distance between us, and I followed her at that distance, and kept looking at her. I had gone a long way from people. Then she disappeared, and I returned to my friends.

Said wants to stand up to her gaze; but humans cannot stand that gaze without losing their mind. At stake is the "testing" of his fear, fear of madness and death, by confronting the *fitna* of a she-demon, who is also a personification of Europe. Said is testing his capacity to resist, not being lost—in the theological sense of *ḍalāl* as perdition, and in the vernacular sense of becoming her prey; but he's also exploring his own fascination and desire. It is an art of danger.[40]

World Ending

Prompted by a violent event the previous night, Kamal and Said start reflecting on death. Death as physical killing. Kamal recalls an event, a dispute between two youths, one stabbing the other with a knife. The victim grabbed Kamal's leg to make a shield with his body, and as Kamal freed himself the other was struck to death. It was the first time he witnessed a violent death, he says, a disfigured death (*mawta mishuha*), obscene, public, a death that, in itself, is a punishment from God. Kamal recalls his own astonishment, "The last rattle of a dying person is like the rattle of a sacrificed lamb (*dhabīḥa*)." In conversation, each recalls the event of a death. They visualize the corpse, the physicality of the body, bleeding until it becomes white and translucent, or rotting in a hole, where it will be found days later (Said says he showered for days without being able to get rid of the smell of death on his skin), or frozen in the refrigerators at the morgue: Said recalls having brought the freezing corpse of a little girl in his arms, from the morgue all the way home for the funeral. To practice "good works," he says.

The visualization of death in their recollection explodes the existential frames of daily life. It inscribes the object-like quality of the corpse in the present as a "remembrance of death," which is not a cultivated attitude, in the sense in which gnostics practice *dhikr*, or at least not explicitly, but something that befalls them, as death does. The experience of death, of the corpse, radically alters the coordinates of the real, tangibly producing a temporality of the afterlife in the here and now of presence.

In *The Book of the Remembrance of Death*, al-Ghazali provides a phenomenological description of the experience of death as the event of a cleavage, a radical dispossession that is a "lapse" into another, incommensurable state. He describes in a profusion of visual details the decomposition of the body in the grave, the fear of the soul, the darkness and smell of the grave, the worms, and the questioning by the angel of death, and invites the faithful to meditate on those images, producing them in the imagination and imprinting them in the soul as both an ethical and an existential bodily experience. Through *dhikr* the living learns to look at the world, and oneself, from the outer-temporal standpoint of the grave: "The dead man sits up and hears the footsteps of those who are present at his funeral, but none addresses him save his tomb, which says, Woe betide you, son of Adam! Did you not fear me and my narrowness, my corruption, terror and worms? What have you prepared for me?"[41]

Seeing the world from the standpoint of the grave is a step towards "unveiling." Yet understanding death is impossible for human beings, "since death cannot be understood by those who do not understand life, and life can only be understood through knowing the true nature of the spirit itself."

The themes of al-Ghazali's "remembrance" are echoed in the conversation with Kamal and Said. In the midst of their recollections of death I asked them the question of the sense of life, the worth of life, whether it still had a meaning, in their neighborhood. Kamal replied, "You see the world, it is like a glass of tea, you drink it and it is empty. You ask me what life is, what the meaning of life is in this [mundane] world (*dunyā*). Life, you enter from one door, and come out from another (*dkhal fi bāb u kharj f bbāb*). The afterlife (*l-ākhira*), life on the side of death, is something else. It is an unveiling, you become aware." But in the banality of everyday life, he continued, in the neighborhood, the first time he witnessed a death, a murder in the street, he couldn't sleep for days. Then one becomes accustomed. Of course he's afraid of dying, despite everything. But he does accept to die in the attempt at migration.

He continues, and the visualization of death in this world lapses to a vision of the Last Day:

> On the Last Day, the day of resurrection, we will all come out in the open, and one person will not recognize another. The kings will come out, Hassan II and Mohammed V, they will come out naked, like everyone else, and no one will know them.

The imagery is reminiscent of Qur'anic reckonings of the Last Day, "the Hour." For in the landscape of the Hour, a landscape flat and without horizon, people will be scattered like moths, barefoot and naked, and none will recognize the other. It is the end of human connectedness, family, community, and nation, and it is the radical aloneness of each person. The condition of life at the "limit," as these youth describe it, in the aftermath of society, necessarily evokes for a person within this tradition the

Qur'anic vision of the end of time. And how could the "passage" itself, the "crossing" of the geographical chasm between the continental fault lines of Africa and Europe, not evoke the *sirāṭ*, the traverse or narrow bridge over the chasm of Hell; the bridge thinner than a blade or a thread, which will widen up like a highway to let across the saved, or instead shrink like a blade to make the damned fall, pushed down into eternal fire.[42]

PART III

The Jurisprudence of the Soul

SEVEN

Overture: A Topography of the Soul in the Vertigo of History

Mais pouvons-nous échapper au vertige? Qui oserait prétendre que le vertige ne hante pas toute existence?

But can we escape the vertigo? And who dares affirm that vertigo does not haunt each and every life?

—Frantz Fanon, "Guerre coloniale et troubles mentaux"[1]

Ammā idhā kānat al-malaka wa aḥkāmuhā bi-l-qahr wa-l-saṭwa wa-l-ikhāfa fa-taksiru ḥīna'idhin min sawra ba'sihim wa tudhhibu al-manaʿa ʿanhum, limā yakūnu min al-takāsul fī al-nufūs al-muḍṭahida kamā nubayyinuhu.

If domination with its rulings is one of coercion, and instills fear as a result, it breaks their fortitude and obliterates their power of resistance (*manaʿa*) because of the apathy that develops in the soul (*nafs*) of the oppressed, as we will show.

—Ibn Khaldun, *The Muqaddima*[2]

"The heart forms an image of life as life burned, life destroyed." The Imam turns a little farther. He gazes outside across the terraced rooftops of his neighborhood, at the narrow alley of makeshift row homes stretching all the way to the ocean, a concrete memory of the layout of a shantytown that dates back to the 1970s. I follow his gaze. The shops are turning on their evening lights, and the cranes of a state-sponsored housing project hover over the horizon, skeletal arms of the state at this abandoned edge of the city that has fostered in recent years its own forms of living and being. The street is slowly emptying from the activity of the afternoon; a man walking home, two women talking, others standing outside in little groups—some

Figure 11.

of the men and women who come to seek the Imam's advice, or ring his doorbell with a request for healing. The Imam is a religious scholar and a healer in the tradition of Qur'anic medicine. We have been talking over a period of over ten years.

People address him as Shaykh, Faqīh, or Imam, depending on the nature of their relationship with him. He is the imam of a mosque in the low-income neighborhood where he lives, and where he is actively engaged in the therapeutics and ethical-religious practice of what is known throughout the Muslim world today as *'ilāj shar'ī*,[3] spiritual-medical cures in harmony with the meaning of the shari'a, including the Qur'anic cures for madness, spiritual and demonic illness. I will refer to him here as "the Imam," to respect the reserve that prefers to clothe itself in the anonymity of a generic appellation, and the one attached to the most public of his functions, which is leading the Friday prayer. He is more accurately a *faqīh* (a scholar of *fiqh*), which along with embracing juridical, spiritual, and ethical knowledge and practice carries for him, as for his fourteenth-century predecessor Ibn Qayyim al-Jawziyya, a concern with medicine. In his own self-description, the Imam is a *murshid* (a religious guide) and *mu'lij* (a therapist, a noun formed from the verbal root *'ilj*, to cure), a specialist in the maladies of the soul in a contemporary tradition of prophetic medicine[4] (*al-ṭibb al-nabawī*) and, more generally, in a living Islamic medical-ethical tradition that draws on a committed reading of the Qur'an and on the legacy of Muslim Scholasticism in its engagement with Islamic jurisprudence.

For the Imam this also entails performing healing acts, above all the liturgy of the *ruqya*, centered on the recitation of the Qur'an, the word of God, and the visible materialization of its effects, and affects, on the soul and the body of the person, and in the case of demonic possession on the elusive ontological being that is the jinn. He often performs the *ruqya* at his home, in this room where we are standing, which for the time of the recital (and the event born of it) becomes a space of manifestation of the Invisible, a stage of the soul, of its torments and battles, attacks and counterattacks, rendered visible in the absenting of a body on the floor, rendered audible in the emergence of a voice and a struggle of voices, in the shadow of the Qur'an's. For, to use the terminology of Ibn Sina and Ibn Khaldun, which finds an echo in the words of the Imam, the senses of that person are disconnected from the physical world, and are turned instead inwards and Outside, towards the world of spiritual realities. *Ruqya*: a term that in the context of healing is translated as "cure" and "incantation," but that in its verbal form, *raqiya*, means to elevate, ascend, and carries the sense of spiritual elevation, the sense that resonates with the practice and pedagogy of the Imam. I will translate it here as "the recital."

The Imam is collecting his thoughts. "The heart forms an image of life as life burned, life destroyed," he finally says, still gazing outside and as if continuing a silent train of thought.

We have been talking about the young men and women in his neighborhood, and other neighborhoods; I shared with him the report I had just read on mental health in Morocco: an epidemiological study by a group of psychiatrists and psychoanalysts highlighting the impact of major depression among the young and middle-aged population. I ask him how he would understand that report in terms of his vision of spiritual life and politics, and his practice of medicine of the soul.

He is of course aware of this state of affairs. He makes reference to the youths he knows, who slash their arms with razors because the physical pain of the wounds, the body bleeding, assuages and anesthetizes the psychic pain, strives to contain it in those cuts; or because the bleeding tests the reality of the body, the fact that the body is not already a corpse. The Imam is concerned about the state of the young men and women who sometimes come to seek his advice, plagued by a forced inactivity, the lack of work raised to ontological and theological significance as a lack of deeds, by apathy, the death of desire—what he describes as the loss of hope and trust in God. He reaches out to them without judging, and, addressing the spiritual causes of existential exhaustion, of despair and suicide, attempts to carve a space of breathing and being.

His therapeutic interventions and much of his teaching are directed at countering the destruction of selves, families, and communities, in the context of dire economic conditions and intergenerational trauma: the broken relationships between fathers and sons, parents and children, where the grounds of parental authority and protection are undermined by the impossibility of providing for the family, and by the psychic and moral wounds of a faltering symbolic transmission; poverty, emotional instability, violence within the family and in the neighborhoods, depression, psychosis, and chronic illness. And there are the hardship and sadness of the home, where men have left or are absent for long periods of time, some at war, stationed in the Western Sahara, and where women are alone to provide for the children (as in the case I discuss in the "Concluding Movement"). Or where husbands are present but in the violence and existential void of moral impairment; where, from the point of view of the children, life in the family home is unlivable, the parental word resonates empty, and attachment is lived on the modality of the double bind—a destructive form of intimacy that can neither be done away with nor embraced; where, from the point of view of the children, the new generation, there is no work and no horizon, only entrapment and void literalized in the "absence" and "coma" (*ghaybūba*), which is the experience of drugs. The Imam himself articulates a political and spiritual critique of the system that reproduces exclusions leading to the self feeling itself like a corpse, losing the sense of existing, or, as in the words of Ibn Khaldun in epigraph, of the kind of rule that "breaks their fortitude and obliterates their power of resistance because of the apathy that develops in the soul (*nafs*) of the oppressed." Treating the apathy of the soul of the oppressed is what the Imam does in his cures. His intervention, as I attempt to trace in this last part of the book, addresses the intimate dual nature of oppression, at once located in the world and in the soul: what we may call—in terms that eschew explicit reference to the life of the soul—the imbrication of politics, trauma, and desire in the life both of the person and the collectivity.

Ibtilā': Trauma and Divine Trial

But for the Imam the point is not just the fact of trauma, the registering of a personal and collective calamity; nor is it simply the mitigation of its effects. It is how we relate to the event as "ordeal," and what a person becomes capable of being in relation to that experience. This is captured by the Qur'anic concept of *ibtilā'* (divine "testing" or "trial"), which encodes the cardinal orientation of his thinking and practice vis-à-vis the theological and existential problem of suffering. From the verbal form *b-l-w* (to be subjected to an ordeal, to be put to test, and to learn from experience), and from the noun *balā'* (affliction and hardship, and the trial and testing they entail),[5] *ibtilā'* is the fact of being summoned by contingency, and being called to respond. The Imam's recourse to this concept poses the question of responsibility in the encounter with the world understood as an ordeal. The ordeal is not just what falls upon us, what breaks our lives and hurls us into bereavement or disablement; it contains an address, the sign of a divine interpellation, even when we don't understand its meaning. It is the encounter with an event that summons us to what the Imam calls a "decision" as for the actualization or the annihilation of an inner potential; *ibtilā' qarār*, he says, "the ordeal is a decision." The state of the neighborhood, the despair of a generation, the risk and the hope of migration, the tragic events and upheavals that keep turning the fate of the region, the destruction of war, the generalization of death—but also what we think as positive events, the enthusiasm of revolt, the satisfaction of a life without need, the pleasure of success, all are examples of such trial, a trial by evil and by good. In his words:

> There is trial (*ibtilā'*) in illness, in migration, in poverty, in madness. In the path (*sunna*) of God the ordeal is ever present in the life of creatures. God tries human beings with happiness and adversity, poverty and plenty, health and sickness, with what brings them pleasure and what brings them pain, as it is said in the Qur'an: "Every soul will have a taste of death: and We test you by evil and by good by way of *fitna*, and to Us you must return" (Qur'an 21:35). *Ibtilā' fīhā l-qarār, li-l-insān, li-l-nafs, ibtilā' ijāban aw salban*: "In the ordeal there is a call for decision, for the human person, for the soul; in well-being and in adversity there is a divine trial."

Ibtilā' is a call to accept the event as it is, confront reality and its hardship; but also, and most important, it is a call to maintain the effort and persist on the path even when our vision is clouded and the world around us is indifferent or hostile. The other side of *ibtilāʾ* is *mujāhada* (effort, struggle), which is the movement of existence.[6] Together, they determine the becoming of the soul.[7]

Welcoming the event as ordeal shifts the coordinates of the real. It means to move from a modality of the world in which things are transformed into objects in order to be "grasped," used, possessed, to a modality in which they are transformed into that which "cannot be grasped." I am here borrowing Blanchot's words, which helped me realize the radical shift implied in an appreciation of the heteronomy of the ordeal, which at once seizes and addresses us in a movement of dispossession, "releasing us both from them and from ourselves."[8] This shift of coordinates is what Blanchot calls the Imaginary space: "To live an event as an image is not to remain uninvolved . . . it is to be taken, to pass from the region of the real where we hold ourselves at a distance from things the better to order and use them into that other region where the distance holds us."[9] In the ordeal received as an image there is the sign of a passage to another side, where life and death are no longer opposed.

I understood this much later, after many attempts at writing and conveying what I learned through my ethnography with the Imam. Paradoxically, or perhaps significantly, it is a personal practice of psychoanalysis and its exploration of the trials of the soul in the space of the transference that disclosed for me the meaning of *ibtilāʾ*. And vice versa. It was by working through the ethnography with the Imam, and struggling to learn from it, that I could understand what change means in psychoanalysis.

And I thought of the words of Marion Milner, a psychoanalyst: "Could it be true that the laws of growth of the heart are not the same as the laws of growth of what we call the mind, those laws of learning by which mental and physical skills are acquired, something which can be done by working to a plan? There seemed to be another paradox here: could it be that change of heart can only really come when one gives up trying to change?"[10]

Modes of the Soul

I am looking at the photograph that I took that day, a view across the rooftops all the way to the towering cranes and the unfinished concrete of a housing development under construction at the limit of the visual field. Spaces and volumes are sharply defined by the shadows of evening approaching, creating the effect of a metaphysical theater that is accentuated by a diffuse purple light with isolated bright green spots, the combined result of the last rays of the sun and the neon lights of the shops as they meet in the lens of my camera. More than other photographs that I took of the Imam and his neighborhood, that image summons me to the scene of the soul as it is evoked in the words, the concern, and the healing work of the Imam, and to a mode of listening where I can become receptive to that scene. It is one of several photographs taken in moments of waiting and absent-mindedness, in the pauses between our conversations and his healing sessions. Looking back at these images I am struck by the resonance of inside and outside, of built space and the space of the soul, of the visible and the invisible.

I often take photographs of urban spaces, outskirts, as in the peripheries of Italian cities in neorealist cinema, Pasolini's peripheries of Rome, and also those where I spent part of my youth. Pasolini traveled the dispossessed peripheries of Italian modernity through the eye of his camera, which transfigured those beings who strode through vacant lots into angelic presences, apparitions on the precocious ruins of Italian consumer capitalism. Later as an ethnographer I was drawn to Pasolini's angle of vision, and that of his Algerian and Moroccan counterparts from whom I attempted to learn the capacity to see otherwise, an angle of vision that may be called anamorphic—listening to the invocations and recitations of Miloud in Lakhdar Hamina's film epic *Chronique des années de braise*, the sage fool who admonishes his contemporaries from the grounds of a cemetery, and recounts the history of Algeria as a commentary in the margins, an address from the gates of the afterlife.[11]

Why, then, this photograph instead of many other images, photographs of healing sessions that I choose not to show? At one level it visualizes a relationship between being and its physical environment: space as marked by the unequivocal presence of modern poverty, the lack of services and care by the state, and the traces of an attempt at the everyday reappropriation of that space in the very zone of neglect ("marginaux, minoritaire et dominés . . . c'est cela même notre chance," Abdelkebir Khatibi wrote at a different time,[12] but with continuing relevance). People making their lives as best they can, also feeling and thinking, debating and organizing, while the state asserts its presence to contain and control the carving of new forms of existence with its cranes—and what it now perceives and construes as the threat of Islam in low-income neighborhoods. This coastline will soon be seized by upscale developers, as is already happening closer to the center of town, and the inhabitants of this neighborhood, already once displaced, will be pushed further inland, to join the growing informal housing sprawls that cover the argillous hills in the hinterland all the way to the formerly rural edges of the city.

The correspondence between the city (*madīna*) and the soul (*nafs*) is important for Muslim cosmological thinkers. The paradigmatic relation between built space, the rise and fall of human civilization (*ʿumrān*), the desire for power (*mulk*), and the forming and de-forming of the soul is central for Ibn Khaldun (d. AH 732/1332 CE), who makes it one of the structuring motifs in his understanding of history.[13] But I am thinking here more specifically and closer to our time of a passage in Kateb Yacine's *Nedjma*, a text that has accompanied me over the years as a guide in my attempt at exploring the intersection of collective history and the life of the psyche and the soul. Rachid, one of *Nedjma*'s four protagonists, is returning to the city of his birth after a long absence. Through the window as the train approaches, the city of Constantine presents itself to him as a mythical landscape, where the inside and the outside, the ruin and the contemporary, the subject and the world, the plant and the machine, the vicissitudes of the soul and the violent history of the land keep exchanging place. In that imaginal mode a human history of conquest and discord is subsumed into the impersonality of geological history and becomes marked as the record of earthquakes: "Citadel of expectation and threat, forever tempted by decadence, shaken by age-old seizures—a site of earthquake and discord, open to the four winds, where the ground shudders and shows itself the master, making its own resistance eternal." It is an allusion, perhaps, to the signs of a divine temporality.[14]

After a long pause the Imam resumes speaking. He addresses me in what I have come to recognize as his more abstract, speculative mode—a mode he sometimes assumes in our reflexive conversations. As he answers my question he moves us back from the epidemiology of depression in the mental health report to the physics and metaphysics of the soul, and the account of its becoming. He describes the soul's movements as a physiological pathos of breathing and choking, opening and closing, expanding and constricting: existential and affective states bordering on theological visions. A phenomenology of the soul in despair. Opening and closing, expanding and choking are ontological terms that carry here a strong Qurʾanic resonance, evocative of God's "expanding" the breast of those He wills to guide (*yashraḥ ṣadrahū li-l-islām*), and "constricting" the breast of those He wills to go astray (*yajʿal ṣadrahū ḍayyiqan*, Qurʾan 6:125). Or, in words of sustenance and hope, as in the Qurʾanic chapter called *al-Sharḥ* ("the opening-up of the heart"): "Have We not opened up your heart and lifted from you the burden that had weighed so heavily on your back?" (Qur'an 94:1–3).

"Choking" and "constricting," as we will see, describe in the words of the Imam the concrete physical and existential state of the person in grief, as well as the medical condition of melancholy—melancholy understood in the Arab medical tradition as a petrifying infiltration of black bile: *al-sawdā*, the black humor. But in his view these terms relate that physical and existential experience, in its despondent concreteness, to the theological problem of salvation and to the soul's capacity for "expansion," in the paradoxical agency that rests in a person's surrender to divine decree (*al-qaḍā' wa-l-qadar*). For the soul's capacity for expansion means also its vulnerability to a disabling loss of moral energy: the human lot is one burdened with the freedom of choice to fulfill God's mission on earth.[15]

Grounded in the Qur'an and in the prophetic sources, this phenomenology of despair for our troubled historical times is articulated by the Imam through a vocabulary inflected with the terms and concepts of a theory of the soul associated with the thought of Ibn Sina (Avicenna) and al-Ghazali, whose writings on the soul the Imam has read and in his own way distilled into a style of thinking and practicing that, as he stresses, is not just a knowledge for the sake of intellectual argument, but a knowing with the heart applied to the task of living. Reinvested in recent years in the works of prominent Muslim scholars in the context of the Islamic Revival (*al-ṣaḥwa al-islāmiyya*), who turned to al-Ghazali and other classical scholars to seek guidance and inspiration in a contemporary reflection on ethics and politics, subjectivity, and the law, the vocabulary of Islamic Scholasticism and its theory of the soul has in many ways been transmitted and kept alive in the study of Islamic philosophy and jurisprudence, and has persisted in the medical-ethical approach to the body and illness in vernacular healing. Yet, what emerges clearly in the discourse of the Imam is that the terms and concepts of Islamic Aristotelianism and Neoplatonism cannot be decoupled from the legacy of the Qur'an and the sunna. Isolating a Greek or Peripatetic legacy, or for that matter an Indian and Chinese one, from *fiqh* jurisprudence and the moral message of the Qur'an is a violence done to the way these traditions have been alive together and have informed the lives of generations of Muslims.[16]

The Imam's reflections are based on a conception of the soul declined in four terms:

— *nafs*, the desiring soul and the worldly self, the "psychic soul," moved by the passions of anger and desire and by the consuming experience of grief, but also the seat of perception, the physical movement of respiration, and the metaphorical movement of aspiration and longing; *nafs*, also, and crucially, as the moral hierarchy of the soul and its states in the Qur'an.

— *qalb*, or "heart," the spiritual soul and metaphysical center of being, site of connection to the divine, the thinking and governing soul, the seat of discernment, the spiritual organ where the person's character is formed, but also the heart as physical organ, which governs the circulation of blood and the pulsating rhythm of life.

— *rūḥ*, or "spirit," at once the corporeal spirit or pneuma of Avicennian medicine and the immaterial soul in the metaphysical world of spirits; the spiritual immortal essence mentioned in the Qur'an, which is a divine inscription in the living soul and the memory of the origin and return to God (Qur'an 17:85: "They asked thee concerning the Spirit [*ruḥ*]: Say: the Spirit is by command of my Lord: Of knowledge is only a little that is communicated to you").

— *'aql*, the intellect or the mind. Whereas the intellect in the psychology of Ibn Sina and others is the seat of the rational faculty and the capacity for judgment, as well as the interface with the world of angelic intelligences, the Imam follows the Qur'an and al-Ghazali (and indirectly Aristotle) in attributing that central place to the heart, rather than to the mind.

The soul conceived and engaged by the Imam in his practice is both embodied and temporal, because we exist and strive in our bodies, and beyond body and time, inasmuch as its essence partakes of the world of the soul and of the mystery of the divine: its journey originates from God and returns to God. It is agonistic and vulnerable—vulnerable to self-deception and "choking," but also capable of "expansion" when anchored in the certainty of faith and transformed through the ethical work of the imagination.

In the account of the soul I strung together from my conversations with the Imam over the years, imagination plays a pivotal role, both as a faculty of the soul and as an autonomous realm of cosmic existence. The Imam stresses its "formative" power—*taṣawwūr*, the formative faculty, and *takhayyul*, the imaginative faculty—in its capacity to configure, form, and de-form; and shows the way images have an effect on the heart (*qalb*), the spiritual center of being. For images, he says, contain the affective form of a life design. They have force and form and can shape and transform a person's life and character or encrypt a trajectory of death instead.

His therapeutic and pedagogical interventions are aimed at a "repossession" of imagination, which is also a decolonization of desire, for he asserts that, in our time, it is through a coopting of the imagination that human beings, Muslim and otherwise, are reduced to captivity and oppression. To understand this plea we need to cast aside the notion of imagination as fancy, phantasy, or mental representation,[17] and instead appreciate the way imagination is here the faculty of the soul that makes possible discernment, knowledge, and a wrestling with truth[18] that is the striving of the subject. It is the stage, one of the stages (but a privileged one in the life of human beings), where unfolds the moral dramaturgy of the soul—at once a perilous being-at-risk and a movement of perfection and vital intensification.

The Imam insists on the importance of cultivating what he calls an "affirmative imagination," "affirmative images" (*ṣuwar ijābiyya*): affirmative in the sense of positive, life affirming, but more fundamentally in the sense of affirming the truth of God as transcendental anchoring point of human life and conduct. *Ijābiyya*, a positive attitude, is a concept emphasized in the classical works of al-Ghazali and Ibn Qayyim al-Jawziyya—and that, in a parallel way, was articulated by modernists such as Sayyid Qutb.[19]

In doing so, the Imam turns towards a classical Islamic theory of the passions and the faculties, the *nafs*, and the heart, which he reads in light of the Qur᾿an, as generations of Muslim scholars have done before him, not only to cite a historical or cultural archive but to embody and embrace it, to illuminate the present historical forms of alienation and loss. In his discussion of anger, melancholy, and pain, and in the energetic and emotional space of his healing sessions (when, as he puts it, "the jinn speaks through the tongue of the afflicted"), he postulates a political and ethical work of the imagination, one that is capable of generating "ethical action" (*ʿamal*) from the midst of a history of trauma. In this phenomenology of imagination the Imam emphasizes the centrality of the heart, as spiritual organ and interiority of the self, distancing himself, he says, from the "scientific theories"[20] that treat the imagination as a faculty of the mind (*ʿaql*). The question is not epistemological, but ethical. And if imagination is the gate of knowledge, it is also an opening to the Invisible.

In our world, the Imam says, we are subjected to the intrusive pressure of destructive images, images of want and images of loss, which insinuate themselves in the heart, or seize the heart with a traumatic and terrorizing force. They are images of war and destruction on television and the Internet, becoming increasingly close to home in recent years and months; scenes of abuse, humiliation, and injustice in one's own immediate environment, in the intimacy of the home or the neighborhood, phantasies of consumption, incited by the shopping centers that keep opening in wealthy enclaves and that are advertised in oversized illuminated posters at major intersections, creating an illusive access to a luxury beyond reach, scornful of living conditions in poor neighborhoods. They are images, above all, in the sense of affective impressions, traumatic inscriptions or poisonous unconscious memories that leave a scar in the heart; "forms" (*ṣuwar*) internalized through habituation, or passed on as a haunting legacy, sometimes actualized in the agency and voice of a demonic presence. *Taḍyīq al-nafs*, "the choking of the soul," is the torment of existence most exemplary of our time, the effect of the impression in the soul and the heart of deathly images that erect the high walls of a claustrophobic space. Those whose soul is "choked" enter a state of spiritual and existential groundlessness, exhaustion of the will and of desire, and lose trust and hope in themselves, in others, in the world, and in God. Soul choking is an existential and moral quicksand, where despair (*ya's*) borders on theological transgression. As said in the Qur'an: "Do not despair of the mercy of God, for none despair of God's mercy except those who have no faith" (12:87), and, "He said: And who despairs of the mercy of his Lord, but such as go astray?" (15:56)

Outside it is almost dark. We are now sitting on the narrow sofas lining the wall in the Imam's reception room. On the small round table in front of us, my recorder tapes his comments as they take on the eloquent and more formal tone of a lesson. The Imam is now elaborating on the agency of evil in the oppression of the soul, and the way evil promptings and suggestions recruit the imagination to its destructive task. He goes on to explain how Shaytan (Satan), the Qur'anic figuration of the trial of evil—at once internal and external to the human soul—"instigates and oppresses the *nafs*," the desiring and resentful personal soul, moved by the passions of anger and desire, and the soul loses ground, loses trust, and starts despairing:

> The *nafs* sends negative images (*ṣuwar salbiyya*) to the heart, destructive images. To the mind and to the heart, but the most important is the heart (*qalb*), not the mind (*'aql*), because the heart is the seat of the formative power, which is also the imaginative power (*li-anna l-qalb huwa mawḍu' al-taṣawwur*

> *wa-l-takhayyul*). This is what is said in the Qur'an: the seat of imagination is the heart (*qalb*), not the intellect (*'aql*), where scientific theories want to put it.
>
> The soul (*nafs*) sends negative and hopeless images of the future, to "form" in the heart (*fa yataṣawwar li-l-qalb*) an image of life as life burned, life destroyed (*ḥayāt muḍrama*). And the person starts imagining that nothing good can happen in the future, only oppression and disaster are foretold, and pain and torture (*'adhāb*), poverty and exclusion, dispossession and destitution (*ḥirmān*) are all there is. . . . And so that human person (*insān*) lives a burning moment. God protect us from harm!

The Imam pauses for me to change the batteries of the recorder. What he is saying is important and he wants us to keep a record. His twelve-year-old daughter comes into the room. He invites her to sit with us and continues:

> And these images that the *nafs* receives in the form of a devilish whisper (*al-waswās*), a destructive and maddening imagining, colonize and murder the heart, which in truth is not the heart of a Muslim. For if faith is present in the heart, the person concentrates on images only when they are affirmative images (*suwar ijābiyya*). But if the heart is deserted by faith, the person accepts those destructive imaginings, welcomes them, and they set the heart ablaze. And choking, the choking of the soul (*taḍyīq al-nafs*), suffocates that human person (*taḍyīq bi-l-insān*). And he or she can no longer aspire to something that might bring renewal, something affirmative, other than his or her own dying; he or she thinks incessantly of the way in which to bring about the limit of death. This is suicide.

In the tradition the Imam is conjuring here, the imaginative faculty is the organ of the soul that mediates between the soul, the external world, encountered through the bodily senses, and the experience of the invisible world beyond sensory perception (*'ālam al-ghayb*, the world of invisible realities). In Islamic cosmology, and particularly in its Sufi formulation, *'ālam al-malakūt* (the angelic or spiritual world) is opposed to *'ālam al-mulk* (the physical world of existence, the Kingdom), and is intermediate between that and *'ālam al-jabarūt* (the world of absolute immensity and sovereignty, the world of Spirit). The *'ālam al-malakūt* (*malak* means angel) is the imaginal realm where the souls, or intellects, and spiritual faculties of the soul reside. The *'ālam al-mulk*, the physical world of existence, is also described as *'ālam al-shahāda*, the visible world, the perceptible sphere of material forms and bodies testified by the five external senses, and is opposed to *ʿālam al-ghayb*, the world of "nonmanifest" or "invisible" realities, encompassing the mystery of the divine.[21]

At one level, and as detailed in the psychology of Ibn Sina, imagination is the cornerstone of a theory of perception in the world of material realities: it is the faculty or "power" (*quwwa*) of the embodied soul that constitutes and preserves the engravings of sense perception in a form, or imprint, making them available as the molds of memory, enabling the combination of forms, and hence thinking and imaginative activity.[22] But at another level, as a spiritual organ,[23] imagination is the faculty of the soul that governs the internal or spiritual senses (*al-ḥiss al-baṭin*) dedicated to a different kind of perception, the imaginal reception of the world of spirits (*ʿālam al-malakūt*, *ʿālam al-ghayb*), inaccessible to human sensory perception and knowledge and approachable only through contemplative vision. At yet another level imagination is an autonomous ontological realm of subtle essences, independent of the seeing and the thinking subject; cosmic existence is identical to imagination. According to Ibn ʿArabi divine essence manifests itself in the cosmos as "nondelimited imagination" (*al-khayāl al-muṭlaq*).[24]

In his account of the phenomenology of "soul choking," the Imam draws from both topographies of the soul. He gestures to the genesis of form through sensory impression in the configurational imagination, storehouse of memory and mold of thinking; and to the ethical engraving of images in the heart, the spiritual organ, the locus of ethical judgment, which connects the human soul to the world of invisible realities and grounds it in its divine essence.

Imagination is both a capacity and a modality of being. It enables the cultivation of "states" of the heart (*aḥwāl al-qalb*), in prayer, for instance, and in the practice of remembrance (*dhikr*), when the internal senses are absorbed in submitting the heart to God, attempting to reconcile the gestures "of the limbs" with the intent of the heart (an attitude that the self should strive to carry into the acts of daily life inasmuch as they are dedicated to God).[25] Imagination mediates what al-Ghazali calls "the actions of the heart" (*aʿmāl al-qalb*), in terms of intention (*niyya*), determination of the will (*ʿazm*), decision (*himma*), and purpose (*qaṣd*), thereby determining the ethical nature and accountability of the act in the afterlife.[26] And it is the imagination that registers the exhortation (*naṣīḥa*) of the preacher and the recital (*ruqya*) of the healer, who seeks to speak directly to the heart, leaving an "impression," as the Imam does with his patients. For when the soul is in the grip of despair, having lost orientation and connectedness, imagination can become the site of a reconfiguration and reconstruction of a "place," to "expand" the soul and reconnect it with its vital source.

As a faculty of the creaturely soul, imagination is the medium of experience, thinking and discernment. As an autonomous ontological realm, it is a space of manifestation (where the jinn and Shaytan are imaginalized as external to the soul). But inasmuch as it is it stirred by the movement of the passions, it is also open to the risk of destruction, calling for the never-ending work of ethical struggle.

At one level this has always been the case. From the early homiletic literature of exhortation to the writings of al-Ghazali and to the Imam, "the battle of the heart" and the human inadequacy to live on the path of God have been central themes in the tradition from which the Imam draws conceptual orientation and resource. In his *Iḥyāʾ ʿulūm al-dīn* (the *Revival*, or better yet the *Revivification, of the Religious Sciences*), al-Ghazali describes the agency of "involuntary suggestions" or thoughts (*khawāṭir*) originating in the desiring self or in demonic insinuations, or instead in angelic messages, and the way these move the imagination and have an edifying or instead a destructive effect on the heart. Yet at another level, the phenomenology of the imagination outlined by the Imam is rooted in his attempt to discern the specific forms of colonization of desire characteristic of the time in which we are living now. Melancholy is not just the effect of dispossession, poverty, and the lack of existential horizon. And even if later on in our conversation the Imam will cite a saying of the Prophet that relates poverty to *kufr*, unbelief and ingratitude towards God, the point here is that despair is not a "natural" occurrence, but a surrender to the insinuations of Shaytan.

The Imam's use of the vocabulary of the soul is not always consistent. In our conversations he sometimes refers to the *nafs* as the lower embodied soul, stirred by the "appetitive" passions of anger and lust, and as the inciter to evil (*al-nafs al-ammāra bi-l-sūʾ*), and sometimes as the spiritual soul understood as "subtle substance" that as such is just another name for the heart. And he refers to the heart as the spiritual center of being, but also as the bodily organ that oversees the circulation of blood and that is affected and agitated by the passions of anger. But this apparent lack of consistency is found in the tradition itself, and grants us an insight into the theological mystery of the unity and multiplicity of the soul with the interlocking of its material and spiritual dimensions. As al-Ghazali makes clear in a passage of his *Marvels of the Heart*, the question is that of the overlapping or folding of the physical and the metaphysical modes of the soul, where the four terms *nafs*, *qalb*, *rūḥ*, and *ʿaql* (soul, heart, spirit, and intelligence) describe specific agencies and bodily organs while referring at the same time to the unity of the soul as autonomous spiritual substance. Each of these terms, al-Ghazali explains, has "two meanings," a corporeal meaning and a spiritual one, and the two are related in ways inaccessible to human reason, for they pertain to the mystery of the divine (*al-ghayb*). Al-Ghazali writes:

> So it is now made clear to you that there exist the following meanings of these names: the corporeal heart (*qalb*), the corporeal spirit (*rūḥ*), the appetitive soul (*nafs*), and intelligence (*ʿaql*). These are four meanings that are denoted by four terms. There is also a fifth meaning, which is that subtle tenuous substance in man that knows and perceives, and all four of these names are successively applied to it. There are then five meanings and four terms, and each term is used with two meanings. . . . Wherever the expression "heart" occurs in the Qurʾan and the sunna, its intended meaning is that [which] in man . . . discerns and comes to know the real nature of things. This might be alluded to metonymically as the heart, which is in the breast, because between the subtle tenuous substance and the physical heart there is a special connection.[27]

This way of conceiving the soul inscribes a long history of the Aristotelian and Platonic tripartite configuration of the soul in Islamic tradition as both "form" and process of "formation" and "perfection," as this is transformed through the vision of the Qurʾan and its exegetical traditions. In the Avicennian and Ghazalian accounts that continue to resonate in the commentary of the Imam[28] the soul has three modes of existence, in a hierarchy from inanimate to animate, from matter to form and from body to spirit. It has as well three "states," or degrees of purification (*tazkiya*), as mentioned in the Qurʾan and in the hadith tradition with reference to the *nafs* and the heart: the parallel hierarchy of *al-nafs al-ammāra* (the soul that orders and incites to evil: Qurʾan 12:53), *al-nafs al-lawwāma* (the soul that reproaches itself and repents: Qurʾan 75:2), and *al-nafs al-muṭmaʾinna* (that soul purified and in peace: Qurʾan 89:27–30).

It is a vegetal soul, the lower form of life endowed with the powers of nutrition, growth, and reproduction; an animal or animated soul, the intermediate and properly "psychical" form of life, seat of the passions of desire and anger and endowed with the powers of movement and sensory perception, and with the higher faculties of common sense, memory, and imagination; and a human or spiritual soul, endowed with the power to project itself into the mode of angelic existence and the desire for God. In this configuration the soul is not just a compound of passions, faculties, and quiddities, but an activity, an "act of being"[29] and the site of a struggle. The theory of the soul is a theory of subjectivity that, however, does not coincide with what we are accustomed to think of as the boundaries and qualities of a human subject. The human soul here is not a given, but is a process of striving and a battle with victories and defeats, where the possibility and risk of "becoming animal," "becoming plant," or even "becoming rock" can never be excluded and is in fact the lot of most of us for most of our lives, for the "becoming human" of the soul is possible only through a work of cultivation and purification—where the qualifier "human" is to be understood as the capacity of accessing a mode of awareness that is the awareness of God, one that, in this vision, often remains unrealized in creaturely life.

The passions and faculties of the soul in its bodily existence are at once an obstacle and the necessary ground, the stage, so to speak, of the life of the soul. "Constriction" and "expansion," in the Qur'anic vocabulary of the Imam, are movements and vicissitudes in this process, connecting the embodied soul and its imaginative activity to the ethical-juridical question of living on the path of God, and opening it to the possibility of transformation. This conception, articulated by the Imam in conversations with me and with some of his more speculatively inclined friends, informs his therapeutic activity as a practical knowledge, a "knowing with the heart" of what a modification of existence might be in the life of his patients, and in the life of each of us.

August 2014

"Are you familiar with *Kitāb al-nafs*, The Book of the Soul?"

The question caught me by surprise. *Kitāb al-nafs* is Ibn Sina's treatise on the soul, also known as his "Psychology," a section of his *Kitāb al-najāt*, Book of Salvation, itself part of the larger work called *Kitāb al-shifāʾ*, The Book of Healing.

The questioner was a friend of the Imam's visiting from Sweden. We were talking in the margin of a larger conversation with the Imam and other visitors, retreating in a corner of the room during a noisy moment of lounging sociality, doing other things at the same time, showing me an application on his phone, and asking me about myself, what I was doing there, why someone like me would be spending the afternoon with his friend the Imam. He called him Shaykh, and the intimacy between them was colored by their many years of friendship and the tender respect characteristic of a relationship of spiritual guidance. "He says you are interested in psychiatry, that you did research at the psychiatric hospital, that's where he met you. What is it exactly you are after?" The question wasn't just inquisitive. He himself was enough of an outsider in the house of the Imam to be able to understand that an outsider such as me would have reasons to be there. It related more to the inkling of a common experience. He was asking me about the nature of my own interest in the maladies of the soul, and the subtle matters of the spirit, which, he said, we had both discussed with our mutual friend.

I mentioned my work with the Imam on the Qur'anic cure, my attempt to relate it to the enigma of madness and the problem of the unconscious in psychoanalysis. He was familiar with the *ruqya*, of course, having accompanied the Imam in his work with patients on many occasions. He saw the *ruqya* both as people see it, as a cure, and as a stage of otherworldly receptivity of the soul. This is also what I had begun to understand in the labor of writing this book.

The key question, he said immediately and somewhat uncannily, was the *nafs*, the soul and its "internal senses." Perhaps our trajectories, searches, or research had a common interest. He had read many books in a quest in which the Imam had been a companion and a guide. He recalled the nights when they were both younger, spent debating until dawn on religious and philosophical questions concerning the states of the soul in its journey and its capacity for knowledge and visionary experience. The Imam had accompanied him through moments of trial and self-doubt, moments of illness, and his guidance had helped him find direction and ground. The sound of children running interrupted our words.

Later he told me about a physical illness and a spiritual crisis, followed by his decision to radically change his life, and to embark on a journey that was also geographical. Reading the Qur'an by himself, he started feeling the presence of God. "When one starts feeling the presence of God it begins to seem as if the world doesn't make sense."

He visited many scholars (*fuqahā'*, the plural of *faqīh*), and could not find help in what they said, until he met the Imam. "He knows how to talk about God; a scholar of great depth who is also modest, lives simply, and doesn't like to use a fancy language." He started studying books on the psychology and philosophy of the *nafs*, and discovering *Kitāb al-nafs* had been a gift. When I myself read Ibn Sina's *Book of the Soul* I understood how he could find there an insight into his experience, and a frame of sorts, with the help of the Imam. In Ibn Sina's topography of the *nafs* I also recognized an articulation that finds an echo in the Imam's vocabulary of the soul, and on the stage of the *ruqya* itself.

Ibn Sina's *Book of the Soul* is at once a phenomenology of sensory perception and of supersensory reception and illumination. It describes the embodied soul in its unfolding in the material world as vegetal, animal, and rational soul, and at the same time reminds us that the embodied soul has two faces, is at once this-worldly and other-worldly: "It is as if our soul had two faces: one turned towards the body . . . the other turned towards the higher principles, and it must always be ready to receive from what is There in the Higher Plane and to be influenced by it."

The animal soul—the soul in its properly "psychic" modality—is described as being set in motion by the "motive powers" (or faculties, *quwwāt*) of desire and anger, and by the motor nerves and muscles, the efficient powers; and as imprinted upon by the "perceptive powers," which include the five "external senses" (sight, hearing, smell, taste, and touch), and the "internal senses," of which the most important is the imagination. While the organs of sense are capable of sensation by directly receiving the imprint of the forms of the sensible world, they are incapable of retaining the forms of that impression: "just as water which has the power of receiving an imprint, but lacks that of retaining it."[30] Only the faculty of imagination (*al-quwwa al-muṣawwira*) has the power to preserve, store, combine, interpret and operate on the forms it receives from the organs of sense, and to perceive "the non-sensible intentions that exist in the individual sensible objects," discerning situations and intentions in a semiotic activity.

Imagination is found at the inception of essential motion itself because it is "when a desirable or repugnant image is imprinted on the imagination, that the powers of desire and repulsion are aroused into movement."[31] The soul is that impression and that movement, which for Ibn Sina is at once a movement of perfectibility and intensification of life, a "becoming more capable of life,"[32] across the three modes of the soul (vegetable, animal, and rational) in the cosmos and within each soul, and in terms of what he calls the soul's fundamental unity, as " a single substance that has many faculties." Such a unity is not just an identity or a quiddity, as in the Cartesian subject of consciousness, but is a coming into being that reverberates as the act of the divine creator.

The purification of the soul opens to illumination and prophecy. Ibn Sina explains: "It must be understood that elemental bodies are prevented from receiving life by their being in absolute contradiction. . . . The nearer they approach the mean, the more capable of life they become."

When this happens to someone, the Imam's friend told me, that experience resembles madness and throws one into a state of confusion. And for that reason it was crucial to have a guide, as he had found in the Imam.

I will return to this phenomenology of the soul, its expansion and its choking,[33] but I choose to begin with it now because it crystallizes the generative core of what I have attempted to trace in the margin of my conversations with the Imam.

For me, listening to the Imam and discussing with him necessarily also meant reading and engaging on my own with his sources: the Qur'an, *fiqh* jurisprudence, the corpus of Arab and prophetic medicine, the classical tradition of ethics known as *akhlāq*, and the religious and philosophical literature on the metaphysics of the soul and the heart. This is what made possible his conceptualization of soul choking and his engagement with it in his practice with his patients, where the work of the imagination is addressed on a stage of the trials and vicissitudes of the soul. I was clear that I could not write only based on his practice, or even his teachings and explications alone. In the watermark of his words, there was an archive that I had the responsibility of addressing, on its own terms, and in terms of the questions and concepts that had guided my own search.

As I began writing I asked myself what it would mean to listen to the Imam and translate his thought and practice in my ethnography. The Imam is speaking of an infraction—the choking—and a melancholic identification, the being morphed into the loss of another. It is a theory of trauma, if the concept can be reclaimed in conversation with and as a challenge to the analytic tradition of the soul that is psychoanalysis. In a little book on the forgotten place of the soul in Freudian thought,[34] Bruno Bettelheim argued that the concept of *Seele* (soul), the soul that is the psyche, was evacuated in its English rendition as "mind" for the Standard Edition. Something disturbing in Freud's approach was brushed aside, and the translation of *Seele* as mind came as an instrumental adaptation to American consumer culture. Bettelheim traces Freud's analytic lexicon, terms such as "Visitation"

(*Heimsucht*), "being visited" by a memory (in "A Disturbance of Memory on the Acropolis"), and argues that for Freud psychoanalysis is a "spiritual journey of self-discovery," not one aimed at the deciphering of the unconscious, but instead an "intimation," and a labor of enabling the "dialectic of the soul" as a process of self-disclosure by which the soul (*Seele*) may become aware of itself. In a somewhat related sense, and taking seriously Freud's and Bettelheim's "intimation," the ethnography of the *nafs* I propose here is not just a description, the phenomenological outline of a life-world, but something that addresses us directly, concerning the possibility of transforming our soul today.

What does it mean to repossess being and to think of life as a commitment to the next generation? For the new generation is endangered in its futuricity by the closure of imagination and the melancholic wound carved by the operation of power, by the violent apparatus of the state and its ability to counterfeit identities and values; and endangered, as well, by the orientation of aspirations and desires, the addiction to consumer goods and their lack, in the new psychic economies of global capitalism at its dispossessed margins, and in its incipient mutations and disintegrations.

Three questions are central in my engagement with the thought and practice of the Imam. The first concerns the nature of subjugation, for a person and a collectivity. It is Ibn Khaldun's question in the epigraph to this section, and what the Imam describes, in theological, political, and existential terms, as the annihilation of being, the "choking of the soul," in the larger context of a society imploding. In Ibn Khaldun's fourteenth-century politico-medical formulation, at issue is a form of domination that rules through coercion and humiliation (*bi-l-qahr*), by disabling, breaking, and instilling fear (*al-ikhāfa*). A form of domination that abducts the desire to resist (*tudhhibu al-manaʿat ʿanhum*), by growing in the soul/*nafs* of the oppressed the deathly vice of apathy (*limā yakūnu min al-takāsul fī al-nufūs al-muḍṭahida*). Resonating with Ibn Khaldun's depiction, "soul choking" is a form of disablement that "breaks the soul," comparable to the intrusion and incorporation of a gaze that murders the self and "sends off the soul" into a realm of the ghostly and the undead. In this sense, it can be conceptualized as a form of failed mourning.

The idea of "failed mourning" is Freud's, via the reinscription of Nicolas Abraham and Maria Torok,[35] for whom melancholy is the haunting by an attachment that consumes the vital space of the self and became incorporated through traumatic identification, or by a "phantom" that is transmitted across generations in the form of a crypt and a corpse within. Inasmuch as the loss is not mourned or symbolized, but just preserved inaccessible in a state of withdrawal or foreclosure, inasmuch as it is resistant to any possibility of experience, even unconscious experience, it cannot give rise to productive new forms and configurations of being. In the Imam's clinical and liturgical work there is an active engagement with such crypts and desires of the unmourned, a therapeutics of melancholia, personal and collective, that I address through his discussion of "cases" and "states"—*ḥālāt*—that involve the desire of the jinn, its specific topology and mode of transmission, and the way it broaches multiple temporal and cosmological realms.

The crypt resonates with the conceptual and experiential core of Fanon's thinking. There are echoes of Fanon's psychopolitics of race as the fate of a being "clad in mourning." Fanon had been a reference for the first postcolonial generation, in Algeria and Morocco, as elsewhere in the Middle East. Muslim thinkers such as Sayyid Qutb in Egypt and Ali Shariati in Iran had engaged with his thought, in a conversation that weighed and displaced the Fanonian questions into another scene of alienation and emancipation that was posed and debated in Islam.

In *Black Skin, White Masks* Fanon pronounces his phenomenological diagnosis of the annihilation of being in the form of a psychodynamics of "intrusion." Sovereignty and domination are located at the core of psychic space, and they are intimately related to desire and the scene of the phantasm. He describes the raced/colonized subject as constituted by the violent intrusion of the other, the colonizer, in the psychic space of the self, an intrusion that evacuates the self and replaces it with the poisonous object of the other's fantasy, an object with which the self will coincide. The intrusion is a seizure of the imagination and of the bodily space of the other; an occupation understood in spatial, almost military terms, as a shrinking of vital space, which snatches the self and pulverizes its corporeal schema, halting the work of the imagination even in the form of dreams, and producing in its place a somatic hallucination.[36] At the center of Fanon's argument is the attack of the Gaze, the look of the Other, the white person, but also the colonial system, the white mythology (with the central role played by the fantasy of the terrifying and sexually powerful African in European culture), and ultimately the white symbolic ("language" and "thought" as powerful European assets). But most important, the attack of the Gaze is also an encounter with a drive to destruction as such: a force of disintegration that is both in the Other, and is found at the traumatic core of the self, inasmuch as the core of the self is born in the Other, and is inhabited by desire.

The second question has to do with the possibility of reorienting the existential and ethical position of the subject in the world by an act of imagination; of interrupting a habitus of entrapment, resentment, and self-reproach in relation to a history of loss, thereby transforming one's relation to that history, opening up the possibility of living again—of futures unforeseen. I will be asking through my ethnography what the nature is of such an opening, which Frantz Fanon (in the epigraph), addressing a set of questions that may be seen as related, called an "authentic arising" (*authentique surgissement*), and which he described as a "leap" (*saut*)—a leap that amounts to introducing invention into the midst of existence, as an open-ended engagement with the entrapment of history, as evinced in his repetitions, metamorphoses, and hauntings.

For, as Fanon reflected in a footnote to his collection of clinical cases from the Blida psychiatric hospital in Algeria, there is no simple exit from the legacy of a violent history, from the entanglement of personal and collective traumas, the intricate transmission and transmutations of symptoms and phantasm. Pondering the case of a former militant awakened to the reality and responsibility to participate in the anticolonial war by a symptom of a recurrent vertigo, a physical-existential dizziness accompanied by sleeplessness and self-destructive thoughts that seized him on the anniversary of an action, Fanon does not dwell on the individual post-traumatic syndrome, but instead turns the question back to himself and us. He calls us into the historical life of the symptom, the "vertigo," which we must feel as our own, and asks: "Mais pouvons nous échapper au vertige? Qui oserait prétendre que le vertige ne hante pas toute existence?" (But can we ever escape the sense of vertigo? Who can affirm that vertigo does not haunt each and every life?).[37] The point for Fanon is not to eschew but to engage the vertigo of existence. For in the experience of vertigo, in the staggering, and by extension in the symptom, the phantasm, the delusion, exists the encounter with the traumatic reality of a collective history. In the blinding and paralyzing context of colonial terror, not so dissimilar from its postcolonial returns, the vertigo of history becomes for Fanon an ethical site of vision. In what follows, I ask what the implications are of interrogating and engaging the historical life of the symptom, the "vertigo of existence" from within a contemporary Islamic tradition, and what can we learn from it for ourselves.

The third question that I raise in this part has do with the relationship of historical time, the time of "soul choking," the time of illness and political oppression, to another time, itself related to the time of trauma and contained in the structure of the symptom, but opening up to the possibility of a "passage," a passage across or beyond; a passage to the unknown and the infinite, beyond the human subject and human temporality, onto an Outside where a reconfiguration of relationships may take place. This is a possibility of traumatic time itself that is explored in the therapeutic practice of the Imam, and in different ways in psychoanalysis, and by Fanon. It has to do with the paradoxical contiguity of repetition and the encounter with the real—Fanon's "vertigo"[38]—that is registered by the lagged character of the time of trauma, a delay that Freud called *Nachträglichkeit* (the fact of being "a posteriori," deferred, belated), and Laplanche translated as *après coup*, "afterwardness";[39] the fact that trauma happens at least twice over, in a prospective and retrospective folding that shatters a linear experience of time and points to a theological dimension of traumatic time itself. In the words of Laplanche, who compared the architecture of traumatic time to the "hermeneutics of the message" in sacred texts, traumatic time contains a "message from the Other":

> Afterwardness is inconceivable without a model of translation: that is, it presupposes that something is proffered by the other, and this is then afterwards retranslated and reinterpreted. . . . This past cannot be a purely factual one, an unprocessed or raw or 'given'. It contains rather in an immanent fashion something that comes before—a message from the other. It is impossible therefore to put forward a purely hermeneutic position on this—that is to say, that everyone interprets their past according to their present—because the past already has something deposited in it that demands to be deciphered, which is the message of the other person. But does not modern hermeneutics forget its very beginning, when it was—in the religious interpretation of sacred texts—a hermeneutic of the message?[40]

In the theological context of the spiritual cures of the "vertigo" of history the point is to make possible a passage, a leap to another time, learning to read illness and the time of calamity as at once a historical condition of our time, and a "sign" and a "passage" (the double sense of the Arabic concept of *ʿibra*, pl. *ʿibar*) in the tapestry of a larger cosmic history, a sign one is called to ponder and learn from. Healing is introducing a pedagogy that implies the ability to read signs in a cosmological sense, to reinstitute the open-endedness of the world.

This is what Ibn Khaldun considered the ethical task of the historian, at once bearing witness to the forms of social and political life that succeeded one another on the revolving scene of the human world, as seized from the historical time of catastrophe, and reading the events and their unfolding as signs and lessons (*ʿibar*), disclosures of nonhuman time; disclosures of the temporality of the hereafter, which opened visibility and insight into the human world. This double movement is captured in a Qurʾanic verse that accompanies this ethnography through its concluding movement: "In their stories there is a lesson (*ʿibra*) for those who are endowed with insight" (*la-qad kāna fī qaṣaṣihim ʿibra li ʿūlī-l-ʿalbāb*) (Qurʾan 12:111).

EIGHT

Faqīh al-Nafs: The Jurist of the Soul

My conversations with the Imam started in 2003, in the company of Dr. A., a young psychiatrist who was completing his residency at the psychiatric hospital where I was doing fieldwork. The Imam had agreed to come and talk with us at the invitation of Dr. A., who had been introduced to the Imam by a patient they had in common. Dr. A. had questions that found no answers in his medical training and searched for answers elsewhere, exploring the world of religious cures. They had met only once before, the psychiatrist and the Imam, and at the request of the patient, who perhaps wanted to ease, through this meeting of her different worlds, the double consciousness that colored her experience of treatment. The three of us met for the first time on a cold winter morning in a small office in the hospital's men's locked ward (*service fermé homme*). That day at the hospital we had a long and somewhat formal conversation on the nature of mental illness and its relation to the problem of evil (*sharr, shayṭān*) through the secondary agency of the jinn and the intervention of *siḥr*, the ancient and yet all too contemporary plague of sorcery.

The Imam outlined the two major causes of insanity in the approach of the Quranic cure, *al-mass shayṭani*, "the demonic touch or demonic infringement," and *siḥr*, "magic" or "sorcery." The first was the harmful bond that jinn established with humans on the mode of encroachment and occupation; the second was the result of a deathly human intervention, a "machine of destruction," as the Imam put it, a machine that was operated and kept running with the fuel (*benzin*) of the jinn. The machine of *siḥr* was both ancient and contemporary; it remained active across generations as a deathly transmission, and could live on "until the end of times," he said, if no attempt was made to stop it. It was by far the most dangerous cause of mental illness, and intermingled with somatic conditions to the point of an uncanny indeterminacy. In the contemporary moment, the Imam explained, *siḥr* has come to the forefront of human illness, because of the generalization of envy in a world where desire is colonized by the possession of consumer goods, and for many by the impossibility to obtain them, as well as the propensity to violence, rendered more acute by social and economic disparities, political abuse, and the absence of justice. He gave us the title of a book on the etiology and cures of *siḥr*, and invited us to read it in anticipation of future conversations.

In his capacity as a *muʿālij sharʿī* (a therapist according to the way of the shariʿa), the Imam is opposed to magical healing, in the sense of the vernacular therapies historically widespread in Morocco and implicated in the arts of divination and magic. This opposition is not simply doctrinal, but is based on a theological interpretation of magic and sorcery as techniques of fetishistic attachment, opposed to the shariʿa cure understood as a practice of freedom.

The Imam is also unsympathetic to Sufism, even though his therapeutic practice and theological thinking are infused with a sensibility indebted to Sufism's concern with the affective life of the soul, first and foremost concerning the centrality of affect and the passions, the place of the heart, and the experience of *wujūd*, or "coming to being," in the therapeutic sessions.[1] In his own way, he is an active member in the local Islamic reform movement, in the sense of the reassertion of a style of theological reasoning and ethical practice that come together in a combination of spiritual medicine, *daʿwa* preaching, pedagogy, and advice; most of all, however, through his exercise of the therapeutic liturgy of the *ruqya*. The *ruqya* is an address to the soul, and the self, in a state of dispossession and intrusion of otherness. It is an address originating in the Qurʾanic utterance, understood as the truthful transmission of divine speech, conveyed in the emotional space of a transference between souls. In the midst of historical dispossession and defacement the sacred space of the *ruqya* and its spiritual and existential aftermath are related to the cultivation of a capacity to become the host of a divine gaze; a capacity that is paradoxically intensified in the proximity of its loss, at a time of trauma, where life, and faith, can be lost and found.

Every day the Imam confronts the particular lives and the painful predicaments of what he calls "the afflicted" (*al-muṣāb*), his patients. His practice as a therapist is paralleled by his activity as a preacher. He delivers the Friday sermon at a small mosque in the low-income neighborhood where he lives, a large informal housing development on the outskirts of the city, where an old shantytown is intermixed with run-down concrete buildings and surrounded by fast-growing housing projects still under construction, part of the state's effort in recent years to eradicate informal housing and shantytowns. The mosque itself, visible from the room where the Imam performs his healing sessions, is a simple white building that on Fridays spills out of its concrete walls, too small to hold the large number of people who come to pray. Mats are laid out in the surrounding area, a loudspeaker projects his voice, and people pray in the open space, the unpaved ground between shops, houses, and shacks. The Imam's sermons and lessons (*durūs*) are valued and recognized by a large circle of people, among whom many are youths who look up to him as a reference point and turn to him in moments of existential crisis. His reputation has grown based on the audio recordings of his lessons that he began copying and sharing during the years we have known each other, and that informally circulate to other parts of Morocco and among communities in Europe.

The Imam was familiar with the hospital grounds from having come to visit some of his patients there. But he never performed the *ruqya* at the hospital, at least not in the form of an explicit session. Aware of the hostile attitude that is dominant in the medical institution, he limited himself to a "silent recitation" of Qur'anic passages (a mode in which the tongue articulates sounds that only the reciter can hear). Yet that hostility was changing somewhat, because of psychiatrists such as Dr. A. and of therapists such as the Imam who attested to the legitimately Islamic character of the liturgy of the *ruqya,* and in general of shari'a healing, grounded in *fiqh* jurisprudence and the medicine of the soul. In this new context Islamic healing could not simply be dismissed in terms of the customary colonial and postcolonial indictment of "traditional therapies." The Imam has never ceased to point out that many patients populating the hospitals are afflicted by an illness of demonic origin, rather than by exclusively organic conditions. Yet unlike other scholars of *'ilm al-nafs al-islāmī* (Islamic psychology) who attempt to lay out the principles of an Islamic psychology for a growing Arabic-reading Muslim public, he has never shown an interest in directly contesting the biomedical claim to knowledge—at least not at the level of a polemic between competing understandings of science.

In his practice, as I came to witness in the course of the years, he is attentive to both the medical-natural and spiritual-religious dimensions of illness and cure, always careful to consider the possibility of a physical illness; reminding a woman that the pain she experiences in her breast may be due to the location of a jinn that found a nesting place there, but that since demonic intrusion can have the long-term consequence of inducing cancer (*saraṭān*), in parallel with his therapy she should have a mammogram. And vice versa, as in the case of a group of women who have had breast cancer often removed by mastectomies and who visit the Imam for spiritual advice and to partake in the *ruqya*, keeping in touch with each other as an informal support group in the shadow of the Qur'an in the protective frame of his presence.

The Imam is also a therapist in the classical Arab tradition of humoral medicine, steeped in natural philosophy; in that mode, which is not apart from, but in dialogue with, the others, with his extensive knowledge of plants he prepares herbal remedies for his patients. He doesn't see a contradiction between a diagnosis of humoral imbalance and one of spiritual and demonic illness; both are subject to the power of God and often blur into one another.[2] Ibn Qayyim's own text on prophetic medicine makes extensive use of humoral and Galenic science, and engages in a debate with the "physicians of natural medicine" from the point of view of *fiqh* and the prophetic sources, emphasizing that there is "a bond of friendship between *al-ḥikma wa-l-sharīʿa*," wisdom (*ḥikma*, the wisdom of the natural physician) and religious law, all the while emphasizing the crucial dimensions of certainty in faith (*yaqīn*) and reliance on God (*tawakkul*). The Imam's own reflection on the destructive influence of the black bile humor (*al-sawdāʾ*), cause of melancholy and existential demise, blurs physical and metaphysical etiologies, echoing a long tradition of medical and later psychological thinking on melancholy peculiar to both sides of the Mediterranean, and pointing to the fact that the uncanny labor of undoing characteristic of the "melancholic temperament" necessarily trespasses the boundaries of the physical body and of natural medical reasoning,[3] and by nature is open onto the metamorphoses and figures of the uncanny that evoke and border on the Invisible.

During the course of the first year of our relationship, the Imam, the psychiatrist, and I met several times together to explore the Imam's therapeutic practice, and to submit our questions to him as one would submit queries to a *mufti* (a scholar of *fiqh* who gives nonbinding legal opinions on matters that range from the intimate dimensions of a person's marital and sexual life to questions of collective concern in the life of a community).[4] We met in the reception room of the well-finished two-story concrete building where the Imam lived with his family. Sometimes he invited us into his more secluded study, a small room on the roof of the house, full of books and with a narrow mattress on the floor.

In our "interviews" (as he called them, *al-ḥiwār*), the Imam's position was often articulated and delivered in the mode of a sermon or a lecture on the particular topic opened by one of our questions. In his answers, he attempted to reach out to the diagnostic vocabularies of contemporary psychiatry in terms of an understanding of madness that is related at once to theological, political, ethical, and biological (or physical) factors, exploring the possibility of faith at the limit of madness, heresy, and damnation. When I asked him a question, the Imam started his answer with a general discussion of the ethical-religious principles of his approach to the cure; he then unfailingly moved to particular cases or specific situations—situations that as such he was able to address, and treat, only by relying on what he called his "experience" (*tajriba*). Yet *sharīʿa* and *tajriba*, the path of ethical-religious principles and experience, were not opposed in his approach. The principles had to do with defining the scope of the lawful cure (*iʿlāj sharʿī*): the authentication of its empowerment by God, which fundamentally relied on the recognition of divine authority and oneness, and on the healer's and the patient's deep acceptance of the just sovereignty of God. The goal was not to obtain a result in this world at all costs, but to seek an ethical efficacy where the cure is subordinated to the well-being of the soul in this world and the other.

For the Imam, the spiritual counselor is also an exemplar, the incarnation of an example, an image or idea, bearing witness to a life on the path of God; an always imperfect witness of an always imperfect life, fraught with struggles and pain, failures and attachments, but one that attests, in its very struggles, to the moral and existential capacity to embrace life, as the Imam often said, in an "affirmative" way, and to transform hardship and the experience of alienation and illness into a spiritual trial for the ethical life of the soul. In his practice as a healer, the Imam attends to those who addressed themselves to him or are brought by their families because of severe psychopathological symptoms. In some cases it is their first attempt at a cure; but most often, they arrive at his door after a long therapeutic quest across healers and sanctuaries for the mad, visits to psychiatrists and in some cases after one or several hospitalizations. He listens, asks questions, always including the family members who had come with the sick person, for he sees the sick as a knot in a larger history of connections, and proposes a cure, through herbal remedies that he prepares himself and through the *ruqya*.

The *ruqya* consists of chanting in the presence of the sick person specific passages of the Qurʾan that bear a direct and effective relation to the person's condition. In some cases the recital causes the temporary unconsciousness of the person, whose corpse-like body becomes the stage for the manifestation of an invisible presence. The Qur'anic utterance opens an eschatological space, a time of the end, where the voice of the healer materializes a prophetic intervention and the soul of the patient opens to a receptivity of the Invisible. (I present the *ruqya* recital as a conjunct creation of eschatological space-time and existential possibility—the "dramaturgy of the soul"—in section 17, through the discussion of a case.)

Many of our conversations are recorded; the Imam doesn't mind, in fact he has encouraged recording since the earliest of our meetings. We both have an archive of our conversations: when we record something, he downloads the audio file from my recorder onto his laptop. For as he once told me, when he answered our questions or my questions, he developed his knowledge into novel argumentations. Recording our conversations became for him the code switch to a specific style of exchange, at once more personal and more intellectual and reflexive, separate from the everyday events of life, from the life of his family, and from the intense emotional happenings in the healing sessions. His language shifts to a more formal classical Arabic vocabulary and pronunciation, and to the rhetorical style of a *dars*, a lesson, argued and offered to a larger imagined audience.

When I returned to see him alone two years later, in 2005, our relationship changed somewhat. Dr. A. had completed his residency and had been appointed to a public hospital in a faraway town. At first I went back to see the Imam with trepidation, as I wasn't sure he would receive me with the same ease that characterized our three-way conversations. He did not usually meet with a woman (especially one alone) who was not from his family or from his circle of regular patients and former patients. Normally with women patients there is always a third, either another woman, a brother, or a son. In one of our first conversations he made it clear that I should wear a headscarf at his home; it was his requirement if we were to talk. He said this to Dr. A. in my presence, not directly to me, and added that it was the case even more since eventually I might take on the practice of healing. The psychiatrist explained that I was doing research and had no intention to become a healer. The Imam replied that one could not ever know for sure.

He was glad to see me, and we resumed our exchange where we had left it, with a renewed emphasis on the philosophical and theological dimensions of his practice that had stayed in the margins of our three-way conversation with Dr. A., focused more specifically on psychopathology and demonological etiology. He invited me to his healing sessions, the experiential field from which his reflection sprang.

Sometimes I visited him in the company of my friend Si Brahim, who had accompanied me in my research many years before in the Wed Draʿa region in the south of Morocco,[5] and with whom I have maintained a friendship over the years. My friend had cancer, and during the months of his chemotherapy in Rabat, he came a few times to visit the Imam with me.

With the Imam, Si Brahim discovered the healing ritual of the *ruqya* in its reformed Islamic liturgy; he had many questions, concerning the relation to evil, the place of saints and sanctuaries, and the proper conduct to observe in the face of illness and death, a question that had become important for him in his illness as an exigency of reckoning with the possibility of his imminent death. The conversations on idolatry (*shirk*), and the Imam's clarifications concerning the importance of discerning the difference between licit and illicit cures, came in part in response to Si Brahim's questions, questions motivated by his illness and his desire to discern and live in conformity to the law of God. Si Brahim died in 2011. We had been friends for more than twenty years through different stages of our lives. We had talked about what the conversations with the Imam had meant for each of us. I am thinking of him as I complete this work.

Over the years, while I remained an intellectual interlocutor for him, the Imam also introduced me to his family; I met his mother and father, who live with him in the family home, his wife and their five daughters, and his sisters, with whom he remains very close. I came to know his mother and her traditional knowledge of herbs, which she used to collect in the countryside to prepare her remedies. She and her son often engaged in debates over their respective herbariums: her knowledge drew from an oral tradition, which she passed on to him in the form of an inclination and a desire. He had learned about plants not from his mother but from works of prophetic medicine and al-Kindi's botanical compendium; but when he gathered plants to prepare a remedy, which he ground at home in a large coffee grinder, sometimes he listened when she offered advice. She respected his scholarship and his authority as a scholar of *fiqh* and Islamic medicine, and had a tender smile for his intellectual passion. She liked me as his interlocutor, perhaps seeing a similar passion in me.

Spending time on the second floor with the family I noticed the way his mother took an interest in his sermons, and sometimes commented on the stories of patients from the sharp angle of her feminine insight. She smiled affectionately at her son's attachment to his Dell laptop. One day, talking with me about him, in a flashback to his childhood she visualized her boy memorizing the Qur'an, in a state of absorption, and other children running out to play in the street in the evening while her boy sat with the Book. He had the nature of a scholar at an early age, she said, back in the region of Wezzane, an old center of learning in northern Morocco, where the family is from.

The computer gave him access to a vast archive of texts in the religious sciences—Qur'an, hadith, *fiqh*, and Qur'anic commentary—that, when the topic was relevant, he passed on to me on a USB drive. It was on that same laptop that we immediately downloaded our conversations, whose file recordings he labeled *ḥiwār*, a term used for debates on Arab satellite TV and appropriate to the tenor of our conversations, at least when we chose to turn the tape recorder on. Sometimes a patient would interrupt our talking, or a friend or relative would come and sit with us and join the conversation.

He was close to his daughters and to his wife. Even closer perhaps after a long illness that almost claimed his life in 2007; an infection of the heart that caused him to have a risky open heart operation, for which he had to ask the financial help of friends in his religious community, and towards which he put all the savings he had accumulated to start a small business. The infection and the operation were the last episodes in a cardiac condition that had rendered him vulnerable since his early youth, and that influenced his decision to interrupt his study of law at the University of Rabat and pursue instead the life of a scholar, a preacher (*dāʿī*), and a Qur'anic therapist.

His illness, and his operation, became a recurrent theme in our conversations. The event was a trial from which he drew examples, guarding against the theological risk of despairing, although he did not see his illness as an initiation through loss, as many healers see the origin of their charismatic gift. In line with his teachings and with the way he attempts to lead his life, his illness was for him a reminder of his vulnerability and a trial of patience (*ṣabr*), in which the strength of his faith (*īmān*) and conviction (*yaqīn*) were tested, and which provided a point of attachment during the hardest moments. He saw it as an allegory of the other collective trials that characterized the daily life of people in his community: extreme poverty, lack of work, lack of the most basic forms of state-provided health care, and the fact of dispossession—feeling demoralized, giving in to despair and melancholy, seeking refuge in drugs and suicide.

These themes keep coming back in the lives of those who seek the help and the advice of the Imam, uttered in the words of the afflicted, or screamed in the tongue of the jinn; and they are present in the ethical and religious advice that the Imam addresses to the youth, in his Friday sermons and in the more personal relations of mentorship, and, most important, through his healing sessions. At one level his practice remains outside the immediate reach of the state, because of the "modesty" of his approach and lifestyle, his fidelity to the marginalized, and his choice not to pursue recognition in the arenas of official public life. Yet his relation to the state is also more complex. As became clear to me during the Middle Eastern uprisings of 2011 and 2012, and despite the critical angle of his moral commentary, which at moments takes on the admonishing character of a *naṣīḥa* ("exhortation," a religiously authorized mode of public speech),[6] the Imam is reluctant to directly challenge the institution of the state, even when he denounces the state as reproducing and fostering injustice and participating in the regime of falsity and oppression that is associated with Shaytan and the jinn. Injustice is in his view an inescapable ill of the human world, and while fighting it is a responsibility of all Muslims, believing in the possibility of an absolutely just order on this earth is a temptation of self-delusion. Revolution can be a misleading hope. And even though he understood the impetus of the crowds that in Egypt gathered in Tahrir Square, he kept telling me that the history of Egypt is different, and that, in any case, even there, the risks of *fitna* and *fawda*, "discord" and "civil war," were lurking. For this reason he accepts operating within and in the margins of the institutional frame provided by the state, in full awareness of its corrupt nature, and one that entails a complex apparatus of surveillance. In his capacity as an imam who delivers the Friday sermon, he is an employee of the Ministry of Islamic Affairs, however small his salary and limited his bureaucratic responsibilities. And like all imams who lead the Friday prayer, he is subject to controls, and each week he receives a prompt with the assigned topics that his sermon will be required to cover (a state practice that has been routine in Morocco since the early growth of the Islamic movement in the 1980s). Within that given frame he still manages to address his community in a way that registers his voice and that can touch them. Perhaps because of his critical views, his sermons, and his commitment to address the despair of the youth, perhaps because of his practice of healing through the *ruqya* recital, he never did obtain the position of imam of a larger and more prominent mosque, which would have come with a much higher salary. He remained assigned to the little mosque adjoining the former shantytown, and pronounced the Friday sermon there.

For a long time I was puzzled by the discrepancy I could observe between the lucid tones of his ethical critique, in the form of commentary, diagnosis, lesson, or exhortation, *naṣīḥa*—in conversation with me, his patients, or members of his community—and the practical advice I heard him give and the decisions I watched him make, which seldom implied directly challenging the authority of the state. I pushed him to make explicit what I saw as a contradiction in the conversations we had—especially in the aftermath of the Tunisian and Egyptian uprisings, in 2011, when Morocco was shaken by large demonstrations, and when the movement of *al-ʿAdl wa-l-iḥsān*, and its guide Shaykh Abdessalam Yassine, a figure who in many ways the Imam admired, had at first taken to the streets, joining forces with the unorganized youth movement. We never did agree on the Arab revolts, which I followed with passion, and in relation to which the Imam remained skeptical. He told me that asking for the fall of the regime was a move he was not sure he could endorse. This was not just because of the literal risk that entailed—one could be arrested or killed, and many were. He considered that the revolts in the East, in Egypt and Syria in particular, were already being undermined, as of the summer of 2011, by the widening of a divisive rift, which he judged to have the potential of engendering *fitna* and discord. The discord among Muslims and between Muslims and Christians was further deepened by what he understood as the pervasiveness of Western interests and intervention, which he traced all the way to the liberal language and the desire spoken in the slogans. Most important, however, his skepticism had to do with what he saw as the risk of forgetting that the true struggle is not located at the level of the state and its structures, but at the level of the soul and its capacity for an ethical life. He saw the state as a secular apparatus, at once centralized and capillary, and did not make much of the fact that it claimed its worldly sovereignty on the basis of religion. He was paradoxically working at its margins, as a different kind of "technician of the sacred,"[7] incommensurable to the very system in which he indirectly participated.

NINE

Shariʿa Healing: "Knowledge of the Path to the Hereafter"

To understand the stakes of the shariʿa cure (*ʿilāj sharʿī*) and its reach into a jurisprudence of the soul in the practice and commentary of the Imam, and to seize the way in which the law is necessary for the cure, and the cure is necessary for the law, we must begin by reading Abu Hamid al-Ghazali's (d. AH 505/1111 CE) plea in his *Book of Knowledge*, the opening statement of his *Revival of Religious Sciences*. The point, as al-Ghazali puts it, is that the Prophet of Islam "did not intend the term jurisprudence (*fiqh*) as you [his contemporaries and we readers] may suppose it to be." Al-Ghazali's tone is polemical and admonishing. He wants to reclaim the spirit of the revealed law from its instrumental exercise within a system of mundane power.

In al-Ghazali's view, "knowledge of the path to the hereafter" comprises two categories: the knowledge of unveiling (*ʿilm al-mukāshafa*), an esoteric knowledge "that is not written in books" and is the prerogative of a few, and the knowledge of proper conduct (*ʿilm al-muʿāmalāt*), which concerns us all, and is the scope of his intervention. The "knowledge of proper conduct," in turn, is divided into "outward knowledge" (*ẓāhir*), which is the knowledge of the senses, and "inward knowledge" (*bāṭin*), which is the knowledge of the "states of the heart."

> The first term: *fiqh*, jurisprudence. The scholars have altered it by making it a specialized field of intellectual endeavor. . . . They have particularized it to denote the knowledge of atypical branches of rulings, the scrutiny of the minutiae behind their reasoning process . . . .
>
> Yet, in the earliest time of this community the word *fiqh* was employed to denote the science of the path to the hereafter, the recognition of the minute evils of the souls or subtle afflictions of the souls (*ʿilm ṭarīq al-ākhira wa maʿrifa daqāʾiq āfāt al-nufūs*), and those defects in one's actions that render

them invalid, as well as [to denote] the overpowering insight into the base nature of this world, the intense perception of the precious gift of the hereafter, and the heart overwhelmed by pious fear [of God].

This meaning is well demonstrated for you in God's statement: *Let them devote themselves to acquiring discernment in the religion (yatafaqqahū), so that they may warn their people when they return to them* [Qur'an 9:122].

[Clearly] that which comprises admonition and warning is the meaning of *fiqh* [as discernment]: it is not the multifaceted opinions dealing with divorce, the freeing of slaves, oaths in matters of adultery, commercial dealings in which payment preceded the delivery of merchandise, and rental agreements: for that there is neither admonition not warning: on the contrary devoting oneself to such a pursuit, without cessation, only hardens the heart and divests it of apprehension [of God], just as we witness in these times among those devoted exclusively to it.

God states: *They have hearts with which they do not understand* [7:179]; and intends the meaning of faith, not legal rulings.[1]

From our first meetings the Imam made it clear that he saw the task of lawful cure and the figure of the healer differently from what is commonly understood. While healing traditionally had been associated with the authority lent by a charismatic gift, he saw healing as a religious task, based on the therapist's unwavering submission to God (*islām*), on the certainty of faith (*īmān, yaqīn*), and on the purity of intention (*niyya*). The healer derived authority through learning, and through an ongoing work on oneself to "expand" and purify the soul. In his view, the required prerogatives of the therapist were the spiritual capacity to provide guidance (*irshād*) and give religious advice (*wa'ẓ*), mastery of the art of Qur'anic recitation (*tajwīd*), and a deep knowledge of the Qur'an as the instantiation of divine speech. In his words:

The person who aspires to be a healer (*mu'ālij*), if he wants to cure, must be a person who is entrusted with a religious task (*muhimma al-dīniyya*). He or she must be committed to the religious path (*iltizām bi-l-dīn*), must be learned in the Qur'an and the hadith, and must be capable of giving guidance (*irshād*) and religious advice (*wa'ẓ*). Now, if that healer is a spiritual guide (*murshid*), and is fluent in hadith literature, he or she must [further] be a scholar of jurisprudence on the path of divine law (*faqīh sharī'an*). Among other reasons, this is necessary [in the context of the cure] because if jinn try to defeat the healer, or corner him (*yajizahu*) in the midst of a healing session, the jinn will then fail in that attempt, because the healer is experienced,

> competent, and secure in his knowledge. For instance, if the healer is reciting the Qur'an, it must never happen that jinn interrupt him because of an error in his recitation. The recitation must be flawless. Because the jinn want to weaken the healer, show him that he is incompetent; they want to laugh at him and break his resolve.

The Imam draws his practice from the Qur'an and the authoritative sources of Islamic jurisprudence,[2] namely the shari'a and the *fiqh*, which he understands in the expansive sense of following the ways of God in the world, preparing for the afterlife, and seeking the generative path of an ethical life and understanding.

Since the early centuries of Islam, *fiqh* jurisprudence is the elaboration and interpretation of norms that translate the revealed law into the world—rules derived from the texts of revelation, and that give ethical and legal qualification to human actions.[3] It is at the same time a founding law and juristic guide applied to the specificity of cases and to the complexity of concrete life situations,[4] a way of regulating and framing the life of local communities that cannot be reduced to what we understand as law in the modern juridical sense. As discussed by classical and contemporary scholars, the scope of *fiqh* is to determine the legal-moral reference for a universal system of justice in relation both to the authoritative sources of revealed law and to the singularity of human situations. *Fiqh* jurisprudence is related to the Qur'an and the sunna in terms of a methodology of norm derivation grounded in rational logics (*uṣūl al-fiqh*, the "sources of jurisprudence"), and based on the principles of analogy (*qiyās*), precedent, and the consensus of the community of scholars (*ijmā'*). But the rational derivation of norms from the sources can never reduce the incommensurability of Revelation, and the heteronomous character of the law itself, a law external to the human world. *Fiqh* jurisprudence at once acknowledges the limits of human understanding and the inevitability of human error, the contingency of cases and the imperfect nature of human judgment, and, by its very reference to the revealed law, points to the incommensurable alterity of the divine.[5]

Now the healer, the Imam says, must be a *faqīh sharī'an*, a learned scholar and one "capable of understanding" (lit. *faqīh*) the path of the divine law. *Fiqh* in this larger sense is insight into a knowledge that al-Ghazali sought to reclaim in his own time as knowledge foundational for the ethical and ontological possibility of the law, against what he criticized as the legal reductionism of his contemporaries.

Al-Ghazali—as today the Imam in his practice—did not see this spiritual dimension of *fiqh* as external or opposed to the exercise of the law as normative ruling in the world, but rather as central to the meaning and practice of the shariʿa and the *fiqh* in their interconnected ontological, ethical, and juridical dimensions. His gesture was an attempt at reclaiming the alterity of the divine in *fiqh* jurisprudence, awakening an experience of the hereafter in the everyday life of his contemporaries, whose hearts, he wrote, were "hardened" and no longer capable of feeling the presence of God. A reflection on the maladies of the soul/self (*āfāt al-nufūs*) was one of the sites where the original and generative meaning of *fiqh* could be reencountered, and reconnected to an experience of the divine in the concrete transactions and deeds of this world.

It is in a similar vein that the Imam abandoned the pursuit of a law degree at the University of Rabat to dedicate himself to the study of *fiqh* and to the medical-spiritual practice of healing, tending to the "minute evils or subtle afflictions of the souls" (*daqāʾiq āfāt al-nufūs*), and attempting to find the words and the images necessary to speak to the hardened and alienated hearts of his contemporaries. He could have become a lawyer or a judge in the courts of modern law, and fought for justice within the juridical idiom of the state; or he could have taught Islamic jurisprudence in a college of Islamic law, where some of the religious scholars contributing today to the debate on shariʿa, ethics, and Islamic psychology have been formed. But partly due to his heart condition, which made him vulnerable from a young age and made it difficult for him to endure the harsh demands of university studies for someone such as himself, who came from a small town in northern Morocco and did not have an affluent family behind him; and partly because the ailment of a bodily organ made him more attuned to the "spiritual organ," to the exercise of the "inner senses" (*al-ḥiss al-bāṭin*) and to perception of the world of spirits, he chose to intervene at the level of the oppression of the soul and to embrace the informal path of *daʿwa*, "the call" to pious conduct that is the calling out to others, both through the practice of religious advice, and his activity as a therapist, which he sees as a central stage for lending guidance and counsel. For there can be no justice and no politics of transformation if the soul is "choked," terrorized, and crippled, and thus unable to undertake ethical work. He is clear about the connection between his commitment to the practice of *daʿwa* and the existential experience of illness; the healing sessions he performs often culminate in a lesson of spiritual exhortation for the benefit of the patient but are addressed, as well, to a larger audience of family and neighbors, and to the community at large.

Opening up to the ethical life of the law as "knowledge of the path to the hereafter" (the Ghazalian exhortation) is not, for the Imam, and for those who revisit this problematic today, a question of negating the world, or the historical casuistry of the law: from marriage to divorce, from contracts to partnerships, or today the new areas of legal interest, such as regulation of the exploitation of natural resources, protection of the environment, juridical reflection on new medical technologies, or on poverty and on the violence of war. It is not a question of retreating into a private spiritual realm of inner life, but of reestablishing the link between worldly activities and awareness of the divine, a link that is fundamentally communal, because in Islam responsibility towards God is necessarily articulated as responsibility towards the world. In the words of Taha Abderrahman, a Moroccan religious scholar who reflects on the relation of law and ethics today, and whose writings directly address issues of planetary concern from a perspective internal to Islam, the question is to awaken in the community the capacity of drawing closer to God, building on the idea that in Islam an activity is dedicated to God if it is performed in light of the fundamental Islamic tenets of sound intention (*niyya*), honesty (*ṣidq*), and sincerity (*ikhlāṣ*), "elevating mundane activity to the station of the sacred."[6]

As a *faqīh* of the soul and a *faqīh* of the law, the Imam connects in his practice two dimensions of *fiqh* that are fundamentally related and increasingly considered side by side by scholars of Islamic law: the inner dimension of "the discernment of the heart" (*fiqh al-qalb* or *fiqh al-bāṭin*), concerning knowledge of the heart's "actions" (*ʿamāl*) and "states" (*aḥwāl*); and the outer dimension of "the jurisprudence of cases" (*fiqh al-aḥkām*),[7] norms and practical legal rulings concerning observable human actions in the world, considered in their relation to revealed law.[8] While the "inner" or "concealed" (*bāṭin*) dimension of the heart is foundational for the moral and ontological possibility of the law, it does not directly enter the normative domain of the jurisprudence of cases, which limits itself to the outer, "manifest" (*ẓāhir*) acts and enunciations, the deeds that can be seen and heard.[9] Crucial aspects of the law, such as the rule of testimony and the discernment of sincerity in a witness, or the definitions of legal capacity (*taklīf*), depend on the probity of the heart as a moral and spiritual quality that as such falls within the realm of the "inner" (*al-bāṭin*) and is beyond observation. The jurisprudence of cases in classical *fiqh*, however, does not cross the external boundary of the "outer" (*al-ẓāhir*), and asserts the vulnerability of human knowledge and judgment vis-à-vis the all-encompassing knowledge of God.

The definition of discernment and good sense (*al-rushd*, to be in one's senses), legal capacity, and personal responsibility (*taklīf*) is directly relevant in the case of insanity (*al-junūn*), and poses a subtle question for the jurisprudence of the soul. Insanity is not addressed directly in the texts of Islamic law, but appears for instance through discussion of the causes of legal interdiction (*ḥajr*) and wardship, as in the assignment of a guardian for a disabled person or an orphan. The highest degree of legal capacity is that of the Muslim who is of age (*bāligh*) and in full possession of his/her faculties of judgment (*'āqil*). This person is fully responsible (*mukallaf*), has the capacity to dispose of property and administer an estate, is under the obligation to perform religious duties, and is subject to criminal law, inasmuch as he or she is capable of deliberate intent.[10] Legal capacity is suspended or reduced in the case of an illness that affects the faculty of judgment (*rushd*). In the Hanafi school of law (though not in the Maliki school predominant in the Maghreb) the person is nonetheless granted full capacity during the periods of remission of the illness, when discernment (*rushd*) and reason (*'aql*) are resumed, however temporarily. A person with partial discernment can marry, through the legal intermediary of a guardian; crucially though, an insane or possessed person's devotional acts (uttering the testimony of faith, prayer, fasting, pilgrimage, alms giving) are invalid, because they lack the lucidity of spiritual intent (*al-niyya*). As Michael Dols and others have noticed, requiring a ruling on devotional (or other) intent is arduous from the perspective of outward legal acts (*al-ẓāhir*), a fact that protects those who have been struck by madness or possession from being arbitrarily denied their status within the community and divested of their rights and property.[11]

Yet, as a scholar of *fiqh* and a therapist, a "discerner of the soul" (*faqīh al-nafs*), the Imam does not limit his intervention to the level of "outward" legal acts (*al-ẓāhir*), but necessarily engages the ethical and ontological register of the jurisprudence of the soul (*fiqh al-bāṭin*). His liturgical intervention is aimed at restoring the spiritual capacity of the soul, repossessing to some degree the lucidity of spiritual intent. This does not mean that in his position as a healer he can claim knowledge of the unknown and the invisible—of the ontological dimensions of *al-bāṭin* (the inner) and *al-ghāyb* (the Invisible or nonmanifest). The human soul and the world of spirits are not an epistemological object of knowledge, but a dimension of the cosmos withdrawn from human perception that under certain circumstances human beings can relate to.

The Imam practices a renewed form of Qur'anic healing known as *'ilāj shar'ī*,[12] "the lawful cure," a cure according to God's law. As this practice has been variously formulated by Muslims today, at issue is the turn to true Islamic healing and virtues, paired with the condemnation or exclusion of what is circumscribed as untruthful Islamic practice. In Morocco, a configuration of cures aimed at controlling, defeating, or appeasing harmful spirits (*ʿilāj al-jinn*, "the cures of the jinn") is today subject to a theological critique as part of a larger move towards Islamic ethics and justice, and away from what, drawing on a classical register of Islamic theology and moral reasoning, is understood as idolatry (*shirk*). The "cures of the jinn" (the old "traditional therapies") are cures of de-possession, involving staging a scene in which the jinn comes to presence and speaks through the body of the sick. In the vernacular version that is today contested the role of the healer is to bring the jinn to reveal its presence, fight the presence to obtain its name, and come to a pact with it, quenching the desire of the jinn through an exchange often sealed by a sacrifice.[13] In this complex scene the world of jinn mirrors that of humans, and healing is made possible by the healer's seeking the intercession of *ṣulṭān al-jinn*, the King (*ṣulṭān*) of the Jinn, and meeting the desire of the jinn, de facto participating in its economy and entering into its service. This is why these cures are treated as a form of idolatry (*shirk*), for they contest the oneness of God and bend to the whim of an idol.

The lawful cure (*ʿilāj sharʿī*) addresses similar afflictions. It doesn't deny the presence of the jinn, for jinn are part of creation as a form of life in the realm of the Invisible, and as such are mentioned in the Qurʾan; but it avoids all forms of negotiation with them, refusing to share in their economy, and considers the vernacular therapists who insist on practicing the cures of the jinn as "false healers" and as magicians who work in the service of Shaytan. The difference is both fundamental and subtle, for the Qurʾanic cures, while practicing a similar form of de-possession, are based on submission to the power of God, and on the engagement in an ethical struggle: *jihād al-nafs*, "the struggle of the soul/self." While the magical cures treat harm as a cosmic agency external to the subject, the Qurʾanic cures locate Shaytan, the figuration of the trial of evil, within the desiring soul, as a heterogeneity that can never be resolved.[14]

In our conversations the Imam drew an explicit connection between his active investment in the lawful cure (*ʿilāj sharʿī*), understood as a renewed instantiation of the practice of faith, and a political critique of the condition of the self and the soul in a state of material and spiritual dispossession, when subjugated by an oppressive state apparatus, and at the limit of despairing of life and abandoning trust in God. This is a time, he said, when human beings everywhere, "in the Arab and the non-Arab world" (*fī al-ʿālam al-ʿarabī wa al-ʿālam al-ʿajamī*) are experiencing a spiritual void, a "vacancy of the spirit" (*al-farāgh al-rūḥī*) that goes hand in hand with other, more concrete afflictions of the time: apathy and disoeuvrement (*al-biṭāla*), poverty (*al-faqr*), depression (*al-ikti'āb*), the anxiety borne of tension within the nuclear and extended family (*mashākil usariyya*), the violence of the economy and the humiliation attached to enduring and returning forms of servitude (*al-khādim wa al-makhdūm*), and social tensions in general.

The cure is at once an intervention into the life of the person in pain, and a mode of collective therapeutics whose larger scope is to heal the heart of the community, and the tradition itself, as experienced in the suspended temporality and affect of "spiritual vacancy" and "soul choking." In this sense the "lawful cure" and the liturgy of the *ruqiya* as conceived by the Imam evoke the pathos of a prophetic genre, literally one of "prophetic medicine" (*al-ṭibb al-nabawī*), where the time of calamity indexes the time of creation, and affliction points to the ordeals of repeated "testing" (*fitnāt*, plural) and "trial" (*ibtilā'*).

As I listen to our recordings the vocabulary of disablement and affliction speaks eloquently for itself: *al-nakba*, affliction, catastrophe; *al-yā's*, despair, giving up hope; *al-ḍīq*, oppression, choking; *al-ẓulm*, oppression, injustice (in a theological sense); *al-ka'āba*, melancholy, grief, depression; *al-biṭāla*, inactivity, apathy; *al-'ubūsiyya*, gloom; *al-tashā'um*, hopelessness, pessimism; *al-'ajz*, cripplehood, spiritual or physical; and more.

The Imam spoke insistently in terms of a certain question, one that gave impetus to his work and shaped every aspect of his life, the question of the possibility of ethical existence in the presence of trauma and madness, and in the shadow of spiritual dispossession. He asked this question at the intimate level of his encounters with the sick and the afflicted (*marīḍ, muṣāb*), from a place at the limit of life and the law. It is a political and yet intimate calling that was the reason why he chose to embrace the life of a religious scholar and healer.

In his Seminar on Ethics, Lacan had addressed a problematic that may be read as related, if from a different place, and as engaging a specifically European tradition of considering destruction and creation between two world wars, one that culminated in Freud's "scandalous" formulation of the death drive. At the empty center of Lacan's seminar is the chasm of the Thing, a Freudian figuration of the problem of evil, at once source and termination of desire, site of horrific visions and primordial projections, and of the ultimate alterity of death. Lacan called the Thing (*das Ding*) "an original division of the experience of reality," "the first outside" and first object, originally lost and impossible to retrieve, an "intimate stranger," "hostile on occasion," an "extimacy" (*extimité*), an externality, unbearability, at the core of intimacy, a crater, in fact, that is also an original inscription "around which the entire trajectory of the subject is oriented . . . in relation to the world of its desires."[15] The Thing, Lacan tells us, which occupies in his reading the place that in Aristotelian philosophy was assigned to the Good, and to the arbitrary rule of the gods, is also the term by which Meister Eckhart referred to the soul, and which, as *causa pathomenon*, wellspring of human passions, points to the fact of destruction, and to "the radical question of evil" as such. Such a Thing, says Lacan, cannot be mastered or dialecticized; it can only be encircled (*cerner la chose*).

TEN

Prophetic Medicine and the *Ruqya*

When he performs the liturgy of the *ruqya*, reciting the Qur'an over a patient, the Imam is skilled in establishing an emotional bond—a bond that Ibn Qayyim al-Jawziyya describes as "a link between souls" in his treatise on prophetic medicine—and relies on it to facilitate and control the coming to presence of the jinn and the state of "absence" (*ghaybūba*) or trance that results in the person. Yet he is never deceived into thinking that his skillful technique may itself be the cause of the cure. The cure is from God. This awareness, conveyed by his posture and words, is reiterated as an aesthetic trait in every aspect of his life.[1] He relies on the guidance of the shariʿa, both for the way the law draws boundaries, contains and enables human life, and for how it points to the Invisible (*al-ghayb*), the unknown and unknowable side of divine reality.

The goal of the cure is the transformation of the soul; recovery from the symptom is never an end unto itself, as is the case with magical or biomedical cures—which the Imam often cites in comparison—where effectiveness is the reason and scope of the treatment. After years of our conversations I better understand how a dimension of incurability is for the Imam the actual ground of an ethical engagement. Unlike the way in which "exorcism" and "deliverance" are often understood, the shariʿa cure is not the elimination of an immunological threat, and a full recovery is not its exclusive outcome.[2] In many cases that would be impossible, because of the nature of the illness, marked by the presence of an intractable jinn, or of what the Imam calls "a mark" (*tabʿ*), the imprint of a melancholic transmission condensed in the elusive figure of a demonic legacy passed on across generations.

But the liquidation of harm is impossible also in another, fundamental sense, for in the understanding of the Imam the destructive potential associated with the jinn is internal to the human soul as the intimate exteriority of desire. Later in this section I will discuss how this topological configuration, at once internal and external to the soul, "extimate" (in the vocabulary of Lacan)—at once vital principle and death drive—may be considered alongside the topology of the drive in psychoanalysis.

Not unlike Lacan's notions of the "localization" of enjoyment and the "encircling" of the drive, the task of the Qur'anic cure is to localize the destructive agency as the condition for reclaiming (to some degree) the spiritual capacity of the soul; a space, we may say, where the subject can exist. In the Imam's own conceptual framework, this means carving an "interval" between the jinn and the soul, an interval that will enable the patient to reclaim a margin of reason and discernment (*ʿaql, rushd*), and hence some degree of spiritual capacity to be absorbed in the remembrance of God. It will then be possible to engage in a spiritual struggle to "expand" the heart, keeping the demonic presence in check, even if its destructive force can never be completely neutralized. Any discussion of the legal capacity of the person (*ahliyya*) in the event of insanity (*junūn*), of personal responsibility (*taklīf*) and the forming of intention (*niyya*) in the performance of devotional acts, as found in the "jurisprudence of cases" (*fiqh al-furuʿ*, *fiqh al-aḥkām*), is secondary to this spiritual-medical question that pertains to the "jurisprudence of the soul" (*fiqh al-qalb*)—the heart of *fiqh*, in the Ghazalian sense inhabited by the Imam.

I understood this point more clearly as I was revising a draft of this section and wanted to ask the Imam for clarification. In trying to formalize the relationship of the jinn and the soul in the way he had explained it to me, I had sketched it in diagrams and in my notes, based in particular on one conversation where he had outlined what he called "three configurations (*taṣawwur*) of the jinn and the soul." These were modes of encroachment that I tried to represent as an overlapping of spaces, and that indicated the incapacity (or relative capacity) of the soul, in terms of the subject being at least partially capable of exerting judgment (*ʿāqil*).

I was far away and missed our conversations; he too was happy to hear my voice. Now on the phone, I asked him about the "configurations," and the state of *ghaybūba*, the coma-like "absence" into which the self is thrown by the event of demonic occupation. And about the deep depersonalization that ensues when, as he had phrased it, the jinn is "fully immersed" (*istaghaqa*) in the mind of the person, and the person "drowns into unconsciousness."

Was that colonized unconsciousness analogous to the "absence" of trance, I asked, or was it something else, more radical, where subjectivity was entirely snatched, and, as he had put it, "you think that you are talking to the person but in fact you are talking to the jinn"? He had stressed this danger many times when talking about cases of patients I had met with him. Thinking in terms of psychopathology, and its resemblance to a psychotic state, I said that I understood this to be the most serious condition.

But instead of following my cue in the direction of a phenomenology of madness, he replied from the perspective of *fiqh*, proposing a jurisprudence of the soul. He said that this configuration was serious, and if left untreated it would destroy the person. But the task of the healer, his task as a healer, was to help the afflicted extract themselves from that state through prayer, through the remembrance of God (*dhikr*), and through a life lived according to the law, on the path of God. And even if the jinn lingered—because jinn do linger—it would then be circumscribed, kept in check, in the unending struggle (*mujāhada*) that is our life in this world. And if the jinn caused the person to "fall," then the healer could help that person "rise" (*qawwum*) with the *ruqya*. And he added:

> If [in his or her life prior to the illness, or in intervals of lucidity] the sick is living in the way of God, obeying God, and with a pure intention, if his heart is pure, if his *nafs* has cheerful disposition, if he doesn't get angry or is not easily irritated, doesn't lose his temper, if he practices the remembrance of God, recites the Qur'an, if he is committed to the treatment, God brings healing. Praise to God, many are healed.

As a liturgy of healing, the *ruqya* is discussed in detail by Ibn Qayyim al-Jawziyya (d. AH 751/1350 CE), whose *al-Ṭibb al-nabawī* was the first work in the genre of prophetic medicine to systematize the statements and advice concerning illness and health, pharmacology and diet found in the authoritative sources of *fiqh*—Qur'an and sunna. Ibn Qayyim, whose medical and juridical corpus is intimately engaged by the Imam, was a prominent scholar of *fiqh* and a theologian, as well as a physician. In his religious-medical compendium he considered the prophetic sources on health and illness side by side with the knowledge and principles of natural medicine (Galenic, Indian, Chinese), and its reconfiguration in Islamic medicine particularly according to Ibn Sina and al-Razi. The opening words of *al-Ṭibb al-nabawī* announce the twofold scope of the work: a study of two types of sickness and remedies, the "medicine of the heart" (*ṭibb al-qalb*) and the "medicine of the body" (*ṭibb al-jism*), outlining differences and symmetries between the two, and the way their science replicates and echoes the relationship of the body and the soul, of the physical and the metaphysical, and of the visible and the invisible. At the center of the work, and throughout his discussion of key medical questions and illnesses, lies a preoccupation with the state of the soul, and with the spiritual capacity of the soul/self to lead a life in harmony with the meaning of the Qurʾan. Ibn Qayyim's compendium inaugurated a prolific literary genre of prophetic medicine that has lived on and is today newly flourishing throughout the Muslim world, through publications and websites in a multiplicity of languages, and where the liturgy of the *ruqya* is considered side by side with the practices of *dhikr*, the remembrance of God, supplication (*duʿā*), and prayer in a time of illness and calamity.

As described by Ibn Qayyim, *al-ruqya al-ilāhiyya* ("the divine cure"), today better known as *al-ruqya al-sharʿiyya* ("the shariʿa cure"), is the fostering of a bond between two souls, with the permission of God. That bond, a link between hearts, makes possible a therapeutic transference, where the soul of the therapist, stronger and purified, connects to the weakened soul of the afflicted, lending itself as a support and a channel, and stands up to harmful spirits on the soul's behalf.

The subtle grammar of Ibn Qayyim's description of the cure, made manifest in the juxtaposition of the nominal and verbal forms of the term *ruqya* (verbal root *r-q-y*) in the passage below, captures the logic of the treatment as a poiesis of action and reaction, active and passive, remedy and illness, between two souls (*nufūs*, sing. *nafs*) and their embodied substance. The soul of the *rāqī* (active form), the one who treats by the *ruqya*, works upon the soul of the *murqī* (passive form), the one being treated by the *ruqya*, and "between their two souls there takes place an action and a reaction as there does between an illness and a remedy."

> The soul of the person reciting the *ruqya* (*rāqī*, active) works upon the soul of the one recited over (*murqī*, passive), and between their souls there takes place an action and reaction, as does between an illness and a medicine: so the soul of the person recited over becomes stronger, gains power by way of the *ruqya*, and becomes capable of dispelling the illness with the permission of God.[3]

The soul of the patient "opens up," it expands, and is no longer "constricted." While the connection, the "action and reaction," and the transfer of power (*quwwa*) between healer and patient may resemble the "rapport" of hypnosis, or even transference in psychoanalysis[4] (and in one sense they do), and while hypnotic states are often produced on the scene of the *ruqya*, the intervention of the healer is only a secondary cause, for the agent of the treatment is God. The transfer between souls made possible by the liturgy opens a third space, a space of alterity and presencing, where the Other can speak and where the divine message can be felt in the heart of the afflicted.[5] The Imam, a *faqīh* and a *mu'ālij*, is also, and most importantly, a *rāqī*. Through his recitation of specific Qur'anic passages—verses that celebrate the power of God, exhort the afflicted to take refuge in God, or verses that make present the torment of Judgment—the *rāqī* summons the afflicted to a temporality of the hereafter, a space of danger and reckoning, a space of trembling, where the illness of the soul may become a site of awakening,[6] and of a reconfiguration of existence.[7]

The *ruqya* opens to the realm of the Invisible. Throughout his *al-Ṭibb al-nabawī* Ibn Qayyim poses the metaphysical dimension of the "world of spirits" (*'ālam al-arwāḥ*) and of the "nonmanifest" or the invisible world (*al-ghayb, 'ālam al-ghayb*), as foundational for both jurisprudence and medicine. Ontologically withdrawn and inaccessible as such to human perception and cognition, *al-ghayb* is the realm of divine reality and its manifestations, which include, as I mentioned earlier, the incorporeal beings that are angels and jinn, as well as the metaphysical essence of the soul itself (*nafs, rūḥ*). Conveyed to the prophet Muhammad in the event of the Revelation—received in part in the form of veridical dreams—the Qur'an has the paradoxical nature of a bridge to the Invisible. For Ibn Qayyim the always-partial consciousness (*shu'ūr*) that human beings may have of the "world of spirits" (*'ālam al-arwāḥ*), and their relation to it, is a measure of the state of their soul, and its capacity for spiritual purification. Coming to this question from the perspective of the shari'a and the *fiqh*, and their sources in the Qur'an, Ibn Qayyim stresses that the relationship of human beings with the Invisible is grounded in the capacity of their souls to be in harmony with the "meaning of *al-Fātiḥa*," the opening sura of the Qur'an, and "with all that *al-Fātiḥa* comprises, sincerity of servanthood, praise of God, commitment of one's affairs in Him . . . seeking refuge and help, expression of need and request, and integration of the highest intentions, namely worship of the Lord alone, and the most noble of means, namely: seeking His help in order to be able to worship Him."[8]

In his discussion of "divinely inspired spiritual medicine" (*al-adwiya al-rūḥāniyya al-ilāhiyya*) Ibn Qayyim poses the reality of the "world of spirits" (*ʿālam al-arwāḥ*) in human life as a fundamental given, and yet one to which most people are oblivious, attached, as they are, to the world of sensory experience and its immediate gratifications, which makes them heedless of God and throws a heavy cloak on their ability to be attentive to the reality of the Invisible. Illness is a breach in the veil, an incursion of the invisible in the visible world.

For Ibn Qayyim, as is the case more generally in this Qurʾanic tradition infused with Muslim Neoplatonism, the world of spirits does not just comprise the invisible beings that are angels and jinn, beings of light and fire mentioned in the Qurʾan. *Al-rūḥ* (pl. *al-arwāḥ*), the invisible spirit (one of the concepts and modalities of the soul), lodges in every person and form of life, vegetal and animal, human, angelic or demonic, and has the power to affect the body (*jism*, pl. *ajsām*) as its "form." Spirits have the power to affect bodies (*ta'thīr al-arwāḥ fī al-ajsām*), as well as the power to affect other spirits. Illness and cure are the result of such spiritual "action" and "reaction," exemplified by the poetic structure of the *ruqya* cure, and that parallels, as Ibn Qayyim suggests, the actions and reactions of natural medicine, the physical medicine of humors and bodies.

It is in this sense that *Medicine of the Prophet* discusses side by side the cure of afflictions as diverse as the "falling sickness" (*al-ṣarʿ*), the attack of the glance (*al-ʿayn*, the "eye"), and the toxic reaction caused in the body by the poison of scorpion and viper bites. Every one of these illnesses is the result of a spiritual injury: in the case of the poisoned bites, an injury caused by harmful "lower spirits," "angry souls" (*al-arwāḥ al-khayba, al-nufūs al-khabiṭa*), made spiritually harmful by the passion of anger that triggered the biting; in the case of the "glance" or evil eye, one caused by the spirit of the envier and that affects the spirit of the afflicted, slowly making her life waste away. And finally, in the case of the "falling sickness" (*al-ṣarʿ*, literally "the annihilation"), which he also references as the "epilepsies" of Hippocratic memory, Ibn Qayyim argues for the need to discern the natural etiology from the spiritual one, a discernment, he writes, that requires the "physician of natural medicine" to have religious faith and be in contact with the ontological reality of the world of spirits. The "falling sickness" of the "natural" kind is related to the brain and is an aspect of melancholy understood as the dominance of the black bile; whereas the "falling sickness" of the second kind, which hurls the afflicted into unconsciousness and makes them drift into melancholy or madness, is an illness that originates in the "world of spirits" (*ʿālam al-arwāḥ*). It takes the form of an attack by lower (animal) spirits, or by spirits (whether human or jinn) that have been drawn to evil by the dominance of their passions, and have struck the soul of the heedless person. Yet, Ibn Qayyim admonishes, the most dangerous type of "falling sickness" is not the one that hurls the person unconscious to the ground, but the fact of heedlessness itself:

> If the veil could be removed, you would find that most human souls are afflicted by these evil spirits, and they are their captives and their prisoners. The spirits drive them where they wish, and they cannot prevent them nor oppose them. This torment is the greatest type of "epilepsy" (*ṣarʿ*).[9]

Unresponsive to natural treatment, the "falling sickness" can be healed by the "power of the soul," by a soul strong and purified, seeking refuge in God: through the *ruqya* performed by the healer, and through prayer and reliance on God on the side of the patient, who "seeks treatment through the power of his own soul by the genuine attention he pays to the Maker and Creator of those spirits, and by truly taking refuge with God, as expressed by his tongue and confirmed with his heart."[10]

ELEVEN

The Jouissance of the Jinn

From where I am sitting the ocean is visible beyond the roofs, and I can see all the way to the horizon. A gentle breeze from the open windows carries the smell of salty water. The ocean in this neighborhood is a constant reference point; it is where the eye escapes to grasp a feeling of space. I am waiting for the Imam to return from the mosque. His younger daughters, their cousins, and other neighborhood children are running up and down the stairs because it's the summer holiday and school is closed; families gather together in preparation for the soon-to-begin month of Ramadan. It is July 2011. I am sitting in the formal sitting room on the second floor of his house, above where the family lives. The sun still shines on the houses and shacks visible from the open windows.

Beyond what my eye can see, the highway runs at the edge of the ocean, where collective taxis stop to pick up passengers, and a few cars speed by. On the other side of the road is an empty stretch of land, the narrow plateau of a cliff that drops sharply into the ocean. In the summer, at day's end, that empty space fills with youngsters playing soccer, or people enjoying the breeze and the open view. Perched on the cliff a few steps away is a sanctuary with a dome, the tomb of a saint, a historical figure, who lived in this town in the fourteenth century. Outside the sanctuary, people sit along its walls, asking for alms or offering to divine the future in the shapes of *aldun*.[1] Inside, women and men sit on mats, resting, sleeping, whispering or shouting supplications to the saint.

It is a sanctuary like many other sanctuaries and domes that punctuate the landscape from the Maghreb to the Mashreq. They are called *sayyid* or *maqām*, *rawḍa* or *zāwiya*, burial sites of a saint or a holy lineage, sometimes adjoining a cemetery, and are often associated with vernacular or Sufi devotional practices. They are sites of retreat and of hope for the sick and the despairing, for which release may come sometimes in the form of a dream—and the wish of a better life may be formulated and sometimes fulfilled. I am remembering one of my first visits to the Imam, when I entered this shrine to seek for myself a moment a peace before going to meet him. A group of women was sitting in silence, a child was playing on the floor mats; a woman was talking to herself leaning on the burial site of the saint.

Uncountable times over the years I have visited saints' tombs and shrines, each time finding there moments of peace. I once went with a close friend in the grip of psychosis, who, for the short length of our visit, seemed to find there a glimpse of relief from the chasing insistence of her tormenting hallucinations and thoughts.

Motivating this work over many years is my attempt to listen to her, and to relate to her experience of madness. Trying to avoid a visit to the psychiatric hospital, I had taken her on a journey south to seek the help of a healer I knew. The healing session did not help, and friends suggested that we visit a sanctuary known for the healing of the insane, where families are invited to accompany family members who had been seized by *l-ḥumq*, madness, and for whom no other treatment had brought relief. I remember standing with my friend on the roof of the building, where we had climbed to get away from the moaning and the screaming in the main interior space of the sanctuary. It was night, the sky was clear. We were seeking the blessing of the place, the spiritual presence of the saint. At least I was, on her behalf; she was not fully there. A man, the father of a boy who was also ill, talked to us kindly and offered advice. Exhausted, I prayed for my friend, for both of us; I cried for both of us, wanting to rest there. That thread of memories came to mind as a reverie, as I waited for the Imam in his living room. By that time I had spent several years doing fieldwork at a psychiatric hospital not far from that shrine by the edge of the ocean in his neighborhood. I had read widely in psychiatry and psychoanalysis; I had learned more, but the enigma of madness remained.

I recall how in one of our very first conversations the Imam formulated a passionate critique of devotional practices in saints' shrines, which he saw as a form of idolatry (*shirk*), sought out by people in pain, people he respected and felt for, but whom he viewed as needing guidance and religious education. In due time I shared with him the story of my friend's illness, and of my implication in it; he listened, asked questions, offered advice. Over the years all that he explained and showed me, in the space of research, addressed questions that remained open in my life, and not just in my work.

The *Ḥāla* of Ḥayyat

At last I hear the Imam's footsteps. Originally we had scheduled a meeting to talk in a more reflective mode about what I had been writing on his therapeutic practice and thinking, and about the uprisings across the region, including Morocco, where demonstrations were still taking place. Although he hasn't been expecting any patients, he comes up the stairs accompanied by a man, a young woman and two children.

A *ḥāla*, "a case" (literally, a "state"),[2] he tells me. But this case is urgent and our conversation will have to be postponed. The woman has recently arrived from Syria, where demonstrations are starting to turn into civil strife and generalized violence. The young woman is from here, but married a Syrian man and moved to Syria, to a little town outside of Damascus, on the way to Darʿa. Her brother, who brings her, was once himself a patient of the Imam.

The woman is a young mother of three. Only two children accompany her, a two-year-old, pale and restless, and a ten-year-old girl. The Imam invites the woman and her brother to sit by his side, with pen and paper, and starts asking her questions. It is the first diagnostic interview (*istijwāb*). He asks her name, Ḥayyat, before beginning with his questions: *Katjik l-khuf*? Are you subject to sudden fright? She replies emphatically that yes, she shakes from fear at night. "Do you eat in the morning?" No, she can never eat in the morning. She adds that in any case it will soon be the fasting month, the holy month of Ramadan, and there is no eating during the day. The Imam interjects, his tone is bitter, "What fasting, what Ramadan!" The holy month has no sense, he adds, when Muslims are killing Muslims.

She describes her symptoms, "I feel ants in my hands and feet, and my feet die"; she feels a heavy weight on her stomach, and a sense of choking, unable to breathe (*ḍīq al-nafs*, the Imam explains, turning to me, "soul choking"); then acute pain in her neck and shoulders. The pain is unbearable. It all comes at once; she has no energy to do anything. The Imam inquires whether she hears a voice from inside her, *wash katsmaʿi shy ṣwt min qalbek*? She replies that yes, multiple voices, and they speak to her, tell her things, sometimes the voices are so loud that she can't bear them. And this last week it was not just voices, but she physically felt the presence of a voice on her, all over her, becoming one with her.

I ask her again about the voices, whether the voices she hears are from inside herself, or from outside (I had asked the Imam with a glance whether

I could intervene in the interview). She replies, "from outside," she hears voices that tell her things, they are not the voices of people she knows, and not her own internal voice; she repeats that in this last week the voice is all over her, hovering over and almost covering her. Her brother interjects that it had been like that for him too, when he was sick, and sometimes he didn't just hear voices, he also "saw them," presences in front of his eyes, apparitions, or hallucinations. And he explains to me that he has been ill with the same illness as his sisters, and the Imam had been able to heal him with the permission of God (*bi-idhni llāh*), and now thank God he's doing well. The Imam continues with his interview, asks Ḥayyat whether in her dreams she sees water, and whether the sight of water pleases her, and makes her feel better. She replies emphatically yes, water, she feels much better when she bathes, she feels in peace when she is near water, finds some moments of rest. The sight of water, the sea, makes her feel better. She points at the sea, outside the window. He nods, says "of course" (the jinn enjoys water), then asks her if in her dreams she is being fed. She says yes, she is fed and loves eating in her dreams, she sees herself eating croissants and all sorts of sweets, and she is happy and fulfilled, and when she wakes up she is not hungry, and sometimes doesn't eat for the entire day, and even can go five days without food. The Imam turns to me: Stefania, did you hear, he feeds her at night (in her dreams) and she is full, and she can go on without eating without being hungry and without losing weight. It is the jinn that feeds her.

Ḥayyat adds that there is something else. She sees the same thing every night in her dreams. She looks at her brother, hesitates. Her son is screaming at her feet. The brother encourages her to speak. She says that every night she sees a young woman, the same young woman. And every night she has sex with her. She says it with difficulty, painfully, and also indicating that in her dreams she enjoys it. The Imam says, "yes," and adds, *leanna jinn lly fik, rajl*, "because the jinn in you is a man." (But this means something different than the case of other women inhabited by male jinn who are their erotic partners. Here the jinn "covers her," becomes her.) He asks her about sex with her husband. She says that they don't sleep in the same in room, in fact, they never did. The Imam asks (confirming something he already knows) if there is hostility between her and her mother and whether they had fights. The brother replies for the sister, and she too confirms it. The Imam explains that all this is part of a larger configuration in which the entire family is caught, and that relates back to the mother and possibly the grandmother.

Ḥayyat turns to the Imam (and to me) and says that even outside of her dreams, when she is awake, even now, she asks herself whether she is a woman or a man. She doesn't know, because she feels like a man. Again her expression is one of pain, being tormented, and in angst. The Imam reassures her, he says that this is in line with her *ḥāla*, her condition, but her condition is difficult, and he will help her. She says that it is unbearable, that she so often feels violence (*ʿunf*) rising inside her, and so many times she has thought of suicide, *shahl min marrat fkkert ʿalā l-intihār*. She almost screams the word *intihār*, suicide, marking it with a gesture of the hand. The Imam doesn't react, I hesitate to speak, and then ask him whether he heard her. He says, yes, it is a difficult condition (*ḥāla*); it is not surprising that she would think of suicide. He then tells her that he will do a *"radio"*[3] to see what's wrong with her. I come closer to her, because her brother has left and I imagine I will have to hold her during the *ruqya*. She asks what will happen to her (she has never been in a *ruqya*). He can't anticipate, he says, but reassures that nothing bad will happen to her. He explains that he will read the Qurʾan to see whether the jinn reacts. It is a test.

He tells her to look straight and concentrate her gaze in the direction of a corner in the room (east, in the direction of the qibla) and to pronounce, *akrahak* (I hate you—to the jinn). She starts reciting and he recites at the same time Sūrat al-Fātiḥa, the opening chapter of the Qurʾan, almost inaudibly. Ḥayyat, the jinn within, starts reacting, her body shakes, her feet start moving, her body as well. She doesn't enter a trance state (*ṣarʿ*), at least not acutely, and doesn't lose consciousness. But she says several times that she is now feeling one by one all the physical symptoms of the illness, the ants in her feet, the heaviness in her stomach and chest. The Imam says: *anā llī jibt l-ḥāla bi-idhni llāh*, "it is I who caused the symptoms to appear, with the permission of God." He keeps reciting, and she reacts in different parts of her body. She is visibly in pain. He says, "Enough for now," and stops reciting. He calls her brother and explains to both of them that it is a difficult condition (*ḥāla ṣaʿiba*); he will prepare herbal remedies for her, and she must follow his prescription with no exception. She must avoid the sea at all cost, and he will see her the following week. She gets up, seems a bit relieved, and her son too has stopped screaming.

Before Ḥayyat and her family leave, the Imam calls Ḥayyat's brother. He will prepare the medicine she should take twice a day before meals. He tells her to take the medicine and return in a week, even though it is the beginning of Ramadan and he usually stops seeing patients at this time. She needs help urgently; he says turning to me, and reiterates to her that he will see her, in any case. He is concerned about her returning to Syria.

I am shaken by Ḥayyat's story, and by the angst in her expression—differently than in other *ruqya* sessions I have attended, where the scene is intensely dramatized as the jinn coming to presence in the fainting of the self; where there is "falling" and screaming, accompanied by facial and bodily contractures. I am perplexed, as well, by the Imam's cursory comment about the situation in Syria—in the summer of 2011 most people including me were not yet imagining what the civil war in Syria was going to become. "Muslims killing Muslims," a violence invalidating in his eyes the holiness of the month of Ramadan. This woman's pain, the jinn, her pull to suicide, the death drive (as I called it to myself), and the anticipation of destruction in Syria, reminding us, as if only by their contextual contiguity, of the implication of the afflictions of the soul in the afflictions of the world, and of the metaphysics of the jinn into larger considerations on war and death.[4] I think of Freud's uncomfortable reflections on the secret implication of our enjoyment in the spectacle of war, the satisfaction of the drive, and the way none of us is immune or external to participating in the violence.

When Ḥayyat and her family leave we sit down to talk. "Do you want to tape-record a little?" he asks. This is code between us, meaning to talk among ourselves, more reflectively, analytically. (I end up not turning the recorder on, and my notes are from memory.) I ask the Imam about what happened during the *ruqya* he performed on Ḥayyat, what he had called a test, and note that she didn't enter a trance (*ṣarʿ*). Differently than in other *ruqya* sessions Ḥayyat's pain was expressed directly, in her own words, not in the words of the jinn. There was a questioning that called for a recognition of her pain and of her confusion as her own, the experience of herself as another, but an experience that filled her with dread, and yet that she could feel and contemplate; the experience of being covered by the other, of feeling like a man, and being conscious of it. I wondered but did not say to the Imam whether there might be another way to address the anxiety that her sexuality arose in her, and whether in the space of a trance that angst and confusion might find an expression; and I asked myself whether her sexuality was a central dimension of the story, or if instead the center was elsewhere, in the bodily torment and the pull to death. I was struck by the polarization of affects, the pleasure and enjoyment in her dreams, and the torment, the violence, and the fate of destruction and death in her waking life. For the Imam it was clear that what gave her pleasure was also what caused her torment, the violence she felt in herself and sometimes spilled out with and towards others, the pain, the choking and suffocation, and the desire to do away with her life were aspects of the same condition. This is why what gave her pleasure should be opposed at all costs, and she should follow the Imam's prescription to the letter, so as not to be trapped in the desire of the jinn, which in the end was a drive to death. The task was to be able to open a space, even just an interstice, to allow a zone of play, to be able to locate the jinn (and its enjoyment) somewhere, localize it, its activity presentified in her body, in an arm or a foot, rather than all over her in totalizing indistinction, to reclaim to some extent the spiritual capacity of the soul in the carving of an interval between the jinn and th self.

The Imam says that because Ḥayyat did go into a slight trance state (*taṣarʿat*) the jinn reacted, and that was the important thing; it was visible in her body trembling. He didn't want to insist; it was clearly painful for her, and he believes it will take time for her to learn. Her reaction, however mild, was the sign of the jinn's responding to the Qurʾan, the sign of a possible spacing between the self and the jinn.[5] The prognosis is not one so much of full deliverance, but, as the Imam will explain a bit later, of localization. Ḥayyat's condition is severe. The jinn, the Imam explains, has completely "claimed and submerged the totality of her mind" (*istaraqa al-jinn jāmiʿ al-ʿaql*), the self disappeared, a land lost to the ocean.[6] But if Ḥayyat persists in the cure she will become capable of entering trance (*ṣarʿ*) and God willing, she will get better.

In the medical-magical texts on the *ruqya*, this moment in the ritual, which from the outside may be described as entering an altered state, is reckoned as "the disappearance of the afflicted" (*inṣaraʿ al-muṣāb*) which can also be rendered as, "the patient loses consciousness."[7] It is a disappearance that announces the coming to presence of an invisible being through the body of the person. It happens when the recitation of Qurʾanic passages forces that being to manifest itself, but it can also happen spontaneously, when the person is struck and falls to the ground because of an attack that was not ritually induced.

The term *ṣarʿ* has also another meaning. In the liturgy the moment of "falling" is followed by a verbal and sometimes physical combat between the jinn and the healer, which ends, if the session is successful, in the defeat and the "vanquishing of the jinn" (*ṣaraʿ al-jinn*), and the return of the subject to presence.

Ḥayyat's learned capacity to fall into a trance within the codified frame of the *ruqya* is for the Imam the path to a partial reclaiming of her inner space from the jinn, because the "falling" or "fainting" of the self represents both the illness and the possibility of a cure: as the Imam keeps reiterating, if the jinn comes to manifest existence (*wujūd*), the healer and the soul of the patient can then engage in a struggle, and if the healer is secure in the grounding of his faith in God, if he is skilled in his recitation of the Qur'an, if he is not afraid of the jinn and of Shayṭan that exists beyond the jinn, the jinn will retreat.

I mention her voices. He says that the voices she hears are the voices of the jinn. I suggest that these voices might be described as a psychiatric symptom (I say *'araḍ mrḍ 'aqli*, symptoms of a mental illness, and *takhayyulāt*, hallucinations, in this case auditory). And he replies that it is difficult to discern whether a symptom is of demonic origin (that is, of spiritual, metaphysical origin) or of psychiatric-natural origin. But that in this case there is no question that the illness is caused by the jinn. It is a difficult illness, he continues, an illness that is not just in Ḥayyat, but is passed on and shared, from the mother or even the grandparents or someone else in the family, and it affects the new generations, the children, and the children's children. In this case, he noticed the symptoms already in Ḥayyat's children. The little boy and the girl are clearly affected.

Magic (*siḥr*), which calls upon and activates the jinn, is the origin of her illness. Unlike other forms of demonic illness, the illness that originates in sorcery is triggered by human intervention, by the propensity for harm and destruction that nests in the human soul (a person manipulated the magic to cause harm, and triggered the jinn). The jinn here is what the Imam characterizes as a *jinn marīḍ*, an "intractable" and quite incurable jinn, of a kind that is impervious, cunning, and versed in the sophisticated arts of simulation. The intractable jinn is dangerous because he or she is capable of enduring torture, without fear and without crying, and resists coming to presence.

Ḥayyat too was inhabited by an intractable jinn (*jinn marīḍ*), "a jinn in love" (*jinn 'āshiq*), the most intractable of jinn, which would not allow her to be intimate with a man and have a family, despite the fact that she was married and had two children. Moreover, in her case it was a jinn passed on from a previous generation, or from her mother, and about whom she knew nothing. One could not know, the Imam said, because when this happens the jinn is passed on as the opaque mark of a bodily legacy, a "deposit" from the past. He called this a "mark" or "signature" (*ṭab'a*); it takes the form of a phantom, an inscription that cannot be deciphered, an inscription that is a radical stranger in the self (*nafs*).

TWELVE

The Psychiatrist and the Imam

I met Dr. A. in 2001, when he was a second-year resident at the psychiatric hospital in Sale. As with many of the younger psychiatrists, I spent time with him in the emergency room and at the morning staff meetings. I sat with him as he evaluated patient after patient, often in the presence of families or family friends. In the ER, time contracts and decisions have to be made quickly; configurations of symptoms must be assessed, the necessary information from different sources gathered, including family history, history of the illness, history of previous hospitalization, if any, and finally a recourse to some form of therapy and a pharmacological prescription. Sometimes, in the short and often nonexistent pauses between a patient leaving, a door closing and opening again with another story of illness, we exchanged a few words about what we saw and heard. Back then, in my eyes, Dr. A. seemed not very different from many of his colleagues in the way he attempted to fulfill the requirements of his position. In fact, I felt a closer intellectual affinity with other psychiatrists, older, more experienced, more vocal in the discussion of the postcolonial predicaments of disaffiliation and estrangement they recognized in themselves and in their patients, and more influenced by psychoanalytic and psychodynamic approaches. But this is a story of generations and not only therapeutic praxis.

I came to know Dr. A. better when two years later he asked me to help him with his *mémoire* in psychiatry, the thesis medical students have to present at the end of their residency. Dr. A. intended to write on the question of culture, religion, and psychiatric care, and as we discussed together I realized that his way of relating to the cultural referent was different from what I had encountered and reflected upon in my work with other, more senior psychiatrists, or psychiatrists trained in France.

Some psychiatrists interrogated their praxis with patients in their own clinic, reflecting on their attempt to grasp, beyond the medical configuration of a symptom, the sense of a life and its disappearance; their own complex relation to the institution vis-à-vis the "mystery" of the patients, as well as the hesitancies and uncertainties of their own diagnostic acts. For others, the dominant sentiment was the melancholic recognition of a loss, and an attachment that made itself felt like a wound. Psychiatrists such as Dr. N. or Dr. M. (as I discuss in part 1) were led to pose the question of culture and disaffiliation at an existential, psychodynamic, and sociopolitical level, and in relation to their own autobiographical trajectories.

For Dr. N., whose consultations I shared for many months, there was only his daily and singular encounter with patients, patients from poor urban and rural areas, who spoke Arabic or Berber and came to the hospital as a last resort. Patients for whom he and others struggled to find free medications and to whom he occasionally even gave money for transportation. A sense of painful renunciation of public voice, and a choice to occupy the institutional margins, in the ethics of a solitary clinical practice; a choice that pointed to the institutional failure to address the question of patients' experience, inequalities, voice, translation. Dr. M. spoke of his daily struggle with himself to follow his patient as far as he could on the territory of strangeness, postponing his diagnostic act, through religious and cultural territories, and as long as things were not so strange for him that he had to stop. Dr. N. and Dr. M. were my interlocutors of choice (it is Dr. M. who introduced me to thinking the hospital through Winnicott), with whom I felt I could connect and share my observations and questions, from whom I knew I could learn, and with whom I wanted to write in dialogue. There were others whose attitude towards the "cassure" of the past—the interruption of cultural transmission—was more pragmatic: the colonial history being what it was, the practices and discourse of institutional psychiatry were their legacy, and psychiatrists had no choice but live with them.

"Psychiatry is in French," Dr. K., a senior psychiatrist told me one day (he was then the head of the female ward, and the one who originally talked to me about writing Foucault's history of madness in Morocco) when I was asking him about the experience of listening to patients in the emergency room, where the residents doing their shifts had no choice but to speak colloquial Arabic, Berber when they could, or to bring in a nurse who could translate from Berber when needed; and yet they were taking their notes in French, because the language of their medical training, of staff meetings and hospital files, was French. He paused. To himself perhaps, just as to me, his words resounded with strident irony. Was it an indictment of the colonial "white mythology" in the sense of Fanon? In

Martinique, Fanon wrote, the French language became the bearer and the signifier of subjugation and loss, woven with the phantasies and torments of perverse enjoyment.[1] Or was it a tacit assent and ultimately a passive endorsement of the postcolonial symbolic? For this reason, he continued, for a psychiatrist such as himself, it was easier to work with patients from the Westernized elites, whose language for the symptom, configuration of thinking and imagining, was not incommensurable with the language of modern medical and psychological science. Psychiatry was French: *"parler une langue c'est assumer un monde, une culture"* (to speak a language is to take on a world and a culture).[2] Where did this leave the large majority of patients at the hospital?

Independent of whatever one thought of "traditional therapies," and whether—as the senior psychiatrist acknowledged—jinn were "real" entities in the lives of patients, they were now the remnants of an inassimilable past and could only belong in the realm of "cultural beliefs"; or, when they came to overlap with a psychiatric symptom, they might at best fit the theme and morphology of a delusion. This is why, Dr. K. continued, whatever we thought of them, whatever I observed and wrote in my ethnography of the hospital, the growth of psychiatry and the imperatives of modern public health, the struggle for a more equitable access to modern medical care, required the eradication of traditional practices. All one could do now was to be careful in listening to the semiological symptom and not diagnose patients as delusional or schizophrenic just because they spoke of their encounters with the jinn.

Dr. A. shared that assessment. The senior psychiatrist had been a mentor for him, and Dr. A. had often urged me to hear the anticolonial tones of his rejection of "traditional" practices, which extended to his harsh critique of Big Pharma and its market expansion into the non-Western world. For Dr. A. the continuity was not cultural: it was found in the Islamic tradition as a tradition that could be learned and relearned. Dr. A. distinguished between shariʿa healing and "traditional" healing. The very possibility of an approach grounded in the authority of the Qurʾan and rooted in the practice of Islamic jurisprudence, as well as Arab medicine and Islamic science, opened anew the transmissibility of tradition, even in the confrontation with its crisis and its aftermath. I discovered a person conversant with the study of the Qurʾan, theology, and *fiqh* jurisprudence, and interested in the growing field of Islamic psychology (*ʿilm al-nafs al-islāmi*). I could then see how in his clinical work his religious disposition played a role, how he had become a reference for numerous youths with psychiatric or psychological problems, who recognized in him an interlocutor and not just an institutional counterpart on the stage of psychiatric power.

Yet Dr. A. did not think that Qur'anic healing and modern institutional psychiatry could actively cooperate. He developed an interest in traditional therapies when he realized that a majority of the patients he saw at the hospital were continuing to seek care from a *faqīh*. He saw and acknowledged that in some cases their improvement had as much to do with the Qur'anic cure as with the psychiatric care and psychoactive medications they received. That very question had been my entry statement to the psychiatric hospital a few years earlier. There was a de facto cohabitation between psychiatry and religious cures. Coming to terms with the world of these cures, acknowledging their existence as de facto contemporary interlocutors was for Dr. A. part of the responsibility of a psychiatrist. It was a matter of listening to patients. His thesis struggles with this double consciousness, which it assumes and attempts to inhabit in a reflexive style, finding a resolution in the sharply critical stance it takes towards magical cures based on the "adoration" or "submission" to demonic beings through magic—seeking to fulfill one's desire (for wealth, health, power, marriage, or vengeance) by surrendering to the desire of the jinn, balanced by a respectful interest in the theological knowledge and the rigorous ethical practices of *'ilāj shar'ī* (that his thesis presents as a modern version of the *faqīh rabbānī*). As the work of a practicing psychiatrist, however, it also asserts the superiority of modern psychiatry, and this most prominently in the context of psychotic symptomatology.

Dr. A.'s interest was further fostered by a theological debate on the nature of mental illness and the ontological and epistemological status of jinn. On the one hand the growth of shari'a- and *fiqh*-based Qur'anic healing was increasingly taking the place of other vernacular forms of cures based on a different understanding of the relation with harm. In that configuration the agency of the jinn intervenes in what classical theology called an "occasion" or "secondary cause," for it is given to both human beings and jinn, as contiguous and different forms of life, to stray from the way of God and to enjoin harm. In relation to both subjects, human and jinn, the Qur'anic cure is addressed as an eschatological and ethical summoning of the afterlife in this life, opening the possibility of choice and of a reconfiguration of existence.

And, there was the theological debate among scholars of *fiqh* and Islamic psychology concerning the status of demonic possession. If the jinn are invisible beings of fire created by God and mentioned in the Qur'an, then in theological terms, no one can deny their existence; but the jinns' ability to come to presence and cause illness by entering the bodies of humans remains a subject of theological controversy. In this controversy Dr. A. stood with the rationalist approach that denied the possibility of bodily contact between human being and jinn, in line with the position of scholars of Islamic psychology (*ʿilm al-nafs al-islāmi*). In contrast with psychiatrists, psychologists, and physicians of Islamic orientations, the Qurʾanic healer who describes himself as *muʿālij sharʿī* (therapist who practices according to the shariʿa) operates on the assumption that the jinn can come into being (*al-wujūd*) through the body of the afflicted, and on the basis of this assumption performs the *ruqya* cure. The altered state itself, within which the jinn comes to presence, is called *al-ṣarʿa*, "absenting of consciousness, fainting or disappearance." In itself the technique of *ṣarʿ* is not specifically Islamic (in the sense in which the term is used by contemporary Qurʾanic therapists); it has been performed for centuries, and is still performed today in ways that the *muʿālij sharʿī* denounces as idolatrous. Yet the *ṣarʿ*, the trance or "fainting" of the self, is central to the efficacy of the treatment, which in many cases lifts the symptom, and could be accounted for in psychodynamic and neurological terms. The association of the cure with the liturgical context of a *ruqya* authenticates its Islamic character and situates the locus of effectiveness in the performative force of what the Imam calls the "miracle" of the Qurʾan itself.

While the modern scholarly field of Islamic psychology (*ʿilm al-nafs al-islāmī*) shares with the discourse of Qurʾanic healing its foundation in the authoritative sources of Islam and the shariʿa, it is explicitly conceived in a dialogue with Western psychology (Freud, Jung, McDougall, and Adler in particular), philosophy (in particular Bergson's intuitionism), psychiatry, and the social sciences, as concerning the nature of the self, perception, emotions, the instincts, human behavior, and the study of society. It is an attempt at discerning, contrasting, and, when possible, reconciling[3] Western psychology and Islamic principles,[4] and defines itself as "the study of the self based on the Islamic imagination of the human being, upon Islamic foundations."[5]

Dr. A. was interested in this debate, and intrigued by the parallels of Qurʾanic healing to his own therapeutic work. The theological arguments of Qurʾanic therapists could not be dismissed by a committed Muslim, and could not be cast aside as superstition, as have traditional therapies and magical rites, which were debased every day at the hospital. The divide between a healer on the path of God (*faqīh rabbānī*) and a healer who worked in the service of Shaytan (*faqīh shayṭānī*) had always existed in practice, and could be traced back to the field of knowledge of "prophetic medicine" (*al-ṭibb al-nabawī*) and to theological and legal ponderings on the nature of the human, the soul, and on the problem of evil. And yet for Dr. A. the renewed rise of Qur'anic healing had the performative force of a novel problematization.

Dr. A. belonged to a new generation of medical students and young professionals that was imperceptibly but decidedly shifting the practice of medicine and the terms of debate, in an international style and reach. He had in this sense something in common with Saad Eddine El-Othmani—a psychiatrist who in 2003 became the head of the Islamic Party of Justice and Development (PJD, *'Adl wa Tanmiya*), and who alongside with his specialization in psychiatry completed a degree in Islamic jurisprudence at the institution of high religious learning in Morocco.

Dr. A. and the Imam had several patients in common, who had at one time or another undergone hospitalization or come for outpatient consultation at the hospital. The Imam did not exclude the possibility of a collaboration of ethical-religious and scientific competencies. In conversation with Dr. A. he argued for the complementarity of *al-'ulama shar'iyyūn* and *al-aṭibbā' ṭabī'iyyūn* ("scholars of religious law" and "physicians of natural law"), and opposed both to what he called the "false healers," merchants of falsehood in the service of Shayṭan. For, inasmuch as nature is a part of creation, science is not external to the oneness of God.[6] It is the jinn and the "false healers" who traffic in unnatural matters; their acts are a violation against God and the created cosmos. As Ibn Qayyim stated in his fourteenth-century medical treatise,[7] and as the Imam argues and practices in his healing sessions with patients and in his preparation and administration of herbal remedies, there are natural (*ṭabī'ī*) and spiritual (*rūḥī*) remedies, and treatment consists in a combination of the two.

But the boundary of the demonic and the organic is blurred. This is why the Imam was interested in exchanging knowledge and reflection with Dr. A.—to better distinguish illnesses caused directly or indirectly by the jinn from situations where the illness was instead caused by a neurological problem, or by chronic substance abuse (*al-mukhaḍḍarāt*)—the two major causes of natural mental illness in the eyes of the Imam. As he explained in one of our first conversations, the brain (*al-dimāgh*) is the principal localization of the jinn in the body, inasmuch as the brain "is the center of perception (*al-shu'ūr*) and feeling (*al-iḥsās*)."

"Take the illness of *al-wahm* (delusion, the delusive imagination, one of the causes of melancholia, *mālikhūliyya*), for instance. *Al-wahm* can be said to be one of the few mental illnesses that are not directly of demonic origin; it has to do with a disturbance in thinking where the person becomes absorbed in her fancies and loses touch of the world. But it can also be a symptom of the intrusion of the jinn in the brain, where it affects the faculty of imagination and thinking (*wahmiyya*) and causes vagaries and drifting of thoughts."

In conversations with Dr. A. the Imam refers to a patient he and the psychiatrist have had in common, and who had been an inpatient at the psychiatric hospital. The person was *mshellel*, the Imam says, frozen or paralyzed; "catatonic," Dr. A. specifies. One possibility is to give a pharmacological treatment that might help that person move again. "If you [at the hospital] give her medications, the patient will seem to get better, but the jinn will remain. As long as the jinn remains the person will not regain her mind (*ʿaql*). She will be left vegetating and disabled, all she will do is sleep, wake up, take her medications and sleep again. There is nothing pharmacology can do, as long as the jinn is there."

Speaking to Dr. A., the Imam adds that in the case of that patient, and other patients with a similar condition, the Qurʾanic cure can help, even if not towards a complete remission. It is a condition he is encountering more and more in his practice, and it is related to the presence of an "intractable jinn" (*jinn marīḍ*), a jinn to a large extent incurable, that is, impossible to expel; a jinn often inherited across generations, as a haunting legacy, what the Imam calls a "mark" or a "signature." In that case, the Imam explains to Dr. A., the harmful presence of the jinn in the brain can only be circumscribed. This kind of jinn can kill the *nafs*—the person and the soul—of those who find themselves in the trajectory of the fate it has inscribed and unfolded. Or it can simulate physical death as a form of ultimate sovereignty, such that even physicians can no longer tell the living from the dead.

The Intractable Jinn

That is what happened to Najat. I met her some years later with the Imam, after Dr. A. had moved to a different city. Najat had been taken to the emergency room in what appeared to be a deep coma, hovering between life and death for several days, to the point where the hospital staff despaired of saving her life. Although she too was, like many of the women who come to see the Imam and seek his help, a Qurʾanic reciter, in recent years she had given up chanting in public, no longer went to the mosque, and no longer met with the group of women who had constituted her sole community in the lonely and painful months after the death of her husband. They too had turned against her. Her life had been marked by a succession of ruinous events that had struck her with the "unwished-for exactitude"[8] of fate: the death of her parents in a car accident; the sudden death of her husband, who left her with two small children and without resources; the loss of her home at the hand of her husband's family, who cut off relations and all her means of support, accusing her of being the indirect cause of their son's death. All around her people became accusatory or frightened, fearful that her misfortune might in some way be contagious and infect them. Each of the men who had approached her after her husband's death had become ill or died.

For the Imam, who was committed to helping her with the Qur'anic cure, the deathly sequence of her losses was the consequence of her *ṭab'*, a "mark" for which she was not responsible but that was active in her nonetheless. It was the signature of an intractable jinn (*jinn marīḍ*), a jinn "in love" (*'āshiq*), who claimed dominion over her life and imposed on her an absolute bond. The jinn had made himself known to Najat when she turned seventeen and had since been a constant presence in her life; the bond with him had added a unique timbre to her voice, an otherworldly sound to her chanting of the Qur'an. According to the Imam, the jinn had been in her family from well before her birth, in the home of her parents, and possibly her grandparents. It was he who made it impossible for a man to become intimate with her. And if some form of intimacy had existed at all, as in the case of her husband whom she had cared for and who had cared for her, the price of that intimacy had been his life.

One day as he was heading to Najat's home for a healing session, the Imam invited me to come along. She was unwell, and the session was tense. When the Imam interrupted his recitation to reassure her young daughter that the screaming and the agitation were the jinn's, and not her mother's, and that her mother would be healed with God's help, I took the girl out to the street to play and didn't come back until the session was over. After the *ruqya*, when Najat came back to herself, we sat in the kitchen and she shared with me what she understood of her story. She believed the jinn connected to her was Muslim, *mu'min*, a servant of God; this is what he professed and she believed him; she could not reconcile or make sense of the fact that he was also the cause of the destruction in her life. Or more precisely, she had an inkling that the jinn's involvement in her life, his attachment to her, had had disastrous effects; but she could not reconcile that realization with the internal image she had of him, that of an intimate friend who had supported her throughout her life. She was perplexed, and at the end of our conversation she asked me what I thought. She was aware that the Imam had a different interpretation of her traumas and her illness, and she herself had asked him to perform the *ruqya*, because she wanted to break the spell in her life for the sake of her children. I told her I didn't know how to answer her question, with a sense of disquiet beyond my inability to understand or to respond. I kept thinking about the effect of that deathly legacy concretely encoded in an attachment that could not be rescinded, a loving bond that yet produced death.

A few days later I was able to discuss her predicament with the Imam. We talked in his car as we drove through parts of the city that I had never seen, through an uninterrupted sprawl of informal and precarious new construction as one by one the neighborhoods morphed into each other. Our conversation was punctuated by the contingencies of the road, the honking and congestion at intersections; but the Imam kept following his train of thought in what became a complex explanation about the character of the intractable jinn, and the modalities of encroachment between the jinn and the self, the jinn and the soul. At some point I turned my recorder on.

The story of Najat had been on my mind, I began. He said that he had noticed my discomfort, and during the *ruqya* he had worried for a moment that I was frightened and vulnerable to the jinn. He disagreed with Najat's interpretation that the jinn in her life was a Muslim; no Muslim, whether human or jinn, would infringe in a person's life and seek such illegitimate intimacy separating a woman from her legitimate spouse. That interpretation was itself an effect of the jinn. It was a dangerous illness, and a dangerous jinn, of the "intractable" type (*jinn marīḍ*), unsubmitted, in the sense of unsubmitted to God, hence non-Muslim; a jinn who could not be treated with the usual means, and required from the therapist a perseverance and a resolve of the highest sort, and a purity of intent without which the therapist would himself be in danger. What was so dangerous in intractable jinn was their capacity to endure torture (the torture that the Qur'anic cure represented for them) and remain hidden, without producing manifest symptoms, and falsely taking on an appearance of truthfulness, even to the extent of simulating that ultimate passage of life in this world, which is physical death. The motive was love, which here meant an unbounded desire for dominion over the object. For, as the Imam explained, non-Muslim jinn are not as such deathly; they became deathly when moved by amorous passion for a human, because they lack the constraint that is the submission to God's law. *Al-ʿishq*, "love sickness," is a primary cause of madness in classical Arabic (as well as Galenic) medicine. But while in the natural medical version of lovesickness the cure was bringing the afflicted to the presence of the beloved—or, if that was impossible, to release the burning passion through a multiplication of erotic investments, distractions, and travel—for the Imam things were more complex, because the bond of love itself (*al-ʿishq*) was the result of an infringement, an invasion that was the totalizing attempt to establish sovereignty and subjugate the soul and its environment of relationships. "Love" here is the name of a form of dominion that admits no other, no alterity, no difference; it absorbs and devours in the kingdom of sameness, ultimately as a drive to extinction.

The Imam explained:

> The intractable jinn will test the strength and rectitude of the healer: to ascertain the healer's power (*quwwat al-muʿālij*) and the truthful orientation of the cure (*ṣidqi tawwajuhihi fī al-ʿilāj*), and if he is convinced, he will begin to leave. By contrast, weak jinn start crying when they see the healer, make the person faint right away and fall into a trance. This is when I know that the jinn is not strong (*ghayr qawiyy*), because he or she makes the person fall [into a trance] at the first inkling of the Qurʾan, and there the jinn begins to plead, and ask for help, and for mercy.
>
> To come back to sister Najat, in truth she is inhabited by an intractable jinn. They know how to trick the healer and are skilled in making the person fall into unconsciousness as if in a coma (*yusqiṭ*) and in hurting her until she stops breathing, until she chokes (*yaqṭaʿ al-nafs*). At the time I understood this: that the jinn simulated her death to make the doctors and the family give up on the possibility of healing (*shifāʾ*); or until they realized that it was too dangerous for them to oppose the desire of the jinn.

Three Configurations of the Jinn and the Self, Consciousness and Unconsciousness

The Imam then went on to outline a typology of what he called three "configurations" (*taṣawwurāt*, sing, *taṣawwur*) of the jinn in relation to the self/soul. All three described a situation of encroachment in which the person was not or could not be completely freed from the jinn.[9] We were talking about the predicaments of Najat and Ḥayyat, as well as other of the Imam's patients who had learned to live a pious life in the vicinity of an intractable jinn, one they strove to keep in check through an art of discernment, but could never completely defeat.

On the semanteme of consciousness and unconsciousness, necessary to understand the Imam's "configurations": the noun *al-waʿī*: consciousness, attentiveness, wakefulness, awareness; the verb *waʿā*, to hold something, to retain within one's memory, to remember; to pay attention, to bear in mind, to heed, to become aware; to enlighten, arouse consciousness.[10] In the negative form, without *waʿī*, to be or become unconscious, to lose consciousness, one of the formulations of the psychoanalytic unconscious. It is a crucial term, both for its resonance within the vocabulary of the psyche and the soul, and for its moral, political, and juridical implications.[11] In its spiritual and psychological usage it is contrastively related to the verb *shaʿara*, to learn or understand intuitively, to realize, notice, perceive, feel, or sense; to be conscious, to be aware, but with an emphasis on emotion. In the negative form, as we encountered earlier, it is one of the terms for the psychoanalytic concept of the unconscious, *al-lā shuʿūr, ghayr mashʿūr*.[12] *Al-waʿī* connects to the concept of responsibility and capacity in Islamic law (*taklīf, mukallaf*), to the state of being *rashīd*, being mature and of right judgment, and *ʿaqīl*, mentally sound.

The first configuration is what the Imam called, by analogy to a concept in modern psychology, *inqisām/infiṣāl shakhṣiyya*, "split or schizoid personality." He used this concept in conversation with me as a spatial image (accompanying his words with a gesture of the hands), the image of a rift and a shared personhood, making a direct reference to Freud, whom he had read when he was a law student in a course on criminology. (I asked him why he used the concept of the split self while in fact he was talking about jinnic intrusion. He replied that psychiatrists and hospital personnel don't understand the presence of jinn, and he had no choice but explain it to them in their own vocabulary, with reference to psychological terminology.)

I understand his use of the term in the sense of cleavage and dissociation, as in hysteria and multiple personality, but more importantly in the direction of what D. W. Winnicott called "encroachment" or "impingement," an intrusion and occupation of vital space by another in early infancy,[13] and of what object relation analysts have called schizoid and borderline personality. The clinical term in Arabic is *infiṣāl shakhṣiyya*, "split, divided, partitioned" personality, or *shakhṣiyya faṣāmiyya*, schizoid personality. *Qasama, faṣala,* and *faṣama* all carry the sense of breaking, cracking, splitting, and dividing. *Infiṣām* is the medical term for schizophrenia. In this configuration, the Imam explains, "the jinn occupies half of the sick person's brain (*dimāgh*), and the self keeps the use of half of the brain; that is, he or she has only half consciousness (*niṣf al-waʿī*)." Madness is located in the physical organ, which is the brain, and affects the capacity for reason (*al-ʿaql*).

The second configuration is the localization of the jinn in the body, in a limb or an organ, so that the sick person may say, "it is here or there," and in that figuration and distancing there opens a space of insight, an interval between the jinn and the self; and the person, as the Imam puts it, "can think," or, in other words, is capable of holding a sense of self. "Thinking," here understood by the Imam as unconscious activity, as a form of relation to the Invisible, requires two scenes.

The third configuration is one of total "submersion" and drowning; the Imam describes it using an underwater metaphor, one that Freud might call "oceanic": "the jinn submerges and occupies the entirety of the mind, and completely claims the person's life" (*istaghraqa al-jinn jāmiʿ al-ʿaql wa-stawlā ʿalā al-insān*), hurling the person into unconsciousness, an unconsciousness that indexes here the annihilation of the self and the soul. In this last case there is no longer any difference or distance between the self and the jinn: the jinn completely snatches the self and the soul, which vanishes under total dominion. This third configuration is the one that from time to time takes hold of both Najat and Ḥayyat. Ḥayyat, who despite her illness maintains remarkable insight, describes how the desire of the jinn "entirely covers her," to become her. Najat is at times completely submerged, and enters a coma-like state that resembles death. Others, the Imam says, have entered that state to never reemerge. In the Imam's own words:

> The first configuration is when the sick person or the afflicted (*marīḍ, muṣāb*) has half of her brain (*dimāgh*) occupied by the jinn, and therefore has access to only half of her consciousness (*waʿī*). The second configuration presents itself when, at moments, the jinn leaves that person alone to think on her own, and he or she has some insight and says: "There it is [the jinn] in my foot, there it is in my hand, there it is in my head," and so forth. But if instead the jinn submerges and occupies the capacity for reason (*ʿaql*) in its entirety (*ʿaql*), and completely claims the person's life, it comes to dominate that human being; he or she is hurled into unconsciousness and all insight is obliterated. This is the third configuration: the person falls into unconsciousness (*yasquṭ fī l-ighmāʾ*) deprived of all awareness (*waʿī*).[14] And when the person is deprived of consciousness the jinn remains, and it is the jinn that speaks, the jinn that moves the limbs and parts of the body, it is the jinn who is the subject of actions and exchanges with other humans in the world. You think that you are talking to that person, but in fact it is the jinn that replies.

And this is how the unconsciousness caused by the jinn is distinguished from mental illness in a book on healing:

> Symptoms that help distinguish between *al-mass al-shayṭānī* and *al-marḍ al-nafsānī* in the course of the *ruqya* cure: the sick slips into unconsciousness (*ghaybūba*), and the words of the jinn are on his tongue. Through that one can observe that his words (*kalāmih*) are different in their nature from the words of the person affected (*al-mamsūs*). Such utterances attest to the fact that [the jinn] impersonates a different personality from that of the afflicted (*yumaththilu shakhṣiyatan ukhrā*). This last trait, or symptom (*ʿaraḍ*), is considered to be more important than the other symptoms. . . . This symptom by itself suffices to reply to those who deny the existence of *al-mass al-shayṭānī*, because this symptom [the fact of speaking through the mouth of another] can be sustained only by "demonic possession" [literally "touch"]. The other symptoms can take place without possession [touch], by way of what is called autosuggestion (*al-iḥyāʾ al-dhātī*) by the sick person herself.[15]

The Death Drive

To dissipate or perhaps confront the anxiety that Najat's story produced in me, I attempted to think it through Freud's formulation of the death drive. In *Beyond the Pleasure Principle*, Freud writes about the repetition of loss and misfortune that seem to happen as if by chance but point to an inexplicable and uncanny necessity, that of finding oneself in the same place, again and again; the man who is betrayed by his friends, over and over; the one whose love relationships always end in the same pattern; the loss that happens twice, as in the story of Tancred, who unwittingly wounds his beloved twice, or the case of a woman whose first, second, and third husbands die of illness, with her nursing them to their death. "We are much more impressed," Freud writes, "by cases where the subject appears to have a passive experience, over which he has no influence, but in which he meets with the repetition of the same fatality."[16] Freud associates repetition with trauma: "A condition has long been known and described which occurs after several mechanical concussions, railway disasters and other accidents involving the risk to life; it has been given the name of traumatic neurosis. The terrible war which has just ended gave rise to a great number of illnesses of this kind, but at least put an end to the temptation to attribute the cause of the disorder to organic lesions of the nervous system brought about by mechanical force." Upon their return from the front, soldiers are tormented by traumatic dreams, repetitions of the traumatic scene, from which they wake up "in another fright." Yet, if the event of trauma hurls the subject into an uncanny zone at the limit of life, trauma per se is not at the center of Freud's reflection so much as the "tendency" (*Trieb*) or "drive" that is the daimon of repetition which fates the subject to return to the "same" situation.

An example insistently visualized for me the symbiotic attachment to the intractable, inherited jinn. In chapter 6 of *Beyond the Pleasure Principle,* Freud lends image to the workings of the death drive through examples from cell biology, and in particular one of an infusorian that dies when left to the toxicity of its own fluids: "For the same animalculae which inevitably perished if they crowded together in their own nutrient fluid flourished in a solution which was over-saturated with the waste products of a distantly related species. An infusorian, therefore, if it is left to itself, dies a natural death owing to its incomplete voidance of the products of its own metabolism." Freud adds, in parenthesis: "It may be that the same incapacity is the ultimate cause of death of all higher animals as well,"[17] and goes on to describe what he calls the "germ cells" as narcissistic in their function, as "retaining libido" with no expenditure into object-cathexes. He concludes with the uncanny remark that "the cells of the malignant neoplasm, which destroys the organism, should also be described as narcissistic in the same sense."

THIRTEEN

Black Bile and the Intractable Jinn: Threshold of the Inorganic

What is the place of the brain (*dimāgh*) in relation to the spiritual centers of being, the metaphysical sites of the maladies and medicines of the soul? This is what triggered the Imam's interest in natural medicine and conversation with Dr. A.

In response to our questions, and in his engagement with Dr. A.'s more focused diagnostic queries (when the psychiatrist kept pushing the Imam in defining the symptoms (*aʿrāḍ*), of a specific demonic illness, and the techniques of discernment for a correct diagnosis), the Imam explained that the threshold between "natural" and "unnatural states," between the brain (*dimāgh*) and the soul (*nafs, qalb*), is epistemologically unstable and sometimes organically blurred. This ambiguity is the subject of the subtle and always imperfect task of discernment, the discernment that carries the literal meaning of *fiqh* jurisprudence, and a discernment that in medieval Christian ascetic practices was called the "discernment of spirits."[1] It situates the practice of spiritual medicine, and of medicine itself, at the slippery and dangerous border of the physical and the metaphysical, the body and the spirit, the physiological and the pathological, in a space where the presence of harm and an encounter with the Invisible in the form of the jinn and Shaytan can never be excluded as such, and where the human being is ontologically *muṣāb*, that is, exposed to injury and loss. This question touches the core of a quandary concerning the body, consciousness, affect, and the status of human life as it is addressed today at the interface of neuroscience, psychoanalysis, psychosomatics, and contemporary philosophy.[2] For the Imam the question is posed in relation to the problem of the soul and its "choking" in the medical, spiritual, and political ailment of melancholy.

One of the figures of the overlapping indeterminacy of body and spirit, demonic and natural illness, is *al-jinn al-khalaṭ*, literally, the "jinn-humor." The Imam traces its medical formulation back to Ibn Qayyim, and cites examples of this hybrid form of illness in his own practice. It is a malign illness that he encounters more and more among his patients—highly dangerous, and in a certain way "beyond" treatment (in the sense in which Freud used the term "beyond"). The jinn-humor, as the Imam describes it, is created when the bodiless spiritual entity of the jinn turns into matter—a jinn that is at one with the body, by becoming the humor of black bile. It causes illnesses that are organic in their nature, and yet demonic in their veritable origin; cancer (*saraṭān*) is one of its possible consequences.

The Imam provided a definition: "*al-jinn al-khalaṭ*," he said, "is *mādda sawdā'*, black bile matter, the stagnating blood that concentrates and lingers in the head. It is organic matter we can locate in the head (*ra's*), in the brain (*dimāgh*)." At first Dr. A. did not understand. He asked whether the Imam was talking about bleeding in the brain, as happens in the case of concussion. The Imam reasserted his point, explaining the nature of the black bile humor in Arab medicine, and it became clear that the transubtantiation of the humor and the jinn was at the site of the uncanny encounter of the spiritual and the material, an indistinction that in this case pointed to an agency of destruction as such.

Mādda sawdā', "black matter" or just *al-sawdā'*, is the black bile humor of Galenic and Arab (and Ayurvedic) medicine, cold and dry, which in high doses becomes toxic, causing life to shrink and lose its vitality. *Mādda sawdā'* is also one of the classical faces of melancholy—al-*mālankhūliya al-sawdāwī* ("black-bile melancholia") in the texts of Ibn Sina (d. AH 428/1037 CE) and other scholars of early Arabic medicine, such as ʿAli b. al-ʿAbbas al-Majusi (d. AH 384/994 CE) and Ishaq Ibn Imran (d. 1087 CE).[3] In these theories, black humor in the brain "oppresses" and obfuscates the natural spirit (*rūḥ*) that preserves reason (*ʿaql*), causing mental confusion (*ikhṭilāt al-dhihn*, or *ikhṭilāt al-ʿaql*) and alteration of thinking, and mood shifting to sadness, fear, and distrust, resulting in anxiety, hallucinations (*takhayyulāt*), and melancholic delusions (*al-waswās al-sawdāwī*). Such melancholia can become "madness" (*al-junūn*, in the sense of mania) when it results from the creation of black bile from "burned" yellow bile and is accompanied by agitation and restlessness. But in its "pure" form (from black bile itself), it is a slow drift into the inanimate—a threshold of the inorganic in human life.

In classical debates on the etiology of melancholic illness, between a theological causality that stressed the metaphysical agency of the jinn and a natural causality that emphasized the toxicity of black bile and the malignant metamorphosis both of the brain and the animal spirit (*rūḥ*), the key point, shared by both approaches, is melancholia's undoing of life. In Ibn Sina's terms, even if melancholia were caused by the jinn, it would still happen "by changing the temperament to black bile, for melancholia's cause is the dominance of black bile. For the cause of black bile may be the jinn or something else." In his compendium of prophetic medicine Ibn Qayyim combines the natural and the theological understanding of the melancholic illness. On the one hand, he mobilizes the same conceptual structure and corpus of knowledge as the physicians of natural medicine centered on humoral theory. On the other, he relates the symptoms of melancholia to magic (*siḥr*), and to the effect of magic on those whose hearts are deserted by the remembrance of God. The weakened heart (*qalb*) of the person bewitched "is attached to something and turns constantly to it" but "the evil spirits only gain control of spirits which they find to be prepared for their control over them."

According to the Imam, who is reinhabiting this tradition from the perspective of his clinical work with patients, what is toxic and dangerous in the materiality of the jinn-humor is the fact that the jinn is no longer active as a "presence" or "being" (*al-wujūd*) that can be summoned and engaged in a therapeutic session, but lingers as an incrustation of coagulated black bile in the brain. When the jinn is no longer active and cannot be brought to presence, we enter a zone of indistinction between life and death, where neither life nor death can be accessed or experienced. This state or condition, the Imam explains, is caused by *siḥr*, the destructive power of sorcery, rather than by direct demonic intrusion (*al-mass*, "the touch"). It appears, as well, in the experience of the youths he seeks to counsel, whose lives are marked by the loss of hope and faith, and so many times cut short by suicide.

For there is a crucial difference between the embodiment that is a coming to presence of the jinn in the body of a person in trance, and the jinn's becoming body in the form of a material encystment—a "crypt," in the sense defined in the psychoanalysis of trauma.[4] It is more than a movement of demonic becoming organic: the toxicity of its material sedimentation causes life to become inorganic. The jinn itself disappears, and what remains is only a trace in the encystment of black matter, its scar, beyond expression and interpretation. As we saw, this encystment is understood by the Imam as the mark of an illness, or a trauma, passed on across generations within a family or a collectivity, which takes on the character of a shared destiny. Many of the "cases" (*ḥālāt*) the Imam sees and attempts to treat bear the trace of such melancholic transmission.

Madness, *l-ḥumq* (in colloquial Arabic; *al-junūn* in classical Arabic), bears the mark for the Imam of such an inorganic beyond of life, of a materiality that is both ghostly and flat. Yet in his view the majority of the conditions he treats and describes are not madness per se, even though a psychiatric or a psychoanalytic eye might recognize some of them as psychotic (because of the symptom of hearing external voices, for instance). This is because as long as the "activity" of a jinn can be registered, even in its work of destruction, there is a space of life that can be reclaimed. *L-ḥumq* instead is an outmost limit. The Imam calls it "the end" (*al-nihāya*), beyond all reclaimable life. The jinn is no longer; only its scar remains in the damaged brain. Its figure is brain death—but it is only a figure, a figure of something that can have no figure. In the Imam's words:

> Because madness (*l-ḥumq*) is the end [the outmost limit], it is a trace, only a trace! The jinn is active until the sorcery is consumed, the *siḥr* comes to an end, everything comes to an end, it reaches the end, and the human being reaches a stage where it is impossible to come back. In other words we say that in the situation of sorcery (*siḥr*) the jinn is still performing its action (*kay'addi fi'l*), working in the service of the magician. But when the jinn goes, the region of the brain (*dimāgh*) where the jinn resided is destroyed, the jinn destroyed that person's brain. And here that person reaches madness! This is clear.
>
> It has never happened that there could be healing at this point. The person reaches a stage where, in fact, there is no longer a jinn. And there is no longer the activity of the jinn.

FOURTEEN

The Argument of *Shirk* (Idolatry)

Several of my conversations with the Imam began with his critical positioning against what he called the "false healers," whose widespread practices infect the terrain of healing in the name of God. It is a polemic against what he calls *ʿilāj ghayr sharʿī* ("cures outside of the law") or *shaʿwadha* (the magic arts, or tricks related to the powers of falsity and therefore to sorcery, *siḥr*). The theme of sorcery is central, and more so than in older approaches to the cure. The tone is reminiscent of the religious-political tone of the Salafiyya movement in Morocco and throughout the Middle East during anticolonial struggles,[1] denouncing the straying into ignorance and the worship of idols that reduce human beings to captivity and alienation (subjugated to the desire for material gain and possessions, and, in the vocabulary of the early twentieth-century Salafiyya, to the fascination for European goods and influence that made Arab countries vulnerable to foreign conquest), and asserting the central tenet of the oneness of God and the possibility of reason in the conviction of faith. It is reminiscent, as well, of several Qurʾanic passages where the operation of magic is addressed directly, as in the narrative of Moses and Pharaoh (Qurʾan 28:1–88). Yet given a closer look, things are more complex.

The imperative is to distinguish the truthful cure from the false one, the Islamic from the un-Islamic, and too to distinguish the jinn from the self, the desire of one from that of the other; to draw a line, a boundary between truthful practice, a life dedicated to God, and the pursuit of falsehood. In the realm of the cure, this amounts to defining the attitude of a Muslim as such. The Imam returns to the question often, as a way of recalling the theological and epistemological coordinates within which his argumentation can move. In the twelfth century, al-Ghazali titled his work on the "limits" of Muslim belonging and faith *Fayṣal at-tafriqa bayna al-islām wa-l-zandaqa,*[2] the discernment of a distinction, a boundary, between Islam and the false believers. On that boundary, he set off to explore the meaning of *al-kufr*, a concept which is usually, if improperly, translated as unbelief or apostasy. The configuration of *kufr* includes the notions of ingratitude (towards God), unfaithfulness, and unbelief (as the antonym of *īmān*, faith); defiance and arrogance towards God (in contrast to *taqwā*, virtue and fear of God); *ṭaghā*, exceeding all bounds and overstepping the norm; *shirk*, idolatry, nonrecognition of the oneness of God (*tawḥīd*), which implies the exercise of unwarranted thinking, conjecture, and speculation (*ẓann*) away from the path of true knowledge; and finally the fact of going astray from the right way (*ḍalāl*), losing or refusing guidance (*ihtidā'*).[3]

The question is complex, because on the one hand false healing is widespread, as the vernacular cures of the jinn are practiced by many, and the difference between false and Islamic cures is elusive and needs to be continuously reaffirmed and rearticulated both in practice and discourse. There is an uncanny mirroring between the actions of the just and those of the wrongdoer, between the truthful and the deceitful; indeed, what may appear to the uninitiated as small differences in the liturgy are highly significant. Most importantly, as became apparent in conversation with the Imam, the boundary is not given once and for all as an abstract principle but is encountered over and over in the experience of illness and healing. It is a boundary that is both external and internal to the definition of the Muslim and that of the self.

The false healing to which the Imam is referring is that of traditional demonology—the array of practices varying from divination, healing, visiting saints' shrines, and what is known as *'ilāj al-jinn*, "the cures of the jinn," based on the principle of reaching out to the jinn, satisfying its desire, and establishing the terms of a pact, often sealed by a sacrifice. The effectiveness of these practices is based on what the Imam calls *istirḍā'*, the attempt at meeting the desire of the jinn, or of calling out for the jinn's help. The Imam does not deny their effectiveness. The question for him is not effectiveness but rather the committed effort to follow God's ways.

In his *Muqaddima* Ibn Khaldun pursues a detailed discussion of the principles of magic healing, based in astrology and the manipulation of cosmological forces, which he contrasts with approaches to healing grounded in the shari'a. He elucidates the workings of magical efficacy and divination side by side with the experience of prophesy, indicating how both approaches testify to an encounter with the realm of the Invisible (*al-ghayb*), but that the question for Muslims is the submission to God and the embracing of a life in agreement with God's law.[4] In a similar sense neither al-Ghazali nor Ibn ʿArabi denies the fact of magical effectiveness, but both state the necessity of discernment between truth and untruth, on a boundary that from the standpoint of human imperfection can only appear as precarious and at times confusing. It is for this reason that reliance upon the revealed law is necessary, inasmuch as it points to the divine decree at the limit of human understanding.

"False healing" participates in the economy of sorcery (*siḥr*). In the Imam's argument, it is contiguous with a form of sovereign power that subjugates human beings and leads them away from justice to error, oppression, and perdition. False healing is therefore associated with more than just magic and the jinn. It is a sign of the state of oppression of the society as a whole, and of the person in it: an oppression that is at once theological, psychological, and political.

The Imam:

> Discussing the question of *ṣarʿ* (the "annihilation" of the jinn) forces us to confront the issue of *shaʿwadha*, that of magic arts and "untruth" in healing. The practice of *shaʿwadha* is a main cause of idolatry (*shirk*) and apostasy (*kufr*). And this is because it is predicated on the recourse to the jinn (*istaghātha*) and the appeal to the intervention of the King of the Jinn. To go about their business, jinn have workers, slaves who work for them, servants whom they have subdued. For jinn put themselves in the service of human beings, but in the perspective of losing them (*ʿan yuḍill*), the perspective of *ḍalāl* (loss, straying). Take a person who visits a sanctuary or a haunted place and seeks proximity with the jinn by way of sacrifice (*dhabīḥa*, *qurbān*), when instead sacrifice and offerings must be presented to God alone. For God has said that prayer and ethical practice, life and death, are intended for God alone, the great and the highest, and [has commanded] do not enter heresy (by way of *shirk*).

The operation of magic (*siḥr*—as at once an ill and a demonological cure) is both that of "false healing" and that of the jinn itself. The world of the jinn mirrors the world of false healing, and it engages in commerce with it.

The Imam continues:

> For what comprises the cure on the side of *shaʿwadha* is the operation of meeting the desire of the jinn, *ʿamaliyya istirḍāʾiyya* (propitiation, satisfaction, pleasing), while instead the [true] cure resides precisely in the opposite, in opposing the desire of the jinn. So the healer, the magician (*al-sāḥir*), or the seer (*al-kāhin*), or the diviner who practices *al-khaṭṭ*, performs certain

> operations and magical calculations, and works with the jinn in an attempt to find information—"intelligence"—disclosing what happened to the sick person [then he explains in vernacular Arabic: *l-jinn kayyjib l-faqīh*, the jinn brings information to the healer]. The jinn will bring "intelligence" relative to when and why the person fell ill, when he or she was "touched" (*mass*) by a jinn and when and how the jinn "clothed" that person (*labisahu*—entered the *nafs*), or when that person encountered witchcraft (*matā taḥatta al-siḥr*), when he or she walked under it [if it was hanging] or over it [if it was buried underground]. In this case the healer on the side of *sha'wadha* tries to meet the desire of the jinn, to find out what the jinn "wants" in order to be satisfied. The jinn says: "I want a sacrifice, or a *ziyāra* (a ritual visit to a certain site) or the healer to burn perfumes," or whatever may please the jinn. When the healer has had the better of the jinn, the person has in fact fallen prey to the Sultan of the Jinn, who is now in command (*ya'mur*) and can now count on that person (*ins*) as his subject, because that person is lost (*ḍāll*). That person is now a property of the jinn, and whenever the jinn wants him or her, the jinn can find him or her.

The image of the jinn who bring "information" to the "false healer" is reminiscent of the *mukhābarāt*—the infamous secret police, and its routine recourse to torture and assassination, in the secret basements of Moroccan police stations. (Echoes here of the torture and secret detention in the experience of many youths associated with the Islamic movement after 2003, as well as earlier detentions, during the "years of lead" under King Hassan II in the 1970s and '80s.) The jinn here is a figure of *kufr*, a materialization of the risk of *kufr*: untruth, ingratitude, contesting the oneness of God. In his study of ethical concepts in the Qur'an, Toshihiko Izutsu argues that the semantic configuration of the concept of *kufr* comprises an array of related yet different meanings, none of which can be reduced to a simple notion of disbelief in the modern English sense of the term.[5] All these variants suggest that the possibility of *kufr* is rooted in basic human dispositions, and hence the position of belief can never be a given, but is an open ethical work—a work, one may add, in whose unfolding one can repeatedly encounter the risk and possibility of *kufr*.

The Imam:

> Human life, human action (*l-'amal*) is dedicated to God. This is the consensus of the Muslims, there is no share for Shaytan, or the jinn, or the Sultan of

the Jinn. Consider for instance that at the occasion of Eid al-Adha [the feast of sacrifice] you find many people who bring a pitcher, or a bowl, and collect in it the blood that sprinkles out of the throat of the sacrificed animal, they collect it, and later drink it. In theological knowledge (*l-ʿilm*), in religion and in the Qurʾan it is stated that blood is impure. It is the spirits (*shayāṭīn*) who drink blood and satiate themselves, and they engage in dealings with people, in the hope of leading them to damnation (*min ajal an tudkhilahum li-l-shaqāʾ*).

The Imam argues that the cause of the recourse to magic (*siḥr*) is coercion (*ikrāh*), the absence of justice, and the impossibility of equitable recourse—in court—for the oppressed; as well as the state of terror and intimidation into which the person is thrown by coercion itself.

Human beings exist in justice (*ādami wujud al-ʿadl*). And justice is violated by way of coercion (*ikrāh*): "there is no coercion in religion (*dīn*)" (Qurʾan 2:256). If there is justice, when I have a problem with another person, I can claim my right, and obtain it. But we have a vulnerable person, a poor person, in the confrontation with a rich and powerful person. In that case, the poor person will have no way to get his right, there is no way. And this is when he turns to sorcery. He will bury sorcery in the ground, at the place where his opponent will step, or in his food, or with his body hair, or with a picture . . .

Dr. A. interjects, as if to clarify the point to himself and to me: "There is no social justice" (*makeinsh ʿadl ijtimāʿī*).

Ijtimāʿī? exclaims the Imam. "No! there is no justice in general. Because justice is the grounding principle of the universe. It cannot be reduced to social justice." He qualifies his statement:

It is not that there is no justice at all. There are laws, but there are people who are too powerful, and interfere with the law to prevent the application of justice. Take a wealthy or powerful person: that person will bribe functionaries in positions of authority to halt the exercise of the law in the courts by pecuniary corruption, or else by coercion and intimidation. In this situation the powerless person turns to magic because he has been offended and hurt (*min ajal al-intiqār*). This is the first reason.

The second reason is envy (*ḥasad*). This is what happens to professionals, teachers, engineers, physicians; they see their neighbors and want to possess

> the same gadgets, the new car, the new phone, the new model (*model jadīd*). There are people who are sick in their heart, and their heart doesn't find peace until they obtain the same possessions as their neighbors.

In Lacanian terms the event of madness "shows." It is an anamorphosis of the apparatus of power and the violence of the state which reveals by disclosing the dominion of the jinn. The event of madness awakens us to the deception of the view, exposing something that was to remain covered, and enabling a different, eccentric angle of vision, an angle of vision that is proper to dreams. The showing happens at the level of the "stain," which necessarily eludes the field of ocular vision and bears witness to the annihilation of the subject. In this sense, the event of madness in the discourse of the Imam occupies the position of the skull in Lacan's famous reading of Holbein's painting *The Ambassadors*,[6] where the insignia of wealth, power, and science are shown as reflected, from a certain angle, into the skull at the feet of the ambassadors—an anamorphic ghost pointing to the ruin of it all. What "shows" in the discourse of the Imam is the anamorphic ghost of the jinn. From its eccentric angle madness makes visible the regime of the jinn, the metamorphosis of the jinn as Shaytan and of the *nafs*/soul as a terrain of conquest.

In other words, the event of madness "shows" the obverse of the subjugation of the subject in the everyday unfolding of social life—a waking life that the Imam describes as a slumber of the soul. Sometimes, as psychoanalyst Piera Aulagnier and others have written, reflecting on their clinical work with psychotic patients, madness is the only path open for the subject, and "people said to be crazy, in the ordinary sense of the term, show us what it was necessary to do in order to survive."[7]

FIFTEEN

Extimacy: The Battlefield of the *Nafs*

> I said that the *nafs* is the yeast, the fertile land that Shaytan cultivates and tills; but he doesn't cultivate grapes, figs, and pomegranates! He cultivates desires, cravings and longings, and with them blasting and bombs . . .
>
> —the Imam

> *L'experimentum mentis* que je vous ai proposé ici . . . a consisté à prendre ce que j'ai appelé la perspective du Jugement dernier, je veux dire de choisir comme l'étalon de la revision de l'éthique à quoi nous mène la psychanalyse, le rapport de l'action au désir qui l'habite.
>
> —Jacques Lacan, *L'éthique de la psychanalyse*

For the Imam the central question is the *nafs*—that is, the soul, in its relation to the heart (*qalb*), which is also the soul, and the perilous stage on which they play out their states and actions.

Because for the healer mindful of the intimate relation of medicine and jurisprudence, and of the twofold character of the law, at once a jurisprudence of the soul and of the world, it is not possible to speak of injustice and violence, of the epidemiology of depression and suicide, or of the wars that are devastating the region without confronting the direct implication of the self and the soul, with their outer actions and inner stirrings, temptations, motivations, and intent. It is necessary to ponder what al-Ghazali in his redefinition of jurisprudence as "knowledge of the path to the afterlife" had called *āfāt al-nufūs*, "the subtle afflictions of the soul"[1]—the soul as the desiring *nafs*, life function and movement of the passions and faculties, and as the heart (*al-qalb*), the spiritual center of being, where character is formed and reformed, and where the ground for ethical judgment resides.

The "inner" and the "outer" (*al-bāṭin, al-ẓāhir*), the jurisprudence of norms and cases and that of the heart and of medicine, are intertwined dimensions of the law, and this awareness shapes the practice of the Imam in his clinical work in cases addressing the jinn and the self, and in his sermons and counseling of the youth. This is why in our conversations the theme of evil and its trials moves between the collective register of a spiritual diagnosis concerning the state of the society as a whole, and the battlefield of the *nafs*, the theater of the struggles of the soul. In the battlefield of the soul longings and passions are vulnerable to the destructive insinuation of Shaytan; but it is also there that the ethical work of spiritual transformation, *al-mujāḥada al-nafsiyya* (the effort or struggle of the soul), takes place, in an engagement with the intimate connection of desire and destruction, the risk of falsification, and the task and responsibility of discernment. This is the core of the Imam's practice, of his thinking and teaching as I understood it in his therapeutic sessions with his patients, in the performative and kinesthetic stage of the *ruqya*, and in his more reflexive conversation with me.

But what *is* the *nafs*?

In the course of a conversation that eventually led to a series of lessons and exchanges[2] on the *nafs*, the heart, the passions of desire and anger, the problem of evil and the illness of grief and melancholy, I asked the Imam a terminological question concerning the difference between the illness of the soul, spiritual illness, and those illnesses that psychiatrists and psychologists call *amrāḍ nafsiyya*, the standard Arabic term for mental or psychological illness. The terms *al-ṭibb al-rūḥānī* (spiritual medicine) and *al-marḍ al-rūḥī* (spiritual illness) are found in some of the classical texts on the maladies of the soul. I noticed their use earlier in the vocabulary of Ibn Qayyim's *al-Ṭibb al-nabawī*, where *rūḥ* and its configuration of related terms are used in the sense of soul or spirit, according to a hierarchy of souls from the lower embodied earthly spirits to the higher disembodied angelic intelligences; *al-Ṭibb al-rūḥānī* (spiritual medicine) is also the title of Muhammad b. Zakariyya al-Razi's medical text,[3] and the term is sometimes used today by scholars of *fiqh* and of Islamic psychology to demarcate the field of spiritual illness and the competence of the religious healer. In this restricted contemporary use of the term, "the spiritual" (*rūḥī*) becomes the specific prerogative of the religious healer. In this way the religious healer can claim a role in a medical distribution of expertise, alongside that of the psychologist, psychiatrist, or psychoanalyst, who treats psychological or mental illnesses (*amrāḍ nafsiyya*) and whose field of expertise is taken to be the *nafs* (here understood as the psyche), and for the psychiatrist also the brain (*dimāgh*); and finally a role parallel with the expertise of the physician, who treats organic illnesses (*amrāḍ uḍuʿiyya*), including those involving the brain.

My question to the Imam was sparked by the way this classification had been positioned and debated a few days earlier at a roundtable broadcast on the question of mental illness in Morocco "between science, religion, and culture."[4] Three professionals and two NGO activists shared the table: a psychiatrist-psychoanalyst, who is also a friend and interlocutor in my research; an endocrinologist at a public Rabat hospital, also member of the Council of Religious Scholars (*ʿulamāʾ*); a scholar of *fiqh*, graduate of the college of Islamic jurisprudence Dar al-Hadith al-Hassaniya, who also, like the Imam, practiced as a shariʿa therapist and performed the liturgy of the *ruqya*; the founder of an advocacy organization for the families of psychotic patients; and finally a student, a member of the organization "Santé Jeunes."

When I started summarizing the debate for the Imam, he seemed distracted and not really interested, but I insisted. It was strange for me to recall that roundtable now in his company and at his home, where he confronted those questions on a daily basis on the bodies and souls of his patients, in an existential depth and complexity that eluded easy characterizations.

The roundtable had opened with an introduction by the convening journalist who evoked the long history of the concept of the *nafs* in Arab and Islamic tradition, and invited participants to consider practices and traditions of healing in Morocco, old and new, as symbolic configurations that should be taken seriously on their own terms, and not just as a subject of disagreement or denunciation. The endocrinologist spoke first, stating his joint commitment to the rationality and truth of both Islam and modern medicine and pointing out how religious faith made a difference for him in his work at the hospital and in his human encounter with patients. The psychoanalyst spoke of his experience of listening to his patients, paralleled with what he had observed at saint shrines, and of the analyst's own relationship with madness in general, where, he said, lay the fulcrum of all therapeutic engagement. The representatives of the associations shared their experiences, each with a mentally ill family member, and spoke of what they saw as the urgent need to educate families on the psychiatric facts of mental illnesses. The onset of psychosis, they said, produced disquiet within the family of the sick, and the widespread tendency to impute odd and aggressive behaviors to demonic or magical etiologies seeking the help of healers was dangerous for both patients and families. All participants, directly or indirectly, in their specific vocabularies, also made reference to the historical crisis resulting in abortive futures and collective mental pain, which manifested itself in illness and an unbearable sense of existential malaise, most visibly through the reality of *l-ḥarg,* "burning," undocumented migration that so often resulted in death.[5]

The scholar of *fiqh* who was also a shariʿa therapist spoke last. He outlined a tripartite typology of illness, and the knowledge associated with each type: organic illnesses (*amrāḍ uḍuʿī*), psychological illnesses (*amrāḍ nafsī*, lit. of the soul), and spiritual illnesses (*amrāḍ rūḥī*). He explained that the first two types originate in the body (*badan*) and are the subject matter of corresponding natural/medical sciences, while the third is different: "Its subject matter belongs in the shariʿa" (*mādda sharʿiyya*), and cannot become an object of positive science in the same sense as the other two (science taught in university lecture halls, as he put it). The journalist seemed confused or impatient, and asked what the difference was, concretely, between the two types of illness, psychological and spiritual. Could he give some examples? The *faqīh* explained that illnesses of the *nafs*—which, by now it was clear, meant for him psychological and mental illnesses—were outside of his competence, and he deferred to the expertise of the psychologist and psychiatrist in the room. But when it came to illnesses whose origin was "spiritual" (*rūḥī*), natural science was powerless. Those illnesses required a different kind of therapist, a therapist with a sound understanding of the Qurʾan, the *fiqh,* and the sunna: one "with subtle insight into the realm of the spirit" (*mutakhaffif fī jihat al-rūḥ*). Illnesses of a spiritual nature were on the rise in the contemporary world, he said. This was because God showed us a way and a method (*manhaj*), but social changes in our historical time were causing people to depart from the way God traced for us, and that straying had become a source of illness and suffering, both for human beings and for the planet writ large.

The journalist did not want to pursue a theological argument; the roundtable was about mental illness. She kept pushing the *faqīh* to specify the contrast: how were the symptoms different from those of psychological or mental illness? The endocrinologist intervened on behalf of the *faqīh*: the diagnosis of "spiritual illness" was necessarily residual, after all other possibilities had been excluded, in the mode of those physical or psychosomatic syndromes that to this day don't find affirmative laboratory evidence.[6] A responsible Qurʾanic therapist, the endocrinologist said, pronounces only residual diagnoses. His comment was both intriguing and troubling: the ontological realm of the Invisible (*al-ghayb*), a central tenet of Islamic metaphysics, was as a "remnant" in the enigma of psychosomatic illnesses, allergies, and other unexplained symptoms.[7] How to speak of the Invisible (*al-ghayb,* the cosmic reality beyond human sensory perception) to an audience that does not share the same metaphysical premises, without resorting to a theological or a cosmological argument? The implicit questions around the table—what is a fact, a symptom, the soul, the psyche, a form of life; what does it mean to move away from the path that God traced—were unbroachable.

The *faqīh* held his ground: psychological illnesses belonged within natural science; spiritual illnesses, on the other hand, were illnesses caused by "the demonic touch" (*mass al-jinn*) and magic (*siḥr*). The demonic touch can have a variety of symptoms, can cause persons to "fall" and lose consciousness while the jinn speaks through their mouth, or may not show any visible signs. "*Mass al-jinn*: *possession*!" the journalist repeated in Arabic and emphatically translated to French. Then she asked the psychoanalyst whether he would defer to the *faqīh* on matters of possession in the same way the *faqīh* deferred to him on matters of the psyche. The psychoanalyst would not defer, and this despite his appreciation of the sharp clinical insight of some traditional therapists. For him, he said, the truth of possession was hysteria. A diagnosis of possession located harm outside the subject, either in the jinn or magic, making it impossible for the subject to come to terms with his or her own history. His own psychoanalytic approach sought to hear the symptom in terms of the individual history of the subject, and posed the question of desire.[8]

Having participated in the working groups on psychosis and symbolic efficacy that this particular analyst had organized, I had an inkling of the depth of his insight. Innumerable times I had discussed with him the possibilities of the subject at the borders of madness,[9] of Lacanian borromean knots and "sinthomes," and how hysteria should be rethought in those terms. Why then, in conversation with a religious scholar, would the psychoanalyst retreat to the normativity of subjectivity's boundaries rather than engaging his own Lacanian thought on psychosis, identification, the drive, "the other enjoyment," and the "makeshift mending" of the sinthome that he explored in his own work? Why not allow that the question of the drive, the unconscious, desire, and responsibility, might be asked otherwise, and in a not-incommensurable form at that? Or, in other (non-Lacanian) approaches, why not consider the analytic research and inquiry on identification and projective identification, melancholy and traumatic transmission, and the multipersonhood and haunting this entailed?[10] These points are raised in a variety of ways in the work of psychoanalysts and psychological anthropologists.[11] In the psychoanalysis of trauma originally inspired by Sandor Ferenczi, traumatic identification was at the heart of the matter. The traumatized was inhabited by a desire that wasn't his or her own, perhaps not altogether differently than the person struck by the "demonic touch." Wasn't the kind of knowledge that "could not be taught in lecture halls," as the *faqīh* had put it, that is, become an object of positive science, not altogether incommensurable with what Lacan had called "the discourse of the psychoanalyst"?[12] Lost in the rift of classification there remained the question of the soul. Not just the *nafs* as psyche, but also the reverse: the psyche as soul, a point made by Bruno Bettelheim in his attempt at reclaiming Freud's *Seele* (soul/psyche) from its English translation as "mind."[13] My work with the Imam over the years and this text on the "jurisprudence of the soul" are my attempt at a reply.

The Imam listened to my account. He recognized much of what the *faqīh* had said, and could relate to the conundrum of referencing the realm of the Invisible (*al-ghayb*) when the interlocutor did not share its metaphysical premise. He himself relied on the psychological vocabulary of dissociation and schizoid states (*inqisām shakhṣiyya*), he said, in order to be understood by mental health professionals when describing the case of a patient or the topography of the jinn's infraction and rapture of the soul. He had used that vocabulary with me, perhaps also to play with an analogy that intrigued him, as if secretly reclaiming the psyche and the brain to map them on the metaphysics of the soul. But he refused to negotiate on the question of the *nafs*.

Was there a difference then between the illness of the soul (*al-maraḍ al-nafsī*), spiritual illness (*al-maraḍ al-rūḥī*), and those illnesses that psychiatrists and psychologists call *amrāḍ nafsiyya*?

For the Imam the question was more complex and foundational, and could not be resolved by a nuancing of terms. He resisted the secular reduction of the psyche and the soul implicit in that distribution of competencies. He saw that position as a disavowal of the perilous terrain of the *nafs*: a disavowal that itself was a symptom of a malady of the soul.

He insisted on the centrality of the *nafs* to the question of illness, the *nafs* in its complex sense of the aspiring soul, the soul of the creature in the journey through life and back to God, as made clear in the Qur'an, and in the dimension of a being of desire, vulnerable to error, exposed to internal upheavals and to the trials (*balā'*) of destruction and evil, open to transformation, and to the experience of the divine. He argued that yes, there was a difference between the illnesses of the soul (*maraḍ nafsī*) and mental illnesses (*amrāḍ nafsiyya, 'aqliyya*), but that mental illnesses as described by psychiatrists and treated in hospitals were themselves and for the most part originally caused by illnesses of the soul. They were illnesses caused by the jinn, but their true origin was a surrender of the *nafs* to the passions of anger and grief:

> Because the *nafs*, what becomes sick in the *nafs*? Does the *nafs* have bones, does it have organs? If we consider the body (*al-jasad*), for instance, it has organs; it has the stomach and the liver, it has the yellow bile (*al-safrawiya*) and the black bile (*al-sawdā*ʾ), the gallbladder and the pancreas, the heart and the circulation of blood (*al-dawra al-damawiyya*), the kidneys, and so on. In other words, something tangible, sensible, and capable of being felt by the senses (*shayʾa malmūsa wa maḥsūsa*) is struck and becomes sick (*tuṣāb*): either by the microbes, or by some kind of cold, what is called rheumatism, or by something that a person has eaten, a poison. But the *nafs*, what makes it sick? Do not become angry (*lā taghḍab*)! It is anger that is the first cause of illness for the *nafs*, anger (*al-ghaḍab*) and grief (*al-kaʾāba*). For the most part the *nafs* becomes ill with what the Prophet said to Abu Dardaʾ: "*Lā taghḍab!*"[14]

The *nafs* is an intangible substance, immaterial, and stirred by the passions. We should keep in mind the cosmology of the soul with which the Imam is working. His description points to its subtle essence as something beyond the body and yet embodied, and describes the movement of passion as at once a fact of creaturely life and the subject of ethical admonition, the admonition of the law in the voice of the sunna: "The Prophet said: Do not become angry."

According to an understanding of the *nafs* grounded in the Qurʾan (*al-nafs al-ammāra bi-l-sūʾ*, "the soul that incites to evil," Qurʾan 12:53) and nurtured by the Imam's familiarity with the thought of al-Ghazali, and by a widespread vernacular and textual use that identifies the *nafs* as the seat of the wrathful and desiring soul, he describes the *nafs* as the impulsive site of passions and desires. It is the seat of the great animal faculties of desire and rage, as well as of the spiritual organs that exercise those faculties. But, as we saw earlier, that description, in its very debasement, opens on the dialectic of the soul, its movement of purification (*al-nafs al-ammāra*, *al-nafs al-lawwāma* [the soul that reproaches itself and repents: Qurʾan 75:2], and *al-nafs al-muṭmaʾinna* [that soul purified and in peace: Qurʾan 89:27–30]).

In the Qurʾanic Neoplatonism of al-Ghazali these two dimensions, the debased lustful and the spiritual, met in the *mujāhada nafsiyya*, "the effort or struggle of the soul." Disagreeing with Ibn Sina, for whom the soul is fundamentally independent of the body and strives to be freed from it, for al-Ghazali the body is the stage of the soul. And differing from the ethical Neoplatonism of, for instance, the Ikhwan al-Safa,[15] for whom the reformation of morals required the purification of the soul from its material bodily substrata, al-Ghazali refers to the body as *markab*, the "vehicle" or "frame" in the journey of the soul towards God. For al-Ghazali, it is in the embodied space of the moral dramaturgy of the soul, a perilous path, stirred by the passions, incited by demonic suggestions (*khawāṭir*) and admonished by angelic ones, that the soul can transform. Only in the turbulence of that "effort" (*mujāhada*) can the heart learn to become accountable to its "actions" and "states," and in that process, be purified and closer to God. Similarly, the Imam sees the body as at once natural—in the sense of natural medicine and cosmology—and as the stage of a trial (*ibtilāʾ*) of affliction and evil, and of a spiritual struggle that can never be reduced to the humoral temperament of the natural soul. In the dramaturgy of the *ruqya* cure, the body is the stage of the soul, its desires and longings, its rage, resentment, and grief, as incited and coopted by the jinn and Shaytan, and as admonished by the words of the Qurʾan in the agonistic and energetic "transfer" between souls.

A description in al-Ghazali's *Marvels of the Heart* is a vivid evocation of this dramaturgy, resonant with the liturgy of the *ruqya*. I cite here the scene of the third typology of the heart, the heart of the majority of us humans:

> The third heart is that in which there appear suggestions to passion that summon to evil. But there follows there a suggestion of faith that summons it to good. The soul with its lust hastens to the aid of the evil suggestion, the lust grows stronger, and enjoyment and delight seem good. But the intellect hastens to the aid of the good suggestion, repels the idea of the lust, and makes doing it appear abominable, attributing it to ignorance and likening it to a beast or a lion in rushing blindly into evil and showing little concern for the consequences. The soul then inclines towards the advice of the intellect. The demon in turn attacks the intellect and makes the call of passion louder, saying:
>
> "What is this cold aloofness? Why do you abstain from your passion and torment yourself? Do you see any of your contemporaries going contrary to his passion, or giving up its aim?" (. . .) Thus the soul inclines to the demon and is turned to him. Then the angel attacks the demon and says,
>
> "Has anyone ever perished save he who followed the pleasure of the moment, forgetting the consequences? (. . .) Or do you think that the pain of

resisting your lust is too great a burden, but do not think the pain of the Fire grievous?" (. . .).

Thereupon the soul inclines to the saying of the angel. The heart continues to sway between the two forces, being attracted to each of the two parties, until there overcomes it that which is dominant therein. (. . .) "The heart of the believer is between two of the fingers of the Merciful."[16]

The Passions

Well aware of the double-edged resonance of the concept of *amrāḍ nafsiyya,* the Imam argues that the maladies of the soul, though not located in the body, are often manifested as physical illnesses, or lie at the origin of physical illnesses. *Amrāḍ nafsiyya* are of demonic origin, but beyond the vernacular representation of harm in terms of jinns; in a more fundamental sense they have to do with the dialectics of the *nafs*.

"Anger," he continues, "is the main cause of malady in the *nafs*; it causes spiritual/psychological illnesses (*amrāḍ nafsiyya*), and even organic illnesses. But anger is not just a passion of the natural soul: it is exposed to the intervention of Shaytan."

> *Lā taghḍab*! Do not become angry! It is anger and grief that are the first cause of illness for the soul (*al-nafs*). The Prophet became angry only when God's boundaries (*ḥudūd allāh*) were violated. ʿA'isha said of the Messenger of God: "each of us humans has his or her devil (*shayṭān*), but his devil submitted to God [entered Islam]." The Prophet, praise be to him, is the only person in the entire world whose soul was never stirred by anger; he never became angry because of a frustrated wish or a disappointment. Shaytan never conquered his *nafs*.

"In my experience," the Imam explains, "jinn are the source of most psychological/spiritual afflictions. Jinn make the *nafs* sick and cause grief and resentment to infiltrate the heart. And when grief enters the heart of a person, that person is no longer herself. An ordinary person in an ordinary family is suddenly thrown to the ground, and "someone else" (*shakhṣ ākhar*) speaks through her or his tongue. That someone else is the jinn."

I ask him to elaborate on the knot of anger in the malady of the soul, and the way it sits on a border of the visible and the invisible.

"Anger is natural," he begins, "it is in the natural constitution of human beings (*al-ghaḍab ṭabīʿa bi-l-insān*). In other words, anger can never be removed (*yaʿnī abadan izzawwāl*)."

He pauses, shifting to his mode of instruction:

> Because the human being is composed (*murakkab*) of three powers or faculties (*quwwāt*): the power of anger, the power of the intellect, and the power of desire. The power of intellect (*ʿaql*) is associated with knowledge and learning, and with polite manners; when the power of anger is stirred instead, violence erupts. Because anger is like the ocean; the ocean is part of nature and is moved by the tides. Anger, like the tides of the ocean, is influenced by the lunar month: there are low tides and high tides. After the twentieth of the lunar month the tide rises, and with it the incidents of crimes and violent events.
>
> When the drive of anger comes to dominate the body, in the heart and in the flow the circulation of blood speeds up, becomes faster and faster in the veins of the person, and that human being comes out of the traced path (*ma'lūfi*), exits the real world (*al-wāqiʿ*), and this causes crimes to happen, or rebellion, or sin; the crimes may be theft, robberies, killings, illicit sex, or gathering of wealth through falsity and usurpation.
>
> The power of desire (*al-quwwa al-shahwāniyya*) is associated with appetites and sexual attraction: when it is aroused in a person it drives that person to steal or to commit violent crimes to obtain what it covets or longs for.
>
> Only the power of the intellect (*al-quwwa al-ʿaqliyya*) eludes this violent set of relations and is capable of restraining the other two, and especially restraining the power of anger.

But it hardly succeeds of its own right, because the key question, the Imam goes on to emphasize, is not reason but faith (*īmān*).

The passion of anger and the sentiment of grief (*al-ka'āba*) are the prime cause of illness—a malady of the soul that also affects the body and can lead to madness, melancholy, or suicide. But while other classical scholars of Islamic medicine, such as al-Rāzī in his *Spiritual Medicine* (*al-Ṭibb al-rūḥānī*), understood anger solely as a bodily affect that causes an imbalance in the circulation of blood all the way to the brain, the Imam sees anger as a passion of the soul that is both in the body and not, and whose imbalance is due to departure from the ways of God and blind attachment to worldly possessions and pride, a delusion of mastery, in fact, and of autonomy of the will.[17] Excessive anger and despair in the face of adversity are ultimately related to a failure to commit one's trust in God (*yaqīn*), and to inhabit one's vulnerability as a reminder of the presence of God ("Verily in the remembrance of God do hearts find tranquility," Qur'an 13:28). For al-Ghazali, however, as well as for the Imam, anger cannot and should not be extirpated in human beings: it is both natural as one of the two passions of the soul, and morally necessary in the dramaturgy of the soul. As passion in nature it is a cosmological force: the example of the tides and the lunar month is eloquent.

"Therefore," he asks, turning to me, "how can we contain our anger or govern our passions?"

> Indeed there is an answer, and it is faith. Faith is the foundation, the ground of everything: faith (*īmān*) and conviction (*yaqīn*). If the foundation is strong we call it in our shari'a *yaqīn*, that is, trust. When something happens in the world, in your life, a misfortune, a loss, you must not become angry. Faith and trust can govern the power of anger. Our trust in God tells us: what has happened is the power of God (*qadar allāh*). And my own volition (*irāda*) is from God.

It is conviction that enables us to welcome the ordeal (*ibtilā'*). "Think of my heart operation."

We had been talking about his operation. When I arrived at his house that morning he was feeling weak and looked frail, and told me that he had not been able to recite the Qur'an at the side of the sick and perform the liturgy of the *ruqya* for several months; the *ruqya* required strength, also physical strength, and he was constrained at home, and thankful to God for his books and his computer that allowed him to keep his heart and mind alert. Almost his entire life had been paced by an illness of the heart, and when some months back he had been taken to the hospital in a mortal emergency because of a cardiac infection, he was told he needed an open-heart operation and had to commit all his savings and resources, ask his friends for financial help, and thought that he might not see his family again. Had he started thinking, "Why this calamity? Why me?" (*li-mādha muṣība*), he would have entered a state of anger and grief. But he has the ground of faith (*yaqīn*) and accepted God's will as his own will (*irādatī min allāh*).

He was lying down and seemed tired. I started to leave, but he said that our conversation put his mind at work and gave him solace. I asked him, then, whether the power of anger originated in the *nafs*.

"Its origin is in the *nafs* and in Shaytan. . . ."

"And Shaytan has a connection with the *nafs*?"

"A major connection: the *nafs* is Shaytan's sister" (*al-nafs ukht shayṭān*). He explained: "The intimate relation of evil in the human self is the *nafs*," because "the *nafs* is the inciter of evil" (*al-nafs al-ammāra bi-l-sūʿ*, Qurʾan 12:53). The *nafs* is its close kin; the one who stirs and agitates it is Shaytan.

Topology of the *Nafs*

What about the *nafs*'s education? I use the term *tarwīḍ*, training or exercise.[18] He corrects me: *tarwīḍ al-nafs lā taghḍab* ("training the soul not to give in to anger"). For the *nafs* is implicated in all the violence that happens in the world:

> I said that the *nafs* is the yeast, the fertile land that Shaytan cultivates and tills; but he doesn't cultivate grapes, figs, and pomegranates! He cultivates desires, cravings, and longings (*shawqān*) and with them blasting and bombs. From the moment of their manifestation they have an effect on the *nafs*, make an impression, and set it ablaze. The one who sparks the ignition is the jinn.[19] But from the gate of the jinn, Shaytan is unleashed. The origin, the cause, is Shaytan, who instigates and terrorizes the *nafs*; but the *nafs* is the great inciter to evil (*al-nafs al-ammāra bi-l-sūʿ*), it commands evil and calamity.

The Imam, for whom the concepts and vicissitudes of the *nafs* are part of a living tradition and a contemporary set of problems, mediates in his thinking and practice between both ways of the *nafs*, the *nafs* as enjoiner of evil and the *nafs* as spiritual substance. In this he is close to al-Ghazali, who writes that "the term *nafs* has two meanings. The one relates to that entity in man in which the power of anger and the power of desire are found. This use is the most prevalent among the Sufis. For them *nafs* means the element in man that includes all the blameworthy qualities . . . The second meaning is that of the subtle entity which is man's true reality, soul (*nafs*) and essence."[20]

On the one hand the Imam remains close to a vernacular sense of the *nafs* understood as desire in its insatiability: sexual desire,[21] the desire for power and possessions, and the passion of anger that causes hatred and violence.[22] It is an understanding that in everyday language is used side by side with the grammatical component of the *nafs* in the sense of reflexivity (*bi-nafsihā*, by herself), the juridical concept of the *nafs* as the individual, the self, or the person, and with the modern psychological sense of the *nafs* as the self and the psyche.

On the other hand the Imam also describes the *nafs* with its connection to the heart as the seat of the faculty of imagination (*taṣawwur, takhayyul*). He understands imagination as the impression and reproduction of forms or images (*ṣuwar*). These forms, just as the soul is form in relation to the materiality of the body as "vehicle" (*markab*), have the character of traces. The forms have an effect on the heart, the sense of being, the capacity for "presence," and for ethical existence on the way of God; their impairment is what the Imam describes as a "choking" (*taḍyīq*) and destruction. The two dimensions of the Imam's analysis are related, and together define the possibility of ethics, politics, and healing.

The *nafs* as desiring soul and personal self is related to the *rūḥ*, spirit and metaphysical soul; to the *ʿaql*, intelligence, seat of thinking and reasoning; to the *waʿī*, consciousness, awareness, and responsibility; and most crucially, to the *qalb*, heart. The heart for the Imam (as also for al-Ghazali and in Sufism) is both the bodily organ that oversees the circulation of blood, and the spiritual and gravitational center of the soul complex. For the heart is the material-immaterial nesting of "being" and the site of connectedness with God. It is the locus of an exchange between the material realities of the mundane world, the body and its attachments, and the truer reality of the invisible world. The ethical dispositions or "qualities" that are usually described as "virtues" are located in the heart, as are the vices that can eventually cause the illness of being, in both the religious and the medical sense. For, as al-Ghazali puts it, "character is a term for the condition and inner aspect of the soul."

Being is located in the heart, which grounds the conviction of faith, as well as the capacity to witness the divine. It is in the disposition of the heart as well that the capacity to be with others in a community resides; and it is in the heart that being loses ground, when the anchoring in the conviction of faith falters and the self/soul drifts into error and delusion, subjugation and unfreedom.

First the question of desire.

The *nafs* is the yeast and the fertile land, the yeast that makes bread rise and grow, and the land that produces the grains. But the work of tilling is one of hollowing, and instead of producing the goods (and good) of life, grapes, figs, and pomegranates, the plants of bliss mentioned in the Qur'an, it produces the ingredients of death: blasting and bombs. The farmer is Shaytan, the angel who refused to submit, but the seeds are already in the *nafs*, desires, cravings, and longings. They are inherent to the passionate nature of the soul, the very drives that register the vitality of being. The life drive of the desiring soul engenders a drive to death. On one side life is natural process of growth, on the other life is another growth that hollows being and causes destruction and death: a growth that in the discourse of the Imam is modeled on the hollowing and murderous work of magic (*siḥr*) and its theological association with the untruth of Shaytan.

At the end of his vivid description of the destructive war-zone economy of the soul, the Imam cites an often-quoted passage in the Qur'an, "the *nafs* is the inciter to evil" (Qur'an 12:53). It is a passage commented upon by al-Ghazali in his discussion of the *nafs* and the spiritual techniques for disciplining, transforming, and training the soul. The hollowing work of Shaytan is at once internal and external to the *nafs*, as the dangerous challenge of an intimate exteriority. That very intimacy is the agonistic theater of struggle. In the words of al-Ghazali:

> Most hearts have been conquered and occupied by troops of demons, and so are filled with incitements to evil, which call for the preference of the swiftly passing world and the casting aside of the world to come, following appetites and desires. After this has taken place the heart cannot be reconquered except by emptying it of the demon's nourishment, which is desire and the appetites, and rebuilding it by means of remembrance of God, which is the place of angelic influence.[23]

And for the Imam, more so than for al-Ghazali, the struggle of the *nafs* is literal and concrete, for it happens in the space of the cure in the confrontation with a "neighbor" of most proximate and violent nature: a desire made present in what the Imam calls the being and coming to presence of the jinn (*wujūd al-jinn*). This fact in itself would not be of such philosophical interest were it not for the ambiguous topological position of the jinn, at once inside and outside, at once the self and its enemy, at once the passion of the soul/self, its longing (*shawq*), and the jinn, at once an urge to life and a drive to death, an ambiguity that closely resembles the topological position of the drive in Freudian and Lacanian theory—and ultimately, of desire itself.

It is here that the plasticity and multidimensional spatiality of the Imam's understanding of the *nafs* is crucial. Unlike the "unlawful" cures (*ʿilāj ghayr sharʿī*), he says, which locate harm outside, with an external and cosmic evil that strikes the person and is magically acted upon by the healer (or by the sorcerer that "caused" the harm), the Imam locates the jinn/desire in the fold of the *nafs*. Yet this is not in the sense of interiority. The jinn and the related work of *tahdhīb* and *tabdīl al-nafs* (the dressing and transformation of the soul) are not treated in the Imam's approach as symptoms of a psychological unconscious, but as an intimate exteriority that is addressed by the heteronomy of a divine command.[24] This is not the case in contemporary approaches of Islamic psychology (*ʿilm al-nafs al-islāmī*) that seek to translate the psychological study of the person into an Islamic perspective,[25] or even in the attempt of a Sufi scholar such as the modern Egyptian rector of the University of Cairo Abu-l-Wafa' al-Taftazani, in his important efforts to think the modern scientific discipline of *ʿilm al-nafs* (psychology) and Freudian psychoanalysis in its articulation and conversation with the ontology and ethical practices of self-transformation and unveiling in Sufism.[26] For the result of such an attempt ends up doing away with the intimate alterity and heteronomy of the subject that are instead central to the thinking and practice of Freudian and Lacanian psychoanalysis.

The Imam's point in citing that Qurʾanic passage, and indirectly al-Ghazali, is that the *nafs* (including human character, desire, and the drive to life/death) is not given once and for all but exists in the mode of an incompleteness that is capable of being transformed. And it is in this sense that the *nafs* is an ambiguous dual entity that is at once an earthly vital principle marked by a propensity to evil that binds life to a risk of destruction, and the subtle substance of the soul, the site of the imagination and realm of forms, which are as such the lieu of ethical activity and can be the site of an encounter with the divine.[27]

For unlike other aspects of the cosmos that are created as complete—that is, inert and immutable—the human soul is given in the mode of a capacity, a potentiality that is not fully formed. The soul is not like a rock or a mountain, whose nature is inert, but like a seed that contains the capacity to engender a tree if given the right conditions, but also the capacity to be wasted: "those things which exist in incomplete form but which are possessed of the ability to get perfected when the condition for this, which may be related to the volition of man, is met. For a seed is not an apple-tree or a date-palm. It has merely been created in such a way as to permit it to become one when it is properly nurtured . . . Therefore, just as a seed is affected by human choice, so it is susceptible of acquiring some qualities and not others, so also anger and desire, which we cannot suppress and dominate entirely so as to destroy any trace of them, can be rendered, should we so wish, obedient and docile by means of self-discipline and struggle."[28]

Al-Ghazali discusses examples of human character more or less disposed to the labor of "struggle" and self-transformation, and ponders the cases of selves given to evildoing by a vagary of fate or by a mischievous propensity for mundane pleasures (and hence afflicted by spiritual illness, whether or not aware of their state). The work of "reshaping" can awaken the capacity for ethical existence and for another enjoyment in the experience of God. The technique of healing the soul in these cases, and in training the soul in general, is to sever the self from its desires and from what gives it pleasure, "the bitter medicine of opposing his desires," a weaning that at first is traumatic and painful, and that al-Ghazali compares to the "extraction of the spirit (*rūḥ*) during the agonies of death."[29] This is also the strategy the Imam pursues with the afflicted, in relation not to themselves, but to that part of their soul that is occupied by the desire of the jinn; the demon that inhabits and is the desire of the self.

The Neighbor

I ask the Imam about the distinction between Shaytan and the jinn. He says:

> Shaytan is the Jinn, and the jinn and the human are mirror images of each other. Yes, [emphatically] they are alike, human beings may rebel, or they may obey, similarly the jinn, may rebel or may obey, obey God the most powerful, but when the jinn gets involved in crimes and harmful actions, it transforms into Shaytan, Shaytan takes over (*inqalaba shayṭān*, as in a violent coup, *inqilāb*). The same for humans: because they are human, but when they begin to act on the way of harm (*shayṭāna*), acting upon temptation, pursuing criminal actions, fostering rumor and falsity among people (*namīma bayn al-nās*), and becoming a cause of crimes, Shaytan takes over. Hence, the origin of Shaytan is the jinn, but more precisely it is his vehicle or means, his connection and intimate friend, because it provokes many crimes, it is his link to [destroy] virtuous activity.

Like humans, jinn are part of God's creation, and are endowed with the capacity to discern and choose. Like humans, they are not inherently bad, but have a capacity for destruction. They resemble humans, the human soul, on the mode of *mathal*—simulacra or more precisely "real images." They can give in to desires that will lead them to the path of evil and rebellion against God, or they can strive to be righteous. Behind the harmful work of the jinn, just as behind the harmful deeds of human beings, there is Shaytan, which manifests itself in their place and "takes over." Shaytan is not independent of God, but is itself internal to God's creation and volition. Evil, in this configuration, and in the understanding of the Imam, is a not a negative force, but an ongoing ontological challenge. It is not an external demon that strikes the person, but an internal enemy, a capacity for evil that is at once internal and external to the *nafs*/soul.

Unlike animals and plants (the Imam says animals are nonetheless subject to *ibtilā*ʾ, the test of affliction and danger), humans have the responsibility of discernment and choice, their souls are the site of a struggle, and can choose to follow God or Shaytan: the neverending risk of evil, and its being nested in the human soul, in the cravings and desires of the *nafs*, marks the space of their specific freedom. It is in this sense that the Qurʾan repeatedly says that Shaytan has power only over those who choose to follow his way: "I had no authority over you, except that I called you and you obeyed me, therefore do not blame me but blame yourselves" (Qurʾan 14:22).[30]

Significantly in a scene of the Sira, the account of the life of the Prophet, Shaytan is presented as debating God's reasons for having created him in full awareness that he would incite humans to harm and destruction. The story is also told, in another passage, of the child Muhammad being visited by two angels, who slit his bosom and his heart, wash his internal organs, open the heart, and extract from it a black pebble. The black pebble in the human heart signals the unending risk of destruction. (In the Moroccan popular imagination this is reckoned as a "black dot" (*nuqṭa khela, suda*), which is seen at the source of both destruction and madness. As we saw earlier, the Imam relates the "black dot" to the melancholy humor.)

According to Ali Shariati's rereading of the dialectic of man and Shaytan, the human is a two-dimensional creature, composed of God (spirit) and clay, and needs both elements to be constituted. Shaytan is not opposed to God as evil is opposed to good; it is included in God's volition, and opposed to the spiritual/divine part of human beings. The element of destruction is ever-present, and is necessary for the human life-form, and for the possibility of freedom: "Within man, Satan wages war against God, and man is their battlefield . . . This constant striving and struggle takes place in man's hidden being, until finally he chooses one of the poles as the determinant for his destiny."[31]

What is important to grasp in this duality, and in the notion of struggle itself, is that the Imam is speaking of a positive challenge, the challenge of a radical heterogeneity that sets the rhythm and pulsation of a form of life engaged with the risk of destruction. Evil in this sense is a revealing element, which at once dis-figures the status quo, providing an always-precarious angle of visibility, and sets a flow of subjectivity in movement, in the punctuation of an ethical life.

It is in this sense that the cure, and the illness itself, can reclaim a space of life in the surroundings of destruction. There, on that border of the inside and the outside, folding the soul with its intimate enemy, is found *jihād al-nafs* ("spiritual effort/exercise"), the central figure of the agonistics of the soul,[32] but also *jihād* in the sense of war.[33] To understand the struggle of *jihād al-nafs* solely in the sense of the refinement or perfectibility of the soul reduces the stakes of what for the Imam is an actual struggle, fraught with danger and the never-resolved risk of a loss without return. Ethical being is precisely that intimate struggle, with a heterogeneity that can never be resolved, and with a violence that is forever lurking. I therefore read the Imam's understanding of *jihād al-nafs* with Lacan's moving "beyond" of the Aristotelian ethics of the good, and towards an ethics of the vulnerable struggle, a kind of wrestling, with an intimate exteriority: an *extimité*.[34]

Inhabiting such a struggle-at-the-limit in his practice with patients, and in a daily confrontation with what he describes as the risk of the two related limits of *kufr* and *ḥumq*, unbelief and madness, the Imam dwells in a space where he can stretch the boundaries of the diagnosis, both theological and medical, and listen for the vibrations of being. For as long as he can register the presence (*wujūd*) and "activity" of a jinn in its "symptoms" (*a'rāḍ*), there is a space of life that can be reclaimed in the midst and at the limit of destruction. On one hand he offered an understanding of madness as an ultimate inert state, fundamentally irreversible and impossible to treat—because it is the last vestige of the destructive work of the jinn who has in the end damaged the brain. On the other he was able to address innumerable intermediate conditions in which the jinn could be heard, in which, as he put it, *"keykhallef al-jinn,"* the jinn could be felt moving, "working," in a process of destruction that the Imam could still seize as a form of life.

For the Imam, it is only when the struggle subsides, when the *nafs* and the heart become inert and are turned into stone, that the ethical being ceases to exist, and all "activity" stops. This is what happens in acute melancholy (*al-ka'āba*),[35] the condition the Imam calls *taḍyīq al-nafs*, "soul choking."

In a different context, pondering what to do, how to think, with and after the butchery of World War I, Freud resorted to the notion of the primary nature of a destructive drive and its radical heterogeneity. His thought on the ineluctability of ambivalence and on the intimate enemy which is the *Todestrieb*, can be read as an engagement with these questions. In his 1915 essay on war and death, Freud had identified a hetero-aggressive propensity of the drives in a murderous displacement of self-destruction, and in the failure to think (subjectivize) "my" death as a radical exteriority. But in *Beyond the Pleasure Principle* (1920) and *Civilization and Its Discontents* (1930), he elaborated this problem somewhat departing from the problematic of paranoia, moving toward an explication of the radical ambivalence of life and death that manifests itself in the form of a struggle—a "battle of giants." The "battle" took place beyond the economic rule of the pleasure principle, in an intermediate zone between the possibility of regeneration and the elasticity of the drive, in its fatal draw to inertia and death. In this sense, ambivalence, and the struggle itself, can be seen as the circuitous paths of life against itself, in the radical heterogeneity of a risk and a certainty, which Freud saw as a return to the inorganic state, beyond the subject and beyond life—an exteriority that is always lurking and comes to be exposed in trauma. For Freud, as in a different sense for the Imam, the space of the struggle in the vision of death defines at once the possibility and the risk of subjectivity. The *Todestrieb* is an existential, political, and ontological lesion at the heart of life,[36] which takes on the connotation of the theological concept of evil.

This resonates, for me, yet beyond the possibility of direct translation, with Lacan's treatment of evil and the death drive in Seminar VII, where ethics is the precarious movement of a being-at-risk, a *sujét risqué*, suspended in a zone between two deaths and two modalities of destruction, between the lead of the drive towards the termination of desire, and the submission to the law as a "service of goods"—between Antigone's assumed martyrdom and Creon's demise by "mistake," in his respect and enforcement of the law of the state.[37]

SIXTEEN

The Writing of the Soul: Soul Choking, Imagination, and Pain

> We should perhaps conceive of pain as a field, which, in the realm of existence, opens precisely onto that limit where it is impossible for a being to move, to escape.
>
> —Lacan[1]

> And whomsoever God will guide, his chest He opens wide with willingness towards self-surrender [unto Him]; and whomsoever He wills to let go astray, his chest He causes to be tight and constricted, as if he were climbing unto the skies.
>
> —Qur'an 6:125

The Imam goes on to reflect on why people today are incapable of feeling the ground of faith. What's happening today, in Morocco and other parts of the world, the Muslim world alike, he says, is similar to what happens to "people in the West": "They want to be the way they themselves want, but life, our life span, is decided by God. They end up clashing with the real (*al-wāqiʿ*—in other words, they dwell in illusion, which engenders delusion). They are hit by reality; and in the end become sick. They are overwhelmed by grief or despair."

The Imam's psychosomatic and spiritual-physiological approach stresses simultaneously the desiring soul's risk of straying (*ḍalāl*: from the path of God, and from ethical existence) in the context of contemporary life, the reality of exclusion (*ḥirmān*), dispossession, and grief, the temptation of evil (*shayṭān*) as a struggle internal to the *nafs*, and the affective impact of the imagination, of "images," on the heart (*qalb*).

So, we repeat, because repetition is good:

The origin, the cause of the problem is Shaytan, Shaytan instigates the *nafs*. The *nafs*, as God said, is the great inciter to evil, that is, it generates and reproduces evil and ills. Shaytan speaks to the *nafs*, orders it around, the *nafs* reproduces injustice and corruption (*fujūr*), and those images we mentioned earlier, the imagination of evil (harmful, foul images, *ṣuwar sayyi'a*), harmful and inflammatory, are transmitted to the heart. The heart is in charge of the circulation of blood (*dawra damawiyya*), and the effects produced by those images, impact the drive of anger (*quwwa ghaḍabiyya*), and it takes over the body. When the drive of anger comes to dominate the body (*musaṭīra fi al-jism*), in the heart and in the flow the circulation of blood speeds up, becomes faster and faster, in the veins and the arteries of the person, and that human being strays from normal, customary life (*yakhruj al-insān ʿan maʾlūf*), comes out of the traced path, exits the real world (*al-wāqiʿ*), and this causes crimes to happen, or rebellion, or sin; the crimes may be theft, robberies, killings, illicit sex, or gathering of wealth through falsity and usurpation.

Faith (*īmān*) is the basis, when associated with conviction (*yaqīn*). Yet there can be faith, trust in God, only if there is activity, in the sense of humanly shared ethical action (*ʿamal*), which is sorely lacking in a community reft by social exclusion, injustice, and by a form of death-in-life. Or, in a related sense, faith and the authenticity of ethical action are inaccessible in a community where the intimate proximity of Islamic ideals has been lost, where there is no justice and the power of commodities and the lure of consumption make vanish the call for the values of reciprocal help and support, the sense of justice, and the remembrance of death in daily life as the foundation of ethical action. In such a world, says the Imam, the heart that receives the affects and visions of the *nafs*, in its worldly desires, as well as in its incurable sadness and grief, is all too often no longer the heart of a Muslim.[2] And the *nafs* becomes prey to the whispering and the terror of Shaytan, and sends its harmful imaginings to the heart—visions of destruction and visions of irretrievable loss.

"What is the cause of suicide (*intihār*)? It is from the choking of the *nafs* (*taḍyīq al-nafs*). And what is the cause of choking? It is Shaytan. Shaytan whispers in the ears of the person, 'You will die, death is your only perspective,' and the human being chokes."

Taḍyīq al-nafs, the oppression or choking of the soul, is the result of an unbearable pain that paralyzes and sculpts in the soul and in the heart, as if in stone, images of destruction that shut the door to all possibility of imagining a horizon, erecting the high walls of a claustrophobic space.

> The *nafs* sends to the heart negative and hopeless images of the future, and the heart forms an image of life as life-burned (*ḥayāt muḍrama*), life-destroyed, and starts imagining that nothing good can happen in the future, only oppression and disaster are foretold, that all that there is is pain and torture (*ʿadhāb*), poverty and exclusion, dispossession and destitution (*ḥirmān*). Only that will be. And so that person (*insān*) lives a burning moment, God protect us from harm [from rising Shaytan].
>
> . . . And these images that the *nafs* receives in the form of a devilish whisper (*waswās*) colonize and murder the heart, which in truth is not the heart of a Muslim. For if faith is present in the heart, the person thinks/remembers those images only if they are affirmative images (*ṣuwar ijābiyya*); if the heart is deserted by faith, the person accepts those images, welcomes them, and they set it ablaze. And choking, the oppression of the soul (*taḍyīq*), instills terror in that person. And he can no longer aspire to something that might bring renewal, something affirmative, other than his own dying, and thinks incessantly of the way in which to bring about the limit of death. This is suicide.

The maddening insinuations of Shaytan to the *nafs* make the self de-realize, lose the sense of ground and connectedness to other beings, entering delusion or sinking into a cadaveric loneliness that, while still among the living, carries the presentiment of death. The "whisper" seizes control of the *nafs* and murders the heart, in the double sense of causing it to lose trust in God in the experience of despair, and becoming mad ("the whisper" is a Qur'anic figure of madness). The hallucination and multiplication of loss in the feeling of melancholy is for the Imam the theological risk of despair, at the threshold of both *kufr* and madness, when life takes the form (the Imam says the "image") of a fatal concatenation of spectral losses sinking into each other and engendering radical doubt, an epistemological quicksand, where the impossibility of trusting the other intersects with a palimpsest of betrayals. Eventually this leads to the annihilation of the soul, in this world and the other. Soul choking describes a world of living dead, where the proximity with death is such that there is no longer a relation, "death" can no longer be "imagined."

In this configuration the imagination itself becomes an agent of destruction, in a soul-snatching that doubles the "torture" (*ʿadhāb*) of the real where dispossession, destitution, injustice, and exclusion are all that the subject has known since a young age. It is a real where engagement can only be "falsified," and where televised images of destruction and the routine instrumentalization of suffering, pain as spectacle, snatch even the possibility of recognizing an authentic expression of pain, rendering the demonic circulation of images the forced and only theater where the *nafs* dwells; indeed a theater of "falsity." In the logic of the Imam's description, the imagination turns into an agent of destruction because it is itself captured, snatched, by an invasion of media images, images of a desire haunted by commodification, by the sense of failure and impossibility, because its capacity for ethical work is disabled; and because, in the larger sense of the *nafs*'s worldly desire, the access to the enjoyment of the global and idealized futures can be experienced only as a maddening lack, in the hallucinatory apparition of a fetish and its alienating effects on the soul.

The soul/self registers those realities, bears witness to them in its pain, in the "impression" they make on the heart, but that registering does not lead to forms of engagement, to ethical and political action (*ʿamal*). Pain is internalized as a wound, incorporated as despair, and the imagination reinforces the subjugation of the subject, which manifests itself as a death drive.[3] "The *nafs* sends to the heart negative and hopeless images of the future, and the heart forms an image of life as life-burned, life-destroyed." There is no protective shield, no countermovement, no possibility of renewal. The Imam is speaking of an infraction, an invasion: the choking "instills terror in the person," holds the person in place, defining a zone where, in Lacan's phrase, being can no longer move, cannot escape, cannot avoid the paralyzing impact.

Soul choking is the Imam's depiction of such acute melancholy, a melancholy described by some of the youths with whom I discussed this question[4] in terms of another figure of despair: *al-qanaṭ*, melancholy-boredom, loss of all hope, which empties the self, and "sends it off" into nothingness.

It is the vanishing of desire and the surrender of struggle. For struggle (*jihād al-nafs*), in this vision of life and the soul, attests to the presence and activity of an ethical subject.

Through an extension of the bodily senses, what might be called, following al-Ghazali, an "analogical" sensorium, the imagination can enable a vicarious experience of aspects and dimensions of the world, visible and invisible, that lie beyond the immediate reach of the embodied soul/*nafs*. The role of the imaginative faculty in apprehending the experience of death (approximating its "tasting") and in the pursuit of witnessing the divine in dreams and other modalities of unveiling is pivotal for the possibility of an ethical life. Yet the same imaginative faculty can also accelerate the demise of the soul/self, on a slope to delusion and annihilation, and away from the truth of revelation. Deprived of its grounding in faith, guarantee of reality and truth, the imagination spins out of bounds, and hallucinates (rather than apprehends or "tastes") the reality of loss and death. (It is perhaps for this reason that in oral poetry the imagination is referred to as "*shayṭānī*," my Shaytan, in its capacity to hallucinate presence in burning loss.)

Somewhat differently than in the classical or Gnostic theosophy of the intermediate imaginal world (*ʿālam al-mithāl*), the Imam approaches the imagination with the pragmatic understanding of a healer and a spiritual guide, listening to the singularity of pain—its unbearability—without normalizing its violence, and its risk, and attempting to provide an anchor, and some spiritual tools, for those locked in the grip of despair. His reformist vision, in a novel inscription that repoliticizes the question of despair, is less interested in the Gnostic or ecstatic aspects of the pursuit of witnessing through imagination and unveiling. Instead, the Imam is concretely concerned with addressing the pain of his community.

It is in this sense that the Imam stresses the concept of an affirmative imagination, "affirmative images" (*ṣuwar ījābiyya*), "fortifying resemblances" (*shabha muqawwī*), which he opposes in his work with the youth to the destructive impact of the images of oppression and choking (*ḍīq*), images of despair (*yaʾs*), and to the picture of a world in which there can be no activity but only pain (*alam*): "The Messenger of God opposed despair, opposed grief. Islam opposed gloom (*ʿubūsiyya*), struggles against sadness. Today many Muslims turn their faces in a petrified sadness, are pervaded by gloom."

Beyond this struggle of images (where the spiritual guide fights on behalf of the melancholic soul with the spear of affirmative images), is the concern with enabling once again *ʿamal*—activity, work, movement, which, the Imam says, is the condition of possibility of faith: "it is impossible to have faith without work" (*īmān bi-dūn ʿamal lā yumkin*). Work is the opposite of *biṭāla*, inactivity, idleness, and in the concrete sense "joblessness"; *biṭāla* conveys lack of all value, and the fact of being inert. In his pragmatic reference to the "affirmative" force of the imagination and its relation with *al-ʿamal*, activity in the world, the Imam echoes the ethical responsibility of the person to hold an "affirmative orientation" to life as part of the "obligation to bear practical witness to Islam."[5]

Yet fulfilling that obligation under conditions of hardship, such as those that characterize life in his neighborhood, as in many similar locations in Morocco and the Muslim world, is not granted. This raises the question of the limits of ethical action in a society where the conditions for material subsistence and for a life of the soul are not met. In the midst of our discussion on imagination and the passions, the Imam cites a much-debated hadith: "*Kāda al-faqr an yakūn kufr,*" poverty leads to *kufr*, it is close to being *kufr*. "Because poverty," he adds, "causes exhaustion and hardship, disaster and ruin." In the words of Farid Esack, "You cannot truly submit to God if you are under the yoke of hunger. Such submission is a form of coercion." The subjugation and annihilation of being is an ethical, but also a political question.[6]

For the Imam the two questions are related. Prior to the possibility of reinstating ethical action and bearing practical witness to faith, it is necessary to guide the *nafs* to reposition its relation to the experience of pain, and to the infraction that caused the soul to choke. It is a question of transforming pain and shifting the coordinates of the real: from a harbinger of destruction to an exercise for thinking/remembering, an exercise where the bodily imagination plays a pivotal role.

Discussing the nature of death and the ethical importance of its frequent remembrance in everyday life, as a practice of "vision" to lure the *nafs* away from heedlessness and loosen its attachment to the greed of this world, al-Ghazali stresses that knowledge of death from the point of view of the living can only be indirect. While the task of the remembrance of death is to "touch and break the heart," to make an "impression" upon and unsettle a person's contentment in the world, this can be achieved only in the form of a meditation on pain, by the intermediary of the faculty of the imagination, because pain is always, necessarily, singular, because it breaks me, and I cannot objectify it (in the words of Jean-Bertrand Pontalis, "I *have* anguish, but I *am* pain").[7] For al-Ghazali pain is a breakage, an intrusion, an infraction, and as such shares a concrete, literal affinity with death. For this reason, if we are to remember death, we must become capable of inhabiting and tasting our pain.

Al-Ghazali invites his readers to meditate upon the death of their loved ones because of the emotional bond that the pain of their passing impressed in my soul: through feeling the pain of their loss, I can come to approximate the feeling of "my" death. And yet "my" soul and "my" death are not mine, for pain is an imaginal bond; it touches me, cannot be displaced, but enables what al-Ghazali calls "an analogical relation" (*qiyās*). It bears witness to something else, opening a connection, establishing a tie. In this paradoxical sense, and by the intermediary of the imagination, pain is relational: it "bears witness" (*shāhid*), in the modality of a gift. I feel/know (my)self by feeling/knowing the pain of the other through "my" pain.

Al-Ghazali invites his readers to meditate on how the departed had "made widows of their wives and orphans of their children," how he used to go hither and thither, and now his joints have rotted away; how he used to speak, and now the worms have devoured his tongue; how he used to laugh, while now the dust has consumed his teeth. This is done through a skilled use of vivid visual images: the visualization of (my) body rotting, of the living disclosing the temporality of the grave. The task is pedagogical, but the method traumatic. For al-Ghazali it is clear that imagining death means to become capable of undergoing its trauma, "for it is separation itself which causes pain."

Later in that text al-Ghazali explicates the relationship of pain and death, in the context of "tasting" (*dhawq*). Pain affects the spiritual soul (*al-rūḥ*) just as death does. Hence pain and death share a quality in the way the spirit is affected by the violent infraction, and are related analogically. He invites people to meditate on the way pain, through its concrete impact on the *rūḥ*, connects with the soul's experience of death.

> Know, too, that the extreme pain of death pangs is known in its fullness only to those who have tasted it. The man who has not tasted it may only come to know it (*yaʿrifuhā*) by analogy (*qiyās*—via the imagination) with the pains which he actually experienced, or by analogy with the pains that can be envisaged through reasoning (*istidlāl*—via the imagination), by analogy with the violent states (*shiddāt*) of other people during their death agonies. Concerning the analogy that bears witness for him (*yashhadu lahu*), and allows him to see, this is as follows: no limb from which the spirit (*rūḥ*) is absent can feel pain. When, however, the spirit is present, then the agency that perceives pain is the spirit. Whenever the limbs suffer an injury or burn the effect makes its way to the spirit, which will feel pain (*alam*) in proportion to the amount that reaches it. The sensation disperses through the blood, the flesh, and the remaining extremities, so that only a certain part of it reaches the spirit itself.[8]

Al-Ghazali gives the example of the pain felt by a person pricked by a thorn. This pain, he says, if we meditate on it, can move us to begin to "taste" another pain, not directly accessible to us, the pain of death pangs. If I inhabit my pain, the pain of the thorn, of the limb, or of the loss of a friend, if I don't flee from it, I can—the soul can—reach through the imagination a partial experience of the tasting of death. This can be only approximate, for it happens from within the space of the living. When death comes, by contrast, the *rūḥ* is assailed directly and entirely, the infraction is total: "The pain felt during the throes of death assails the spirit directly, and engulfs every one of its fractions. The dying man feels himself pulled and jerked from every artery, nerve, part and joint, from the root of every hair and the bottom layer of his skin from head to foot."

For al-Ghazali as well as, in a more pragmatic sense, for the Imam, who is concerned with addressing the theological-medical affliction of soul choking (*taḍyīq al-nafs*), the point is that inhabiting pain in this second sense, bearing witness to pain without succumbing to it, can engender an opening of the soul. Pain, in this sense, crosses a limit, beyond the paralysis of being, the impossibility of movement; it transforms. Such an opening to death as a way of "seeing" and "tasting" is a different modality of melancholy from the closing up of the horizon, the generalization of the death drive in the affliction of soul choking. Inhabiting pain in the bodily imagination, connecting to others in that space, is both unbearable and expansive. And yet the two modalities are contiguous, like the topological reversal in the inside-out structure of a glove.[9]

The unbearable remains. It can never be overcome. And the bereavement of acute melancholy is always at the risk of choking the soul, and make being inert. We should not forget the risk: the Imam never does; the two related risks, in his reading and in his clinical practice, of heresy (*kufr*) and madness (*ḥumq*). The question should resonate for us: What does it mean to not forget that risk?

SEVENTEEN

Concluding Movement: The Passion of Zulikha, a Dramaturgy of the Soul

> And indeed she desired him, and he desired her (*hammatu bihi wa hamma bihā*); [and he would have succumbed] had he not seen [in this temptation] an evidence of his Sustainer's truth. Thus [We willed it to be] in order that we might avert from him all evil (*al-sūʾ*) and all shameful deeds (*al-faḥshāʾ*). For he was one of our servants, sincere and purified.
>
> —Qurʾan 12:24

> In their stories there is a lesson (*ʿibra*) for those who are endowed with insight.
>
> —Qurʾan 12:111

Z. has taken leave from herself. She lays now on the floor in another consciousness, her body the host of an invisible presence. She fell quickly when the Imam asked her to repeat the invocation, *bi-smi llāh al-ḥamdu li-llāh* ("in the name of God and in gratitude to God"). He had instructed her to utter her words aloud, in a firm and calm voice, as he pressed a ballpoint pen on her chest, a simple Bic pen that he always keeps in his pocket. It is an opening gesture of the *ruqya*. The pen is an indirect form of touching. It is also a literal remainder of the sacred writing of the Qurʾan, a word that touches and discerns.[1] For, as we saw described by Ibn Qayyim al-Jawziyya, the *ruqya* is a transfer between souls with the permission of God.[2]

In repeating the invocation her voice must betray no fear (*Ghwwt! b-ṣawt murtaḥ*, "Shout!" he told her, "in a calm and reassured voice"). It is the invocation to God that forces the jinn to manifest itself. As she kept repeating the words she started gasping, struggling for air, her vital space progressively occupied by the jinn. He inquired gently, "What do you feel?"

and then, "Don't you have a feeling of oppression or tightness (*makatziy-yersh*)?" She indicated that she did. "Where?" She pointed to her chest, by her left breast, and he pushed there with his pen as he recited the Qur'an. He asked me to put a pillow under her head and went on chanting in silence. Her voice started changing, splitting into two voices, one voice making its way, cutting through, occupying, and the other voice striving not to be choked. It was a battle of voices, and the emergence of a counterpoint. As the one voice struggled to continue uttering "In the name of God," the other rose, gaining presence and force in the form of a moaning, interrupting and displacing the first, while a third voice, the voice of the revealed Qur'an, provided the frame and the force, disclosing a temporality of the hereafter and enabling and regulating the proliferation of voices and the very possibility of that counterpoint.

The first voice lost breath and surrendered. The Imam instructed Z., now a dimming consciousness, to spit out "that thing" (*dak shiy'*). She coughed several times, physically signaling the emergence of the thing. It was not an expulsion, but a coming to presence. Z. was now gone. And the Imam could address the invisible presence directly: "*A'ūdhu bi-llāhi min* . . . I am invoking God against you. *La'nuka bi-la'nati llāhi wa tāmma,* I curse you by God's damnation." *Ma-smuk*? "What is your name?"

She seemed lifeless for a time. Motionless, her eyes closed, she was drawn into a distance beyond reach. This phase of the cure is traditionally described by the term *ṣar'*: eclipse, falling, disappearance, lapsing into nothingness. *Ṣar'* is the "eclipse" of the subject. And this is why *ṣar'* also means epilepsy in today's medical usage, as also in classical Arab medicine. The two conditions, the neurological and the spiritual, sit on a blurred and uneasy border.

> *Katṣra'i*: that is, you make the patient fall, and he or she is gone, muted, unconscious, and rigid like a piece of wood; like a corpse. The *ṣar'* resembles death. But when you examine the body you see that the heart is beating. You hear a rattling like a person who is dying—a person in the pangs of death. It is the sign that they are there, still inside the person.[3]

The annihilation of the jinn is the other meaning of the term *ṣar'*, and marks the return of the subject to presence. But in the grammar of the ritual the two dimensions of the *ṣar'*—the eclipse of the subject and the vanquishing of the jinn—are not simply opposed. The cipher of their relation is the metamorphosis and the struggle of the soul, at once singular and plural, active and passive, perpetrator and victim.

In the classical dictionary *Lisān al-ʿarab*, the constellation of words related to the root *ṣaraʿa* is shown to have an intimate relationship with the torpor of sleep, and with the inertia of death, the return to an inanimate state, prior to life, in the material physical sense. "The sleeper is almost like a dead man—for sleep is the brother of death" (Ibn Qayyim). As stated in the Qurʾan, sleep is a temporary death, which delivers the soul to a beyond of worldly life, to a region of the limit, an Outside: "God takes the souls at death, and those who die not, [He takes] during their sleep; He keeps those on whom he has passed the decree of death, and the others he sends back [to their bodies] for the term appointed" (Qurʾan 39:42). Death, as cultivated in the practices of "remembrance" (*dhikr*), is both a break—a radical detachment of the soul—and the event of awakening. "The Prophet said, 'People are asleep, and when they die they awake.'"[4] This theological homology of sleep and death is also the reason why the rite of the *ṣar*ʿ is related to the experience of dreaming, inasmuch as dreaming has an intimate relationship with death.

Ibn ʿArabi distinguishes between two kinds of sleep: one that is bodily rest, and another that he calls "transferal" (*intiqālī*). Transferal sleep is the sleep in which there are dreams. Dreams, he says, are a deathlike experience of the limit given to all humans irrespective of background, spiritual training, and abilities. Through the experience of dreaming, transferal sleep exposes each of us to a presentiment of the Invisible (*al-ghayb*), the divine Real that remains inaccessible to human perception and that can only be grasped as imagination. In transferal sleep "the instruments of the soul are transferred from the manifest side of sense perception to the non-manifest side (*bāṭin*) in order to see what has become established in the treasury of imagination (*khizānat al-khayāl*); . . . I call this state a 'transferal' because meanings are transferred from their disengagement (*tajrīd*) from substrata into a state of being clothed in substrata, like the manifestation of the Real in the form of corporeal bodies, or of knowledge in the form of milk, or similar things."[5]

The radical and deathlike detachment of the subject from the spatial and temporal coordinates of life has some of the qualities of transferal sleep, though truthful dream visions cannot be compared to experiences of the Invisible in demonic possession. Possession, at least from the point of view of the Qurʾanic healer, and of the Qurʾan itself, is associated with ontological untruth. It cannot be confused with an experience of the divine. The Imam makes this clear in our conversations: the reality of the jinn, as a form of life on its own account, or as the "extimate" alterity of desire in the human soul, comes with a fundamental risk of unreality: the hollowing of life into a play of simulacra. This is even more the case, as the Imam never ceases to repeat, in the historical conditions of our time, and its violent and alienating psychopolitical regimes of speculation, destitution, and desire. Sometimes the border of possession and piety is perplexing, and the spiritual task of discernment is taken on by the Imam, in recognition of the limits of human knowledge, and of the fact that only God knows "the real nature of things."[6] As for the patient, she is not in a position to know, at least not as herself. Her "disappearance" opens onto another life, one that is not hers but the life of another, a life in which her soul and her body are "shared," and where the isomorphic states of death and the torpor of sleep border with a metamorphosis of consciousness.[7]

Summoned to the sacred space of the *ruqya* by the recitation of Qur'anic speech, the subject retreats from the human world. *Kunti ghayba*? "Were you gone?," the Imam asks Z. at the end of the session. That state of "being gone" is called *ghaybūba*, unconsciousness, which in modern medical language also means coma, and in the context of healing is sometimes translated as trance. The verbal root of *ghaybūba*—*gh-y-b*—which spans the vocabulary of absence from fainting, to the absence of exile, to the theological concept of the nonmanifest (*al-ghayb*), is the semanteme of absence and invisibility, of being in retreat and suspended. In the being-gone of the subject, an almost literal coma suspended between life and death, what comes to the fore is existence as such, giving itself in imaginal form. Jinn, like angels and dreams, partake of that imaginal realm. Elaborating on the Quranic formulation of the limit, as at once the barrier that separates and the interval between the lines, Ibn 'Arabi calls that imaginal realm *barzakh*: a region of the boundary and a domain of imagination in which contraries come together, bodies are spiritualized, and spirits become manifest in corporeal form.[8] But the limit is also the "separation" of the law itself: the impassable barrier between life and death, the line between night and day, made visible at dawn in the thread that announces the beginning of fasting during the month of Ramadan, the distinction of truth and untruth (Qur'an 23:99–100, 2:187). It is the law's capacity to cut and discern, its nature as "knowledge of the path to the afterlife" (al-Ghazali), that inaugurates the imaginal stage of the *ruqya* and the experience of the limit it makes possible.

The state of *ghaybūba* is such a *barzakh* of the subject—at once an absence and a coming to presence, a paradoxical form of simultaneous sleep and waking. In the midst of demonic arousal and spiritual wrestling, in the "coma" that is also an awakening, and in the unfolding vicissitudes of the soul, the *barzakh* of the *ruqya* becomes a site for an encounter with the divine, and the training of a renewed capacity to cultivate and host a divine gaze.

When the Imam starts chanting aloud, the body on the floor becomes animated by the invisible being[9] that is summoned by his recitation, and that now shapes her limbs into contracted postures, in a visible, painful, and ecstatic attestation of its presence. The presence makes itself felt but refuses to speak. Resistant, it instead throws the body into a passion without words. It is midday, just after the *ẓuhr* prayer. The open windows in the Imam's receiving room bring in a breeze from the ocean.

The Imam had called me that morning making quick reference to the case (*ḥāla*) of a woman he wanted me to meet. I waited for him in his sitting room. He climbed the stairs of the house with a woman in her early forties, or perhaps younger, accompanied by a teen. There was no time to fill in the details, I found myself in the scene, putting a pillow under her head, holding her in her being-gone. The Imam had performed the *ruqya* for Z.'s daughter the night before. They had called him in emergency, as the girl had fallen into a spell of unconsciousness and restless agitation, and the family feared that she might never return. He had recited the Qur'an before an anxious group of relatives and neighbors. The girl had reacted to the recitation promptly, and had returned to herself, but the Imam knew that the respite would not last. This is why he had asked her mother to come. He explained to me later that the illness was only secondarily in the girl. At the center of it there was Z., the mother herself. Z. had come that morning accompanied by a teenage boy, the son of a neighbor. She had come, she said, "on behalf of her daughter." Her three daughters in fact, because they were all affected, even though the youngest, Dunya, who is thirteen, was today most visibly ill. She had not come to the Imam with the intention of seeking her own healing, just to talk about her girls. But when he started reciting the Qur'an and touched her chest with a pen, she felt her consciousness retreating to a familiar yet unfamiliar place, a place she knew and did not knew, but for which her senses and bodily memory were clearly trained. In her absence, the jinn haunting her family could manifest itself in form and voice.

That the invisible presence had been summoned by the Qur'anic utterance meant that its manifestation was not involuntary, as in the event of the illness of possession; rather it was ritually induced, in the dangerous and yet regulated space of the session. The jinn might always be with or in the proximity of the person, in latent form, in this case in Z.'s breast; or potentially there, and concealed. It might come to presence on specific occasions, striking the person in the mode of illness, or ravishment, or both. And this too happened to her, at other times. But now its manifestation took place under the constraints of the liturgy, and in the space of a struggle, inaugurated by the proclamation of the sovereignty of God. And unlike other cases, when a person sought healing unambiguously from the position of the sick, as an "afflicted-I," Z.'s indirect request, on behalf of her daughters, indicated that the subject was plural: it was a family, a collectivity. She was at once its kernel and its medium.

By the end of that day the crisis of illness had disclosed itself as the enigmatic knot from which radiated the secret threads that connected the multiple lives of the family: present and past, potential or failed, impossible or unlived, with their desires and longings, their load of resentment and hope. Their threads and their parallel unfolding were made manifest and could be heard in the voice of the invisible entities with whom those lives intersected and exchanged their places, in a tangle of oppression, violence, desire, and companionship. A companionship forced upon, or longed for.

Four moments, or movements, are turning points of this story, at least as I could witness it on that day and on following days, in the immediacy of the event, and in later conversations with Z. and the Imam. The movements are related to the structure of the liturgy, which provides the syntax and the forms of an imaginal experience. The recitation of Qur'anic verses—in Arabic, *āyāt*, literally "miraculous signs," or "examples"—stages a succession of scenes that unfold in the *barzakh* of the ritual. They inaugurate the site of a struggle, dramatizing the vicissitudes of the soul "astray."

The first movement, which is also the opening scene, is the summoning of an eschatological vision in the proclamation of the power of God. Over the body on the floor the Imam recites Sūrat al-Fātiḥa, the opening chapter of the Qur'an:

> In the name of God the most gracious, the dispenser of grace.
> All praise is due to God alone, the sustainer of all the worlds,
> The most gracious, the dispenser of grace,
> Lord of the Day of Judgment!
> Thee alone do we worship; and unto Thee alone we turn for aid.
> Guide us the straight way—the way of those upon whom Thou hast bestowed Thy blessings, not of those who have been condemned [by Thee], nor of those who go astray! (*ḍāllīn*).[10]

The Imam pauses and marks the last word, *ḍāllīn*, Astray! and repeats the chapter three times, each time asking the presence to deliver its name, to no avail. The third time the recitation is as if in slow motion. The last words resonate with the weigh and density of perdition and loss, being-astray: *ḍāllīn* . . .

In this space of the End, and in the evocation of pious fear of divine judgment of human deeds, the Imam asks the presence to speak and, again, to identify itself: "Are you a Christian, a Jew, or a Muslim?" He forcefully exhorts it to repent and surrender to God, joining the community of Muslims. But the presence refuses to speak, while the body on the floor, wheezing and blowing, laughing and roaring, alternating between agony and defiance, seems to mime the torments of the soul of the damned in hellfire.

"Are you Christian (*naṣrānī*) or Muslim? If you are Christian, you must be in love (*'āshiqan*). Are you lovesick? Speak! Are you afraid? Are you willing to bear witness that there is no God but God? Speak with the permission of God."

The Imam's recitation, from a selection of verses from Sūrat al-Dukhān (the Smoke, Qur'an 44) and al-Fuṣṣilat (Clearly Spelled Out, Qur'an 41), is a visualization of "The Day of Distinction (*yawm al-faṣl*—between the true and the false) . . . when no friend shall be of the least avail to his friend, and when none shall be succored" (Qur'an 44:40–41). The Hour, when the truth of the soul will be disclosed and human limbs and skins will attest to the sins of their bearers.

The recitation opens a vision of the Tree of Zaqqum, at 'the bottom of hell fire':

> "Verily [in the life to come] the tree of deadly fruit will be the food of the sinful: like molten lead will boil in the belly, like the boiling of burning despair!"
>
> [And the word will be spoken]: "Seize him [O you forces of hell], and drag him into the midst of blazing fire: the pour over his head the anguish of burning despair. Taste it—thou who [on earth] hast considered thyself so mighty, so noble!" (Qur'an 44:43–49)

Breathing and silence. The Imam throws "I invoke God against you," towards the presence that is emerging, and repeats the phrase several times. Speak! (*inṭaq!*) "What is your name?"

Without waiting for an answer, as an enjambment on the word *inṭaq*, "speak," and on the gift of speech from God (*antaqanā*), he resumes chanting:

"They will say to their skins: Why bear you witness against us? They will say: God has given us to speak (three times)—He who gives speech to everything" (*Qālū antaqanā Allāh* [3 times] *alladhi antaq kulli shay'an*, Qur'an 41:21).

The context is again the Hour: the verse just preceding refers to the scene of judgment, "The enemies of God will be gathered together to the Fire, and when they reach the Fire their sight, their hearing, and their skin—their senses—will bear witness against them" (Qur'an 41:21).

For a long time still, the presence refuses to speak. There is only the moaning of a wordless pain, and the body contracting on the floor. With a sharp change of tone the Imam intervenes in that scene of mute passion, no longer speaking to the soul astray, the soul of the sinner in torments of fire and in the vision of judgment, but directly addressing the lovesick in her passion: *Nṭaq bi-idhni llāh, yā l-'āshiq*! "Speak, the one in love, with the permission of God!"

Again enjambing on the *'āshiq* ("the lover, the one in love"), the Imam's recitation resonates with a Qur'anic verse (*āya*, sign) of *'ishq*, a scene and example of passionate love. As I listen to the recording we made that day, I am struck by the sudden shift in tone, and by the nature of his interpretation. I hear the Imam's turn as a (psychoanalytic) interpretation, as the concept is used in the context of analytic sessions. It is an interpretation borne of the "transfer between souls" in the space of the liturgy, and of the unconsciousness in which the divine speech can be heard; an interpretation that is an event, in the sense in which Ibn 'Arabi speaks of imaginal manifestation (*ḥadrat al-khayyal*),[11] and Lacan says that analytic interpretation "is made to generate waves": "A psychoanalytic interpretation must in no case be theoretical or suggestive, in other words imperative. It must be ambiguous. Analytic interpretation is not made to be understood; it is made to generate waves."[12]

The Imam starts chanting without any pause a verse from the story of Yusuf in the Qur'an, "the best of narratives" (*aḥsan al-qaṣaṣ*, Qur'an 12:23–27). It is the scene of Yusuf and a woman designated as "she" (Potiphar's wife from the biblical narrative, who remains unnamed in the Qur'an):

> *wa rāwadathu llatī huwa fī baytihā ʿan nafsihi . . .*
>
> And [it so happened] that she in whose house he was living [conceived a passion for him] and sought to make him yield himself (his soul/*nafs*) unto her; and she bolted the doors and said: "Come thou unto me!" [But Joseph] answered: "May God preserve me! Behold, goodly has my master made me stay [in his house]. Verily, to no good end come they that do such wrong!"
>
> And indeed she desired him, and he desired her (*hammat bihi wa hamma bihā*); [and he would have succumbed] had he not seen [in this temptation] an evidence of his Sustainer's truth. Thus [we willed it to be] in order that we might avert from him all evil (*al-sūʾ*) and all shameful deeds (*al-faḥshāʾ*). For he was one of our servants, sincere and purified.
>
> And they both rushed to the door; and she [grasped] and rent his tunic from behind—and lo! They met her lord at the door! Said she: "What ought to be the punishment of the one who had evil designs [on the virtue] of thy wife—[what] but imprisonment or a yet [more grievous] chastisement?"
>
> [Joseph] exclaimed: "It was she who sought to make me yield myself unto her!" Now one of those present, a member of he own household, suggested this: "If his tunic is torn from the front, then she is telling the truth, and he is a liar; but if his tunic has been torn from behind, then she is lying and he is speaking the truth."
>
> And when [her husband] saw that his tunic was torn from behind he said . . .

The second movement has to do with the "waves" of that recitation, and the resonance of a story (Qur'an 12:23–27) that directly addresses the experience of erotic passion, the transport of love, and the conundrum and vicissitudes of the soul, between its worldly desire and the striving for purification in the devotion to God.

"Is this a matter of love?"

The Imam introduces this turn with a question, directly addressed to the jinn: sharply different in tone than the opening intimation of hellfire, the verse from the story of Yusuf and Zulikha evokes a scene of desire and moral uncertainty, yet not unrelated to the theme of divine judgment. Judgment now is further qualified, to disturb the presumption of knowledge and the righteous certainty of moral judgment in the human world, the judgment of those who too quickly believe they "understand." For in the intricate emplotment of this story all those who claim to speak from a position of righteousness are proven wrong over time by the disclosure of a larger plot whose logic and unfolding eludes human agency and calculation.

The verse chosen by the Imam is the scene of a missed carnal encounter between Yusuf, the prophet and beautiful clairvoyant youth abandoned by his brothers and adopted by an Egyptian courtesan, and the woman who remains unnamed in the Qur'an, but who in the Bible and in other versions of the story bears the name of Zulikha.

The evocation of the passion of a woman for a man who "would have desired her," and did desire her, but struggled to fulfill the truth of his God as reflected in the purity of his own soul, opens on a scene of human vulnerability, beyond all easy judgment, one that stresses the complexity of human vicissitudes, passion and attachments, and the opacity of divine design. Differently than in the biblical version, the Qur'anic story of Yusuf foregrounds the spiritual vicissitudes of the soul and the enigma of fate, where the reasons for events and feelings are not immediately discernable, and must remain invisible, even for the ones who can "see" them in veridical dreams, as Yusuf does, and has the gift of allegorical reading of divine signs. For, as it is stated multiple times in this section, understanding "the inner meaning of happenings" is not an easy task, in all cases one only partly accessible to human beings; discernment is possible only with the guidance of God and through a painful apprenticeship of trials and errors. As Muhammad Asad notes in his translation of this Qur'anic chapter, "The whole of this surah might be described as a series of variations on the theme, 'judgment [as to what is to happen] rests with none but God. In him I have placed my trust. For all who have trust must place their trust in him alone'" (Qur'an 12:67). Openness to the meaning of things, of fate, and its unfolding, requires the capacity to suspend judgment, and the presumption to know. In writing the story of the woman I call Z., of her daughters, their illness and their life, I came to realize that the mention of Sūrat Yūsuf was more than a liturgical element of the ritual. It provided the narrative and existential frame within which the pathos, trajectory, and possibility of their lives could be heard and come to the fore.

The chanting resonates:

"If his tunic is torn from the front, then she is telling the truth, and he is a liar; but if his tunic has been torn from behind, then she is lying and he is speaking the truth.

"And when [her husband] saw that his tunic was torn from behind he said . . ."

It is at this point—in the hiatus open between the evocation of the Hour and divine judgment, and the hermeneutic suspension of judgment in the pondering of human vulnerability and passions, in the surrender of the faithful soul to the justice of God's design, that the invisible presence finally can speak.

First an imperceptible bodily movement. I don't notice it, myself transported by the chanting. The Imam calls for my attention:

"*L-istislam*! Submission!—Look! What is the meaning of that gesture? It is submission. The jinn is submitting, is asking, 'What do you want from me?'"

She asks for silence: Shhhhh.

—Are you a woman, a female presence?

Half-voice, the jinn discloses her name to the Imam. He receives and repeats aloud. ʿAʾisha.

—Speak with the permission of God, where are you settled [in the body] (*ayna taskuni*)?

She points to her belly.

He wants to localize more. Finally she points to a specific place. Laughter. She is finally responding.

The Imam starts questioning ʿAʾisha about the woman she inhabits.

—Is that woman divorced? The jinn nods.

—Did you separate her from her husband?

—Yes.

—What kind of deed is this (*ʿamal*), to enter between a woman and her spouse?

He beats her gently. Is this the result of magic? She nods. He beats her again, very gently, and when he does she rumbles.

—*Matʿaddebnish*! Stop torturing me.

—Tell us then where is the magic. She spits, keeps spitting.

—In [Western] Sahara [the former Spanish territory that Morocco annexed in 1974].

—Where in the Sahara? Speak with the permission of God!

Spitting.

He counters her spitting by repeating, "I invoke God against you!" many times. Finally she admits that the woman—Z.—carried the magic on herself, in the form of an amulet, but that the magic is no more; the actual bundle is gone. The Imam asks, then, what she is still doing there, inside that woman. In reply to his questions she embarks in a passionate monologue, at once lament and accusatory speech.

The jinn's tone rises, on a crescendo, affected, angry, pained, high pitched.

The third movement, then, is the lament of the jinn, which is also, in the proximity and distance of a dance, the lament of the soul. In the hiatus between the jinn and the woman, in the subtle shift of pronouns, is the encounter with an ambiguous history of violence, pain, and desire. As in the story of Yusuf and Zulikha, it has to do with the vicissitudes of the soul, its vulnerability and error, and the uncertainty and fallibility of human interpretation and judgment when confronted with the opacity of the ways of God. It is from that position of infinite distance—the point of divine address, beyond vision and knowledge—beyond human life and consciousness, beyond subjectivity and personhood, that the liturgy addresses the subject. This is the point the Imam conceptualizes theologically as the absolute unknowability of God, foundational for the possibility of the commitment of faith (*yaqīn*) and for the ethical and existential effectiveness of the healing acts of the *ruqya*.

ʿAʾisha delivers an account of Z.'s life. She speaks of a man who had sought to bind his spouse to him by the knots of magic (*siḥr*) in a now distant past, and in a faraway region of the south, the Western Sahara, which was then, and still is today, a war zone. And she speaks of Z.'s suffering, her solitude and oppression, and of her own pain, she, ʿAʾisha, who is bound to Z. in (almost) flesh and blood, destined by that magical writing to become her life companion, her other herself, enduring the same affliction, the same violence, and the same humiliation. She speaks of her rage against that man, Z.'s husband, who had ruined their lives, both lives, the life of the woman and the life of the jinn, and whom she finally sent away, off, expelled from their lives, rendering him as lonesome and derelict as he had caused them to be. Halfway between a rant and a lament, ʿAʾisha's monologue is a condensation of pathos, of rage and pain, where the voice of the jinn so overlaps with the voice of the person as to become one, in the memory and retrospective account of a life of loss. In the words of the jinn:

> She used to cry, subjugated, and defeated (*mqhūra*) . . . I have been with her for twenty years, twenty long years that I have been with her. Her husband told her, take "that thing" (*dak shiʾ*) with you and she took it, and she wore it on herself . . . This is how I became attached to her (*muʿalleqa maʿahā*), bonded to her, and for more than twenty years I have been her companion. But that man who tortured me along with her, I sent him off, off . . . That man is gone . . . it is he who bewitched me (*huwa lly saḥrni*), he who attached me by magic, he told her, "tie that thing," and she tied it, and I remained tied to her, bonded to her for so long, twenty years I have been attached to her, tied up with her . . . It is that man who tortured me. I have been her companion, it is he who made her entire life into a torment, and tormented me along with her (*u'adhdhebni ḥatta ānā maʿahā*), it is he who attached me to her, it is he who gave her that piece of cloth and that magical inscription. But I sent him off and he is GONE! For so many years I have been living with her, I have accompanied her through life (*ānā ghāda maʿahā*) . . . I will not accept to be separated from her. I will not be separated from her; I will not be separated from her [screaming]. Her children will remain with me. She will remain with me. And if you [to the Imam] hurt me, if you try to subdue me I will throw her and her children into madness! (*u ilā 'athart ʿalya ghadi nḥammaq hiya u nḥammaq wladhā*).

The lament of the jinn speaks of the intimacy of attachment, through the literal term "attached to her," the companionship with another who is almost oneself in pain and sorrow, who, more than oneself, can see, feel, and speak the torture of being. It is a description, "she cried, subjugated and defeated" (*kent katbki mqhūra*), which at moments almost slips into the first person, "it is he who bewitched me" (*anā mqhūra*)—the ambiguity of the "me," in the "shared" and "mixed" utterance of the one in the other. And yet moments later the voice is splitting itself off again, casting itself against, and uttering threats against Z. and her daughters, a curse of madness: if anyone (the Imam) tries to separate us, "I will throw them, this woman and her children, into madness" (*nḥammaq hiya u nḥammaq wladhā*).

The Imam repeats the threat in a flat and ironic tone, as if to measure the absurdity of the statement: "You will throw them, this woman and her children, into madness."

—Everyone will go crazy, everyone will go, everyone will be lost, everyone, she and her children, everyone, I will destroy them.

—So you, the jinn, can push humans to madness?

But the identity of the jinn is ambiguous.

—He made me mad (*ḥammaqni*), when he tied me to her. She's innocent, she did nothing wrong. He wrote down my name and the name of my family and gave it to her to wear. But now he is paying. He is suffering, can't sleep. He tortured me and I am torturing him in turn . . . [crying].

—What is his name?

She cries, finally says a man's name, ʿAbdallah.

—And her daughter?

She was in the house, ʿAʾisha says, the previous night, when the Imam performed the *ruqya* for Z.'s daughter. It is time to leave the girl alone, the Imam says; free to move on with her life. The jinn counters that she still has not obtained what she wants. She wants the Imam to visit her hometown and bring a sacrifice. The animal doesn't matter, whatever Z. can afford. She only wants the blood. The hometown is a sanctuary for the mad; her family lives there. But when the Imam asks the names of her children, she rebels, becomes threatening, and refuses to respond. The ritual becomes a counseling session: having ascertained that ʿAʾisha is separated from her husband, and that her children are alone without a father, the Imam proposes to bring order in their lives, to restore a lawful situation, where the families might be reunited.

—Leave that woman and her children alone, and go back to your children; you are a Muslim!

—I am a Muslim but I refuse to pronounce the testimony of faith.

—Then you are not a Muslim, and just hide yourself behind a Muslim name. Are you an unbeliever who just pretends to be a Muslim?

The Imam asks her whether she prays (she doesn't), and exhorts her to take on praying at the proper times. She doesn't reply, but says that she is tired and wants to come out. He insists that she pronounce the testimony of faith. She repeats after him, *Ashhadu*. . . , "I bear witness . . ."

Something is choking her. Spitting and as if vomiting.

—ʿAʾisha, do you want to come out?

The Imam starts chanting again, the verse of the Throne (Qurʾan 2:255):

> There is no God save Him, the Alive, the Eternal. Neither slumber nor sleep overtakes Him. Unto Him belongs whatsoever is in the heavens and whatsoever is in the earth. Who is he that interceded with Him save by His leave? He knows that which is in front of them and that which is behind them, while they encompass nothing of His knowledge save what He will. His throne includes the heavens and the earth, and He is never weary of preserving them. He is the Sublime, the Tremendous.

ʿAʾisha is holding onto the ground with her hand.
—I am burning (*kanthạrq*), she says with a thread of voice.
—Burn! Burn with the permission of God.
—It's enough, I want to come out.
—I will continue with the recitation till you come out.

> It has been revealed to me that a group of jinns listened (to this Qurʾan). They said: We have really heard a wonderful Recital.

Sūrat al-Jinn (Qurʾan 72:1–9) speaks of the submission of jinn to the oneness of God, their being converted by the beauty of the sound of the Qurʾan. It is a chapter often read during the *ruqya*, along with Sūrat al-Fātiḥa and the verse of the Throne. (The Imam's recitation stops at verse 9, not because he decides to stop but because the jinn has come out and Z. is speaking.)

> It guides to the Right Path, and we have believed therein. We shall never join [in worship] anything with our Lord.
>
> And exalted is the Majesty of our Lord; He has taken neither a wife, nor a son.
>
> There were foolish among us who used to utter extravagant lies against God.
>
> But we thought that no men and jinn should utter a lie against Allah.
>
> And true, there were persons among mankind who took shelter with persons among the jinns, but they increased them in oppression and folly (*rahaqan*).
>
> And they thought as you thought, that Allah will not raise up anyone [to Judgment].
>
> And we have sought to reach the sky; but found it filled with stern guards and flaming fires.

And we used to sit there in stations, to [steal] a hearing, but any who listens now will find a flaming fire watching him in ambush.

And we know not whether harm is intended for those on earth, or whether their Lord intends to guide them to the Right Path.

Silence, a long pause, and then "she" turns to us, with a different gaze. Z. looks at the Imam, then me.

—ʿAʾisha, ʿAʾisha, or instead Z.?

—Z. . . .

The Imam greets her, and offers her a glass of water over which he recited the Qurʾan.

Z. awakens from the session without remembering much. When I ask her, she says that she had felt herself "falling," becoming lightheaded and then falling, and had awakened with knowledge neither of what happened nor of the passing of time. The experience is a familiar one, the thread of consciousness slowly vanishing, and then the lapse into absence.

Turning to me from time to time, and asking me to confirm his account as a witness, the Imam revisits the scene with her, telling Z. what ʿAʾisha has said, double checking the two versions of the story, the woman's and the jinn's, and asking about that time in the Sahara, when she was a young bride and her man was a soldier stationed there in the Moroccan army. And the story is told again by the Imam, as he reports on the version offered by the jinn in the scene from which Z.'s presence was missing.

He now speaks with Z. in a very different tone, with the kindness and politeness he certainly didn't use in addressing the jinn that spoke through Z.'s mouth. He asks her whether she feels better now, offers her breakfast, as one would address an acquaintance that has come for advice. He asks her about her daughter, and whether she wanted to go home, and proposes to go with her. He tells her that he has ordered the jinn to leave her family alone (*sharṭ ʿalayhā tferq maʿa l-bint u maʿa l-ʿayla kullhā*).

—Is your husband's name ʿAbdallah Ben Hammou?

—Yes.

—And did he perform magic on you? (*ken der lik suḥr huwa?*).

—It happened so long ago (*bkri*).

—Did he give it to you, the magical writing, to wear, or was it instead hung somewhere?

—He gave me a silver amulet and there was writing on it.

—Why?

—He told me to wear it to protect the baby in my womb.

The Imam addresses her in a tender, brotherly tone: "sit up and be in peace." She gets up, adjusts her scarf back on her head, and realizes the mess on the floor; wants to mop the water, but he refuses. He tells her that he made a recording and took some photos so that she too can become aware of the nature of her condition (*besh tʿrf ḥetta hiya ashnu ʿandhā*). The video recording the Imam wanted to make with his phone didn't work, but the pictures were there. She looks at the pictures, *"Tahat l lard!,"* I fell on the ground . . .

The Imam turns to me. He asks me, smiling but serious, about a moment during the ritual when I got up suddenly, in the midst of his recitation. What happened to me? What did I feel? I seemed emotional, and emotion (*ʿaṭifa*) makes a person vulnerable. "You were not in yourself when you got up." He was about to start reciting over me. It was the moment when Z. had fallen on the ground. I explain that yes, I felt the intensity of the moment, but had not been afraid. Did I seem afraid? A bit, he said. We laughed, Z. laughing with us.

As we walk he keeps talking with Z. about what ʿAʾisha has said. "You are not aware of this, but the jinn told us that ʿAbdallah Ben Hammou—he was your husband, you didn't tell me—did the magic so that you would love him." She explains that at the beginning when she was pregnant with her first daughter—the girl who is now twenty years old—during the time of *wuham* (the period of "envies" during the first months of pregnancy), she stopped liking her husband sexually, rejected him. . . . The Imam interjects, *"Kraḥtih,* you hated him, he didn't do magic to protect the pregnancy, he did it so that you would love him."

Z. remembers that time in the Western Sahara, when she became pregnant and was still a young bride. The Imam tells her that ʿAʾisha, the jinn, is not alone. She works in the service of another, more powerful jinn, a male, who has been with her from that distant past, who desires her, and wants to be with her. She nods. A "man" (jinn) comes to her at night. In recent times she has started focusing closely on prayer and good deeds, and he has left her alone somewhat, but then her daughters started getting sick. He asks if her daughters pray, if they wear the hijab. And he says that according to ʿAʾisha, her husband now is sick—Z. confirms—he is depressed and ill, and lives with another woman out of wedlock. She nods. Of course he is sick, it has been six years since he last visited his children! And they are now grown up. The Imam looked at her fondly and smiles. He concludes: "All things considered the jinn told us a little bit of truth."

The fourth movement is the interior community.

The session resumes in the afternoon at the home of Z. and her daughters, where, in a small sitting room filled with relatives and neighbors who have been helping and caring for the sick girl, the Imam tends to the mother and her daughters, who keep "falling" as they respond or echo each other; and he listens to the invisible presences that speak, scream, and bear witness through their bodies. Dunya, the youngest daughter, falls first, immediately, as the Imam walks in the door. It is not because of his personal charisma, he explains to me, but because of the digital Qur'an in his cellphone, and the Qur'an that he himself embodies. As he starts reciting Sūrat al-Fātiḥa over the girl, Z. "falls" once again, the two bodies side by side on the carpet. But while the daughter remains inert and as if lifeless, her mother's body is animated by a presence that for a long time only expresses itself in moaning, roaring, and restless agitation. It takes two women to hold her down, her older daughter and a neighbor. The Imam recites, increasingly hoarse from fatigue. Then a voice, a coarse masculine voice, claims dominion over the home and its inhabitants. The voice screams: *anā mul ddar*, "I am the Master of the home."

The Imam sprinkles water, and then begins reciting Sūrat al-Fātiḥa. Dunya, the girl, starts breathing, laughing-crying. The recitation again emphasizes the last word, *ḍāllīn* ("those who go astray").

Long silence.

Dunya, the youngest daughter, is crying and breathing heavily. The Imam touches Z. on her breast with his pen, and she screams, she says not to touch there, screaming, as if she is being burned. The daughters say that she is sick there, in her breast, but that she has been seen at the hospital and there is nothing medically wrong.

—We reached the place of haunting, where the jinn resides (*hna wuṣlnā fī hadak l-makān dyal sakan*).

Dunya sits down, back to herself. The Imam greets her, and asks her how she is feeling.

He calls ʿAʾisha, and the voice screams acutely, as the voice of someone in acute pain.

—What is your name? A roaring voice emerges from Z.'s body: *Anā huwa mul ddar* ("I am he the Master of the home"), and as the Imam insists on his questioning the voice changes, and becomes thicker and sharply masculine. *Anā mul ddar, mul ddar, lly sakn f-had ddar* ("I am the Master of the home, the Master, the one who lives in this house").

At the end of the afternoon, when mother and daughters are slowly returning to their waking selves, when everyone is exhausted, and the Imam's voice is coarse from fatigue, he addresses those in attendance with words of moral exhortation, in the form of a lesson (*naṣīḥa*) drawn from the example of life we just witnessed. With Z.'s body still lying on the floor, resting and slowly coming back to presence, her older daughter holding her mother's head and caressing her face, with people sitting around in circle, the Imam addressed us. The experience of illness becomes a summoning and a witnessing of the ways of God, and the ritual gives way to a *daʿwa* session. He speaks in colloquial Arabic and in simple words and figures, different from the words he uses in his sermons, or in his formal conversations with me. He says:

> Please listen and understand what I am saying: God, high be His praise, created the human and the jinn, two worlds (*khalaq allāh al-ins wa al-jinn, ʿalamayn*). Imagine the example of Europe and the Maghreb, two separate worlds and continents, neighboring each other, but different. Such are the jinn and the human. They are distinct, but one always overpowers the other. If we don't conquer the jinn, the jinn conquer us (*imma nkunw hna kanghalbuhum, wa imma ikunw huma yghalbuna*). How can we conquer the jinn? With religion (*dīn*), with pious fear of God (*taqwā llāh*), with prayer and remembrance (*dhikr*). The more we fear God, the more the jinn fear us. But if we are fearful of our fellow humans, if because of our fear we seek the help of magic and false healers, and through them of the jinn (*shayāṭīn*), we empower and strengthen the jinn, and the jinn end up conquering us. So to come back of the story of this household, this is what happened . . . .

He goes on to offer an interpretation, by stringing in a single narrative the fragments of the story that in the course of the day had been told in multiple voices and perspectives, human and jinn. His account situates the experience of the family—within which he counts the jinn as nonphysical beings—within a trajectory that reflects the vulnerability of life and the entanglement of passions. He speaks of the losses and the pain, not in the mode of judgment, but as an invitation to reflect back on the very human failures that had been at the origin of this suffering, the failure to trust in God, and to be attentive and just with our fellow humans—a spouse, a child, a neighbor; the fact of falling into the trap of suspicion, a kind of sickness of relations that resulted in a catastrophic loss of confidence. It is such a loss of trust—in God and consequently in fellow humans—that causes people to resort to witchcraft, furthering the tangle and the imprisonment. But his tone was not one of simple condemnation. Listening to the testimony of the jinn, a speech of pain and delusion, meant for the ones involved to take responsibility for the history of suspicion, and ponder the other potential lives and failed encounters, truthfully submitting to God. In that submission there was the ground for reencountering the violence of that past in a new form, the capacity to encounter others in their vulnerability and error, which was also one's own.

It is from this perspective that he relates to us the testimony of the jinn, the female jinn who had spoken in the morning session during Z.'s "absence," and who mentioned events in the past that took place in the Sahara, where her husband was a soldier in the Moroccan army stationed there and she was a young bride. That scene contained the example, and the lesson, of the development of suspicion, the longing for love, the fear of its loss, and the sense of being crippled in life. Large numbers of people from what is now three generations have had their lives uprooted or suspended in interminable waiting because of the Saharan war. Men sent to an elusive front, protecting an elusive border that itself was the result of multiple colonial and postcolonial occupations, sent to a life of exile away from their families, or taking their families to what seemed like a bottomless chasm. The solitude born of the war, for all the parties involved. The resentment, the sense of impotence. As the Imam is speaking I remember vividly a visit I made to a family in a housing sprawl in the barren land surrounding a southern town. Unfinished concrete buildings on land given by the state to soldiers stationed on the Saharan frontier, homes built piecemeal with money sent sporadically, and the taste of abandonment, resentment, and solitude.

The Imam continues his retelling in the style of a parable. The jinn—a feminine presence—had spoken of a man, disoriented and fearful of losing his spouse, who sought to bind her to him for life by the knots of magic (*siḥr*). And she had spoken of Z.'s suffering, her solitude and oppression, and of her own pain and her rage against that man, Z.'s husband, who had ruined their lives, and whom she finally sent away. But that man too, the Imam says, raising his tone, has suffered; he has paid a high price for his acts, and was now lonesome and sick, estranged from his family and children. He now asks us to remember the scene that we (the attendees) have directly witnessed in the afternoon, in that same room, during the intensely emotional session that has involved Z. and her daughters. He revisits the events with us, all the way through his recitation. He asks the audience to reflect on the example of those lives, and see how they all, including the man and the jinn, could choose to transform, and to truthfully engage on the path of God. It is a lesson literally spoken over Z.'s fallen body, as she was slowly returning to presence.

Postscript

Fadoua Laroui died on February 23, 2011, in a Casablanca hospital after setting herself on fire in front of the city hall of her rural town in central Morocco. She was twenty, a single mother of two. Her shack had been razed by the bulldozers that came to enforce an administrative order of the city; she had been denied the assignment of social housing for which she had filed a request. She stood in front of city hall screaming her indictment; the injustice to which she bore witness, of a world and a regime, and not just for herself. She lit a match and set herself ablaze. Three YouTube videos recorded her lament: a young woman in jeans and a white shirt, her turning into the light of fire, and her refusal to be saved. The third video, her funeral procession—the whole town in a cortege of mourning, pain, and rage, images posted on the web side-by-side with videos of the demonstrations that had been shaking Morocco since mid-February. Her immolation followed that of the Tunisian Mohamed Bouazizi, who is said to have literally ignited the wave of uprisings that swept across the Middle East, toppling authoritarian regimes in Tunisia, Libya, Egypt, and Yemen. Like Bouazizi, Fadoua has been called a *shahīda*, and her act, discredited and ignored by the state media as the lunacy of a psychopath, was seen not as a suicide but as a form of witnessing. The Libyan writer Ibrahim al-Koni spoke of Bouazizi's role in the revolutions as that of a saint, a spiritual and otherworldly exemplar, pointing to the double dimension of martyrdom and gift, witnessing and healing; and to the transformative force of pain, showing that it can be generative of political-spiritual action.

But the Imam disagrees. *Fitna aw thawra*?, he asks me, "discord or revolution?" *Fitna*, the theological term of error and discord, the term I could not predict he would suggest as a frame for understanding the uprisings. He calls instead for the need of "discernment"—in a sense not unlike the "discernment of spirits" he practices on the ritual stage of the cures of the jinn. I am surprised, disturbed, as I understand the uprisings in light of all I have learned with him and from him, in his work with the youth, with his patients, in the refinement of his political-spiritual critique, from his courage, and in the way in which, in his practice, he embodies an overcoming of fear. I realize that the entanglements are complex. Discernment for the Imam meant pondering the risks of discord, partition, and splintering within the community of Muslims. In Egypt and Syria, he noticed, this had already begun. He warned that the language of revolt was imbued of words and values that spoke of a desire to resemble the West, and he found that desire to resemble the West, like all desire, is a desire of the *nafs* that can take the person astray. He called for vigilance in interrogating desires, and for a containment of enthusiasm, which in his view was too close to the neighboring affect of despair. He saw the immolations as acts of despair that should be seen and mourned as suicides and not as acts of martyrdom. They were the outcome of the choking of the soul. He understood despair: melancholy is at the center of his practice of healing. Pain can be generative, he said, but the path to transformation is arduous. And the way is long.

I am left pondering, through the impersonal and enigmatic dreams of a history that folds back into the future.

ACKNOWLEDGMENTS

Knot of the Soul happened over many years. Its life is intertwined with lives and places, resonance of voices, injunctions, summonings, demands, gifts, debts, love, and loss, and of course the life of its author, which at times found in it a home. Acknowledging this debt is more than just mentioning the names of those who have marked the book the most. It means to register the wrinkles and the whispers, the movements and hiatuses of life in the many versions and voices, that are recognizable and faded signatures of the living and the dead.

I hope that my debts and gratitude will be felt in the writing. *Knot* is itself an acknowledgement: the transmission of speech that was given to me on "consignment," as an *amāna*. *Amāna* (from the Arabic root ʾ*-m-n*) is a term of fidelity and care: something that is not ours but with which we are entrusted: words, children, possessions, our very lives.

I hope this work won't betray the trust of those who left their words and thoughts with me: the trust of Kamal and Jawad, who asked me to record their experience of "burning" in a book: their attempt at migration, their sense of suffocation and their quests for a horizon; or of Amina, who in one of our last meetings at the psychiatric hospital asked me to turn my tape recorder on and register the witness of her life and her desire. Or of Ilyas, for whom entrusting the paintings of his visionary inner world to this book was also a way of sharing his story for the sake of others struggling with mental illness and the torments of the soul; or of the psychiatrists and psychoanalysts, who welcomed me into their world in an exchange that in some cases became a critical debate. Or of the Imam.

The Imam welcomed me into his life and therapeutic practice and shared his learning and thought on the law, the soul, and the trials of madness. I owe him more than I can acknowledge. He opened a path for me into the Islamic medical-religious tradition that he embodies, and speaks in the singular-plural voice of his search and research, developing it into what we jokingly called a "general theory" of the self-body-soul in the polity and the cosmos. As we sat in his home during this recent month of Ramadan, he told me of his desire to write a book himself, at this time of trial and uncertainty for subjects and communities, in Morocco and the planet at large.

My gratitude goes first and foremost to the protagonists of the book, necessarily mentioned by their pseudonyms: Amina, Hind, Reda, Dr. N., Dr. B., Dr. M., Dr. S., Dr. A., Ilyas, Samia, Kamal, Jawad, and the Imam; as well as all the others, visible and invisible, named and unnamed.

At the Hôpital ar-Razi in Salé at the time of my fieldwork: I am grateful to the staff, psychiatrists, residents, nurses, as well as the patients, who welcomed and included me in their daily activities for extensive periods of time between 1998 and 2003, and especially Dr. Mehdi Paés, Dr. Jamal Eddine Ktiouet, Dr. Mustapha Laymani, Dr. Munaim Zenati, Dr. Selwa Kjiri, Dr. Abdelhaq Belaouchi, Dr. Jalal Toufiq, and Dr. Kamal Raddaoui. In particular, the time spent with Mustapha Laymani, Munaim Zenati, Selwa Kjiri, and Abdelhaq Belaouchi, in consultations with patients, in the emergency room, or in individual conversation has been invaluable. Without them, each in their particular orientation and style, part 1 of this book would not have been written.

The psychoanalysts and psychotherapists of L'Espace tiers, and what is today called L'Association Marocaine de psychanalyse and Le Cercle freudien, have been crucial interlocutors over the years. In particular, Fouad Benchekroun has been an inspiration, a constant challenge, an unsparing critic and a caring friend; as well I would like to thank the late Martyne Medejel, Abdallah Wardini, Farid Merini, Hakima Lebbar, and, finally, Selwa Kjiri, whose clinical creativity I admire.

The Seminaire du symbolique has been an intellectual and spiritual home in Rabat for twenty years; I thank the friends and colleagues there who shared their work and thinking, and offered their comments: Abdelhai Diouri, Abdelahad Sebti, Mohammed Hamdouni Alami, Halima Ferhat, Abdelfattah Kilito, Abderrahmane Moudden, and the late Mohammed Ayyadi as well as the psychoanalysts mentioned above.

Abdelahad Sebti's important work on history and memory in Morocco, our conversations, and his friendship have nourished and sustained my work through the years. Driss Ksikes and Omar Berrada have been interlocutors and friends with a unique literary and political poetic gaze, and were kind enough to include me in conversations and debates they organized. Abdallah Laroui's thought on Arab modernity shaped the questions at the inception of this work. The late Abdelkebir Khatibi is still a source of inspiration, as is Edmond Amran Al-Maleh, who shared the gift of his literary imagination and his lucid perspective on politics and life.

For having engaged deeply with this work over the years, in some cases reading it at every step, and for making life and writing possible because of their friendship, I am grateful to the following:

Mohammed Hamdouni Alami lived with this book from beginning to end, lending his critical gaze at times of hesitation, and sharing with me his writing and his discoveries of the early Arab and Islamic texts of Al-Jahiz and Ikhwan al-Safa's theory of the soul and visual meaning. His companionship, intelligence, and love are everywhere present in the book.

Luca D'Isanto, generous interlocutor and critic, shared with me his love for the work of Certeau, and his deep knowledge of the European mystical tradition. Soraya Tlatli, companion in writing, and in the passion for Kateb Yacine, read the entire manuscript with stunning intelligence. Shahla Talebi's writings at the limit of life have inspired this work, holding the bar very high. Maria Letizia Crevetto has been present for me throughout with her reflections on fidelity and transmission. Their friendships have sustained me.

Emily Ng, Saleem al-Bahloly, and Basit Iqbal have read and corrected drafts of the manuscript with care and insight, adding to the craft of editing their investment in the meaning of the work, which they helped clarify and refine. Cecile Pineda lent me her wisdom and literary artistry at a crucial moment, taking time away from her own book to help me when I most needed it.

Milad Odabaei, Saleem al-Bahloly, Khashayar Beigi, Emily Ng, Youssef Belal, Basit Iqbal, Raphaelle Rabanes, Michael D'Arcy, Patricia Kubala, Ashwak Hauter, Rosa Norton, and Jeremy Soh, fellow scholars, graduate students, and friends, who have shared with me almost every moment and dimension of this work, have made it resonate with their own work (on religion, trauma, politics, time, madness, medicine, Islam) and have encouraged me to make it better, in a process of both learning and teaching. This book would not be the same without them.

Antonio Maone, Anne Lovell, and Roberto Beneduce have been interlocutors on the question of madness, institutionalization, and exclusion. I have benefited immensely from their conversation, their writings, their friendship, and their constant reminder that the implications of our research exist also concretely in the world. Anne Lovell spearheaded a collective book on the theme of madness that brought together Veena Das, Sandra Laugier, herself, and me, which became the occasion for a fascinating set of conversations on madness and the everyday, conversations that were also joined by Pierre Henri Castel and Richard Rechtmann. To all of them goes my gratitude.

Omnia El-Shakry's and Leïla Kilani's arrival in my life, and their friendship, have been a gift. Since our first encounters in Rabat 2005 around the work of the Instance Equité et Reconciliation, and even more today, Leïla's courageous vision and her films (*Tanger, le rêve des brûleurs* and *Nos lieux interdits*) have resounded deeply in my work and left their mark, prompting me to experiment with new forms of encountering the real. Omnia's research on psychoanalysis and Islam in Egypt, and her exploration of the Sufi genealogy of the unconscious, have been a crucial site of encounter and discussion, from which I learned and where I found a second home for my book. Etel Adnan and Simone Fattal, their vision and their art, the journey of their lives, have been an example and an inspiration for me through the years.

Youssef Belal, in Berkeley and Rabat, accompanied me through the archive of *fiqh al-nafs*, "the jurisprudence of the soul," in its legal and spiritual dimensions. David Marriott's intellectual companionship, his work on race, politics, and psychoanalysis, and his poetry, made of my work a better book.

Annie Topalov taught me that madness can sometimes be traversed.

David Brent, editor and friend, who has the uncanny ability to see what is invisible on the page, can bring out the latency of form in a work and cares about the ethical task of writing and publishing. His personal interest in psychic life and the active imagination made his gaze on my book even more enriching.

In different ways Veena Das, Talal Asad, and Gananath Obeyesekere have each been a reference point and an inspiration, and represented for me the possibility of dwelling in anthropology. Through Veena Das's spiritual and intellectual investment in the questions that animate her research, her own conversations with the dead, her confidence in the living, the figure of the child in her books, and her friendship. Through Talal Asad's truthful questioning, at once as an engagement with the Islamic tradition—as a world, worlds, enduring, asserted, and repeatedly undone—and as the impossibility of disentangling work and life. And through Gananath Obeyesekere's explorations of the psyche and the soul in psychoanalysis, ethnography, and religious traditions, his love for poetry, his friendship, his willingness to take risks and traverse boundaries, and the way he read a letter that was addressed to me by a young man in the grips of psychosis in 1989.

The conversations with Saba Mahmood and Charles Hirschkind over the years, their writings on Islam, their commitment to the Middle East, and our reciprocal engagement with each other's work left traces across this book. The seminar on violence and death that I taught with Samera Esmeir in 2009 set the foundations for the reflection on violence and the unconscious that I pursue here, as I also recall the time spent with her and Lena Meari in Palestine. Mario Biagioli and Kriss Ravetto have been present for me with care and insight, respectively from the angle of the history of science and that of visual theory. Brinkley Messick offered his support and advice on *fiqh* jurisprudence and its relevance to the practice of prophetic medicine.

I felt the inkling of a common language with friends and colleagues whose writings and concerns resonated with mine and interrupted the solitude of writing. From early on, conversations on madness with Tanya Luhrmann and Vincent Crapanzano contributed to the making of this book. Jocelyne Dakhlia and Rosalind Morris offered perceptive readings of a draft of the manuscript, and fostered an enriching exchange with their own work. Michael Jackson and Angela Garcia have been companions in writing, working through spaces of death and healing. Joan Copjec made me feel that it was possible to engage with Lacan in ethnography.

Natasha Schull, Cristiana Giordano, Lisa Davis, Lisa Stevenson, Anand Pandian, Tarek Elhaik, Tahir Naqvi, and Eduardo Kohn were active interlocutors at a formative stage of this work, and continued our conversation through their own remarkable books. The dialogue and friendship with Vyjayanthi Rao, and the spaces she created at the intersection of anthropology and contemporary art, opened new directions for thinking.

Nouri Gana's writings on Arabic poetics and the anti-elegy of violence, his interest in psychoanalysis, and his sense of humor have been a gift. Amira Mittermaier, Bhrigupati Singh, Naveeda Khan, Peter Skafish, Stuart McLean, Satyel Larson, and Christian Suhr Nielsen have been insightful interlocutors and fellow travelers through neighboring regions of thinking and imagining.

The dialogue with Byron Good, Mary-Jo Del Vecchio-Good, and Ellen Corin accompanied my work through the years. Byron and Mary-Jo included me in the generative spaces they created, including the collective work that was *Postcolonial Disorders*. Arthur Kleinman offered comments and reflections on a draft of the manuscript.

Maria Pia Di Bella and Baber Johansen have been interlocutors and caring friends. The conversations with each of them enriched dimensions of the book. The dialogue with Tassadit Yacine and the space she provided with Francis Zimmerman in their seminar at L'École des Hautes Études en Sciences Sociales shaped the inception of this work.

Giorgio Agamben, Didier Fassin, Achille Mbembe, Catherine Malabou, and Pierre Henry-Castel have been critical interlocutors at different critical moments.

The psychoanalysis group at UC Berkeley has been a precious and unique space of discussion. I am grateful to Peter Goldberg, Francisco Gonzales, Deborah Melmann, Alan Tansmann, Irina Paperno, Thomas Zurfluh, Paula Varsano, Soraya Tlatli, Omnia El Shakry, Jake Dalton, Alice Robinson, and Jed Sekoff, for their presence, and for their remarkable reading of *Knot*.

The graduate students and fellow scholars who participated in my seminars at UC Berkeley between 2010 and 2016 ("Madness and Culture," "Violence and Subjectivity," "Trauma and History," "On Psychoanalysis and Islam," "The Temporal and the Intemporal") contributed in a collaborative ethos to the reading and thinking related to the writing and revising of *Knot of the Soul*.

For their insight, inspiration, friendship, comments, art, scholarship, companionship, and for just being there, I am grateful to Niklaus Largier, Lawrence Cohen, Nancy Scheper-Hughes, William Hanks, Helène Mialet, Laura Nader, Mariane Ferme, Alexei Yurchak, Donald Moore, Cori Hayden, Rosemary Joyce, Beth Berry, Eric Glassgold, Abdul JanMohamed, Asad Ahmed, Emily Gottreich, Gil Anidjar, Robert Kaufman, Heriberto Yepez, Damir Arsenijevic, Simona Taliani, Katherine Ewing, Monica Nunes de Torrenté, Tiago Pires Marques, Omar Berrada, Sarah Riggs, Jalal Toufic, Itto Barrada, Zohr Sahli, Abdallah Dagdid, Chris Cochran, Jocelyn Syderlberg, Philip Gerard, Ramzi McGlazer, Shaul Setter, Emilio Spadola, Nadia Guessous, Christopher Polk, Ned Garrett, and, collectively, the colleagues and staff of the Department of Anthropology at Berkeley, which has been one of my homes for the last many years.

At the University of Chicago Press, in addition to David Brent, I am grateful to Michael Koplow, who edited the manuscript of *Knot* with understanding and a skillful touch, and Priya Nelson, who oversaw the book in the final stages and cared for it with attention and engagement.

And my families, in Italy and Morocco. *Knot of the Soul* is also for them. Nives Riccio and Arturo Pandolfo, my parents, who can't read English but are related to this book in invisible ways. Mariachiara, Andrea, and Paolo, my siblings. Dino Riccio, who died in 2009, a psychoanalyst, who introduced me to the unconscious before I knew what it meant, and with whom I feel I can still talk, and al-Hajja Rabi', the late Hajj Abdesalam, Nouzha and Lami'a, and of course Yassine Hamdouni Alami, my son, to whom I dedicate this book.

The author wishes to acknowledge the following publishers for granting permission to reproduce revised versions of sections originally published in their respective journals and books.

Section 1, "Testimony in Counterpoint," is an extensively revised version based on material previously published as "'*Bghit nghanni hnaya*' (Je veux chanter ici): Parole et témoignage en marge d'une rencontre psychiatrique," in "La nouvelle anthropologie du Maghreb" (in French), special issue, *Arabica* 53, no 2 (2006): 232–80 (Leiden: Brill). It was first published in English as "Testimony in Counterpoint: Psychiatric Fragments in the Aftermath of Culture," "Thinking Alterity, Reprise," special issue, *Qui Parle* 17 (Fall/Winter 2008): 63–123 (Lincoln: University of Nebraska Press).

Section 2, "The Hospital," contains a few paragraphs of material that was previously published in "The Thin Line of Modernity: Reflections on Moroccan Debates on Subjectivity," in *Questions of Modernity*, ed. T. Mitchell, 115–47 (Minneapolis: University of Minnesota Press, 2000).

Section 3, "The Jinn and the Pictogram" is a revised version of "'*Nibtidi mnin l-hikaya* (Where Are We to Start the Tale?)': Violence, Intimacy, and Recollection," *Informations en Sciences Sociales/Social Science Information* 45, no. 3 (2006): 349–71 (in English).

Section 4, "The Knot of the Soul," is a revised version of "The Knot of the Soul: Postcolonial Conundrums, Madness, and the Imagination," in *Postcolonial Disorders*, ed. B. Good and M. J.e Del Vecchio Good (Berkeley: University of California Press, 2008), 329–58. It was originally published in French as "Le Noeud de L'Ame," *A partir de Michel de Certeau*, special issue, *Rue Descartes* 25 (1999): 107–24.

Section 5, "*Ta'bīr*: Figuration and the Torment of Life," is an extensively rewritten version of material that was published in "Ramz: La passion d'Ilyas," in *Face aux désastres: Une conversation à quatre voix sur la folie, le care, et les grandes détresses collectives*, edited by Anne Lovell, with Veena Das and Sandra Laugier (Paris: Editions d'Ithaque, 2014), 70–120.

Section 6, "The Burning," is a revised version of material that appeared in "The Burning: Finitude and the Politico-Theological Imagination of Illegal Migration," in "Religion and Globalization," ed. T. Csordas, special issue, *Anthropological Theory* 7, no. 3 (2007): 329–63; and in "The Burning: The Politico-Theological Imagination of Illegal Migration," in *Transnational Transcendence: Essays on Religion and Globalization*, ed. T. Csordas (Berkeley: University of California Press, 2009), 145–84.

Part 3, "The Jurisprudence of the Soul," is an extensive development of material that was published in "Soul-Choking. Maladies of the Soul, Islam, and the Ethics of Psychoanalysis," in "Islam," special issue, *Umbr(a): A Journal of the Unconscious* (2009): 71–103.

Section 17, "Concluding Movement: The Passion of Zulikha, a Dramaturgy of the Soul," is a revised version of material that was previously published in "The Barzakh of the Image and the Speculative Scene of Possession," in *Speculation, Now: Essays and Artwork*, ed. Vyjayanthi Venuturapalli Rao, Prem Krishnamurti, and Carin Kuoni (Durham, NC: Duke University Press, 2014), 168–87.

NOTES

INTRODUCTION

1. Jacques Lacan, "Fonction et champ de la parole et du langage," in *Écrits I* (Paris: Seuil, 1999 [1966]), 279, English translation by Bruce Fink, *Écrits* (New York: Norton, 2006), 232, translation modified.
2. Abū Ḥāmid al-Ghazālī, *The Book of Knowledge* (*Kitāb al-ʿilm*), Book 1 of *The Revival of the Religious Sciences* (*Iḥyāʾ ʿulūm al-dīn*), translated by Kenneth Honerkamp (Louisville: Fons Vitae, 2015), 87.
3. The term *cosmomorphism* is Maurice Leenhardt's in *Do Kamo: la personne et le mythe dans le monde melanésien* (Paris: Gallimard, 1947), translated as *Do Kamo: Person and Myth in the Melanesian World*, trans. Basia Miller Gulati (Chicago: University of Chicago Press, 1979). Post-shaman is from Heriberto Yepez's introduction to *Eye of Witness: A Jerome Rothenberg Reader* (Boston: Black Widow Press, 2013), pointing to an aftermath of prophetic force, when the shaman is left in the position of the witness to the disaster.
4. I am thinking here of the work of psychoanalysts who were engaged in the psychotherapy of psychosis and schizophrenia, in dialogue with phenomenology and anthropology, and for whom the spatiality of the bodily image grounds the fundamental symbolic orientation of self in the world, as, to borrow Gisela Pancow's expression, a first symbolic "rule of exchange": Gisela G. Pancow, *Structure familiale et psychose / L'Être-là du schizophrène* (Paris: Aubier-Montaigne, 1982), 211–22; Piera Aulagnier, *La violence de l'interprétation: Du pictogramme à l'énoncé* (Paris: PUF, 1975).
5. Omnia El Shakry, *The Arabic Freud: Psychoanalysis and Islam in Modern Egypt* (Princeton: Princeton University Press, 2017). El Shakry's work is a crucial contribution to the study of this archive, and to this debate, in Egypt but also in general, inspired by a double immersion and engagement with both psychoanalysis and Sufism, one that is not just historical but also analytic and existential. Through a close engagement with the work of the Egyptian psychoanalyst Yūsuf Murād, and the journal he coedited from 1945 to 1953 (*Majallat ʿilm al-nafs*), and a parallel exploration of the writings of Abū al-Wafāʾ al-Ghunaymī al-Taftazānī and Muḥammad Muṣṭafā Ḥilmī, prominent Egyptian Sufi intellectuals who attempted to inscribe the unconscious within Sufi tradition in the newly founded discipline of psychology, El Shakry poses the question of what might it mean to think the relation of psychoanalysis and

Islam, while also mindful of "the ontological stakes," the place of the divine, in this conversation. Our dialogue through the writing of our respective books has left permanent traces in my work.

6. El Shakry, *The Arabic Freud*; Ibn ʿArabi, *Fuṣūṣ al-ḥikam*, translated as *The Ringstones of Wisdom*, trans. Caner K. Dagli (Chicago: Kazi, 2004); also cited in Fethi Benslama, *La psychanalyse à l'épreuve de l'Islam* (Paris: Aubier, 2002).
7. Jung, of course, but also others in the Freudian lineage (Lacan, Marion Milner), as well as Bettelheim with his *Freud and Man's Soul* (New York: Knopf, 1983). And of course the work of Michel de Certeau, especially *The Mystic Fable*, to which this book is indebted more than I can say.
8. Sigmund Freud, *Civilization and Its Discontents*, trans. James Strachey (New York: Norton, 1961 [1930]), 16–19.
9. Ibid. This point is nicely developed by Michel de Certeau in "Psychoanalysis and Its History," in *Heterologies: Discourse on the Other*, trans. Brian Massumi (Minneapolis: University of Minnesota Press, 1986), 3–16.
10. Freud, *Civilization and Its Discontents*, 11n2, and Freud's letter to Rolland, 19 January 1930. See David James Fisher, "Sigmund Freud and Romain Rolland: The Terrestrial Animal and His Great Oceanic Friend," *American Imago* 33 (1976): 1–59; William Parsons, *The Enigma of the Oceanic Feeling: Revisioning the Psychoanalytic Theory of Mysticism* (New York: Oxford University Press, 1999); and Certeau's discussion of Freud, psychoanalysis, and mysticism in *La fable mystique II* (Paris: Gallimard, 2013), 36.
11. Jacques Lacan, "Tuché et automaton," in *Le séminaire XI, Les quatres concepts fondamentaux de la psychanalyse* (Paris: Seuil, 1973), 53–68.
12. Jacques Lacan, video of lecture at the Catholic University in Louvain, cited in http://www.lacanonline.com/index/2015/07/what-does-lacan-say-about-jouissance/.
13. Michel Foucault, *Histoire de la folie à l'age de raison* (Paris: Gallimard, 1972), translated as *The History of Madness*, trans. Jonathan Murphy and Jean Khalfa (New York: Routledge, 2006).
14. Frantz Fanon, "Racisme et culture," *Présence africaine* (June–November 1956), as the text of Fanon's speech at the first conference of black writers and artists in Paris, reprinted in *Pour la révolution africaine* (Paris: Maspero, 1964), and in *Oeuvres* (Paris: La Découverte, 2011), 713–35, translated as "Racism and Culture," trans. F. H. Chevalier, in *Toward the African Revolution: Political Essays* (New York: Grove Press, 1967); 33–34 of translation quoted here with modification.
15. Fanon, "Racisme et culture," in *Oeuvres*, 717.
16. Ibid.
17. Fanon, "Médecine et colonialisme," in *L'an cinq de la révolution algérienne*, in *Oeuvres*, 361, and "Le syndrome nord-africain" (1952), in *Oeuvres*, 691–703.
18. "Where do you hurt? Everywhere, Doctor." "Today the North African patient who comes to a consultation bears on his body the dead weight of all of his compatriots." Fanon, "Le syndrome nord-africain," 696, 700, my translation. These reflections on "agony" in Fanon are inspired by a discussion of these two texts with Achille Mbembe.
19. Fanon, *L'an cinq de la révolution algérienne*, in *Oeuvres*, 351. My translation.
20. Fanon, "Racisme et culture," in *Oeuvres*, 717, 726.
21. On this point, Gananath Obeyesekere, *The Work of Culture: Symbolic Transformation in Psychoanalysis and Anthropology* (Chicago: University of Chicago Press, 1990). Obeyesekere thinks the "work of culture" in South Asia, between Buddhism and

psychoanalysis, and defines it with Freud and Ricoeur, as a movement of symbolic "progression" and "regression" between the sublimation of culture and the depth of unconscious motivation, on a continuum of symbol and symptom that is the work of the symbol itself. His ethnography traces the agency of cultural symbols when they come to shape lives in unique configurations of "personal symbolism" gravitating for some towards the regressive level of "symptom" and for others towards the progressive level of culture and religious practice. The cases of Abdin (Obeyesekere's informant and friend of many years) and his personal symbolism at the border of psychopathology and the priestess's successful sublimation and creative production of shared religious symbolism are paradigmatic of his approach. The book however does not raise the Fanonian question of a culture in agony as the impairment of the work of culture itself.

22. Fanon, "Racisme et culture," 718. "Ce pseudo-respect s'identifie en fait au mépris le plus conséquent, au sadisme le plus élaboré. La caracteristique d'une culture est d'être ouverte, parcourue des lignes de forces spontanées, généreuses, fécondes."
23. This is a question raised, albeit in a different way, by Veena Das in her book *Affliction: Health, Disease, Poverty* (New York: Fordham University Press, 2015), and in "What Does Ordinary Ethics Look Like?" in *Four Lectures on Ethics: Anthropological Perspectives,* by Michael Lambek, Veena Das, Didier Fassin, and Webb Keane (Hau Books, 2015).
24. Frantz Fanon, *Peau noir, masques blancs* (Paris: Seuil, 1952). I discuss this point in part 3 of the book. A remarkable discussion of this Fanonian question is found in David Marriott, "Inventions of Existence: Sylvia Winter, Frantz Fanon, Sociogeny, and the Damned," *New Centennial Review* 11, no. 3 (2011): 45–90.
25. Fanon, *Peau noire, masques blancs,* in *Oeuvres,* 249–50.
26. Michel de Certeau, *La fable mystique I* (Paris: Gallimard, 1982), 170, my translation.
27. Ibid., 15.
28. I discuss this point and the relevant exceptions (most prominently the work of Fethi Benslama) in the interlude to this volume, "Islam and the Ethics of Psychoanalysis."
29. Adnan Houballah, "La psychanalyse et le monde Arabe," *La celibataire,* no. 8 (Spring 2004).
30. See Maurizio Ferraris, *L'Immaginazione* (Bologna: Il Mulino, 1996), for a history of the faculty of imagination from Aristotle to Freud, with a particular concern for the theme of the trace/imprint.
31. Sigmund Freud, *The Interpretation of Dreams* (New York: Avon Books, 1980), 581 (footnote added in 1914).
32. Jacques Lacan, *Le Séminaire VII, L'Éthique de la psychanalyse, 1959–1960* (Paris: Seuil, 1986), translated as *The Seminar of Jacques Lacan (Book VII): The Ethics of Psychoanalysis, 1959–1960,* trans. Dennis Porter, ed. Jacques-Alain Miller (New York: W. W. Norton, 1997), in particular chapter 11: "Courtly Love as Anamorphosis."
33. Michel Foucault, *Histoire de la folie à l'age classique* (Paris: Gallimard, 1972), 231–32.
34. Particularly through the lens of Henri Collomb and the Dakar (Fann) school of ethnopsychiatry. Collomb was also read at the hospital. See, for instance, "Les bouffés délirantes en psychiatrie africaine," *Psychopathologie africaine* 1, no. 2 (1965): 167–239.
35. Foucault, *History of Madness,* see especially Ch. 1, "Stultifera Navis"
36. Ibid., xxviii.
37. Gladys Swain, *Le sujet de la folie: Naissance de la psychiatrie* (Paris: Calman-Levy, 1997

[1977]), *Dialogue avec l'insensé* (Paris: Gallimard, 1993), and (with Marcel Gauchet) *La pratique de l'esprit humain* (Paris: Gallimard, 1980), translated as *Madness and Democracy: The Modern Psychiatric Universe*, trans. Catherine Porter (Princeton: Princeton University Press, 1999).

38. Michel Foucault, "Dream, Imagination, and Existence," introduction to Ludwig Binswanger's *Dream and Existence* (Atlantic Highlands, NJ: Humanities Press, 1993 [1955]).
39. Muhammad Asad's translation.
40. This is how Muhammad Asad translates the term *al-ghayb*.
41. Freud, *The Interpretation of Dreams*, 129.
42. Sayyid Qutb, *In the Shade of the Qur'an*, vol. 10, trans. Adil Salahi (Leicester: The Islamic Foundation, 1965). On Qutb's modernist realism, see Jane Idelman Smith and Yvonne Yazbeck Haddad, *The Islamic Understanding of Death and Resurrection* (Oxford: Oxford University Press, 2002).
43. In the Bible, but also in the Sufi retelling of the story of Yūsuf and Zulaykha, as in the fifteenth-century mystical poem by Jami, and described in an appendix to Abdullah Yusuf Ali's translation of chapter 12 of the Qur'an.
44. See variously Eric Ormsby, *Theodicy in Islamic Thought: The Dispute over al-Ghazali's Best of All Possible Worlds* (Princeton: Princeton University Press, 1984); Sherman A. Jackson, *Islam and the Problem of Black Suffering* (New York: Oxford University Press, 2009); Navid Kermani, *The Terror of God: Attar, Job, and the Metaphysical Revolt*, trans. Wieland Hoban (Cambridge: Polity, 2011); and Nasrin Rouzati, *Trials and Tribulation in the Qur'an: A Mystical Theodicy* (Berlin: Gerlach Press, 2015).
45. Ibn 'Arabi, *The Ringstones of Wisdom*, 98.
46. Sigmund Freud, *Project for a Scientific Psychology* (1885); *Case Studies in Hysteria* (1895); *The Uncanny* (1919); *Beyond the Pleasure Principle* (1920); *Civilization and Its Discontents* (1930).
47. Sigmund Freud, letter 197, cited in Nata Minor, "Vienna ou le lieux des naissance," an appendix to Serge Leclaire, *On tue un enfant: un essai sur le narcissisme primaire et la pulsion de mort, suivi d'un texte de Nata Minor* (Paris: Seuil, 1975), translated as *A Child Is Being Killed: On Primary Narcissism and the Death Drive*, trans. Marie-Claude Hays (Stanford: Stanford University Press, 1998).
48. Jean-Bertrand Pontalis, "Le travail de la mort," in *Entre le rêve et la douleur* (Paris: Gallimard, 1977).
49. Jacques Lacan, "Le problème du style et la conception psychiatrique des forms paranoiaques de l'expérience," *Revue Minotaure*, June 1933, reprinted in Lacan, *De la psychose paranoiaque dans ses rapports à la personnalité* (Paris: Seuil, 1975). I use the term "countermove" in a Benjaminian sense: the countermove of "historical materialism when it enlists the services of theology," from his first thesis on history.
50. Lacan, "Propos sur la causalité psychique" (1946), translated as "Presentation on Psychical Causality," in *Écrits*, trans. Bruce Fink (New York: W. W. Norton, 2002), 123–60.
51. Lacan, *Écrits* (Paris: Seuil, 1966), vol. 1, 175; English translation, 144.
52. I was inspired to revisit the early writings of Lacan by Soraya Tlatli's insightful work, *Le psychiatre et ses poètes: essai sur le jeune Lacan* (Paris: Tchou, 1999). See also her *La folie lyrique: Essai sur le surréalisme et la psychiatrie* (Paris: L'Harmattan, 2004).
53. Maurice Blanchot, *L'espace littéraire* (Paris: Gallimard, 1955), translated as *The Space of Literature*, trans. Ann Smock (Lincoln: University of Nebraska Press, 1982).

54. William Chittick, *The Sufi Path to Knowledge: Ibn al-ʿArabi's Metaphysics of Imagination* (Albany: State University of New York Press, 1989), 116 ff.
55. Muhsin Mahdi, *Ibn Khaldun's Philosophy of History* (London: Ruskin House, 1957), 63–73.
56. Marion Milner, *The Hands of the Living God: An Account of a Psycho-Analytic Treatment* (New York: Routledge, 2011 [1969]), and Adam Phillips, introduction to the volume.
57. Frantz Fanon, "Guerre coloniale et troubles mentaux," in Fanon, *Oeuvres*, translated as "Colonial War and Mental Disorder," in *The Wretched of the Earth*, trans. Richard Philcox (New York: Grove Press, 2004).
58. David Marriott, "Inventions of Existence," 64.
59. Ibn Khaldun, *The Muqaddima: An Introduction to History*, 3 vols., trans. Franz Rosenthal (Princeton: Bollingen Series, 1956), vol. 1, 64–65.
60. See Didier Fassin and Richard Rechtman, *The Empire of Trauma: An Inquiry into the Condition of Victimhood* (Princeton: Princeton University Press, 2009), and Janet Roitman, *Anti-Crisis* (Durham: Duke University Press, 2014).
61. Albert Hourani, *A History of the Arab People* (Cambridge: Harvard University Press, 1991); Marshall Hodgson, *The Venture of Islam: Conscience and History in a World Civilization*, 3 vols. (Chicago: University of Chicago Press, 1974); Eugene Rogan, *The Arabs: A History* (New York: Basic Books, 2009); Abdallah Laroui, *Les origines sociales et culturelles du nationalisme marocain (1830–1912)* (Paris: Maspero, 1977).

ONE. TESTIMONY IN COUNTERPOINT

1. Fanon, "Racisme et culture," 34–35, translation modified.
2. Jacques Lacan, *Le Séminaire III: Les psychoses, 1955–1956*, ed. Jacques-Alain Miller (Paris: Seuil, 1981), 29; translated as *The Seminar of Jacques Lacan (Book III): The Psychoses, 1955–56*, trans. Russell Grigg (New York: Norton, 1993), 20, translation modified.
3. See, for instance, Allan Young, *The Harmony of Illusions: Inventing Post-Traumatic Stress Disorder* (Princeton: Princeton University Press, 1997); Didier Fassin and Richard Rechtman, *The Empire of Trauma: An Inquiry into the Condition of Victimhood*, trans. Rachel Gomme (Princeton: Princeton University Press, 2009).
4. Walter Benjamin, "The Task of the Translator," in *Illuminations*, ed. Hannah Arendt, trans. Harry Zohn (New York: Schocken, 1968); and Lacan, *The Psychoses*.
5. *Qātil r-rūḥ* in a poetic idiom means a "murderer," but I prefer to preserve the letter of the phrase in translation. *Rūḥ* (spirit, soul) is a common way to refer to life.
6. According to the law that regulates psychiatric hospitalization (*Dahir Royal* of April 30, 1959, to which I will return), hospitalization in the form of a "mise en observation" cannot exceed fifteen days (art. 14), but it can be extended by the decision of the psychiatrist in charge for up to two months, in view of completing the treatment (art. 18).
7. In classical Arabic *al-ḥumq* means foolishness or stupidity, unsoundness in the intellect or want thereof, and it also connotes intoxication (Edward William Lane, *An Arabic-English Lexicon* [London: William & Norgate, 1863], 646). In the vernacular use, however, this term merges with the more radical meaning of *al-junūn*: madness, insanity, and possession.
8. The nouns *al-junūn* and *al-jinna*, from the verbal root *j-n-n*, are translated as "madness," or in some cases "possession." For a discussion of the semantic configuration of *j-n-n* see section 3 below.

9. In Arabic humoral medicine, madness (*al-junūn*) is caused by burned yellow bile (Arabic *al-ṣafrā'*), the dry and hot humor, which in its burned and hence corrupt version affects the brain, causing illness to occur, or by burned and hence corrupt black bile (*al-sawdā'*), which infiltrates the brain and causes hallucination and fury, or instead falling and loss of consciousness in the case of burned yellow bile, and anxiety, obsession, and melancholia associated with loss of reality in the case of burned black bile. See Michael W. Dols, *Al-Majnūn: The Madman in Medieval Islamic Society* (Oxford: Clarendon Press, 1992). I address this question in some detail in part 3 of this book, and specifically in section 13, "Black Bile and the Intractable Jinn."
10. In her ethnography of mourning rituals in Greece, Nadia Seremetakis elaborates an "ethics of antiphony," underscoring the weaving of the social fabric made possible by the communal act of singing laments. "In Greek the concept of *antifonisi* (antiphony) possesses a social and juridical sense in addition to its aesthetic, musical, and dramaturgical uses. Antiphony can refer to the construction of contractual agreement, the creation of symphony by opposing voices." *The Last Word: Women, Death, and Divination in Inner Mani* (Chicago: University of Chicago Press, 1991), 102.
11. Ibid.
12. I borrow the contrastive pair miracle/catastrophe from chapter 4 of Giorgio Agamben's *Lo stato d'eccezione* (Turin: Bollati Boringhieri, 2003), translated as *State of Exception*, trans. Kevin Attel (Chicago: University of Chicago Press, 2005), where Agamben opposes Carl Schmitt's theologico-political notion of the miracle to Benjamin's messianic and anomic vision of catastrophe.
13. "*Shahāda* [is] the general term for both the form and the content of 'witnessing.' As form, *shahāda* refers both to the initiating act of witnessing as sensual perception and to the subsequent act of witnessing as verbal production, that is, as testimony in court. As content, *shahāda* refers to the substance of what is perceived, carried, conveyed and recorded." Brinkley Messick, "Evidence: From Memory to Archive," *Islamic Law and Society* 9, no. 2 (2002): 235.
14. Jacques Lacan, "Fonction et champ de la parole et du langage," *Écrits* I (Paris: Seuil, 1966), p. 297, translated in Bruce Fink, *Ecrits: A Selection* (NY: Norton, 2002), 84, translation modified.
15. Michel de Certeau, *La fable mystique (XVIe–XVIIe siècle)*, vol. 1 (Paris: Gallimard, 1982), 257–73. "Cet esprit est en quête d'un lieu, comme vacant . . . L'imaginaire fournit à cet esprit un lieu métaphorique, une demeure empruntée. Ce sera une fiction de l'âme, la production d'une 'demeure' (*morada*) qui n'est pas la sienne, un lieu fictif permettant l'expression d'un parler qui n'a pas de lieu propre où se faire entendre." Translated as *The Mystic Fable, Vol. 1: The Sixteenth and Seventeenth Centuries*, trans. Michael B. Smith (Chicago: University of Chicago Press, 1992), 189.
16. Sigmund Freud, *Beyond the Pleasure Principle*, trans. James Strachey (New York: Norton, 1961 [1921]).
17. Melanie Klein's account of her psychoanalysis of a ten-year-old boy during World War II is a prominent exception. Klein, *Narrative of a Child Analysis* (The International Psychoanalytic Library, 1961), as well as the work of Abraham and Torok and others that I discuss later in the book.
18. Kateb Yacine, *Nedjma* (Paris: Seuil, 1956), trans. Richard Howard (Charlottesville: University of Virginia Press, 1991), 232 (of English translation).
19. Ibid.

20. Ibid., 174 (French).
21. The oneiric dimension of traumatic memory takes the forefront of the scene in literary works in the Maghreb and the Middle East, and has been taken up in some anthropological works. We see here the central place of the phantasm in *Nedjma*, as well as its relationship to a primordial violence, colonial or otherwise. The space of the dream is also in the forefront of Mohammed Dib, *Qui se souvient de la mer* (Paris: Seuil, 1963), translated as *Who Remembers the Sea*, trans. Louis Tramaine (Washington, DC: Three Continents Press, 1984), where the Algerian war is transfigured into the mythical tale of an underground world, for the horror, Dib tells us, can be represented only through mythical or legendary forms. In Morocco, Edmond Amran El Maleh's *Parcours immobile* (Paris: Maspéro, 1980) depicts the disaster of memory, its vertigo and shattering into fragments, through an autobiography compiled in geological "strata" in which the stories of the individual characters intertwine with collective historical ruptures of the country, giving way to a metamorphic exchange of life with death that has been the experience of the subject in Morocco in the aftermath of colonization.
22. Kateb Yacine, *Nedjma*, 176 (French), 234 (English).
23. Sigmund Freud, "Thoughts for the Times on War and Death," *The Standard Edition of Complete Psychological Works of Sigmund Freud*, vol. 14 (1914–16), trans. James Strachey (Psychoanalytic Electronic Publishing, 2015).
24. I use foreclosure (*forclusion*) in the Lacanian sense as an exclusion/repudiation/obliteration from the order of what can be thought and experienced. Distinct from the Freudian mechanism of "repression" (*Verneinung*), related to the Freudian concept of *Verwerfung* (rejection or repudiation), and associated with the mechanism of psychosis, foreclosure is the exclusion of a thought or an experience, from the realm of what can be symbolically elaborated, even unconsciously. What is foreclosed can return only in what Lacan called "the real," as a delusional fragment and an inassimilable traumatic return. See Lacan, *The Psychoses*.
25. The expression "dictatorship of health" (*la dictature de la santé*) is taken from Dr. Jules Colombani, *Le Ministère de la santé et de l'hygiène publique au Maroc* (Rabat: Blanc et Gauthier, 1924). See also Richard C. Keller, *Colonial Madness: Psychiatry in French North Africa* (Chicago: University of Chicago Press, 2007).
26. Inasmuch as this part 1 of the book addresses an instance of radical questioning of symbolic references, Geertz's thought on culture must be taken into account for its contribution to the study of the loci of symbolic reference in Morocco. See Clifford Geertz, *Islam Observed: Religious Development in Morocco and Indonesia* (New Haven: Yale University Press, 1968), as well as his "Centers, Kings, and Charisma: Reflections on the Symbolics of Power," in *Local Knowledge: Further Essays on Interpretive Anthropology* (New York: Basic Books, 1982), 121–46, and "Suq: The Bazaar Economy in Sefrou," in *Meaning and Order in Moroccan Society: Three Essays in Cultural Analysis* (Cambridge: Cambridge University Press, 1979). But it also, and more importantly, must be attended to because of the secret yet foundational relationship that his thought of culture entertains with the loss of all sense and the experience of madness. For Geertz, culture as a symbolic form is the anchorage and guarantee of meaning, and of the possibility of the human, yet it is also the trace of an always lingering threat that the system of references may fail, unleashing an affective experience of radical insecurity, the realization of "being adrift in an absurd world." Clifford Geertz, "Religion as a Cultural System," in *The Interpretation of Cultures* (New York: Basic Books, 1973), 87–125. Geertz never stopped pondering this

fundamental fragility of the human, seeking to understand how other "cultures" ask the question of meaning and represent the anguish of its loss. See, for example, Geertz, "Person, Time, and Conduct in Bali," in *The Interpretation of Cultures*, 360–411. Yet his preoccupation with a totalizing conception of meaning, inscribed in a fundamental cognitive matrix, a cultural "blueprint" upon which human beings are assumed to be psychophysically dependent, is exposed to the danger of radical madness: contrast the discussion of the figure of *fitna* in "Suq: The Bazaar Economy in Sefrou" with that of the *fitna* of life-death in Pandolfo, *Impasse of the Angels: Scenes from a Moroccan Space of Memory* (Chicago: University of Chicago Press, 1997), 81–103. It is also a major obstacle to apprehending subjectivity in situations of historical transformation, where one must be able to think the self in the midst of failing symbolic references, and where meaning is born, if at all, as the work of mourning of a "present in ruins." A certain cultural absolutism is also at work in the renaissance of ethnopsychiatry, and the painful questioning of belonging that is expressed in the illness can seldom be heard. See, for example, Tobie Nathan, *L'influence qui guérit* (Paris: Odile Jacob, 1994).

27. See Stefania Pandolfo, "The Thin Line of Modernity: Some Moroccan Debates on Subjectivity," in *Questions of Modernity*, ed. Timothy Mitchell (Minneapolis: University of Minnesota Press, 2000), 115–45; and Cristiana Giordano, *Migrants in Translation: Caring and the Logics of Difference in Contemporary Italy* (Berkeley: University of California Press, 2014).
28. On this point I refer to the work of Piera Aulagnier and Gisela Pankow, *Structure familiale et psychose* (Paris: Aubier-Montaigne, 1983).
29. Piera Aulagnier, *La violence de l'interprétation* (Paris: PUF, 1975), 192.
30. In Moroccan law, prior to the October 2003 reform of the *Mudawwana* (family code), if a woman had been repudiated because she was found not to be a virgin while she was supposed to be one, the woman's father would have been required to return the dowry. However, if the woman's virginity was attested by a medical certificate of virginity (*shahādat al-bakara*), divorce could not take place on this basis. Amina is reclaimed in marriage by the spouse's family because the certificate of virginity she produced forced them to pursue the divorce on different terms. Once the marriage is consummated, the woman has the right to keep the dowry.
31. Per Moroccan family law prior to the reform, Amina or her father may not oppose the divorce, since the husband has a unilateral right to divorce (this is also what Amina says: "Women don't have a chance; if he wants to divorce, he divorces"). The *Mudawwana* that was ratified by the Moroccan parliament in 2003 changes the law on this point, at least in the text, since a husband no longer has the unilateral right to divorce nor can he repudiate his wife, while a woman on the other hand has the right to ask for divorce. Divorce becomes a civil transaction, which can be pronounced only at the tribunal and by a judge. It is the judge who decides the conditions. In Amina's case, according to the new law, the judge could have found her in her lawful right, accorded her a pension, and sentenced the husband to pay it. The new law does not mention virginity (*al-bakara*), which nonetheless remains customary, and is routinely mentioned in marriage contracts. For a discussion of Moroccan family code and its relationship with the shariʿa, see Jamila Bargach, *Orphans of Islam: Family, Abandonment, and Secret Adoption in Morocco* (Lanham: Rowman and Littlefield, 2002).
32. For an ethnography of the vocabularies of dreaming and poetry in the Moroccan south, see Pandolfo, *Impasse of the Angels*, as well as Vincent Crapanzano, "Saints,

Jnun, and Dreams," in *Hermes' Dilemma and Hamlet's Desire: On the Epistemology of Interpretation* (Cambridge: Harvard University Press, 1992), 239–59.

33. Refer to part 3 for further discussion of "falling."
34. The sanctuary, as *zāwiya* or simply *sayyid* (place of a saint, *sayyid* or *walī*) and in general the institution of sainthood understood as protection, mediation, and symbolic reference point, is also a classical topos in the anthropology of the Maghreb, from the colonial period onward. Edward Westermark, *Ritual and Belief in Morocco* (London: Macmillan, 1926); Edmond Doutté, *Magie et religion dans l'Afrique du Nord* (Paris: Geuthner, 1908); Émile Dermenghem, *Le Culte des saints dans l'Islam maghrébin* (Paris: Gallimard, 1954); as well as Clifford Geertz, *Islam Observed*; Vincent Crapanzano, *The Hamadsha: A Study in Moroccan Ethnopsychiatry* (Chicago: University of Chicago Press, 1978); Jalil Bennani, *La psychanalyse au pays des saints* (Rabat: Eddif, 1996); Halima Ferhat, *Le soufisme et les Zaouyas au Maghreb* (Casablanca: Toubkal, 2003); and Abdelahad Sebti, *Ville et figure du charisma* (Casablanca: Tubkal, 2003).
35. See Janis Jenkins, "Ethnopsychiatric Interpretations of Schizophrenic Illness: The Problem of *Nervios* within Mexican-American Families," *Culture, Medicine, and Psychiatry* 12, no. 3 (1988): 106–24.
36. Abdallah Laroui, *L'idéologie arabe contemporaine* (Paris: Minuit, 1969).
37. Donald W. Winnicott, *The Piggle: An Account of the Psychoanalytic Treatment of a Little Girl*, ed. Ishak Ramzy, *International Psycho-analytic Library* 107 (1980): 2 (sec. vii), http://icpla.edu/wp-content/uploads/2013/02/Winnicott-D.-The-Piggle-pp.1-201.pdf/.
38. Michel de Certeau, "The Historiographical Operation," in *The Writing of History*, trans. Tom Conley (New York: Columbia University Press, 1988), 56–113.
39. Kateb Yacine, *Nedjma*, 124 (French).
40. According to the Moroccan law governing the institution and regulation of psychiatric care (Dahīr of 1376/1959, "relating to the prevention and treatment of mental illnesses and the protection of the mentally ill"), hospitalization takes place "either at the request of the patient (*malade*), or that of any public or private person acting in the interest of the patient, his family, or the public order" (article 9). When the request is made by a close relative, and against the consent of the patient, it is filed at the local police station or at the *gendarmerie*. The law specifies that such a request must identify the nature of the relationship or how closely related the parties are, and precisely describe the anomalous behavior displayed by the patient. Following this request the patient is brought to the psychiatric emergency by "police order" (*réquisition de police*), and often in an official vehicle (ambulance of the *protection civile*). Crucially, however, according to this modernist law, conceived for the protection of the rights of the sick, only a psychiatrist can order hospitalization. It often happens that after clinical evaluation patients brought by police order are released.
41. The national identity card having been instituted by the colonial administration, Moroccans were forced to choose a surname (*kunya*), often arbitrary, which in rural or working-class milieux (never in the families of the urban aristocracy) corresponded to an occupation, craft, or desired connotation.
42. Peter Geschiere, *The Modernity of Witchcraft: Politics and the Occult in Postcolonial Africa*, trans. Janet Roitman and Peter Geschiere (Richmond: University of Virginia Press, 1997). The classic ethnography by Jeanne Favret-Saada, *Les mots, la mort, les sorts: La Sorcellerie dans le Bocage* (Paris: Gallimard, 1977), could be rethought in this sense (particularly in light of the appendix on paranoia and collective delusion,

where the discourse of witch accusations is read as a counterdelusion). On the discourse of witchcraft in today's Morocco, and on the context of contemporary Qur'anic cures, see part 3 of this book.

43. *Siḥr* is the bundle in which the witchcraft is hidden, often buried or hidden.
44. See in this context Giorgio Agamben's reflections on the paradox of testimony as at once the possibility and impossibility of speaking, in *Quel che resta di Auschwitz: L'archivio e il testimone* (Turin: Bollati Boringhieri, 1998), translated as *Remnants of Auschwitz: The Witness and the Archive*, trans. Daniel Heller-Roazen (New York: Zone Books, 1999).
45. See Baber Johansen, "Signs as Evidence: The Doctrine of Ibn Taymiyya (1263–1328) and Ibn Qayyim al-Jawziyya (d. 1351) on Proof," *Islamic Law and Society* 9, no. 2 (2002): 168–93. This article brings to light the hermeneutic dimension of oral testimony (by the *shuhūd*) and of evidence in the *fiqh* and in the juridical practices of classical Islam (until the thirteenth century) vis-à-vis what the author regards as an epistemological break in which the concept of circumstantial evidence is introduced—an "indiciary sign" that furnishes objective proof, independent of the oral testimony of the witnesses.
46. Walter Benjamin, "On Language as Such and on the Language of Man," in *Walter Benjamin: Selected Writings, vol. 1 (1913–1926)*, ed. Marcus Bullock and Michael W. Jennings (Cambridge: Harvard University Press, 1996), 62–74.
47. Veena Das, *Life and Words: Violence and the Descent into the Ordinary* (Berkeley: University of California Press, 2006). In a related sense Heonik Kwon has traced the geography and the socio-logics of the uncanny encounters with the ghosts of the dead left unburied in the ravaged aftermath of the Vietnam War. Kwon, *Ghosts of War in Vietnam* (Cambridge: Cambridge University Press, 2008), traces the encounters between soldiers and displaced villagers who died away from their homes, whose bodies were never found and could not be properly mourned, and the residents of distant communities who became directly concerned by their pain and become hosts and adoptive kin for the displaced and homeless souls. In the case of the (ghost) Lotus flower and her relationship with the teenager Bien, it is the experiential and conceptual accessibility of the experience of *xac*, the state of lending one's body to a spirit, and the openness of the surviving community to such an experience of alterity, that makes possible the reburial of the displaced dead and a collective coming to terms with the destruction and the losses of war.
48. Seremetakis, *The Last Word*, 102.
49. Kateb Yacine, *Nedjma*, 176 (French), 234 (English).
50. Many *shaykhāt* were and are artists, women poets and musicians, in communities that reserved an ambiguous status to poetry, song, and the performing arts. The genre of *l-'ayṭa* ("the calling") and some of its great twentieth-century figures, such as Shaykha Hajja Hamounia, Fatma Bint Lhussein, and lHajja Hamdawiya, and in a more general sense the popular music known as *sha'bī*, are related to the music and compositions of *shaykhāt*.
51. Walter Benjamin, "On the Concept of History" [1940], in *Walter Benjamin: Selected Writings, vol. 4 (1938–1940)*, ed. Howard Eiland and Michael W. Jennings (Cambridge: Harvard University Press, 2006), 390–411. See also Giorgio Agamben, *Il tempo che resta* (Turin: Bollati Boringhieri, 2000), translated as *The Time That Remains: A Commentary on the Letter to the Romans*, trans. Patricia Dailey (Stanford: Stanford University Press, 2005).
52. See in this context the work of Nicolas Abraham, a psychoanalyst of trauma, on

rhythm, the cipher, and the symptom-symbol in psychoanalysis and poetics, *Rythmes* (Paris: Flammarion, 1985), and in particular on the notion of "la conscience rhytmisante," in the chapter "Pour une esthétique psychanalytique: le temps, le rythme, et l'inconscient."

53. See Stefania Pandolfo, "Rapt de la voix," *Awal: Cahiers d'études berbères* 15 (1997): 31–50, for an analysis of the technique of *ṣar*ʿ (annihilation, of the patient *and* the jinn).
54. See Robert Castel, *L'ordre psychiatrique* (Paris: Minuit, 1976); Erving Goffman, *Asylums* (New York: Anchor Books, 1961); Franco Basaglia, *Scritti*, vols. 1 and 2 (Turin: Einaudi, 1981); Michel de Certeau, "Language Altered: The Sorcerer's Speech," in *The Writing of History*, 244–68; Certeau, *The Possession at Loudun*, trans. Michael B. Smith (Chicago: University of Chicago Press, 2000); Michel Foucault, *Psychiatric Power: Lectures at the Collège de France, 1973–74*, trans. Graham Burchell (New York: Palgrave, 2006); Mohamed Boughali, *Sociologie des maladies mentales au Maroc* (Casablanca: Afrique-Orient, 1988), chap. 2, "La Folie hospitalisée"; and Alain Ehrenberg and Anne Lovell, *La maladie mentale en mutation* (Paris: Odile-Jacob, 2001).
55. Cf. Pandolfo, *Impasse of the Angels*, 246–95.
56. I owe this comparative reference as well as the development of the notion of *al-ṣawt* in classical Arab literature to Mohammed Hamdouni Alami, *Art and Architecture in the Islamic Tradition: Aesthetics, Politics, and Desire in Early Islam* (London: IB Tauris, 2011), 50–51.
57. Adonis, *An Introduction to Arabic Poetics*, trans. Catherine Cobham (Austin: University of Texas Press, 1990).
58. Theodor W. Adorno, "The Function of Counterpoint in Modern Music," in *Sound Figures*, trans. Rodney Livingstone (Stanford: Stanford University Press, 1999), 127.
59. Ibid., 129.
60. Ibid., 128.
61. Ibid., 126–27. One might compare Amina's song and its relationship to a sociocultural code that is simultaneously perceived as dispossessing/annihilating the subject and as instantiating the law (in the case of Amina, the dispossession is literal), with the impromptu poems sung by the Egyptian women from the western desert, as reckoned by Lila Abu-Lughod, *Veiled Sentiments: Honor and Poetry in a Bedouin Society* (Berkeley: University of California Press, 1986). In my reading of the story of Amina, however, and by the notion of "voice," I place the accent on an irreconcilable tension, one that can never be resolved as complementarity, of a multiplicity of conflicting institutional codes, and an impossibility of inhabiting the locus of symbolic reference, which is experienced as threatening and potentially lethal. I interpret Amina's song as the crystallization of such a tension.
62. Donald W. Winnicott, "Fear of Breakdown," in *Psychoanalytic Explorations* (Cambridge: Harvard University Press, 1989), 82.
63. Ibid.
64. In Fanon's letter of resignation to the "Ministre Resident," he writes: "La folie est l'un des moyens qu'a l'homme de perdre sa liberté. Et je puis dire que, placé à cette intersection, j'ai mesuré avec effroi l'ampleur de l'alienation des habitants de ce pays. Si la psychiatrie est la technique médicale qui se propose de permettre à l'homme de ne plus être étranger à son environnement, je me dois d'affirmer que l'Arabe, aliéné permanent dans son pays, vit dans un état de dépersonnalisation absolue. (. . .) Une société qui accule ses membres à des solutions de désespoir est une société non viable, une société à remplacer." Fanon, *Œuvres*, 734–35.

65. Byron Good, with Subandi and Mary-Jo DelVecchio Good, "Le sujet de la maladie mentale: Psychose, folie furieuse, et subjectivité en Indonésie," in *La Maladie mentale et mutation: Psychiatrie et société*, ed. Alain Ehrenberg and Anne Lovell (Paris: Odile Jacob, 2001), 163–96; as well as Mary-Jo DelVecchio Good, Sandra Teresa Hyde, Sarah Pinto, and Byron J. Good, *Postcolonial Disorders* (Berkeley: University of California Press, 2008).
66. Certeau, *La fable mystique, vol. 1*, 41.
67. A poet from the Wad Draa region, cited in Pandolfo, *Impasse of the Angels*, translation from Arabic modified.

TWO. THE HOSPITAL

1. Abdallah Laroui, *L'idéologie arabe contemporaine* (Paris: Maspero, 1967), 37, 66, my translation.
2. He later with some of his colleagues published a useful account of the colonial and postcolonial history of Moroccan psychiatry: M. Paés, J. Toufic, A. Ouannes, and F. El Omari, "La psychiatrie au Maroc," *L'information psychiatrique* 81 (2005): 471–80.
3. "Rien à faire de durable, en matière d'assistance publique si la mentalité ambiante n'évolue pas, et c'est cette évolution dont il faut ausculter le degré tous les jours. Je ne citerai, pour exemple, que les difficultés multiples auxquelles nous nous sommes heurtés pour transformer le régime des aliénés, difficultés non encore résolues." Jules Colombani, *Le ministère de la santé et de l'hygiène publique au Maroc*, (Rabat: Blanc & Gauthier, 1924), 16.
4. Antoine Porot, "Notes de psychiatrie musulmane," *Annales Médico-psychologiques* (1918); see also Robert Berthelier, *L'Homme maghrébin dans la littérature psychiatrique* (Paris: L'Harmattan, 1994); Jalil Bennani, *La Psychanalyse au pays des saints* (Casablanca: Editions Le Fennec, 1996), republished as *La psychanalyse en terre d'Islam. Introduction à la psychanalyse au Maghreb* (Toulouse : Le Fennec/ERES, 2012); Françoise Vergès, *Monsters and Revolutionaries: Colonial Family Romance and Métissage* (Durham: Duke University Press, 1999).
5. Lucien Lévy-Bruhl, *Les fonctions mentales des sociétés inférieures* (Paris: Alcan, 1910), 19.
6. In *La psychanalyse au pays des saints* Bennani analyzes the history and legacy of the Groupe d'étude de psychologie de l'inconscient et de médecine psychosomatique. Even though my discussion relies directly on articles from *Maroc Médical*, I am obviously indebted to Bennani's research and reflections.
7. Maurice Igert, "Introduction à la psychopathologie marocaine," *Maroc Médical*, no. 360 (1955): 1324.
8. Ibid., 1329.
9. Ibid., 1319–21.
10. Colombani, *Le Ministère de la santé et de l'hygiène publique au Maroc*, 1924; *La Protection sanitaire de l'indigène au Maroc*, Conférence faite aux Journées Médicales Coloniales de Paris, 1931. This is how Colombani defined the "Dictatorship of Health": "Civil and military personnel, civil and military equipment, are in the same hands; the entire organization of health obeys a single directing mind, all the beams of the medical network, whose knits grow to cover Morocco in its entirety, are oriented towards a single optical center" (*Le Ministère*, 16). The scope of this all-seeing "health dictatorship" are, according to Colombani, to "recognize the pathological dangers," establish a "medical topography" through a systematic work of "*reconnaissance médicale*" performed by the Groupe Sanitaire Mobile, and above all, keep watch over the movements of population from the "bled," the back country, and develop what he

called *dispositifs de désinfection* ("disinfection devices"), both mobile and stationed at neuralgic geographical junctures, in order to "neutralize all the carriers of errant germs, half-starved, jobless; assemble these crowds outside of the city limits, and send them back in small groups to their respective home regions" (32). While in Colombani's view, "the stage of defense" must precede in the colonies that of *pitié humaine*, the issue of indigenous mentality is central: "Our administrators must have the better of fatalism, smiling or melancholic, both indomitable, must have the better of an ancient milieux, older and more cristallized in its ancient forms than our own . . ."(my translation).

11. I use the notion of incommensurability as it is used in the history of science. Cf. Mario Biagioli, "The Anthropology of Incommensurability," *Studies in History and Philosophy of Science* 21, no. 2 (1990): 183–209.
12. Sigmund Freud, "The Uncanny" (1919), in *The Standard Edition of the Complete Psychological Works of Sigmund Freud*, trans. and ed. James Strachey, vol. 17 (London: Hogarth Press, 1955).
13. The diagnosis of hysteria is still current in French psychiatry. Even though Moroccan psychiatrists are increasingly conversant with the American system, and with the series of DSM diagnostic manuals, a main difference from the US system is the centrality of the category of hysteria.
14. Cf. Josef Breuer and Sigmund Freud, *Studies on Hysteria*, trans. James Strachey (New York: Basic Books, 1987 [1895]).
15. Suggestion works *per via di porre*, as Leonardo said of painting, and analysis *per via di levare*, like sculpture—for, says Freud, "it takes away from the rough stone all that hides the statue contained in it." "On Psychotherapy" (1904), in *Therapy and Technique* (New York: MacMillan, 1963).
16. Jacques Lacan, "The Function and Field of Speech and Language in Psychoanalysis."

THREE. THE JINN AND THE PICTOGRAM: "THE STORY OF MY LIFE"

1. *Lisān al-ʿarab*, by Ibn al-Manẓūr (circa 1311), first printed edition 1892; see Stefania Pandolfo, *Impasse of the Angels: Scenes from a Moroccan Space of Memory* (Chicago: University of Chicago Press, 1997), 158.
2. E. W. Lane, *Arabic-English Lexicon* (London: Williams and Norgate, 1863), 463.
3. Sigmund Freud, *Massenpsychologie und Ich-Analyse* (Leipzig: Internationaler Psychoanalytischer Verlag, 1921), translated as *Group Psychology and the Analysis of the Ego*, trans. James Strachey (New York: Norton, 1959).
4. I develop this point extensively in part 3 of this book, "The Jurisprudence of the Soul."
5. Quoted from the hospital file.
6. Deborah Kapchan, *Traveling Spirit Masters* (Middletown, CT: Wesleyan University Press, 2007); Abdelhafid Chlyeh, *Les Gnaouas du Maroc: itinéraires initiatiques, transe et possession* (Casablanca: Le Fennec/La pensée sauvage, 1999); Timothy Abdallah Fuson, "Musicking Moves and Ritual Grooves across the Moroccan Gnawa Night," Ph.D. dissertation, University of California at Berkeley, 2009.
7. She was for a time at the Sanctuary of Bouyya 'Omar in the region of Marrakesh, where for decades patients with severe psychiatric conditions were taken by their family and left with the caretakers of the saint in exchange for a monthly pension. In 2015 more than 700 patients were evacuated by the police under orders of the Ministry of Health, and the facilities were closed (on the charge of fraud and false therapeutic promise). Following the evacuation, however, only a few of those

patients could be absorbed by the psychiatric system and receive care. As mentioned in the press, the majority have not, and many have become homeless ("Au Maroc le martyre des fous enchainés du mauselé de Bouya Omar," *Le Monde*, June 17, 2016). On the sanctuary as effective and controversial center of healing, see the ethnography by Khadija Naamouni, *Le culte de Bouya Omar* (Casablanca: EDDIF, 1993).

8. A jinn that is *mu'min*, which literally means "faithful Muslim," and hence "submitted to God," is a less dangerous jinn.
9. This is both a somber Moroccan reality and a figure of speech that evokes sexual violence and abuse by the powerful. It is known that wealthy Saudi men like to vacation in Morocco, where many have built villas and palaces, to be entertained by Moroccan woman, sometimes against their will.
10. This a phrase by which Abdel Halim Hafez was referred to in Egypt and, similarly, in Morocco.
11. She is alluding to the tale of Prince Qamar Zaman and princess Badur. But she is also playing with the word *zamān*, and its meaning as part of her own name.
12. Sylvie Le Poulichet, *L'art du danger: De la détresse à la création* (Paris: Anthropos, 1996), 8–9.
13. Freud and Breuer, *Studies on Hysteria*.
14. Piera Aulagnier, *La violence de l'interpretation*, 78.
15. Cf. Ellen Corin, "Living through a Staggering World: The Play of Signifiers in Early Psychosis in South India," in *Schizophrenia, Culture, and Subjectivity*, ed. Janis Jenkins and Robert Barrett (Cambridge: Cambridge University Press, 2004), 110–45; and Janis Jenkins, "Schizophrenia as a Paradigm Case for Understanding Fundamental Human Processes," in Jenkins and Barrett, *Schizophrenia, Culture, and Subjectivity*, 29–61.
16. Sigmund Freud, *Moses and Monotheism* (New York: Vintage, 1967 [1939]).

FOUR. THE KNOT OF THE SOUL (AND THE CERVANTES STAGE)

1. See Didier Fassin, "Santé et immigration: Les verités politiques du corps," *Cahiers de URMIS* 5 (1999); Fassin, "Politique du vivant et politique de la vie: Pour une anthropologie de la santé," *Anthropologie et Société* 24, no. 1 (2000); Fassin, "The Biopolitics of Otherness: Undocumented Foreigners and Racial Discrimination in French Public Debate," *Anthropology Today* 17, no. 1 (2001); Fassin, *Humanitarian Reason: A Moral History of the Present*, trans. Rachel Gomme (Berkeley: University of California Press, 2012).
2. In Fassin's view biolegitimization is not a tactic of resistance, but a strategy of power on the shifting terrain of European capitalist and postnational societies. Its rules are dictated by the ideological and juridical reconfiguration of the republican state, which reproduces inequality and racial exclusion as it promotes the values of *égalité*, and which has come to confer an absolute moral primacy to the nonproductive life of the suffering foreign body. In a context in which eligibility to basic rights is argued and granted on the basis of incurable illnesses (such as AIDS or lead poisoning), one must question the ideological-legal structure of a democratic state to which migrants gauge their bodies in a mortal exchange.
3. Morocco has since had the experience of a truth commission, which concluded its proceedings in December 2005. L'Instance Equité et Reconciliation (IER, *al-Inṣāf wa al-muṣālaḥa*) was created in April 2004 by royal decree with the mandate to investigate and record human rights violations committed since national Independence, and during the kingdom of the late king Hassan II (1956–99). The IER collected

hundreds of testimonies of "victims" (*al-ḍahiya*, the official term) or relatives of deceased victims, and received reparation requests from over twenty thousand victims. See note 29 in section 6, "The Burning."

4. See Philippe Lacoue-Labarthe and Jean-Luc Nancy, "La panique politique," in *Retreating the Political*, ed. Simon Sparks (New York: Routledge, 1997), 1–28; Mikkel Borch-Jacobsen, *Le lien affectif* (Paris: Aubier, 1991), translated as *The Emotional Tie: Psychoanalysis, Mimesis, and Affect*, trans. Douglas Brick and others (Stanford: Stanford University Press, 1992).
5. As was pursued in European phenomenological psychoanalysis, and has recently been attempted, on the basis of different premises, in American cultural psychiatry. See Ellen Corin, "Living through a Staggering World: The Play of Signifiers in Early Psychosis in South India," in *Schizophrenia, Culture, and Subjectivity*, ed. Janis Jenkins and Robert Barrett (Cambridge: Cambridge University Press, 2004), 110–45, and Janis Jenkins, "Schizophrenia as a Paradigm Case for Understanding Fundamental Human Processes," in Jenkins and Barrett, *Schizophrenia, Culture, and Subjectivity*, 29–61.
6. The Moroccan university curriculum for the scientific disciplines, including mathematics, is entirely in French. The social sciences, as well as literature and philosophy, are instead taught in Arabic. At the schools of medicine, architecture, and engineering, instruction is in French.
7. In 2002 illiteracy in Morocco was 62 percent for women and 34 percent for men, with 67 percent of the rural population being illiterate. In 1960 the rate of illiteracy was 87 percent. Secretariat d'Etat Ministère de l'Education Nationale (Bilan, 1997–2003).
8. Reda's accusations mirror and echo the critique of "charlatanism" by Moroccan psychiatrists, for which see above, "The Hospital," and the critique of "false healing" (*al-shawada'*) by the Imam below, on the basis of an argument grounded in Islamic Fiqh (in part 3, "The Jurisprudence of the Soul").
9. In the sense pursued by Victor Turner and Gananath Obeyesekere. See for instance the latter's *The Work of Culture: Symbolic Transformation in Psychoanalysis and Anthropology* (Chicago: University of Chicago Press, 1990).
10. In an essay on Schreber's *Memoir of My Nervous Illness*, Vincent Crapanzano describes a comparable struggle against annihilation, in which "space," "occupation" and "distance" play a fundamental role. Crapanzano, "'Lacking Now Is Only the Leading Idea, That Is—We, the Rays, Have No Thoughts': Interlocutory Collapse in Daniel Paul Schreber's *Memoirs of My Nervous Illness*," *Critical Inquiry* 24, no. 3 (Spring 1998): 737–67.
11. See for instance Bryant L. Creel, "Theoretical Implications in Don Quixote's Idea of Enchantment," *Bulletin of Cervantes Studies* 12, no. 1 (1992): 19–44.
12. Personal communication, Abdelfattah Kilito.
13. Michel de Certeau, "L'opération historiographique," in Certeau, *L'écriture de l'histoire* (Paris: Gallimard, 1975), translated as "The Historiographic Operation," in *The Writing of History*, trans. Tom Conley (New York: Columbia University Press, 1988), 56–113.
14. Fethi Benslama, *La nuit brisée: Mohammad et l'énonciation islamique* (Paris: Ramsay, 1988).
15. Gilles Deleuze, *Critique et clinique* (Paris: Minuit, 1993), translated as *Essays Critical and Clinical*, trans. Daniel W. Smith and Michael A. Greco (Minneapolis: University of Minnesota Press, 1998).

16. The case of Reda has some resemblance with the case of Abdin in Obeyesekere's *The Work of Culture*. Unlike Reda, however, Abdin has at his disposal the symbols of his cultural tradition that allow him to elaborate the destructive relationship with his mother by way of a double identification of the mother: with the vengeful goddess Kali, and a loving mother.

INTERLUDE. ISLAM AND THE ETHICS OF PSYCHOANALYSIS

1. M. Fouad Benchekroun, Radio T Marocaine, August 5, 2008, "Arène génération: La psychiatrie entre tradition et modernisme," roundtable with members of patients associations, a psychoanalyst, a religiously minded physician, and an imam.
2. The Societé Psychanalytique Marocaine, SPM, was founded in Rabat in December 2007, by Drs. Jalil Bennani, Leila Cherkaoui, Abdeslam Dachmi, Farid Merini, Abdellah Ouardini, and Hachim Tyal. Bennani was its first president, followed by Merini. The period between 2001 and 2005 was one of great ferment and activity on the psychoanalytic scene in Morocco and in the Midde East, a fact also generative of tensions between different orientations and groups (as has been the case in the history of the psychoanalytic movement in Europe as well). Some of the founders of the SPM were originally participants in this seminar on psychosis. The convener of the seminar and the "groupe de refléxion" I am discussing here is Dr. Mohammed Fouad Benchekroun, former chef de service of the Hôpital Arrazi in Salé, former president of the Moroccan Psychiatric Association, and psychoanalyst of Lacanian orientation, who, however, chose to remain in the margins of the institutional struggles of this period.
3. Enquête Nationale: Prévalence des troubles mentaux dans la population générale. Ministère de la Santé Mentale et des Maladies Degéneratives, Rabat, Morocco.
4. Association Lacanienne Internationale, Colloque Paris November 2002, "La psychanalyse et le monde arabe"; Association Lacanienne Internationale, Colloque de Beirut, 2004, La psychanalyse dans le monde arabe et islamique, "La psyché (Al-nafs) dans la culture arabe et son rapport à la psychanalyse," Colloque Beirut, May 20–23, 2004, which was also the founding event of the Congrès international des psychanalystes de langue arabe. Association Lacanienne Internationale, Colloque Fes, May 5–8, 2005, "Les trois monothéismes, ce qu'ils ont aujourd'hui en commun."
5. There is an important growth of activities related to the attempt to establish the presence of a psychoanalytic voice in Morocco, in terms of the transmission of knowledge through seminars and conferences, as well as analytic training. See Jalil Bennani, "Histoire d'une transmission: La psychanalyse au Maroc," *Prologues* 33 (Spring 2005); Bennani, *La psychanalyse au pays des saints* (Casablanca: Le Fennec, 1995).
6. For a discussion of the predicament, and the *unheimlich* status of *"les thérapies traditionnelles"* in postcolonial Morocco, see Stefania Pandolfo, "The Thin Line of Modernity: Reflections on Some Moroccan Debates on Subjectivity," in *Questions of Modernity*, ed. Timothy Mitchell (Minneapolis: University of Minnesota Press, 2000), 115–48. Psychoanalysts "comprehended" the symbolic efficacy of these cures in terms of suggestion and a one-to-one correspondence with hysteria, and rejected them as alienating for the subject.
7. In a related sense, see Saba Mahmood, "Secularism, Hermeneutics, and Empire: The Politics of Islamic Reformation," *Public Culture* 18, no. 2 (Spring 2006): 323–47.
8. The Colloque de Fes, "Les trois monothéismes, ce qu'ils ont aujourd'hui en commun"—with Ibn Rushd, St. Thomas Aquinas, and Maimonides in the analytic plat-

form as landmark figures of a kind of critical reason that no longer exists in today's Islam—is symptomatic of this concern.

9. The recent work by Omnia El Shakry develops some of Abdel Qader's history and insight.
10. Hussein Abdel Qader, "La psychanalyse en Egypte entre un passé ambitieux et un future incertain," *La celibataire*, no. 8 (Spring 2004): 61–73.
11. "Avec la mémoire de cet échec, l'Association lacanienne internationale a décidé de valoriser cet héritage de la logique antique et médiévale, non pour le commémorer et s'en tenir à des déclarations de bonnes intentions, mais pour le renouveler en le traitant avec les moyens nouveaux apportés par Sigmund Freud et Jacques Lacan. En redonnant sa valeur à la parole, et donc une place prépondérante à l'altérité, l'un comme l'autre ont fortement contribué à séculariser le champ des croyances tout en permettant de l'analyser scientifiquement, autant dire sans recourir à la passion."
12. Gilles Deleuze, *Critique et clinique* (Paris: Minuit, 1993).
13. Omnia El Shakry, *The Arabic Freud: Psychoanalysis and Islam in Modern Egypt* (Princeton: Princeton University Press, 2017).
14. Ebrahim Moosa, *Ghazali and the Poetics of Imagination* (Chapel Hill: University of North Carolina Press, 2005), 229–31.
15. Adnan Houballah, "La psychanalyse et le monde Arabe," *La celibataire*, no. 8 (Spring 2004), 27, my translation.
16. Moustapha Safouan, *Pourquoi le monde arabe n'est pas libre: Politique de l'écriture et terrorisme religieux* (Paris: Denoel, 2008), 72; translated as *Why Are the Arabs Not Free? The Politics of Writing* (London: Wiley-Blackwell, 2007). In 1995 the members of this group had organized a symposium entitled "Du Droit à la parole," where Moustapha Safouan had presented the basic argument of what was later to become this book on the question of "voluntary servitude" in the Arab world.
17. Ibid., 72, 155.
18. Ibid., chapter 7: "La fraude de l'Etat Islamique et le terrorisme," 147–62.
19. Jacques Lacan, *Le Séminaire VII, L'Éthique de la psychanalyse, 1959–1960* (Paris: Seuil, 1986), translated as *The Seminar of Jacques Lacan (Book VII): The Ethics of Psychoanalysis, 1959–1960*, trans. Dennis Porter, ed. Jacques-Alain Miller (New York: W. W. Norton, 1997), 351 (French), 303 (English).
20. See for instance Charles Melman, *L'homme sans gravité: Jouir à tout prix* (Paris: Gallimard, 2005), and Charles Melman and Jean-Pierre Lebrun, *La nouvelle économie psychique* (Paris: Editions Erés, 2009).
21. See for instance Sylvie Le Poulichet, *L'art du danger*, and, more specifically on the clinic of addictions, *Psychanalyse de l'informe* (Paris: Aubier, 2003); Massimo Recalcati, *Clinica del vuoto: Anoressie, dipendenze, psicosi* (Milan: Franco Angeli, 2002); Jacques Hassoun, *La cruauté mélancolique* (Paris: Aubier, 1995).
22. This line of thinking has been developed by Fahrad Khosrokhavar in his works on martyrdom and suicide in Iran: *Les nouveaux martyrs d'Allah* (Paris: Flammarion, 2002), and *L'Islamisme et la mort* (Paris: L'Harmattan, 1995). Khosrokhavar's diagnostic reading of what he describes as "martyropathy" during the Iran-Iraq War and later in Iran is predicated on the assumption of a "failed" and "oneiric modernity" that entraps the unrealized subject in a self-destructive fantasy that can find violent fulfillment only in death.
23. See for instance Benslama's discussion of Freud's *The Future of an Illusion*, in *La psychanalyse à l'épreuve de l'Islam* (Paris: Flammarion, 2004) translated by Robert Bononno as *Psychoanalysis and the Challenge of Islam* (2009).

24. Ibid., 53 (French). The conceptual imagery Benslama deploys in his text is resonant (perhaps by design) with the hallucinatory corporeality he attributes to Islamist discourse. It would be useful to reread some of the examples he provides in light of an understanding of the body, the organs, the heart, and the soul in the Islamic medical tradition. Already in *La nuit brisée* (Paris: Ramsey, 1988), Benslama seized the articulation of subjectivity in Islam as both specific to the Qur'anic context (as the subject of Revelation) and in dialogue with the Freudian Lacanian subject of desire (via Kierkegaard), and the concept of *parole*. Along those lines Benslama discusses, in the second part of *La Psychanalyse à l'épreuve de l'Islam*, how in Islamic tradition the radical alterity of God guarantees the *Spaltung* of the subject. But that is precisely the configuration of the Muslim subject he sees as collapsing in the Islamic Revival.
25. Talal Asad's *On Suicide Bombing* (New York: Columbia University Press, 2007) dissects the construction of the object "terrorism" and "suicide bombing" in the ever-growing field of terrorism studies in the US, from the idea of "just war" versus terrorist action to the hypostatization of an Islamic "culture of death" with its modern logics of jihād. Asad's is an acute analysis of the (paranoid) imaginary of terrorism and the horror the suicide bomber triggers in "us" (the "us" interpolated by the presymbolic encounter with horror as experienced by the Western liberal subject), as structured by the unthinkable contiguity and irreducible duality of compassion and cruelty, humanism and destruction.
26. Benslama, *La psychanalyse à l'épreuve de l'Islam*, 27.
27. Ibid., 275 (French); 182 (English).
28. Ibid., 274 (French); 183 (English).
29. Cf. for instance the reflection of Nicolas Abraham and Maria Torok on this point, *L'Ecorce et le noyau* (Paris: Flammarion, 1987), translated as *The Shell and the Kernel*, ed. Nicholas T. Rand (Chicago: University of Chicago Press, 1994); and Nicolas Abraham, *Rythmes: De la philosophie, de la psychanalyse et de la poésie* (Paris: Flammarion, 1999). For Abraham and Torok, the capacity to assume a posture open to the transmutation of its own knowledge is defining of psychoanalysis (and subjectivity) as such.
30. One need only think of Freud's acknowledged debt to Aristotle (in the interpretation of dreams, and for the notion of the mnesic trace) as well as to the Neoplatonist tradition of the imagination and the phantasm. Cf. for instance Giorgio Agamben, *Stanze: La parola e il fantasma nella cultura occidentale* (Turin: Einaudi, 1977), translated as *Stanzas: Word and Phantasm in Western Culture*, trans. Ronald L. Martinez (Minneapolis: University of Minnesota Press, 1992).
31. Jacques Lacan, "Le temps logique et l'assertion de certitude anticipée" [1945], republished in *Écrits* (Paris: Seuil, 1966).
32. Saba Mahmood, *Politics of Piety: The Islamic Revival and the Feminist Subject* (Princeton: Princeton University Press, 2004).

FIVE. *TA'BĪR*: FIGURATION AND THE TORMENT OF LIFE

1. See Leïla Kilani's poignant documentary on sub-Saharan and Moroccan undocumented migration, the dream of Europe, and the waiting in Morocco, *Tanger, le rêve des brûleurs* (Rennes: Vivément lundi productions, 2003).
2. See Omnia El Shakry, *The Arabic Freud*.
3. Abu Hamid al-Ghazālī, *The Remembrance of Death and the Afterlife*, trans. T. J. Winter (Cambridge: Islamic Texts Society, 1989).

4. Qurʾan 6:93, 8:52, 9:102. See also Jane I. Smith and Yvonne Haddad, *The Islamic Understanding of Death and Resurrection* (Oxford: Oxford University Press, 2002), 43 ff.
5. Guy de Maupassant, *Le Horla* (Paris: Albin Michel, 1984).
6. Gladys Swain, *Le sujet de la folie: Naissance de la psychiatrie* (Paris: Calman-Levy, 1977), 29, 118–22, 123–30.
7. Hans Prinzhorn, *Artistry of the Mentally Ill: A Contribution to the Psychology and Psychopathology of Configuration*, trans. Eric von Brockdorff (Heidelberg: Springer, 1972 [1923]).
8. Prinzhorn's idea of aesthetic comparability was coopted by the Nazi regime in the 1938 exhibition entitled "Degenerate Art," where the work of banished modern artists such as Klee were debased as mentally deranged. See Bettina Brand-Claussen, Inge Jádi, and Caroline Douglas, *Beyond Reason: Art and Psychosis: Works from the Prinzhorn Collection* (Berkeley: University of California Press, 1998).
9. Ibid., 31.
10. Jean Starobinski, preface to Hans Prinzhorn, *Expressions de la folie: Dessins, peintures, sculptures d'asile* (Paris: Gallimard, 1984).
11. In his reaction there was recognition of a common concern, and of parallel worlds they visited, and perhaps of commonality in the mode of perception. Originally from Marrakesh, Abbès Saladi (1950–92) lived in Casablanca and Rabat. In a video interview recorded shortly before his death he recounts how he began drawing and painting as child in a low-income family, learning as an "*autodidacte.*" In many of his paintings, he suggests, there is the staging of parallel worlds, incommensurable with the world in which we live, where the characters are in a search for truth. In the 1980s Saladi was a patient in the same hospital where Samia sees her psychiatrist as an outpatient, and where I conducted fieldwork in the late 1990s and 2000s. See Farid Zahi, *Abbès Saladi: un monde féerique, 1950–1992* (Casablanca: Marsam Editions, 2006), 43.
12. Edward William Lane, *An Arabic-English Lexicon* (London: William & Norgate, 1863), 673.
13. See for instance the discussion of the concept and practice of *al-wajd* in Gilbert Rouget, *La Musique et la transe* (Paris: Gallimard, 1990), 449 ff.
14. See the introduction to this book, and Ibn al-ʿArabī, *The Ringstones of Wisdom*, trans. Caner K. Dagli (Chicago: Kazi, 2004), "The Ringstone of the Wisdom of Light in the Word of Joseph."
15. Viviana Pâques, *L'Arbre cosmique* (Paris: L'Harmattan, 1995).
16. Aby Warburg, "Dürer and Italian Antiquity," in his *The Renewal of Pagan Antiquity: Contributions to the Cultural History of the European Renaissance*, trans. David Britt (Los Angeles: Getty Research Institute for the History of Art and the Humanities, 1999), 553–731.
17. I take the phrase "poem of life" from Nicolas Abraham and Maria Torok, *The Wolf Man's Magic Word*, trans. Nicholas Rand (Minneapolis: University of Minnesota Press, 1986). That book is their joint rereading or restaging of the case of the Wolf Man, the Russian aristocrat Sergei Pankejeff, who was unsuccessfully analyzed by Freud. Abraham and Torok's work on cryptonomy and poetics in the surrounding of trauma, as well as their attempt to imagine the rhyming of lives, is relevant to my reflection here.
18. Nicholas Abraham and Maria Torok, *The Shell and the Kernel: Renewals of Psychoanalysis*, trans. Nicholas Rand (Chicago: University of Chicago Press, 1994), 153.

19. *Al-fann al-shaklī* is "figurative art," and Ilyas is familiar with this term even though his use of the term *ashkāl* is related to a metaphysical vocabulary of the image.
20. See Sigmund Freud, *The Interpretation of Dreams*, and Georgio Agamben, *Remnants of Auschwitz: The Witness and the Archive*. Agamben moves beyond the simple opposition of witness (as survivor) and witness (to event) in his theory of "signatures": *The Signature of All Things: On Method*, trans. Luca D'Isanto with Kevin Attell (Cambridge: Zone Books, 2009).
21. In Seminar 11 Lacan speaks of the character of "emergence" and "stain" of the images that come to the fore in the dream. Jacques Lacan, *Le Séminaire XI: Les quatre concepts fondamentaux de la psychanalyse* (Paris: Seuil, 1973), translated as *The Seminar of Jacques Lacan (Book XI): The Four Fundamental Concepts of Psychoanalysis*, trans. Alan Sheridan (New York: Norton, 1981).
22. William Chittick, *The Sufi Path to Knowledge: Ibn al-ʿArabi's Metaphysics of Imagination* (New York: SUNY Press, 1989), 115 ff.
23. See Anne Lovell's discussion on fictive genealogies among the homeless mentally ill in New York City, and how what she calls "delusion of identification" does not fit standardized diagnostic criteria, and cannot be considered a "constructed syndrome" (in Ian Hacking's sense). Lovell reads the symptoms as a form of life and collectivity in the space of the city, and as a (psychotic) strategy of life in a context of racialized exclusion and social annihilation. Lovell, "Les Fictions de soi-même ou les délires identificatoires dans la rue," in *La Maladie mentale en mutation: Psychiatrie et société*, ed. Alain Ehrenberg and Anne Lovell (Paris: Editions Odile Jacob, 2001), 127–62.
24. Hans Wehr, *Arabic-English Dictionary: The Hans Wehr Dictionary of Modern Written Arabic*, ed. J. Milton Cowan (Urbana, IL: Spoken Language Services Inc., 1979).
25. On this question of the *ʿibra* as example or admonition, see also the Arabian Nights, where the story/life also functions as example, and its writing of the story "in the corner of the eye," as the tattoo of a moral instruction that shapes the gaze: Abdelfattah Kilito, *L'Oeil et l'aiguille: Essais sur "les mille et une nuits"* (Paris: La Decouverte, 1992), and Elliott Colla, "The Porter and Portability: Figure and Narrative in the Porter's Tale," in *Scheherazade's Children: Global Encounters with the Arabian Nights*, ed. Philip Kennedy and Marina Warner (New York: New York University Press, 2013), 89–107.
26. Ibn al-ʿArabi, quoted in Chittick, *The Sufi Path to Knowledge*, 122.
27. "Par example le dome, la bougie, l'oeil. Ce sont des elements impregnés d'un sens sacré que je percois. C'est pour cela qu'on les retrouve répétés dans tous mes travaux." Zahi, *Abbès Saladi*, 43.
28. Jacques Lacan, *Le Séminaire VII, L'Éthique de la psychanalyse, 1959–1960* (Paris: Seuil, 1986), 58 ff.
29. Giorgio Agamben, *Infancy and History: On the Destruction of Experience*, trans. Liz Heron (New York: Verso, 2007), 24.
30. See Michel Foucault, *History of Madness*, trans. Jonathan Murphy and Jean Khalfa (London: Routledge, 2006).
31. Jalal Toufic, *Credits Included: A Video in Red and Green* (1995).
32. Georges Didi-Huberman, *L'image survivante: Histoire de l'art et temps des phantomes selon Aby Warburg* (Paris: Les Éditions de Minuit, 2002); Aby Warburg, *Images from the Region of Pueblo Indians of North America*, trans. and introduced by Michael Steinberg (Ithaca: Cornell University Press, 1997); Phillippe-Alain Michaud, *Aby Warburg and the Image in Motion* (New York: Zone Books, 2007).

33. Didi-Huberman, *L'image survivante*, especially the part "L'image symptome" and the chapter "Warburg chez Binswanger: Construction dans la folie."
34. Ludwig Binswanger, "The Existential Analysis School of Thought," in *Existence*, ed. Rollo May, Ernest Angel, and Henri F. Ellenberger (New York: Basic Books, 1958), 213.
35. The cases of Ellen West and Ilse are found in "The Existential Analysis School of Thought." The case of Lola Voss is found in Binswanger, *Being-in-the-World: Selected Papers of Ludwig Binswanger*, trans. Jacob Needleman (New York: Basic Books, 1963), 266–341. Cecile Munch and Dr. Ambuhl are patients discussed in Binswanger's *Mélancolie et manie: Études phénoménologiques*, trans. J. M. Azorin and Y. Tatoyan (Paris: PUF, 1987), translated from the German *Melancholie und Manie: Phänomenologische Studien* (1960).
36. A fact that necessarily distanced his "analysis of existence" from Heidegger's emphasis on the shared quality of the quotidian. Binswanger, "The Existential Analysis School of Thought."
37. Ludwig Binswanger, "Dream and Existence," in Binswanger and Michel Foucault, *Dream and Existence*, trans. Jacob Needleman, ed. Keith Hoeller (Atlantic Highlands, NJ: Humanities Press, 1993), 81–83.
38. Michel Foucault, "Dream, Imagination, and Existence," in Binswanger and Foucault, *Dream and Existence*, 54.
39. Ibid., 59.
40. Binswanger, "Dream and Existence," 102.
41. Ibid., 85.
42. Ibid., 90.
43. Ernesto de Martino's concept of "crisi della presenza," in *Morte e Pianto Rituale* (Turin: Bollati Boringhieri, 1998 [1961]).
44. Binswanger, "The Existential Analysis School of Thought," 194.
45. Giorgio Agamben, "Warburg o la scienza senza nome," in *La Potenza del Pensiero* (Vicenza: Neri Pozza, 2005), translated as "Warburg and the Nameless Science," in *Potentialities: Collected Essays in Philosophy*, trans. Daniel Heller-Roazen (Stanford: Stanford University Press, 1999), 98.
46. Aby Warburg (and W. F. Mainland), "A Lecture on Serpent Ritual," *Journal of the Warburg Institute* 2, no. 4 (April 1939): 291.
47. Agamben, "Warburg and the Nameless Science," 98.
48. An emergence of form, as in Botticelli's birth of Venus. Around that image, Warburg traces the nymph and her avatars, all the way to Charcot's hysterical postures and bodies. In *The Signature of all Things*, Agamben proposes a conceptual development of this Warburgian notion in the theory of the signature, understood as codes or ciphers that can activate networks of forces (cosmic and others), an insight that is relevant here. And in *Il percorso e la voce: Un'antropologia della memoria* (Turin: Einaudi, 2002), Carlo Severi offers a reading of Warburg's Pueblo ethnography of forms, with an emphasis on the chimera, suggesting that the image of the chimera is a compound sign/emblem that can activate a reaction through association, channeling the work of the imagination, and that in this sense the Pueblo rituals as well as Warburg's images are devices to "capture the imagination," in turn generating contexts and worlds. See also Severi, "Capturing Imagination: A Cognitive Approach to Cultural Complexity," *Journal of the Royal Anthropological Institute* 10, no. 4 (December 2004): 815–38.
49. Agamben, "Warburg and the Nameless Science," 98.

50. Warburg, "A Lecture on Serpent Ritual," 277, 281.
51. William James, *The Varieties of Religious Experience* (New York: Random House, 1994), 182–83.
52. See Lacan, *The Four Fundamental Concepts of Psychoanalysis*, part 2: "Of the Gaze as *petit objet a.*" For a discussion of the *ʿayn*/eye/source in Moroccan vernacular tradition, see Pandolfo, *Impasse of the Angels*, 25; Abdelkebir Khatibi, *La blessure du nom proper* (Paris: Denoel, 1974); and of course a multitude of Arabic magical texts, as well as an Islamic pietistic literature that addresses the healing of illnesses caused by sorcery (*siḥr*) and the (evil) Eye (*ʿayn*).
53. My use of the concept of "interruption" (the interruption of a divine violence) is inspired by Walter Benjamin, "Critique of Violence," in *Reflections: Essays, Aphorisms, Autobiographical Writings* (New York: Schocken Books, 1978), 277–300. Lacan also made use of the concept of "interruption," which recurs in his writing and is at the heart of his theory of the signifier.
54. Louis Lafont, *L'Apocalypse de Saint Jean* (Paris: Tequi, 1975), sections 12–13. Thanks to Rachid Benzine for pointing out the presence of St. John's Apocalypse in the painting.
55. The question is complex, however, because the line between suicide and martyrdom is sometimes blurred (as explored by ʿAli Shariati in his writings on *shahādat*); and because, as shown in historical and recent legal debates on taking life, inasmuch as suicide (*al-intihār*) can only be determined by the intention of taking one's life, and only God has full access to human motives, the fact that a death is a suicide in many cases is impossible to establish. Cf. Jonathan E. Brockopp, ed., *Islamic Ethics of Life: Abortion, War, and Euthanasia* (Columbia: University of South Carolina Press, 2003).
56. ʿAlī Aḥmad Taḥṭāwī, *Aḥwāl al-qubūr wa mā baʿda l-mawt* ("States of the Grave and What Follows Death") (Cairo: Dār al-Bashīr, 1987).
57. The expression is Veena Das's, in *Life and Words: Violence and the Descent into the Ordinary* (Berkeley: University of California Press, 2006).

SIX. THE BURNING

1. D. S. Marriott, "Only Sleeping," in *Hoodoo Voodoo* (Exeter: Shearsman Books, 2008), 12.
2. Diana K. Davis, *Resurrecting the Granary of Rome: Environmental History and French Colonial Expansion in North Africa* (Athens: Ohio University Press, 2007).
3. Transcript of a conversation tape-recorded in June 2003, in Rabat.
4. Muhammad Khalid Masud, "The Obligation to Migrate: The Doctrine of *Hijra* in Islamic Law," in *Muslim Travellers: Pilgrimage, Migration, and the Religious Imagination*, ed. Dale F. Eickelman and James Piscatori (London: Routledge, 1990), 29–49. And see Qurʾan 4:97–100: "Lo: as for those whom the angels take [in death] while they wrong themselves, the angels will ask: In what were you engaged? They will say 'We were oppressed [weak and humiliated].' The angels will say, 'Was not Allah's earth spacious that you could migrate therein?'"
5. Marshall Hodgson makes this point in *The Venture of Islam: Conscience and History in a World Civilization* (Chicago: University of Chicago Press, 1977), vol. 1.
6. The question of whether eschatological reasoning and imagining presuppose the closure of hermeneutics in the certainty of the end of time, which is also the fulfillment of prophecy, is once again at the center of debate. Most secular interpretations argue in this direction, postulating a fundamental incompatibility between the "closed future" of eschatology and the "open future" of modernity; cf. Reinhart

Koselleck, *Futures Past: On the Semantics of Historical Time*, trans. Keith Tribe (New York: Columbia University Press, 2004). Karl Löwith, however, whose reflection on eschatology and history shaped the early configuration of this debate, points out that eschatological time is hermeneutically open, and more so than the time of modern science understood as calculability and predictability, inasmuch as human beings have no access to the designs of God. Löwith, *Meaning in History: The Theological Implications of the Philosophy of History* (Chicago: University of Chicago Press, 1957). In *The Time That Remains: A Commentary on the Letter to the Romans*, trans. Patricia Dailey (Stanford: Stanford University Press, 2004), Giorgio Agamben revisits this question through a close reading of St. Paul's letter to the Romans with Walter Benjamin's "Theses on the Philosophy of History"—Benjamin's visionary reflection on the experience of *Jetztzeit*, the messianic "now," in which time is interrupted, as a coming of the temporality of the End. In a chapter on the figure of the "apostle" (whose features Agamben recognizes in both St. Paul and Benjamin), which is contrasted with the figure of the "prophet," Agamben distinguishes "eschatological time" from "messianic time." The first is static and incommensurably "distant" in the future, he argues, as the End of Time, while the second is dynamic and "near," immanent, and can be understood as "the time of the end," as experienced in the present moment. Messianic time, in his view, is an intermediate temporality—a "limit" and an "excess"—between sacred eschatological/apocalyptic time, and profane chronological time. Here I implicitly engage with Agamben's discussion of messianic time, but attempting, at least in the context of my ethnography, to overcome the dichotomy.

7. In the last section of *Imaginative Horizons: An Essay in Literary-Philosophical Anthropology* (Chicago: University of Chicago Press, 2002), and as an engagement with the work of Ernesto de Martino in *La fine del mondo*, Crapanzano constructs a comparable opposition between "open" and "closed" millenarianisms and eschatological horizons.
8. Forty-five people were killed in the bombings at five different sites in the business center of downtown Casablanca. Most of the dead were Moroccan nationals. This includes thirteen youths who carried the bombs on themselves. They were all from the same shantytown in Casablanca, Sidi Moumen (population 130,000), and were later described as belonging to a local neo-Salafist group.
9. The Moroccan press from this period, from May 17, 2003 and for several months, was primarily dedicated to attempting to understand, document, and diagnose the situation that might have produced the bombings in Casablanca. The primary concerns were the realization of urban poverty; exclusion, and lack of future for a generation of young Moroccans; and the representation of urban poverty as a factory of violence and religious radicalism. The association of poverty, violence, and terrorism was most prominently made in *Maroc Hebdo*, *la Gazette du Maroc*, *Aujourd'hui le Maroc*, and *al-Ṣaḥīfa*, while other weeklies such as *Le Journal* and *Tel Quel* tried to resist what they called *"l'amalgame."*
10. As documented in the Amnesty International report of May 2004, and later also in the Moroccan press.
11. In recent years there has been a vast literature published on border crosssings in Europe and Mediterranean migration and its tragic forms. As an example of interest here, see Maurizio Albahari, *Crimes of Peace: Mediterranean Migrations at the World's Deadliest Border* (Philadelphia: University of Pennsylvania Press, 2015). A useful compendium of voices and developments is found in the special issue on

the European crisis in *Near Futures*, "Europe at Crossroads: Managed Inhospitality," no. 1 (March 2016).

12. Mohammed Hamdouni Alami, "Gestion urbaine et accés aux services de base" (2006), in "Rapport sur le Développement Humain du Cinquantenaire de l'Indépendance du Maroc," http://www.rdh50.ma. See also SNAT, *Schema National d'Amenagement du Territoire*, bilan diagnostique (Rabat: Direction de l'Amenagement du Territoire, 2004).
13. These points are documented and argued in Hamdouni Alami, "Gestion urbaine et accés aux services de base." Thanks to Mohammed Hamdouni Alami for sharing his vast knowledge of the politics of planning in Morocco.
14. Abderrahmane Rachik, *Casablanca, l'urbanisme de l'insurgence* (Rabat: n.p., 2002).
15. Achille Mbembe, *De la postcolonie* (Paris: Karthala, 2005 [2000]), translated as *On the Postcolony* (Berkeley: University of California Press, 2001).
16. A hadith of al-Bukhārī reports the Prophet's saying, "Let none of you hope for death," cited in a note by T. J. Winter in his translation of al-Ghazālī, *The Remembrance of Death and the Afterlife* (Cambridge: Islamic Texts Society, 1989), 8.
17. Ibn Miskawayh, *Tahdhīb al-akhlāq wa taṭhīr al-a'rāq*, translated into French as *Traité d'éthique*, trans. Mohammed Arkoun (Damascus: Institut Français de Damas, 1969), 166.
18. A literal translation of *al-iḥsān* would be "practicing the good." Mohammed Tozy proposes the translation of "gift of self," as the more precise theological connotation than "bienfaisance," in his *Monarchie et islam politique au Maroc* (Paris: Presses de Science Po, 1999). See also Youssef Belal, *Le cheikh et le calife: Sociologie religieuse de l'islam politique au Maroc* (Casablanca: Tarik Editions, 2012).
19. While the reference to al-Ghazālī remains foundational, the shaykh and the movement as a whole reject today any kinship with Sufism, choosing instead to be associated with modernist currents in the international Islamic Revival. Abdessalam Yassine had, however, earlier been a disciple at an important Sufi *zāwiya* in northern Morocco.
20. Michael Cook, *Commanding Right and Forbidding Wrong in Islamic Thought* (Cambridge: Cambridge University Press, 2001). Note that in her book *Le divan des rois: Le politique et le religieux dans l'islam* (Paris: Aubier, 1998), Jocelyne Dakhlia has questioned the notion that all dissent in Middle Eastern history was cast in religious terms. See also Talal Asad, "Thinking about Tradition, Religion, and Politics in Egypt Today," *Critical Inquiry* 42, no. 1 (Autumn 2015): 166–214.
21. In his book on the practice and the implications of Qur'an cassette listening, Charles Hirschkind argues that the kind of listening associated with this modern and reproducible medium is not passive, but instead constitutive of an ethical self. Listening-performing, or chanting, is an irresolvable couple, and it is in fact understood as such in the Arabic concept of *samā'*, listening (with the heart), which presupposes an active role and creative function. Hirschkind's text engages with the representation of physical death and the relation to eschatological time conjured by Qur'anic recitation, whether live or mechanically reproduced in cassette recordings. Hirschkind, *The Ethical Soundscape: Cassette Sermons and Islamic Counterpublics* (New York: Columbia University Press, 2006).
22. Literally, *l-qarqubi* indicates the agent by which one is turned over (*qarqab*, vernacular onomatopoeic), inside out, or upside down.
23. Their contiguity is reckoned by a much-cited hadith: "Our Prophet said to some people who had just returned from a *jihād* [war]: Welcome, you have come from the

lesser to the greater *jihād.* O emissary of God, he was asked, and what is the greater *jihād*? The *jihād* against your soul, he replied. And he said, The real *mujāhid* is he that wars with himself for the sake of God." Abū Ḥāmid al-Ghazālī, *Kitāb riyāḍat al-nafs wa kitāb kasr al-shahwatayn,* books 22 and 23 of *Iḥyā' ʿulūm al-dīn,* translated as *Disciplining the Soul & Breaking the Two Desires,* trans. T. J. Winter (Cambridge: Islamic Texts Society, 1995), 56. "God has ordained *jihād,* which is of two kinds: fighting the enemy with the sword, and fighting passion and the self with the sword of renouncing one's own will. As recompense for the former struggle, He has promised Heaven, and for the latter, attainment unto Him. For when a man fights an enemy and is killed, he finds the path to Heaven and rejoices in his delight; as for he who fight the self and passion until they are dead, he finds the path to the Throne, to the place of Proximity." Al-Ḥākim al-Tirmidhī, commentary on the hadith above, cited in T. J. Winter's introduction to his translation (lxiii).

24. Al-Ghazālī, *Disciplining the Soul & Breaking the Two Desires,* 25. For further elaboration of the theological concepts discussed in this section, see part 3.
25. *Yakaddar ʿalā al-insān al-ladhdhāt wa al-shahawāt,* [death] spoils for human beings pleasures and longings.
26. In *The Politics of Piety: The Islamic Revival and the Feminist Subject* (Princeton: Princeton University Press, 2004), Saba Mahmood provides a description of contemporary religious pedagogies and a world of practice that share a remarkable resemblance with al-Ghazālī's reflections on spiritual exercises. The book does not engage in a discussion of al-Ghazālī's theological-ethical universe per se, but shows how that tradition is alive in contemporary pedagogical practices in the Egyptian female "mosque movement." Her book attempts to demonstrate the inherent coherence (and specific rationality) of these practices with reference to the discourse from which they draw their orientation. At a moment in which the very possibility of recognizing the existence—and the right to continue to exist—of life forms that draw their ethical and political reason from the universe of Islam, Mahmood's contribution is crucial. While in dialogue with that work, my approach here does not focus on the coherence of a discourse, but on the way this tradition is articulated with and in the lives of particular people, who at times push that discourse to its "limit" (which in a theological sense borders heresy). Second, I suggest that ethical practices in the tradition of al-Ghazālī are predicated on a guided encounter with alterity. This requires a reflection on the limits of reason, and an exploration of what, in William James's terms, might be called the existential edge of experience.
27. Jawad's position could be supported by the literal interpretation of a hadith reported by al-Nawawī: "Actions are but by intentions (*innamā al-aʿmāl bi al-niyyāt*) and every man shall have but that which he intended. Thus he whose migration was for Allah (*hijratuhu ilā llāh*) and his Messenger, his migration was for Allah and his Messenger, and he whose migration was to achieve some worldly benefit (*hijratuhu lil-dunyā*) or to take some woman in marriage, his migration was for that for which he migrated." An-Nawawi, *Forty Hadiths,* trans. Ezzeddin Ibrahim and Denys Johnson-Davies (Cambridge: Islamic Texts Society, 1976), 26. But for Kamal, who is giving a theologico-political reading of the situation from which he seeks to migrate, the "worldly benefit" to be gained in the endeavor is also, as he attempts to show, a spiritual struggle. In his intention (*niyya*), the lower world (*dunyā*) can be the site of a struggle.
28. "Liberating his character from the inherited norms of his race and the conventions of his society—all of which are relative and the product of the environment—and

discovering eternal and divine values, he takes on the characteristics of God and attains the nature of the absolute. He no longer acts virtuously as a duty imposed upon him, and his ethics is no longer a collection of restraints forced upon him by the social conscience. To be good has become identical with his nature." Ali Shariati, "The Ideal Man," in *On the Sociology of Islam*, trans. Hamid Algar (Oneonta, NY: Mizan Press, 2000), 123.

29. It should be added that at around the time when I was conducting these interviews, a truth commission was officially instituted in Morocco to investigate, document, and record human rights violations committed since the early years of Independence, and during the reign of the late king Hassan II (1956–99). L'Instance Equité et Reconciliation (IER, in Arabic *al-Inṣāf wa al-muṣālaḥa*), created in April 2004 by royal decree, collected hundreds of testimonies of victims or their relatives and received over 20,000 requests for reparations by the state. In spring 2005 a number of public hearings were organized by the IER in several cities, widely covered by the media and (for the first time) broadcast on Moroccan television. This process stirred much debate and produced complex and sometimes unintended reactions. For several months it captured public attention, contributing to the feeling (already fostered by the growing importance of reportage and first-person accounts in the programming of Arabic satellite televisions) that the posture of "witness" is a pivotal step in the claim for rights. In spring 2005, public hearings were held by the IER in several cities, covered by the Moroccan and international media. The process stirred many hopes and a heated debate, with complex and unintended outcomes. Yet in the Moroccan situation the equation of witnessing, injury, and citizenship (based on human rights) is less obvious than in other international contexts. Among large unprivileged sectors of the Moroccan population, less conversant than the political elite with the international idiom of human rights, skepticism colored people's perception of the work of the IER, as well as the notion of accessing citizenship through witnessing. The powerful and moving documentary film by Leïla Kilani, *Nos lieux interdits* (Tager: Soccochico Films and Paris: INA, 2008), captures some of this complexity.
30. Cf. Abdellah Hammoudi, *Une saison à la Mecque: Récit de pèlerinage* (Paris: Seuil, 2004), 286: "Chacun était donc parti à la découverte de la vie, dans le parcours qui nous séparait de la mort."
31. See my discussion of dreaming in Pandolfo, *Impasse of the Angels: Scenes from a Moroccan Space of Memory* (Chicago: University of Chicago Press, 1999), esp. 165–98.
32. "Desperation absolute and complete, the whole universe coagulating about the sufferer into a material of overwhelming horror, surrounding him without opening or end. Not the conception or intellectual perception of evil, but the grisly blood-freezing heart-paralysing sensation of it close upon one, and no other conception or sensation able to live for a moment in its presence. How irrelevantly remote seem all our usual refined optimisms and intellectual and moral consolations in presence of a need of help like this! Here is the real core of the religious problem: Help, Help!" William James, *Varieties of Religious Experience* (London: Routledge, 2002 [1902]), 129, cited in part in Charles Taylor, *Varieties of Religion Today: William James Revisited* (Cambridge: Harvard University Press, 2003), 35.
33. Ibn Qayyim al-Jawziyya, *Medicine of the Prophet*, 142–47; some sections of Ibn Qayyim's text are cited in Moroccan oral vernacular poems of an eschatological nature, inciting people to become aware of the unimportance of the material world. Cf. "Inhabiting the Vanishing," in Pandolfo, *Impasse of the Angels*, 275–79.

34. Fethi Benslama, *La nuit brisée* (Paris: Ramsay, 1988). Benslama comments on a passage by Muḥammad b. Jarīr al-Ṭabarī (d. AH 310/923 CE) where it is said that the Prophet had a moment of doubt concerning the true nature of the revelation, for the voices he heard frightened him and made him fear he might be possessed.
35. Al-Ghazālī, *al-Munqidh min al-ḍalāl*, translated by R. J. McCarthy as *Deliverance from Error* (Louisville: Fons Vitae, 1999); one can also think comparatively of Søren Kierkegaard's *The Sickness unto Death* (Princeton: Princeton University Press, 1983 [1849]). See also Abdessalam Cheddadi's chapter on the Qur'an and its fundamental paradox of truth, in *Les arabes et l'appropriation de l'histoire* (Paris: Sindbad Actes Sud, 2004).
36. As found in the twenty-volume dictionary of Muḥammad b. Mukarram Ibn Manẓūr (d. AH 711/1312 CE), titled *Lisān al-ʿarab* ("The Arab Tongue").
37. For instance, Martin Lings, *A Sufi Saint of the Twentieth Century: Sheikh Ahmad al-ʿAlawi, His Spiritual Heritage and Legacy*, 3rd ed. (Cambridge: Islamic Texts Society, 1993).
38. Al-Ghazālī, *Disciplining the Soul & Breaking the Two Desires*, 63–64.
39. James, *Varieties of Religious Experience*, cited in Taylor, *Varieties of Religion Today*, 59.
40. Sylvie Le Poulichet, *L'art du danger: De la détresse à la création* (Paris: Anthropos, 1996).
41. Al-Ghazālī, *The Remembrance of Death and the Afterlife*, 135.
42. Ibid., part 2; and see Jane I. Smith and Yvonne Haddad, *The Islamic Understanding of Death and Resurrection* (Oxford: Oxford University Press, 2002 [1981]).

SEVEN. OVERTURE: A TOPOGRAPHY OF THE SOUL IN THE VERTIGO OF HISTORY

1. Frantz Fanon, "Guerre coloniale et troubles mentaux," in *Les Damnés de la terre* (Paris: Maspero, 1961), reprinted in *Oeuvres* (Paris: La Découverte, 2011), 627, translated as "Colonial War and Mental Disorder," in *The Wretched of the Earth*, trans. Constance Farrington (New York: Grove Press, 1963), 249, 253 (quoting translation with modifications).
2. Abū Zayd ʿAbd al-Raḥmān b. Muḥammad Ibn Khaldūn, *al-Muqaddima, Tārīkh al-ʿallāmat Ibn Khaldūn* (Beirut: Dar al-Kitāb al-Lubnanī, 1967), vol. 1, 220, translated as *The Muqaddimah: An Introduction to History*, trans. Franz Rosenthal, abridged and ed. N. J. Dawood (Princeton: Princeton University Press, 2015), 96 (translation modified).
3. "Sharīʿa healing" should be understood here as lawful and God-empowered healing.
4. *Al-Ṭibb al-nabawī*, "Prophetic medicine," for which see the eponymous text by Ibn Qayyim al-Jawziyya (d. 1350), and its contemporary reinvestment worldwide via the internet. Justin K. Stearns, *Infectious Ideas: Contagion in Pre-Modern Islamic and Christian Thought in the Western Mediterranean* (Baltimore: Johns Hopkins University Press, 2011); Fabrizio Speziale, *Soufisme, religion et medicine en Islam indien* (Paris: Kathala, 2010).
5. "Trial, as meaning a probation, or a test, and as meaning particularly a trouble or an affliction of any kind by which one's patience or any other grace or virtue is tried, proved, or tested; The act of trying, proving, or testing, by or with good, and by or with, evil, a trial, or an affliction, which is its original meaning." Edward William Lane, *Arabic-English Lexicon* (London: Williams & Norgate, 1863), 256–57. *Lisān al-ʿarab*, *f-t-n* (*fitna*); translated from the Arabic in Pandolfo, *Impasse of the Angels: Scenes from a Moroccan Space of Memory* (Chicago: University of Chicago

Press, 1997), 161: "Do men think they will be left alone on saying, We believe, and they will not be tested (*la yuftanun*)? (Qur'an 29:1–2). And in the Commentary this means that they must be tested (*yubtalūn*) in their person/soul (*anfusihim*), and in their wealth, and through the endurance of calamity and evil (*al-balā'*) will be possible to discern sincere from insincere faith."

6. This is not of course just specific to the Imam, or even to the Arabic language, and despite the resonance of this concept in the modulation of the term *balā'*. While making the last round of copyedits to the book I was talking one day with a Senegalese tailor in Paris in his shop, a gentle elderly man. As we talked about the present state of the world, he lamented the resentment and inability to be grateful by which human beings came to see themselves as invulnerable: "It is enough for a tiny fly to enter a person's nose to make that house of cards collapse. They don't understand," he said, "that 'illness is a grace' (*la maladie est une grace*). It makes us realize our place in relation to God."
7. Christian Jambet refers to the becoming of the soul as "the act of being": *L'Acte d'être: La Philosophie de la révélation chez Mollâ Sadrâ* (Paris: Fayard, 2002); translated as *The Act of Being: The Philosophy of Revelation in Mulla Sadra*, trans. Jeff Fort (New York: Zone Books, 2006).
8. Maurice Blanchot, *L'espace littéraire* (Paris: Gallimard, 1955), translated as *The Space of Literature*, trans. Ann Smock (Lincoln: University of Nebraska Press, 1982), 98.
9. Blanchot, *The Space of Literature*, 261.
10. Marion Milner, *The Hands of the Living God: An Account of a Psycho-analytic Treatment* (New York: Routledge, 2011 [1969]), 294.
11. Mohammed Lakhdar-Hamina, dir., *Chronique des années de braise*, 70 mm [1975] (Algeria: Arab Film Distribution, 1997), Panavision Film. The character of Miloud is played by Lakhdar-Hamina himself.
12. Abdelkebir Khatibi, *Maghreb pluriel* (Paris: Denoel, 1983), 17: "Marginalized, minoritized, and dominated . . . this is precisely our chance."
13. For the centrality of the concept of *mulk* (power), see also Abdesselam Cheddadi, interviewed by Olivier Mongin, "Reconnaissance d'Ibn Khaldūn," *Esprit* 11 (November 2005), trans. David Macey as "Recognising the Importance of Ibn Khaldun: Interview with Abdesselam Cheddadi," available online at http://www.diplomatie.gouv.fr/en/IMG/pdf/Cheddadieng.pdf. And see Ibn Khaldun, *Le Livre des exemples*, ed. and trans. Abdessalam Cheddadi, 2 vols. (Paris: Gallimard, 2002–12).
14. Kateb Yacine, *Nedjma* (Paris: Seuil, 1956); trans. Richard Howard (Charlottesville: University Press of Virginia Press, 1961), 202.
15. As stated in multiple places in the Qur'an (e.g., 4:115; 8:53; 13:11). And see Fazlur Rahman, *Major Themes in the Qur'an* (Chicago: University of Chicago Press, 1980).
16. And indeed, as noticed by Wael Hallaq, Muslim thinkers remade Aristotelianism by taking some aspects and rejecting others. On this point see the important new insight from the perspective of Indian and Eastern Islam, and related critique of the colonial and Orientalist Greek-centric focus, by Speziale in *Soufisme, religion, et medicine* and "Linguistic Strategies of De-Islamization and Colonial Science: Indo-Muslim Physicians and the Yunani Denomination," *International Institute for Asian Studies Newsletter* 37 (2005).
17. I have already touched on the status of the imagination in the Islamic tradition in section 5 of this book, where I discuss figuration and creation in Ilyas's paintings.
18. I borrow here an expression from Lacan, who himself takes it from Plato, "le judo avec la verité," wrestling with truth.

19. Sayyid Qutb, *Muqawwimāt al-taṣawwur al-Islāmī* (Cairo: Dar al-Shuruq, 1982 [1962]), translated as *Basic Principles of Islamic Worldview*, trans. Rami David, ed. Hamid Algar (North Haledon, NJ: Islamic Publications International, 2006). Qutb develops here the notion of *ijābiyya*, "positive orientation."
20. Ibn Sīnā (Avicenna) but also, and more importantly for the Imam, Western philosophy and psychology. In the *Book of the Soul* Ibn Sīnā situates the "animal internal faculties of perception," and "the faculty of fantasy," i.e., sensus communis, in the forepart of the front ventricle of the brain. Ibn Sīnā, *Kitāb al-Najat* (Book of the Soul), translated as *Avicenna's Psychology*, trans. Fazlur Rahman (London: Oxford University Press, 1952), 31.
21. Cf. Ibn ʿAṭā'illāh, *Kitāb al-Hikam: Sufi Aphorisms*, trans. Victor Danner (Leiden: Brill, 1984).
22. As intended in the Aristotelian sense conveyed and reinterpreted by Ibn Sīnā, *Avicenna's Psychology*, book 2, chap. 6.
23. As shown in al-Ghazālī's and Ibn ʿArabī's topographies of the soul, as well as in Ibn Sīnā, for whom, as we will see, "the soul has two faces: one turned toward the body, the other turned towards the Higher Principles" (*Avicenna's Psychology*, 26).
24. William Chittick, *The Sufi Path of Knowledge: Ibn al-'Arabi's Metaphysics of Imagination* (Albany: SUNY Press, 1989), 117. For an ethnography of imagination in Egypt that touches on some of these questions through an exploration of dream interpretation and especially the ethical use of visionary dreaming among a Sufi community, see Amira Mittermaier, *Dreams That Matter: Egyptian Landscapes of the Imagination* (Berkeley: University of California Press, 2010).
25. Youssef Belal's unpublished book in progress on "The life of Shariʿa" where much attention is given to the place of the heart and the disposition of the self, between the heart and the "limbs."
26. Abū Ḥāmid al-Ghazālī, *The Marvels of the Heart: Science of the Spirit* (*Kitāb sharḥ ʿajā'ib al-qalb*), book 21 of *Iḥyā ʿulūm al-dīn/The Revival of the Religious Sciences*, trans. W. J. Skellie (Louisville: Fons Vitae, 2010), 118–19.
27. Al-Ghāzalī, *The Marvels of the Heart*, 9–10.
28. The Imam borrows eclectically, for the task of understanding the present, from schools of thought considered rival or incommensurable by academic scholars. We should note, however, that contemporary scholarship on al-Ghazālī has pointed to a much larger interface between his thought and the Avicennian tradition, namely in the theory of perception and manifestation. See for instance a special issue of *Muslim World* 101, no. 4 (October 2011) on the 900-year anniversary of al-Ghazālī, especially the article by Jules Janssens, "Al-Ghazālī between Philosophy (*falsafa*) and Sufism (*taṣawwuf*)," 614–32.
29. Jambet, *The Act of Being*.
30. Ibn Sīnā, *Avicenna's Psychology*, 31.
31. Ibid., 26.
32. Ibid., 67.
33. See sections 15, 16, and 17.
34. Bruno Bettelheim, *Freud and Man's Soul* (New York: Knopf, 1983).
35. Nicolas Abraham and Maria Torok, *The Shell and the Kernel*, ed. and trans. Nicholas T. Rand (Chicago: University of Chicago Press, 1994).
36. Frantz Fanon, *Peau noire, masques blancs* (Paris: Seuil, 1952), translated as *Black Skin, White Mask*, trans. Richard Philcox (New York: Grove Press, 1998).
37. Fanon's references to the arising (*surgissement*) and the leap (*saut*), a term high-

lighted by Fanon to lend it the status of a concept, are to be found in *Peau noire, masques blancs*, 6 (arising) and 186 (leap). The "vertigo" of history is in "Guerre colonial et troubles mentaux." An insightful reading of the temporality of the "leap" is David Marriott's "Inventions of Existence: Sylvia Wynter, Frantz Fanon, Sociogeny, and 'the Damned,'" *New Centennial Review* 11, no. 3 (2012): 45–90. "To leap is to escape and yet to remain, to continue to relate to the historical and yet never abandon the possibility of the open-ended traveling, where reaching towards the universal is to reach for oneself as other, not the performance of some mask or illusion" (86). On the question of "opening," *éclosion* (bursting open, springing out) and *déclosion* (opening, dis-enclosing) in the aftermath of the colony, see Achille Mbembe, *Sortir de la grande nuit: Essai sur l'Afrique decolonisée* (Paris: La Découverte, 2010).

38. Jacques Lacan, "Tuché et automaton," in *Le séminaire XI, Les quatres concepts fondamentaux de la psychanalyse* (Paris: Seuil, 1973); *The Seminar of Jacques Lacan: The Four Fundamental Concepts of Psychoanalysis*, trans. Alan Sheridan (New York: Norton, 1998).
39. Jean Laplanche, *Essays on Otherness* (New York: Routledge, 1999).
40. Ibid., 238–63.

EIGHT. *FAQĪH AL-NAFS*: THE JURIST OF THE SOUL

1. He sees Sufism has having compromised itself with worldly power and collaboration with the state (both colonial and postcolonial) and having been corrupted by idolatrous practices related to the worship of saints.
2. On the relation of spiritual and physical cures, between medicine of the heart and medicine of the body and its humors, I refer to the remarkable work of Fabrizio Speziale in the context of Islam in the Indian Subcontinent. *Soufisme, religion et médécine en Islam indien* (Paris: Kathala, 2010), and "The Persian Translation of Tridosa: Lexical Analogies and Conceptual Incongruities," *Asia* 68, no. 3 (2014): 783–96. Speziale demonstrates the lively interaction and interpenetration of physical (humoral) medicine of Greek and Galenic origin, Muslim medicine inflected with Ayurvedic humoral concepts, and spiritual medicine based on *fiqh* jurisprudence and the Qur'an, in the tradition of prophetic medicine, practiced most prominently in the context of Sufi devotion at sanctuaries (*mazār*). And he uncovers the colonial history of what he calls the "de-Islamization of medicine," which aimed at representing humoral medicine and the Galenic tradition as de facto "secular" and rational, and opposed to the irrationality of religious cures. By studying the transmission of medical knowledge (physical and spiritual), he shows that humoral medicine itself, grounded in natural law, was profoundly religious.
3. Jean Starobinski, *L'encre de la mélancholie* (Paris: Seuil, 2013). A physician trained in psychiatry and a scholar of literature and poetics, Starobinski reflects on the medical history of melancholy in European culture and its relation to demonic and metaphysical interpretations; he points out that the dark humor necessarily exceeds the safe boundaries of medical pathology, and in its uncanniness opens onto a metaphysical, demonic space.
4. See Brinkley Messick, *The Calligraphic State: Textual Domination and History in a Muslim Society* (Berkeley: University of California Press, 1996); Hussein Ali Agrama, *Questioning Secularism: Islam, Sovereignty, and the Rule of Law in Modern Egypt* (Chicago: University of Chicago Press, 2012); Norman Calder, "Al-Nawawī's Typology of Muftīs and Its Significance for a General Theory of Islamic Law," *Islamic Law and Society* 3, no. 2 (1996): 137–64.
5. Pandolfo, *Impasse of the Angels*, 377.

6. See Talal Asad's remarkable discussion on the concept of *naṣīḥa* vis-à-vis the concept of *naqd*, which could be translated into the modern sense of critique within a space of debate: "The Limits of Religious Criticism in the Middle East: An Islamic Public Argument," chapter 6 in *Genealogies of Religion: Discipline and Reasons of Power in Christianity and Islam* (Baltimore: Johns Hopkins University Press, 1993). The *naṣīḥa* as also a mode of scorching political admonition during the Moroccan anticolonial struggle is remarkably discussed by Abdallah Laroui in *Les origines sociales et culturelles du nationalisme marocain (1830–1912)* (Paris: Maspero, 1977), 328–36. Laroui closely reads and comments on a sermon by the Moroccan nationalist and scholar of *fiqh* Muḥammad b. Jaʿfar al-Kattānī, *Naṣīḥat ahl al-islām* (Fes, 1908). For the contemporary place of *naṣīḥa* in Morocco, see the description of the exercise of *naṣīḥa* and its regulation within the *Jamāʿat al-ʿadl wa al-iḥsān* in Youssef Belal, *Le shaykh et le calife: Sociologie religieuse de l'Islam politique au Maroc* (Casablanca: ENS, 2011), 168–70.
7. Mircea Eliade, *Le Chamanisme et les techniques archaiques de l'extase* (Paris: Payot, 1951), translated as *Shamanism: Archaic Techniques of Ecstasy*, trans. Willard R. Trask (Princeton: Princeton University Press, 1964).

NINE. SHARIʿA HEALING: "KNOWLEDGE OF THE PATH TO THE HEREAFTER"

1. Abū Ḥāmid al-Ghazālī, *Kitāb al-ʿilm*, The Book of Knowledge, book 1 of *The Revival of the Religious Sciences, Iḥyāʾ ʿulūm al-dīn*, trans. Kenneth Honerkamp (Louisville: Fons Vitae, 2015), 87.
2. The sunna, literally the clear path and sanctioned tradition, which includes the record of the spoken pronouncements of the Prophet Muhammad (hadith), and his actions, as well as the narrative account of his life (sīra), treated together as a generative source of examples and normative orientation.
3. Cf. Baber Johansen, *Contingency in a Sacred Law: Legal and Ethical Norms in the Muslim Fiqh* (Leiden: Brill, 1999), 28.
4. Cf. ibid.; Messick, *The Calligraphic State*; Wael Hallaq, "What Is Shariʿa?" *Yearbook of Islamic & Middle Eastern Law* 12 (2005): 151; Hallaq, *Shari'a: Theory, Practice, Transformations* (Cambridge: Cambridge University Press, 2009); Roy Mottahedeh, *The Mantle of the Prophet* (New York: Pantheon Books, 1985).
5. Thanks to Youssef Belal for his comments on an earlier version of this section and our conversations on the relationship of *fiqh al-qalb* and *fiqh al-furūʿ*. Cf. his dissertation, "The Life of Shariʿa," University of California, Berkeley, 2017.
6. Abderrahman writes: "By means of this Islam has been able to expand the concept of *religious activity* to incorporate that which had not been previously considered part of its domains; as such that which was not technically an act of worship becomes one thereby, and that which was not technically a means of becoming closer to God becomes such." Taha Abderrahman, "A Global Ethic: Its Scope and Limits," Tabah Papers Series no. 1 (Abu Dhabi: Tabah Foundation, June 2008), 15. See also Wael Hallaq, "Knowledge as Politics by Other Means: An Interview with Wael Hallaq, Part I," and "Muslims on the Path of Intellectual Slavery: An Interview with Wael Hallaq, Part II," interview by Hasan Azad, *Jadaliyya*, May 16 and June 7, 2014.
7. Or *fiqh al-furūʿ*, literally the "jurisprudence of branches."
8. In terms of the legal categories of the prescribed (*farḍ*), the forbidden (*ḥarām*), the recommended (*mustaḥabb*), the permissible (*mubāh*), and the discouraged (*makrūh*).
9. Brinkley Messick, "Indexing the Self: Intent and Expression in Islamic Legal Acts," *Islamic Law and Society* 8, no. 2 (2001): 151–78.
10. Joseph Shacht, *Introduction to Islamic Law*, 124–25, cited in Michael Dols, *Majnun:*

The Madman in the Medieval Islamic World (Oxford: Clarendon Press, 1992), chapter 14: "Insanity in Islamic Law."

11. Messick, Asad, and Agrama have written on how the inner, *al-bāṭin*, is in practice inferred from the observable, *al-ẓāhir*. However, the *ruqya* is different, for the inner or nonmanifest is engaged directly, not epistemologically as knowledge but rather as a transformation of the soul. See Talal Asad, *Formations of the Secular: Christianity, Islam, Modernity* (Stanford: Stanford University Press, 2003); Hussein Agrama's discussion of the role and discernment of the *mufti* in the Egyptian personal status courts, in chapter 5 ("What Is a Fatwa?") of *Questioning Secularism: Islam, Sovereignty, and the Rule of Law in Modern Egypt* (Chicago: University of Chicago Press, 2012); and Messick, *The Calligraphic State*, on the evaluation of the "just witness" and the information gained through "established notoriety" (*istifāḍa*): "Like 'social honor' (*iḥtirām*, *sharaf*) and 'justness' (*ʿadāla*), the inverse, established notoriety and, more technically, the status of 'sinner'/'unjust' (*fāsiq*), are products of collective attribution and somewhat relative in content" (180).
12. Literally "*sharīʿa* healing"; but here the term *sharīʿa* should be understood as "being on the way of God."
13. Stefania Pandolfo, "Rapt de la voix," *Awal: Cahiers d'études berbères*, no. 15 (1997): 31–50.
14. Parallel to Qurʾanic healing is the rise of a scholarly field of Islamic psychology (*ʿilm al-nafs al-islāmī*—literally, Islamic science of the *nafs*) that directly engages with Western psychological theories by selectively reinscribing them within an Islamic vision of human life, knowledge, and truth as empowered by God. Māhir Saqqā Amīnī, *Qirāʾāt fī ʿilm al-nafs al-islāmī*, 2 vols., vol. 2: *ʿIlm nafs shakhṣiyya* (Beirut: Dār al-Nafāʾis, 2004).
15. Jacques Lacan, *Le Séminaire VII, L'Éthique de la psychanalyse* (Paris: Seuil, 1986), 65, translated as *The Seminar of Jacques Lacan: The Ethics of Psychoanalysis (Book VII)*, trans. Dennis Porter, ed. Jacques-Alain Miller (New York: W. W. Norton, 1997).

TEN. PROPHETIC MEDICINE AND THE *RUQYA*

1. I borrow the formulation from Ibn ʿArabi, and from William C. Chittick in his commentary in *The Sufi Path of Knowledge: Ibn al-Arabi's Metaphysics of Imagination* (New York: SUNY Press, 1989).
2. Emilio Spadola, *The Calls of Islam: Sufis, Islamists, and Mass Mediation in Urban Morocco* (Bloomington: Indiana University Press, 2013).
3. Muḥammad b. Abū Bakr Ibn Qayyim al-Jawziyya, *al-Ṭibb al-nabawī* (Beirut: Dār al-Kutub al-ʿIlmiyya, 2007), 184, translated as *Medicine of the Prophet*, trans. Penelope Johnstone (Cambridge, UK: Islamic Texts Society, 1998), 135 (translation modified). Ibn Qayyim uses the nominative (*fāʿil*) and accusative (*mafʿūl*) forms of the noun (the "doer" and the "done to," *rāqī* and *murqī*) and active and passive forms of the verb, for healer and patient, illness and remedy (*adwa'* and *dawa'*, again different forms of a given word).
4. See for instance the discussion of hypnosis in Henri Ellenberger, *The Discovery of the Unconscious: The History and Evolution of Dynamic Psychiatry* (New York: Basic Books, 1970), 70 ff.; Chastenet de Puységur, *Mémoires pour servir a l'histoire et a l'établissement du magnétisme animal* (London, 1786).
5. This is also arguably the case in hypnosis and psychoanalysis, if one is to follow F. Roustang, Mikkel Borch-Jacobsen, Éric Michaud, and Jean-Luc Nancy in their rethinking of hypnosis as a radical exposure of the subject to a beyond of

subjectivity: *Hypnoses* (Paris: Galilée, 1984). As for psychoanalysis, Lacan made it clear that what manifests itself in transference is the alterity of the Other, and not the person of the analyst. See also Borch-Jacobsen, "Hypnosis in Psychoanalysis," in his *The Emotional Tie: Psychoanalysis, Mimesis, and Affect* (Stanford: Stanford University Press, 1993), 39–61.

6. This is discussed through a case in section 17.
7. The connection established through the "divine cure" has an affinity with a ritual of connectedness practiced within the community of Shaykh Yassine in Morocco, known as *du'ā al-rābiṭa*, "the supplication of the link." Cf. Youssef Belal, *Le shaykh et le calife: Sociologie religieuse de l'Islam politique au Maroc* (Casablanca: ENS, 2011).
8. Ibn Qayyim al-Jawziyya, *Medicine of the Prophet*, 134.
9. Ibid.
10. Ibid., 48.

ELEVEN. THE JOUISSANCE OF THE JINN

1. *Aldun* is lead, which diviners melt in small amounts on the fire and then pour in a bowl of cold water to interpret the shapes that form in relation to the person's life.
2. See part 2 for an in depth definition and discussion of *ḥāla*.
3. French for X-ray, used in Moroccan Arabic as well. It is here a metaphor for the *ruqya* performed as a test, to see whether a jinn would manifest itself under the pressure of the Qur'anic word.
4. Sigmund Freud, "Thoughts for the Time, on War and Death," in *The Standard Edition of the Complete Psychological Works of Sigmund Freud*, vol. 14 (1914–16), ed. James Strachey (Psychoanalytic Electronic Publishing, 2015), based on *The Standard Edition*, trans. E. C. Mayne, vol. 4, 288–317.
5. Happening here in the form of a developing dissociation. In this case the dissociation marks the beginning of healing.
6. *Ghariqa*, to dive, to be or become immersed, to sink, to claim completely, to occupy: Hans Wehr's *Arabic-English Dictionary*, ed. J. M. Cowan (New York: Snowball Publishing, 2011).
7. Muḥammad ibn Muḥammad Ibn al-Ḥājj al-Maghribī, *Kitāb Shumūsh al-anwār wa-kunūz al-asrār al-kubrā* (Cairo: al-Maṭba'ah al-Milījiyyah, 1329 [1911]).

TWELVE. THE PSYCHIATRIST AND THE IMAM

1. Frantz Fanon, *Peau noire, masques blancs* (Paris: Seuil, 1952), 7.
2. Ibid., 30.
3. See Omnia El Shakry's *The Arabic Freud: Psychoanalysis and Islam in Modern Egypt* (Princeton: Princeton University Press, 2017) on the intellectual history of the concept of the self and the unconscious in turn-of-the-century and early twentieth-century Egypt, in relation to Freudian psychoanalysis, Bergson's philosophy of intuition, and Sufism. What are the stakes of translating, as Yūsuf Murād did with a concept drawn from Ibn 'Arabī, the Freudian "unconscious" as *al-lā shu'ūr*, and of reformulating the "drive" as *al-gharīza*, summoning the vision of al-Ghazālī on the struggle of the *nafs*? By returning to us the Egyptian translations of the unconscious as divine unknowing, and of the drive as ethical self-transformation, El Shakry allows the archive of the unconscious to disclose its secret connections with the problematic of the soul. See El Shakry, "The Arabic Freud: The Unconscious and the Modern Subject," *Modern Intellectual History* 11, no. 1 (2014): 89–118.
4. "And in this regard we use the term 'Islamic psychology,' and with that we mean

the scientific study of the self that is based on Islamic fundamentals, to distinguish it from Western study of the self, which in itself is based on secular (*'ilmānī*) fundamentals that bear no relation to the knowledge that has come out of godly intuition (*al-waḥī al-ilāhī*)." Muḥammad Najati, *Madkhal ilā 'ilm al-nafs al-islāmī* (Beirut, 2001), 18.

5. Ibid., 14.
6. In the Islamic reinscription of Aristotelian and Neoplatonic tradition, *al-'ulūm al-ṭabi'iyya* is the sciences of Nature (which includes physics, astronomy, medicine, geography) and is related to *al-'ulūm al-rūḥiyya*, the sciences of the spirit, of which the first level is *al-ma'rifat shar'iyya*, the knowledge of the rules of law; above it there are the more spiritual dimensions of disclosure of the divine. The key point is that both the "sciences of nature" and the "sciences of the spirit" are part of the knowledge of the cosmos and subjected to the sovereignty of God.
7. Muḥammad b. Abū Bakr Ibn Qayyim al-Jawziyya, *al-Ṭibb al-nabawī* (Beirut: Dār al-Kutub al-'Ilmiyya, 2007).
8. The phrase is from Sigmund Freud, *Beyond the Pleasure Principle*, trans. James Strachey (New York: Norton & Co, 1961 [1921]).
9. In a condition of permanent *sakan*, or inhabitation, one we encountered earlier in the story of Hind (section 2).
10. Wehr, *Dictionary of Modern Arabic.*
11. I discuss some of the resonance of this term in section 6.
12. El Shakry, "The Arabic Freud."
13. For instance, D. W. Winnicott, "Fear of Breakdown," *International Review of Psychoanalysis* 1 (1974): 103–7.
14. *Yasquṭ fī l-ighmā'*: *al-ighmā'* is a swoon or a fainting spell, the fact of suddenly becoming unconscious. In this configuration however the Imam is describing a condition in which the jinn has entirely taken hold of the mind. Here, fainting is closer to a falling into a coma, a death-like state from which there might be no return.
15. Muḥammad Ṣāliḥ al-Shaykhāni, *Ṭuruq ṣar' al-jinn* (Ḍār al-Bayḍā': Maktabat al-Taysīr, 2004), 54.
16. Freud, *Beyond the Pleasure Principle*, 24.
17. Ibid., 58.

THIRTEEN. BLACK BILE AND THE INTRACTABLE JINN:
THRESHOLD OF THE INORGANIC

1. See Niklaus Largier, "Praying by Numbers: An Essay on Medieval Aesthetics," *Representations* 104, no. 1 (2008): 73–91, and "Mysticism, Modernity, and the Invention of Aesthetic Experience," *Representations* 105, no. 1 (2008): 37–60; as well as Nancy Caciola, *Discerning Spirits: Divine and Demonic Possession in the Middle Ages* (Ithaca: Cornell University Press, 2003), and Carol Thysell, *The Pleasure of Discernment: Marguerite de Navarre as Theologian* (Oxford: Oxford University Press, 2000). The discernment of spirits is also practiced and conceptualized in contemporary charismatic Christian healing, as discussed for instance by Thomas Csordas in *The Sacred Self: A Cultural Phenomenology of Charismatic Healing* (Berkeley: University of California Press, 1994). See also Tanya Luhrmann, "The Art of Hearing God: Absorption, Dissociation, and Contemporary American Spirituality," *Spiritus* 5, no. 2 (2006): 133–57.
2. The work of Antonio Damasio precisely addresses this intersection, and can be

said to struggle with an ambiguity and indeterminacy between the brain and the passions, registering and exploring the ways in which the brain is transformed and shaped by the relational (social and cultural) processes of subjectivity, as mediated by affect and emotions; between the individual brain understood as an organ, and the brain as the site of inscription and transformation of something beyond the organic, which Damasio understands as the collective dimension of cultural transmission. Antonio Damasio, *Descartes' Error: Emotion, Reason, and the Human Brain* (New York: Quill, 1994), and *The Feeling of What Happens: Body and Emotion in the Making of Consciousness* (New York: Harcourt Brace, 1999). And see Catherine Malabou, *Ontologie de l'accident: Essai sur la plasticité destructice* (Paris: Léo Scheer, 2009); Malabou, *Les Nouveaux blessés: de Freud à la neurologie, penser les traumatismes contemporains* (Paris: Bayard, 2007), translated as *The New Wounded: From Neurosis to Brain Damage*, trans. Steven Miller (New York: Fordham University Press, 2012).

3. Michael Dols, *al-Majnūn: The Madman in Medieval Islamic Society* (Oxford: Clarendon Press, 1992), 81–86; see also Abū 'Alī al-Ḥusayn Ibn Sīnā, *al-Qanūn fī-l-ṭibb*, 3 vols. (Būlāq, 1877), and Muḥammad b. Abū Bakr Ibn Qayyim al-Jawziyya, *al-Ṭibb al-nabawī* (Beirut: Dār al-Kutub al-ʿIlmiyya, 2007).
4. Nicolas Abraham and Maria Torok, *L'écorce et le noyeau* (Paris: Aubier-Flammarion, 1978), translated as *The Shell and the Kernel: Renewals of Psychoanalysis*, trans. and ed. Nicholas T. Rand (Chicago: University of Chicago Press, 1994), especially Abraham's "Notes on the Phantom: A Complement to Freud's Metapsychology," 171–76.

FOURTEEN. THE ARGUMENT OF *SHIRK* (IDOLATRY)

1. Abdallah Laroui, *Les origines sociales et culturelles du nationalisme marocain (1830–1912)* (Paris: Maspero, 1977), chap. 7, "Aux sources du salafisme"; Albert Hourani, *A History of the Arab Peoples* (Cambridge, MA: Harvard University Press, 1991).
2. Abū Ḥāmid al-Ghazālī, *Fayṣal al-tafriqa bayna al-Islam wa al-zandaqa*, translated as *On the Boundaries of Theological Tolerance in Islam*, trans. Sherman Jackson (Oxford: Oxford University Press, 2002).
3. As discussed in Toshihiko Izutsu, *Ethico-Religious Concepts in the Qur'an* (Montreal: McGill-Queen's University Press, 2002 [1966]).
4. Ibn Khaldūn, *al-Muqaddima*, vol. 1, trans. Franz Rosenthal (Princeton: Princeton University Press, 1958), 194–207.
5. Izutsu, *Ethico-Religious Concepts*.
6. Jacques Lacan, *Le séminar Livre XI, Les quatre conceptes fondamentaux de la psychanalyse* (Paris: Seuil, 1973), 82–83.
7. Françoise Davoine and Jean-Max Gaudillière, *History beyond Trauma*, trans. Susan Fairfield (New York: Other Press, 2004).

FIFTEEN. EXTIMACY: THE BATTLEFIELD OF THE *NAFS*

1. See section 9.
2. The series of conversations on the *nafs*, the heart, and the question of Shaytan started in August 2008 and continued over the next two years, at the Imam's home. The conversations were just between the Imam and me. In 2009 I started attending the *ruqya* healing sessions, through the summers of 2011 and 2012.
3. Muḥammad Ibn Zakariyya al-Rāzī, *al-Ṭibb al-rūḥānī*, translated as *La Medicine spirituelle*, trans. Rémi Brague (Paris: Flammarion, 2003). Al-Razi writes, "The scope

of spiritual medicine, *al-ṭibb al-rūḥanī*, is the reformation (*iṣlāḥ*) of the character of the soul."

4. On Moroccan radio, "Arène des generations," August 5, 2008.
5. This was in 2008, well before the Middle Eastern uprisings and the destruction that ensued.
6. We may think of how certain autoimmune or otherwise unexplained or unexplainable conditions, such as irritable bowel syndrome, allergies to unspecified allergens, or mysterious illnesses like "sick building syndrome," cause chronic fatigue, migraine, insomnia, crippling symptoms that do not reveal any pathology through conventional laboratory tests, at least with the present scientific capability.
7. Of interest with reference to this point is Eric Santner's notion of semiotic distress, in "Miracles Happen: Benjamin, Rosenzweig, Freud, and the Matter of the Neighbor," in Slavoj Žižek, Eric L. Santner, and Kenneth Reinhardt, *The Neighbor: Three Essays in Political Theology* (Chicago: University of Chicago Press, 2005), 76–133.
8. See Stefania Pandolfo, "Rapt de la voix," *Awal: Cahiers d'études berbères*, no. 15 (1997): 31–50.
9. See section 5, above.
10. Harold Searle, *Collected Papers on Schizophrenia and Related Subjects* (New York: International University Press, 1966); Melanie Klein, *Envy and Gratitude and Other Works, 1946–1963* (New York: Free Press, 1963); Piera Aulagnier, *La violence de l'interprétation* (Paris: Presses Universitaires de France, 2003 [1975]); Wilfred Bion, *Attention and Interpretation* (London: Kamac Books, 1984 [1970]). The work of Egyptian analyst Sami Ali, *L'espace imaginaire* (Paris: Gallimard, 1974), is important here for its focus on the formative imagination and the spatiality of the body, projection, and identification, as reflected upon through his practice and research in Egypt.
11. Among others, Gananath Obeyesekere, *The Work of Culture: Symbolic Transformation in Psychoanalysis and Anthropology* (Chicago: University of Chicago Press, 1990); Vincent Crapanzano, *Hermes' Dilemma and Hamlet's Desire* (Cambridge, MA: Harvard University Press, 1992); Jeanne Favret-Saada, *Deadly Words: Witchcraft in the Bocage*, trans. Catherine Cullen (Cambridge: Cambridge University Press, 1980 [1977]); Ellen Corin, but also of course Lévi-Strauss's important discussion of the "effectiveness of symbols," in *Structural Anthropology* (New York: Basics Books, 1963).
12. Jacques Lacan, *Le Séminare Livre XVII, L'envers de la psychanalyse, 1969–1970* (Paris: Seuil, 1991); *The Other Side of Psychoanalysis*, trans. Russell Grigg (New York: W. W. Norton, 2007).
13. Bruno Bettelheim, *Freud and Man's Soul* (New York: Knopf, 1982). I must thank Arthur Kleinman for reminding me of Bettelheim's important text in relation to this work.
14. On the authority of Abū Hurayra (may Allah be well-pleased with him), who said:

    > A man said to the Prophet (may the blessing and peace of Allah be upon him), "Counsel me." He said, "Do not become angry (*lā taghḍab*)." The man repeated his request several times, and he said, "Do not become angry." Related by al-Bukhari (al-Nawawi, *Forty Hadiths*, hadith 16).

15. A remarkable discussion of "the ethics of arts and crafts," and the purification of the soul in the transformation of matter in the "reformation of ethics" of Ikhwān aṣ-Ṣāfa' (eleventh-century) is found in Mohammed Hamdouni Alami, *The Origins of Visual Culture in the Islamic World: Aesthetics, Art, and Architecture in Early Islam* (London: I.B. Tauris, 2015).

16. Abū Ḥāmid al-Ghazālī, *The Marvels of the Heart: Science of the Spirit* (*Kitāb sharḥ ʿajā'ib al-qalb*), Book 21 of *Iḥyā ʿulūm al-dīn/The Revival of the Religious Sciences*, trans. W. J. Skellie (Louisville: Fons Vitae, 2010), 134–35.
17. al-Rāzī, *al-Ṭibb al-rūḥānī*; Ibn Qayyim al-Jawziyya, *al-Ṭibb al-nabawī*; Abū Ḥāmid al-Ghazālī, *Kitāb riyāḍat al-nafs wa kitāb kasr al-shahwatayn*, books 22 and 23 of *Iḥyā' ʿulūm al-dīn*, translated as *Disciplining the Soul & Breaking the Two Desires*, trans. T. J. Winter (Cambridge: Islamic Texts Society, 1995).
18. *Rawaḍa*: *rāda*, to tame, domesticate, break in, train, practice, exercise; *riyāḍāt*, religious exercises; *riyāḍī*, sportive/mathematical (Wehr).
19. *Al-sharāra*, spark, evil trigger; from *sharr*, to be evil, malignant.
20. Al-Ghazālī, cited in Sara Sviri, "The Self and Its Transformation in Sufism: With Special Reference to Early Literature," in *Self and Self-Transformation in the History of Religions*, ed. David Shulman and Guy S. Stroumsa (New York: Oxford University Press, 2008), 195.
21. In some cases the sexual organ itself may be referred to as *nafs*, as in the colloquial expression *mat lih nafsu*, his *nafs* died, meaning, he became sexually impotent.
22. As in the expression *nafs beynathum*, meaning the (passion of) hate between them.
23. Al-Ghazālī, *Marvels of the Heart*.
24. See Ebrahim Moosa's discussion of the heteronymous self in *Al-Ghazālī and the Poetics of the Imagination* (Chapel Hill: University of North Carolina Press, 2005).
25. For instance, Maḥmūd al-Bustānī, *Dirāsāt fī ʿilm al-nafs al-islāmī* (Beirut: Dār al-Balāgha, 2000), and Muḥammad Najati, *Madkhal ilā ʿilm al-nafs al-islāmī*. See Omnia El Shakry, *The Arabic Freud: Psychoanalysis and Islam in Modern Egypt* (Princeton: Princeton University Press, 2017).
26. Abū al-Wafā ʿ al-Ghunamī al-Taftazānī, "Sikulujiyyāt al-taṣawwuf," *Majallat ʿilm al-nafs* (1950), whose thought and writing are discussed in El Shakry, *The Arabic Freud*.
27. The ambiguity of the concept of *nafs* is discussed by Sviri in "The Self and Its Transformation in Sufism," where she traces a bifurcation in the early Islamic literature on the *nafs*. According to Sviri, Sufism presented a third way: starting from the premise that the *nafs* is a negative and earthbound force as in the homiletic tradition, it postulates the possibility of transformation, hence meeting the Aristotelian and Neoplatonic tradition (which treats the *nafs* as a subtle and transcendent substance) in the sense of ethical transformation and the possibility of visionary experience. For the Imam at the outset the *nafs* has both dimensions: it is a vital principle that is earthly, driven by desire/enjoyment and the passion of anger, and as such the theatre of a struggle understood as a "greater jihād." But it is also the soul understood as the complex *nafs/qalb* (soul/heart), the locus of the ethical work of the active imagination.
28. Al-Ghazālī, *Disciplining the Soul*, 26.
29. Ibid., 45.
30. Maḥmūd Ḥusayn, *al-Sīra*, vol. 1 (Paris: Grasset, 2005).
31. Ali Shariati, *On the Sociology of Islam*, trans. Hamid Algar (Oneonta, NY: Mizan Press, 1979), "Man and Islam," 74.
32. On *jihād al-nafs*, al-Ghazālī's *Disciplining the Soul* is a crucial reference, both for the Imam and in contemporary debates.
33. El Shakry, *The Arabic Freud*.
34. Jacques Lacan, *Le Séminaire VII, L'Éthique de la psychanalyse* (Paris: Seuil, 1986), 167, translated as *The Seminar of Jacques Lacan: The Ethics of Psychoanalysis (Book VII)*, trans. Dennis Porter, ed. Jacques-Alain Miller (New York: W. W. Norton, 1997), 139.
35. The insight of some contemporary psychoanalysts working on psychosis and addic-

tion is relevant here, as an attempt to address destructiveness itself as a reclaimable form of life. For instance, Sylvie Le Poulichet, *L'art du danger: de la détresse à la création* (Paris: Anthropos, 1996).

36. On the notion of the friend/enemy knot as life against itself, see Massimo Recalcati, *Sull'odio* (Milan: Mondadori, 2004), as well as Mikkel Borch-Jacobsen, *The Emotional Tie: Psychoanalysis, Mimesis, and Affect* (Stanford: Stanford University Press, 1993).
37. Lacan, *The Ethics of Psychoanalysis*, chaps. 9–11: "The Essence of Tragedy: A Commentary on Sophocles's *Antigone*."

SIXTEEN. THE WRITING OF THE SOUL: SOUL CHOKING, IMAGINATION, AND PAIN

1. Jacques Lacan, *Le Séminaire VII, L'Éthique de la psychanalyse* (Paris: Seuil, 1986), 74, translated as *The Seminar of Jacques Lacan: The Ethics of Psychoanalysis (Book VII)*, trans. Dennis Porter, ed. Jacques-Alain Miller (New York: W. W. Norton, 1997), 60: "Nous devrions peut-être concevoir la douleur comme un champ qui, dans l'ordre de l'existence s'ouvre précisément à la limite où il n'y a pas possibilité pour l'être de se mouvoir."
2. Note that when the Imam speaks of "the heart of a Muslim" he does not treat "Muslim" as an identity or a "religion," which would then be followed by the qualified "faithful." It is an active position vis-à-vis God and the community, and the heart that is incapable of taking that position is no longer Muslim.
3. In *L'écorce et le noyau*, Nicolas Abraham and Maria Torok rethink melancholia and the intergenerational transmission of trauma in terms of the two movements of "incorporation" and "introjection." These describe two positions, or modalities, of the subject in its relation to the object—two different kinds of melancholies. Incorporation succumbs, introjection is a transformative inscription in the psychic space of the subject of trauma. The question remains of whether the two principles can be separated in actual life; their limen, always blurred, is here also the site of a struggle.
4. See section 6.
5. Sayyid Qutb, *Khaṣā'iṣ al-Taṣawwur al-islāmī wa-muqawwamātuh* (Cairo: Dār al-Kutub al-ʿArabiyya, 1965), translated as *Basic Principles of Islamic Worldview*, trans. Rami David (North Haledon, NJ: Islamic Publications International, 2006), chap. 7, "Positive Orientation." "He is required to bear practical witness to this religion—not witness of the tongue or even witness of the heart—with every act he undertakes. It is practical witness of this type that confirms the existence of real, visible and palpable faith" (172–73).
6. Farid Esack, "Qurʾan, Liberation, and Pluralism: An Islamic Perspective on Interreligious Solidarity against Oppression," in *Liberating Faith: Religious Voices for Justice, Peace, and Ecological Wisdom*, ed. Roger S. Gottlieb (Lanham, MD: Rowman & Littlefield, 2003), 142. Esack stresses that there is a requirement of socioeconomic justice that is beyond all ethical possible adjustments.
7. "There is no metaphor here, creation of meaning, but instead analogy, direct transfer from one register to another. . . . It is as if, under the effect of pain, the body transforms into the psyche, and psyche into the body. Ordinary language can guide us here: pain awakens, and sometimes wakes us up. . . . I *have* anguish, but I *am* pain." Jean-Bertrand Pontalis, *Entre le rêve et la douleur* (Paris: Gallimard, 1977), 261.
8. Abū Ḥāmid al-Ghazālī, *Kitāb dhikr al-mawt wa-ma baʿdahu*, book 40 of *Iḥyā' ʿulūm al-dīn* (Beirut: Dār al-Kutub al-ʿIlmiyya, n.d.), 490, translated as *The Remembrance of*

Death and the Afterlife, trans. T. J. Winter (Cambridge: Islamic Texts Society, 1989), 38 (translation modified from Arabic original).

9. A topological figure recurrent in Lacan.

SEVENTEEN. CONCLUDING MOVEMENT: THE PASSION OF ZULIKHA, A DRAMATURGY OF THE SOUL

1. The pen is a direct gestural reference to Sūrat al-Qalam, "The Pen," Qur'an 68: 1–6. "Nūn. By the pen and what they inscribe. You are not [O Muhammad], by the favor of your Lord, a madman" (68: 1–2).
2. See above, section 10 for a discussion of Ibn Qayyim al-Jawziyya's definition.
3. This is quote from a *faqīh* in the Wed Dra' region of Morocco, also the imam of a mosque there, who first explained to me the *ṣara'* and the experience of demonic possession.
4. Ibn 'Arabī, cited in William Chittick, *The Sufi Path of Knowledge: Ibn al-'Arabi's Metaphysics of Imagination* (Albany: SUNY Press, 1989), 120.
5. Ibid.
6. The phrase is al-Ghazālī's, in *Marvels of the Heart*, 10.
7. Jean-Luc Nancy, "Identité et tremblement," in *Hypnoses* (Paris: Galilée, 1984), 32. "In hypnosis the soul is a body given to existence in another person" (*dans l'hypnose, l'âme est un corps offert à l'existence dans autrui*).
8. See Stefania Pandolfo, *Impasse of the Angels: Scenes from a Moroccan Space of Memory* (Chicago: University of Chicago Press, 1997), 188.
9. I follow Muhammad Asad in translating *al-jinn*, here and in some other places, as "invisible beings."
10. Muhammad Asad's translation: *The Message of the Qur'ān* (Bristol: Book Foundation, 2003).
11. Ibn 'Arabi, *Fuṣūṣ al-ḥikām*, and the question of figural interpretation in relation to the unconscious, as discussed by Fethi Benslama in *Psychoanalysis and the Challenge of Islam*, 181–84.
12. Jacques Lacan, "Conferences et entrétiens dans des universités nord-américaines," *Scilicet* nos. 6/7 (Paris: Seuil, 1976), 32. Cited in Barbara Cassin and Alain Badiou, *Il n'ya pas de rapport sexuel* (Paris: Fayard, 2010), 28.

INDEX OF CHARACTERS

INDEX OF QUR'AN CITATIONS

GENERAL INDEX

204, 224, 267, 273, 283, 297, 303, 306, 361n4, 367n24, 376n2, 380n23, 397n35. *See also* public health
public health, 5, 25, 39, 43–44, 50, 81, 85, 101, 109, 122–23, 251, 282, 367n25, 372n3, 372n10, 373n7. *See also* clinic; emergency room; hospital

qalb (heart), 10, 27, 50, 64, 230, 232–36, 260, 266–67, 274, 294, 296, 304, 316, 323, 397n27. See also *ʿaql; nafs; rūḥ*
qanaṭ. *See* despair
Qurʾan, 14–17, 26, 30, 37, 55, 61, 90, 110–11, 115, 119–20, 125, 127–28, 131, 133–35, 147, 149, 157, 174, 186, 188, 194, 201, 203, 211–12, 217–18, 223, 225, 228–33, 236–38, 240, 245, 247–53, 257–58, 262, 265–70, 276, 278–79, 282–84, 289, 298, 301–2, 307, 309–11, 314–20, 323, 325, 331–40, 344–48, 382n4, 384n21, 387n35, 388n5, 388n15, 390n2, 393n3 (sec. 11), 399n1. See also *balāʾ*; eschatology; *ibtilāʾ*; torment; *and individual Qurʾan citations*
Qurʾanic cure. See *ruqya; ṣraʿ*
al-Qurtubi, Abu Abdullah, 188
Qutb, Sayyid, 15, 134, 201, 231, 242, 364n42, 389n19, 398n5

Rabat, 12, 100, 106, 109, 115, 121, 127–28, 131, 136, 143, 154, 191, 196, 198, 202, 215, 252–53, 259, 306, 376n2, 379n11
racism, 7, 24, 46, 49, 77, 81–84, 98, 144, 362n14, 363n22, 374n2, 380n23
rage. *See* anger
Ramadan, 272, 274, 276–77, 334, 354
ramz (cipher), 147, 150, 152, 166, 172–75, 184. See also *ʿibra; taʿbīr*
al-Razi, Ibn Zakariyya, 79, 267, 305, 313, 395n3 (sec. 15)
Real, the, 17–18, 23–24, 174–75, 177, 216, 226, 244, 323, 328, 333–34, 367n24. *See also* reality
reality, 8, 39, 41, 49, 73–74, 93, 98, 119, 172, 190, 192, 236, 282, 313, 320, 323–26. *See also* delusion; illusion; Real; *taʿbīr*
reason, 13, 52, 80, 90–91, 102, 113, 127, 184, 205, 236, 298, 377n8, 385n26. See also *ʿaql*; unreason
reformism. *See* Islamic Revival
refuge. *See* sanctuary
refugees. *See* migration
remembrance. See *dhikr*
representation, 27, 35–36, 38, 44–46, 60, 62, 74, 81–82, 84, 97, 113, 135, 147, 156, 162, 168–70, 173, 176, 182, 184, 189, 205, 213, 215, 231, 266, 288, 312, 367n21, 368n26, 384n21, 390n2. *See also* painting; *ramz*; sign
responsibility, 10–11, 190, 198, 201, 240, 243, 287; in healing, 45, 65, 77–78, 81–84, 87, 122–23, 130–31, 283, 307; individual, 21, 23, 201, 207; in Islam, 30, 128–29, 150, 163, 201, 212, 225, 254, 260–61, 266, 290, 305, 308, 316, 320, 327, 350. *See also* struggle; witnessing
revelation, 14–15, 17, 91, 111, 114, 124, 134, 211, 258, 269, 327, 378n24, 387n34
revivalism. *See* Islamic Revival
revolution, 7, 28, 124, 201, 212, 254, 351. *See also* protests; uprising
rights, 25, 35, 50–51, 77–78, 101, 103, 131, 196, 261, 369n40, 374n2, 374n3, 386n29
risk, 2, 15, 19, 21, 27, 30, 40, 68, 72, 77, 110–11, 119, 122, 130–31, 137, 144, 149, 165, 169, 192–95, 198–201, 203, 209–13, 216, 225, 231, 235, 237, 253, 255, 267, 269, 288, 292, 301, 305, 318, 320–27, 330, 334, 368n26. *See also* struggle; witnessing
rūḥ (spirit), 36, 186, 188, 190, 203, 209, 212, 230, 236, 263, 269–70, 285, 295–96, 305, 307, 309, 313, 316, 319, 329–30, 365n5, 394n6, 395n3 (sec. 15). See also *ʿaql; nafs; qalb*
ruin, 1, 4, 7, 9, 41–42, 63, 93, 107, 128, 184, 187, 193, 227–28, 287, 303, 328, 342, 350, 368n26
ruqya, 9–10, 14, 26, 186, 223, 235, 238–39, 247–52, 254, 265, 267–69, 271, 276–78, 284, 287–88, 292, 305–6, 311, 314, 331, 334–35, 342–45, 392n11, 393n3 (sec. 11), 395n2 (sec. 15). *See also* possession (jinn); shariʿa healing

Lightning Source UK Ltd.
Milton Keynes UK
UKHW012339260919
350528UK00001B/10/P

9 780226 465081